PC Magazine
Guide to Connectivity
Third Edition

PC Magazine
Guide to Connectivity
Third Edition

Frank J. Derfler, Jr.

Ziff-Davis Press
Emeryville, California

Development Editors	Eric Stone and Lyn Cordell
Copy Editors	Glen Becker and Lyn Cordell
Technical Reviewer	Steve Rigney
Project Coordinators	Cori Pansarasa and Barbara Dahl
Proofreader	Carol Burbo
Cover Design and Illustration	Regan Honda
Book Design	Paper Crane Graphics, Berkeley
Screen Graphics Editor	Charles Cowens
Technical Illustration	Peggy Smith and Sarah Ishida
Word Processing	Howard Blechman
Page Layout	M.D. Barrera
Indexer	Ted Laux

Ziff-Davis Press books are produced on a Macintosh computer system with the following applications: FrameMaker®, Microsoft® Word, QuarkXPress®, Adobe Illustrator®, Adobe Photoshop®, Adobe Streamline™, MacLink®Plus, Aldus® FreeHand™, Collage Plus™.

If you have comments or questions or would like to receive a free catalog, call or write:
Ziff-Davis Press
5903 Christie Avenue
Emeryville, CA 94608
1-800-688-0448

ISBN 1-56276-274-5

Manufactured in the United States of America
10 9 8 7 6 5 4 3 2

To Marlene, Shandra, Steve, and Stephen: a small family, but growing.

■ Contents at a Glance

■ Table of Contents

■ Acknowledgments

This team has gone to the plate three times and this, I'm sure, is our third home run! My sincere thanks to the many people at Ziff-Davis Press who contributed to this third edition. Special thanks go to Lyn Cordell for her editorial expertise and infinite patience, to Eric Stone for insight and persistence, and to Barbara Dahl who picked up some pieces and guided this project through the production maze. Back in Florida, both Steve and Shandra Rigney did much of the hard work of adding value to the book. Continuing thanks are due to those who worked on the first edition, which forms the foundation of this book: Glen Becker, Dr. Marvin Schwartz, and Eric Stone for their humor, encouragement, and technical skills. Kimberly Maxwell, Gerard Kunkel, Ames Kanemoto, Kim Haglund, Cherie Plumlee, Katja Amyx, and Jeff Green provided the outstanding "look and feel" of this book.

■ Introduction

Connectivity! Convergence! The Information Superhighway! The Internet! What is it all about and how do you do it? My goal in writing this book is to show you the both the big picture and the pieces and parts you need to make computer connections within your office or home and outside. In a sense, I want to make you a hero. I want to help you solve problems in your company or organization, improve productivity, and save money. That's the stuff of modern heroes. With the information I've given you in this book, you can amplify, release, and focus the power that is available in modern PCs when you connect them to synthesize and distribute information.

I've written this book with managers in mind, not just technicians or PC power users. I assume you're "PC-savvy" enough to understand DOS subdirectories and that you know how to plug a printer into the parallel port of a PC, but otherwise you don't need any special information, background, or experience to use this book.

The book you have in your hands is different from most books, because it is more than just printed pages of text. The stories, the diagrams, and the Connectivity Decision Tree chart bound into the back of the book lead you to important information and recommendations that can help you make decisions without forcing you to wade through oceans of words.

■ What's in This Book

The first chapter introduces the concept of information as the raw material, inventory, and finished product of many organizations. Chapter 2 takes you through the Connectivity Decision Tree, an innovative device that can help you find economical and effective ways to design, install, and operate a connectivity system. Chapter 3 discusses a variety of ways you can link computers to share printers, exchange files, and use networked applications.

The connectivity field is broad. No other logical division of the computer industry encompasses so many different technologies. The world of local area networks—only one portion of the connectivity galaxy—includes many specialized elements such as cables, connectors, interface adapters, connecting software, and management tools. Chapters 4 through 10 give you an overview, specific details, and practical hints about all these different network elements.

Chapter 11, "Telephone Modems and Network Remote Access," looks at how using modems can extend the service area of local area networks. You'll find hints on buying and using modems, as well as information on the latest developments in modem technology.

Chapters 12 and 13 explore a rapidly evolving aspect of the connectivity market: interoperability. This deals with the problems of connecting computers that use different architectures and operating systems, often in different locations. An arena of challenges, interoperability draws in some of the most arcane leading-edge technologies used in the computer industry. We'll work through concepts such as ISDN, satellite WANs, and even an ATM that doesn't mean "automatic teller machine!"

Chapter 14 opens the new world of convergence—the merger of high-speed processing and high-speed connectivity to deliver sound and images to your PC. We'll work through the ideas and techniques that have gotten so much financial, political, and editorial attention.

The Appendix contains a database of connectivity products and vendors, including all those that are mentioned in the book. Near the back of the book you'll find an extensive glossary covering topics ranging from modems to the definitions of the IEEE 802.X standards.

Throughout this book, I've clustered information together into related areas—sometimes allowing overlap between those subject areas—to make the concepts and hints as readily available to you as possible. You don't have to read this book from cover to cover or even from front to back. It's designed to act as a quick reference, a tutorial, and a friendly consultant. Please enjoy it.

- *Connectivity Is Dead*

- *An Open World and Everybody's World*

- *Networks and LANs*

- *Layers of a Structured Market*

- *The Future of Connectivity*

Society + Commerce = Connectivity

TECHNICAL TALE

"This is a day for me to philosophize," Paul Cannon told the students in his Business Theory 400 class. "Here are five truths to ponder."

"Number one: Moore's Law has changed business and commerce forever. At the start of the microprocessor revolution, Intel's Gordon Moore observed that the number of transistors on new integrated circuits doubles every 18 months. With more processing power, data storage and communications speed have about the same cycle.

"Number two: You'll get what you want when you want it! Mass production will give way to mass customization. As the connectivity links between the buyer, the manufacturer, and the designer of products get faster, the buyer will place an order for a product that will be fabricated on-demand, customized from within a wide set of options, and shipped overnight.

"Third: Virtual corporations need business connectivity. Modern enterprises survive by reacting speedily to opportunities. Maintaining internal corporate speed requires a network of external links to suppliers, distributors, customers, lawyers, and accountants. This group forms a changing and responsive 'virtual' corporation that can grow into and withdraw from business areas in response to market pressures and opportunities.

"Fourth: An increasingly large percentage of workers won't go to work. Improved connectivity makes it effective and economical for people to work at home or at neighborhood work centers equipped with appropriate technology.

"Finally, my personal favorite: The 'ilities have met the 'ologies and nothing will ever be the same. The '...ilities' of business, including manageability and sustainability, have met information technology and have inevitably changed. For example, manageability will continue to evolve from dictatorship to leadership. Sustainability, the ability to keep business in the future, is very difficult to achieve as modern corporations profit from fast reactions and speed. Customers will be increasingly fickle because it's so easy for them to develop new sources of supply."

As Paul lectured, he backed into his desk and knocked a thick book onto the floor. It landed flat and loud and everyone jumped. "Oh," punned a senior in the back row, "I guess that's the end of the Cannon report."

THE INTERNET, THE INFORMATION SUPERHIGHWAY, TELECOMMUTING, information-based management...these are the hot buzzwords of the mid-1990s, and they are all about networking. Puzzled, but willing? Intrigued, but anxious? I'm here to help! You don't have to be a corporate networking guru to be interested in linking computers to each other or to benefit from the synergy they provide. As the Workgroup Systems editor of *PC Magazine*, I receive any number of letters from people who work in offices with five or six PCs and want to know the best way to connect their computers in order to share data or printers.

Similarly, you don't have to be a power programmer to install a printer-sharing device or even a full network for a dozen or more PCs. Modern networking products make it easy and economical to install powerful and flexible networking systems.

From surveys of the readers of *PC Magazine*, I know that more than half of the PCs our readers own are connected to modems, mainframes, or local area networks (LANs). The interconnected organization that relies on a flow of information is the commercial role model for the mid-1990s. In this book, we'll explain how these things work and how they relate to buzzwords like the information highway.

Commerce and society in the United States and in many other countries are increasingly based on information. Information replaces the need for inventory in the "just-in-time" production lines. In the bustling city of Atlanta, Georgia, the airport is the largest employment center. But without the information grid underlying the airline, air traffic control, car rental, and metropolitan transportation systems, the entire operation and the peripheral businesses it supports would grind to a halt in an hour.

In some organizations, information is a necessary lubricant for trade. In others, it is both a raw material and a crafted product. Information technology has been the grease that has allowed modern corporations to slide out from under management pyramids to become flatter, more streamlined, and more profitable organizations.

Computers hold and sort information, and communication networks transport information among computers. Computers and their networks form the manufacturing and transportation infrastructure of modern organizations and societies.

At certain stages in the development of a society, the majority of the people need practical skills in such areas as agriculture, herding, or fishing. As societies industrialize, a large percentage of the populace must learn how to drive a car, and many people master mechanical trades. In the United States, we are now at the stage when many of us must master the information trades. Most people have to know how to use information-delivery tools such as television sets, and an increasing number have to be able to put information into and take information from a computer. The need to use a computer connected to a communications network follows quickly after that.

Not every member of society will need the skills taught in this book to select, install, and manage connectivity systems, but someone in practically every commercial office and workgroup must have these skills for the enterprise to run efficiently and effectively. A hundred years ago, commercial organizations relied on horsepower and the skills of teamsters and farriers as they moved their products by horse-drawn wagons. Fifty years ago commerce was based on the train and the truck, and on the skills of drivers and mechanics. Today, commerce is increasingly dependent on computers and their communications systems and on the skills of the professionals who create, install, and maintain them. Now is the right time for you to learn about computer connectivity systems. In fact, if you work with or around computers and aren't familiar with most of the material in this book, you're almost too late!

■ Connectivity Is Dead

I used to begin my speeches to groups of PC users and managers by announcing, "Connectivity is dead!" Since I carried the title of Connectivity Editor of *PC Magazine* at the time, my audiences thought this was a strange thing to say. My point was that Connectivity, with a capital C, is an IBM term describing a method of interconnecting computers that inexorably laced people into IBM's proprietary web. Once you connected using Big Blue's signaling, cabling, and software systems, it was difficult to integrate products from other manufacturers into your network.

That type of Connectivity is dead. The new world of connectivity, with a little c, allows interconnection between computer systems made by many different manufacturers. Today, you can shop for components on the basis of features, price, service, support, and availability and generally know that the software and hardware products you buy will work together.

■ An Open World and Everybody's World

The escape from the "closed" meaning of Connectivity was an uphill trek. Many companies, institutions, and even governments took thousands of small steps to reach a system of "open" connectivity. In 1977, the International Standards Organization (ISO) established a subcommittee to define standards for products used to link heterogeneous computers.

The world of open connectivity specifications, or *protocols*, is a paradise with rules, where all products work together in harmony because they conform to published standards for interoperability. The first real footsteps of mortals echoed in this paradise in 1987, when companies like AT&T, Digital Equipment Corp., and others began announcing and releasing products conforming to certain sections of the ISO specification for Open Systems Interconnection (OSI).

An interesting thing happened on the way to paradise. Many companies learned to get along with each other even without conforming exactly to the ponderous ISO OSI model. While companies learned how to create products for the structure of the open systems, they also learned that it was relatively easy to create products for each others' systems. So aggressive companies such as Microsoft, Performance Technology, and Artisoft created software that let their network operating systems interoperate with Novell's popular NetWare. Novell fielded software allowing networks that use NetWare to interoperate with those using Microsoft's Windows NT Advanced Server and with computers running the Unix operating system.

Modern network managers can mix network pieces and parts from different companies in a variety of ways. The open world, designed to be open according to certain guidelines, became everybody's world. Particularly in the United States, but also in other pragmatic countries, following the rules of openness became less important than working together directly.

■ Networks and LANs

An organization usually takes some time to evolve to the point where it needs large open systems, or at least cooperative computer systems made up of pieces supplied by many vendors. The need for connectivity often begins with a simple desire to share a single printer between two PCs, or to move a file from one person to another without writing it to a floppy disk and walking it down the hall. These modest problems don't always require solutions with miles of wire and megabytes of programs. Some connectivity problems cry out for local area networks, but others yield to simpler solutions.

The word *network* and the phrase *local area network* (LAN) are both overused and abused, so we should be sure we have the same frame of reference. A *network* is any type of interactive information-carrying system. There are networks of sensors and nerve fibers in your body, and there are information and entertainment networks displayed on your television set. The information-carrying aspect of networking is important. Information-carrying networks are the infrastructure—the roads and highways—of modern societies. Computer communications networks carry information between different computers and between computers and their peripherals.

A *LAN* is a computer communications network that spans a limited geographical area—usually no more than a few miles, and often much less.

Other types of computer communications networks include the *metropolitan-area network* (MAN) and the *wide-area network* (WAN). Technical factors force these computer communications networks to trade speed for distance. In a LAN, the data moves at tens or even hundreds of megabits per second within an office, throughout a factory, or across a campus. By contrast, data in a WAN typically moves at 1.5 megabits per second or less, but this kind of network can span continents and oceans. This book will focus primarily on local-area-network connectivity alternatives, but we will also consider networking over longer distances in Chapter 13.

■ Layers of a Structured Market

Overall, buyers of connectivity products seem to fall into four categories, based primarily on the complexity of the systems they need. Figure 1.1 illustrates how these layers overlap.

Figure 1.1

The buyers of LAN systems divide themselves among those with simple resource-sharing needs, people who need to link 2 to 20 PCs in a network, managers of larger networks with 20 to 200 nodes or even more, and the new priests of computing who practice the arts of interoperability.

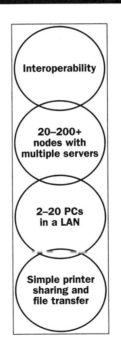

The first level of connectivity buyers are innovators who see a need to link computers and share information, usually in a small organization or workgroup, and who take action to fill that need. These buyers often include PC-savvy managers and people who are genuinely enthusiastic about personal computers. They often shop with a limited budget and look for practical solutions that don't involve a lot of training or support. Usually they don't have to coordinate their decisions with a lot of technical specialists. These people often buy the products they use through catalogs or directly from magazine ads. They can buy printer-sharing and simple file-transfer systems and have them installed and operational in just a few hours.

The second level of buyers are those who know they need a high-speed network for a group of 2 to 20 users. These people are often engaged in what has been called "guerilla networking." They bring in small networks in an underground guerilla operation, sometimes under the noses of unresponsive corporate data-processing professionals.

The networking hardware and software for a group of 2 to 20 PCs runs about $200 per PC. This is within the discretionary limits of a middle manager, so these buyers aren't strapped for cash, but they must carefully account for what they spend. There are several good networking products, including Microsoft's Windows for Workgroups, Performance Technology's POWERlan, and Artisoft's LANtastic, that allow these people to install a network for 2 to 20 PCs in one afternoon, spend a couple of hours configuring the applications and batch files, and enjoy a functional network on the third day.

This class of network doesn't need a full-time person dedicated to the job of network management. But someone usually emerges or is appointed as the caretaker of the LAN.

The next category of connectivity buyers includes many graduates of the guerilla school of networking and some of the corporate data-processing professionals who understand the importance of networked PCs. These folks need a multiserver network for 20 to 200 users or more. They operate from funds specially budgeted for the network, and they worry about speed, reliability, and support much more than cost.

Buyers of networks with 20 to 200+ nodes might hire professional system integrators to supply and install their networks, but the buyers typically dictate the brands and components of a system. Increasingly, organizations with networking requirements on this scale have a professional staff dedicated to maintaining and expanding the network.

Interestingly, contributions to the budget for the operation of larger networks often come from managers of the business side of an organization. In a growing number of companies, the business managers control line items in their budgets for services such as copy machines, telephones, and the LAN, which gives them a lot of input into the activities of the technical staff.

Finally, at the top of the stack are those managers who must integrate multivendor networks. The people involved in this sphere of interoperability, as I've named it, come from several disciplines. First, there are the PC-savvy zealots who have hiked a long trail and learned many lessons. Second, there are people who specialize in communications systems and are often schooled more in telephone networks than in corporate computing networks. Then there are corporate data-processing managers and people whose whole line of work depends on computers, like structural or mechanical engineers who use computers as tools every day. They have to learn the technology of their tools in order to use them well.

In many ways these people are today's priests of computing, and they chant a litany that would be lost on managers and buyers of the lower-level systems. The step into the technology of interoperability is much bigger than the one from small- to medium-sized networks. The words are different, the concepts are sometimes arcane, and the arguments between factions supporting different protocols, architectures, and vendor-backed systems are fierce. Yet once you've mastered this technology of openness and interoperability, it really works.

The priests of interoperability often control their own budgets, but they must work with network systems servicing and financed by business managers, so they worry about productivity and economy more than the corporate data-processing professionals of the 1960s and '70s ever did. They usually write the specifications for their own systems and often buy directly from manufacturers.

All of these consumers of connectivity products are trying to solve the problem of how to tap their organizations into the volume and type of information they need for successful operation. Working in and building up the infrastructure for modern commerce and society are the tasks of the modern connectivity worker.

Whatever category you fall into, when you are ready to make buying decisions you look for products. These products will conform to certain protocols and follow certain technical strategies, but the buying decision finally comes down to a company name, a product name, and a price.

■ The Future of Connectivity

It's easy to predict the future, but making those predictions come true is often much more difficult. Here are some of today's connectivity trends and some projections of where I think they will take us.

- Interoperability: Interoperability will continue to replace "openness" as companies deliver an increasing number of products pragmatically designed to work together.

- Distributed processing: In distributed-processing systems, a program executes tasks on many processors spread around the network. In several ways, this architecture makes more sense than the use of "super servers" that have multiple processors in one box, which is a common system configuration marketed today.

- Diversity: The industry will continue to offer a variety of alternative ways to share information and resources. There won't be a single big winner among the competing wiring schemes and network operating systems, but rather a rich blend of offerings.

- Wireless connections: This technology poses many problems, including overcrowding the radio frequency spectrum, but you'll see an increase in the number of wireless alternatives for LAN, MAN, and WAN connectivity.

- Direct sales: The majority of buyers will be sophisticated enough to bypass higher-cost sales channels for everything from cables to software in favor of buying direct. As products become more interoperable, people will shop primarily for price, differentiating features, and availability.

The mid-1990s are a rich time for people who manage and use computer networks. Many new careers have already been launched, and the technology will continue to multiply in its complexity. The *PC Magazine Guide to Connectivity* is designed to help newcomers get started and to help experienced people stay current in the critically important field of connectivity.

- *Connection = Sharing*

- *Distance Makes the Difference*

- *Media-Sharing LANs*

- *Making Outside Connections*

- *Linking LANs*

- *LAN-Management Tools*

- *Making the Right Choices*

More than a Dozen Good Ways
to Connect Computers

TECHNICAL TALE

"Down the rabbit hole, right after Alice," Gail muttered to herself. "This is as bad as the mad tea party." The tea party Gail was attending was a committee meeting. The committee included people from across the corporation who were supposed to select a corporate networking system. But what they found were dozens of existing networks, purchased by managers at all levels, that linked two to twenty computers in different workgroups but never talked together. The committee either had to stop the party by throwing out all the existing equipment or try to get everything to sing from the same sheet of music.

"Look," Gail said to the group, "it breaks down into layers. First, there are the LAN adapter cards and the cables: They're related to each other, but independent of everything else. Next, there's the networking software—we've got six different brands' releases. Then, there are the network communication devices like gateways into mainframes, remote access servers, and fax servers. Those things are pretty much independent, too. So we can work on this problem in different layers."

"The networking software ties it together, right?" asked the representative from marketing. "So we should start there."

"Yes, but the network-layer protocols must be compatible," pontificated the MIS manager.

"Ahhh, yeah, whatever that means," Gail said. "Can't you ever speak English?"

"Whatever it is, it's got to run my applications," interrupted accounting. "We spent a lot of time and money developing that accounting system software."

"Okay, wait a minute. Let's take the diagram of the headquarters building and annotate it with the cards and cables, networking software, communications gateways, application programs, and that network-layer protocol stuff to see what we've got."

"Curiouser and curiouser," muttered the sales manager from the back of the room.

When Gail followed his gaze, she saw a white rabbit nibbling on the carefully tended corporate lawn.

I DESIGNED THIS CHAPTER FOR FOLKS WHO KNOW (OR PERHAPS JUST SUSPECT) that they need to link their PCs together, gain access to mainframe computer systems, or simply share printers, but aren't sure how to do it. You've probably heard about local area networks (LANs), and you might even use one now. Yet, beyond what you'll learn to call media-sharing LANs, there are lots of different ways to link PCs to each other, to other kinds of computers, and to shared devices such as printers and modems. Some of the alternatives cost less than traditional LANs and provide more flexibility. This chapter will lead you through the alternatives and guide you toward other references in this book.

The heart of this chapter is a chart called the Connectivity Decision Tree, bound at the back of the book. The chart consists of a series of yes-or-no questions leading to recommendations. At each branch of the Connectivity Decision Tree, I suggest an alternative connection scheme or service. Boxed comments indicate the major advantages and drawbacks of each alternative. I'll give you a brief explanation of the major connectivity alternatives in this chapter; later chapters contain detailed explanations of nearly all of the alternatives.

As we examine these alternatives, you can use the Appendix near the back of the book to find companies offering products in each category I describe. The Appendix includes phone numbers and addresses so that you can contact the companies for further information.

■ Connection = Sharing

The need to share inspires all of the connectivity systems, techniques, and alternatives discussed in this book. You link computers together to gain shared access to resources such as printers, files, and communications gateways.

The most common initial reason for linking computers is to share printers. Even though the prices of very capable laser printers have declined in recent years, it still makes economic sense to share printers among PCs if you can do this without too much technical and managerial overhead.

Connecting to Print

Let's start with the question in the upper-left corner of the Decision Tree: "Need to share more than printers?" If you answer no to this question, it means that sharing printers is all you need to do. Several kinds of products give you low-cost printer sharing.

You can share printers among a few people using a manual switch to route the printer connection from one PC to another. Typically, however, you would automate the process through a *printer-sharing buffer.* Such devices—usually small boxes roughly the size of this book (see Figure 2.1)—can give up to ten people shared access to the same printer at a cost of about $65 per connection.

Figure 2.1

Printer-sharing products, like the PrintDirector from Digital Products, Inc., provide an inexpensive way to share several printers among as many as 32 PCs without adding LAN adapters or networking software to the computers.

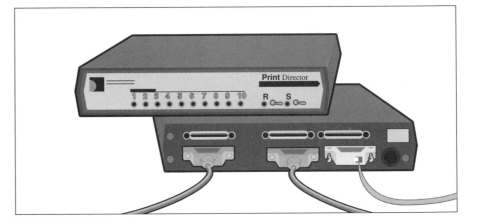

When a PC has something to print, the printer-sharing buffer routes the job to the printer. The person using that PC simply invokes an application program's print function in the usual way, and the buffer does all the work. Buffers often include their own internal memory to hold or spool print jobs until the printer can handle them. Some printer-sharing buffers include a small pop-up terminate-and-stay-resident (TSR) program or a Windows program that allows you to select the desired printer, but others use no software in the PCs.

Printer-sharing buffers attach to serial or parallel ports on each PC and to one or more printers. When you buy one of these products, you have to choose a model that has the appropriate types of ports for the PCs and printers you want to link. The dealers and manufacturers of these devices have a good handle on the technical specifications of any devices you are likely to have, so do ask for help in selecting the right buffer.

Refer to the Appendix near the back of this book for a list of companies offering these products, and see Chapter 3 for more detailed information on printer-sharing techniques.

Sending the Mail

After printer sharing, the most common reason people report they want to link PCs together is to exchange files and send electronic mail (e-mail). Surveys of *PC Magazine's* readers have revealed that electronic mail now equals printer sharing as a justification for local area network installations. As you have seen, you don't need to invest in a full LAN to share printers; savvy managers also know that they don't need a sophisticated network to establish a first-class electronic-mail system, either.

Electronic-mail programs are relatively simple pieces of software. Primarily, they transfer files (messages) from one subdirectory (mailbox) to another. Programs that let people share database files simultaneously or that provide shared access to mainframe computers are complex pieces of software, but e-mail packages are simpler programs that don't need a lot of sophisticated shared resources or network support.

Since e-mail programs primarily transfer small files, they will work over a wide variety of connection schemes. Simple cables connected to a PC's serial port, modems connected to telephone lines, and high-speed LAN cables all can carry e-mail messages. Later branches of the Decision Tree will help you make more decisions about your connection options.

■ Distance Makes the Difference

When you get to the question "All within 1,000 feet?" in the Decision Tree, we've established your commitment to the concept that you need a connectivity scheme fast enough to provide multiuser, concurrent access to the same data files. Only the question of the distance between devices remains.

The laws of physics make it much more difficult—and therefore expensive—to send a fast signal over a long distance than to send a slow signal over a long distance or a fast signal over a short distance. If you want high-speed service over a mile or more, you'll have to pay for special signaling techniques and circuits, but it is relatively easy and economical to maintain a signaling rate of 10 megabits per second over 1,000 feet.

ISDN Moves Data over Distances

One technique you can use to link PCs over a distance is called the *Integrated Services Digital Network*, or ISDN. The ISDN program, supported by funds from many governments and international companies, has the goal of digitizing the analog telephone systems of the world. You'll find ISDN available in the major cities of North America, Europe, and Japan.

The links between ISDN and personal computers are still emerging, but as new hardware and software reaches the market, ISDN promises to provide 128-kilobit-per-second computer-to-computer communications across thousands of miles at reasonable prices.

Refer to the Appendix to see a list of companies selling ISDN products and services. Read Chapter 3 for more detailed information.

The PBX Alternative

If you want to link computers over a distance of a mile or so, then a digital *Private-Branch Exchange* (PBX), or the telephone company's similar offering, called Digital Centrex, is a good alternative. One of these devices will often serve as the voice telephone switch for an organization, but they also have the ability to move data between computers at 56 or 128 kilobits per second across a "campus" or large installation.

Refer to the Appendix near the back of this book for a list of companies making telephone switches with computer data-switching capabilities.

If ISDN and digital PBX systems don't meet your needs for high-speed long-distance computing, don't despair. You can divide your resources into several local area networks and then link the networks at high speed over long distances. If you are interested in this technique, continue on through the Decision Tree to select your local network alternatives, and then refer to Chapter 13, where we discuss how to link your LANs across the miles.

■ Media-Sharing LANs

Fasten your seat belt and tug on your helmet strap; we're about to enter the fast lane. Now you're in the world of *media-sharing LANs*. These networks use special adapter cards to let each computer on the network share access to high-speed cables or *media* connecting them together.

The next stops on the Connectivity Decision Tree involve the selection of cabling schemes, adapter cards, and LAN software. (Figure 2.2 shows examples of some typical networking products.) Soon you'll have to be familiar with terms such as *Token-Ring*, *Ethernet*, *DOS-based operating systems*, and *gateways*. Don't worry though; you'll find the information you need in Chapter 5, which provides an introductory overview of media-sharing LANs. Later chapters cover topics such as adapter boards in even more detail.

Video on LANs

The next section of the Decision Tree asks if you want desktop videoconferencing. What we're getting at is the need to move a lot of data across the LAN without the delays caused when computers contend for the network cable. If you don't need videoconferencing, you can look at the traditional Ethernet and Token-Ring options that follow. If you do think you'll use videoconferencing and you want the lips to move in synchronization with the voice, then you'll need some networking schemes that are a little more expensive, but offer faster throughput.

If you have an existing Ethernet network system, then you should consider adding an Ethernet switch. An Ethernet switch provides each network station with a full 10 megabits-per-second throughput without contention. You can add an Ethernet switch to the network without changing the adapters or other components.

Figure 2.2

Media-sharing LANs use internal adapter circuit boards, cables, and wiring hubs. These products from Thomas-Conrad Corp. provide connections for networks using Token-Ring wiring.

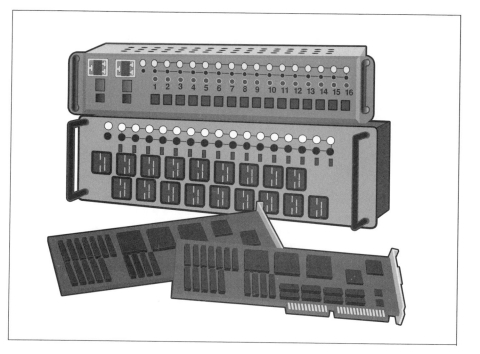

If you don't have an existing Ethernet network and need high speed connections, then you should investigate 100Base-X and 100VG network systems. These architectures carry data at 100 megabits-per-second, but they require new adapters and other network equipment.

Cables for Mainframe Connections

One important question is whether the PCs on your network will need access to an IBM mainframe; hence the question "Need IBM mainframe connections?" in the Connectivity Decision Tree. You should make this decision early, because IBM designed one cabling and access scheme—Token-Ring— as the primary way to link mainframes to a network. If you choose not to use Token-Ring (as well you might, because it is ugly and expensive), there are other good ways to link PCs to mainframes, but Token-Ring is clearly the primary route IBM wants you to use for this purpose. If your organization will ever need connections between PCs and IBM mainframes, choosing a Token-Ring architecture now gives you the option to use special IBM connection equipment later. Chapter 6 describes LAN wiring alternatives.

If Token-Ring access to IBM mainframes is not critically important to you, the two other wiring schemes you should consider are ARCnet, and a general family of standards known as Ethernet.

You have many factors to consider when you select LAN cabling. The construction of the building, existing wiring, the experience and knowledge of the people doing the installation, and several more factors influence this decision. In later chapters, we'll discuss other, less critical aspects of various LAN wiring systems, but the questions in the Decision Tree cover the most important considerations.

On to Software

The next question on the Decision Tree is "More than a dozen users of the same files?" The number of people simultaneously sharing the same data files is a rough indicator of the workload placed on the computer that acts as a file server. Heavily loaded servers—those handling more than a dozen simultaneous users running word processing, spreadsheet, and accounting applications—need an operating system that is able to handle several tasks at a time. Lightly loaded servers can run efficiently using the single-tasking operating system MS-DOS.

Multitasking Server Operating Systems

A server carrying the load of many busy client stations can receive hundreds of requests for file actions per second. The operating systems in these servers need special multitasking techniques to queue and satisfy these requests. The three most widely used server operating systems are Novell's NetWare, Microsoft's Windows NT Advanced Server,and Banyan Systems's VINES. These high-quality products have comparable prices, capacities, and performance ratings, so choosing between them is largely a matter of selecting the product with the right features for your organization, bearing in mind the expertise of the local installers and support people.

DOS-Based Servers

Lightly loaded servers—those handling only a few simultaneous users—can run effectively with DOS or Windows as their operating system. Because the PC acting as a server runs DOS, it can also perform as a local workstation for someone running applications. The server tasks and the local workstation tasks interact to slow each other down, but this arrangement works in organizations with light network loads or with many computers configured as servers.

When you choose between multitasking server operating systems and DOS-based servers, you can base your decision on a number of factors, including cost and the question of centralized versus distributed structure. But the primary difference between these types of server operating systems is the number of simultaneous users of the same files they can support.

The Appendix lists companies providing network operating systems. You'll find a lot more information on these operating systems in Chapters 4, 7, and 8.

■ Making Outside Connections

The next series of questions in the Connectivity Decision Tree deals with extending the network beyond the limits of its local high-speed cable. Extended links can go to mainframe computers, to other local networks, and to unlikely sounding devices like distant facsimile machines. Since few companies do business in just one place anymore, developing extensions to other operating areas, to suppliers, to dealers, and even to customers is a critically important part of networking in business. In large part, this is what the highly touted and little explained "information highway" is all about—extending beyond physical limits to do business wherever the business might be.

Mainframe Links

At this point in the Decision Tree, we again raise the question, "Need mainframe connections?" If you selected IBM's Token-Ring wiring scheme when this question came up earlier, you already have a path to the mainframe.

If you don't have Token-Ring wiring, there are several other LAN-to-mainframe connection alternatives. If the computers follow the IBM 3270 communications architecture, you can establish a network gateway, or give each PC the ability to emulate a 3270 terminal and connect directly to the mainframe through coaxial cable or over modem-equipped telephone lines. Some of these terms may be new to you; if so, you'll find detailed information on linking to mainframe computers in Chapter 12. The Appendix provides listings of companies selling LAN gateway products under the menu selection "Mainframe Links."

A negative reply to the question "Only IBM mainframes?" opens a path to the subject of linking computers with architectures designed by many companies through the *TCP/IP protocol services*. TCP/IP (Transmission Control Protocol/Internet Protocol) is a standard set of communications protocols developed by the U.S. government and adopted by many companies and institutions around the world. If you properly select communications software designed to meet the TCP/IP standards, you can link computers with many different kinds of operating systems and internal architectures. TCP/IP utilities let you exchange files, send mail, and store data on different types of computers connected to local and extended networks.

Talking Fax

Faxing has become a critically important part of how we communicate. People operating LAN client stations can use the network to link to distant facsimile machines. One PC on the network acts as a special type of communications server called a *fax gateway*, which can send and receive the images of fax documents. People working at individual client PCs can view fax messages on their screens and send files created by word processing software as fax messages.

Chapter 7 contains more information on network fax servers. Refer to the Appendix near the back of this book to find a list of companies offering these products.

■ Linking LANs

Organizations that have offices in many locations face the problem of linking widely separated local area networks. The Decision Tree question "Want to link LANs?" introduces more questions relating to how far apart the LANs are and how much data will flow between them. Solutions range from connections made over fiber-optic links (Figure 2.3) to the use of ISDN.

Figure 2.3

Fiber-optic cabling provides long-distance connections between PCs and between discrete networks of PCs using more typical copper wiring.

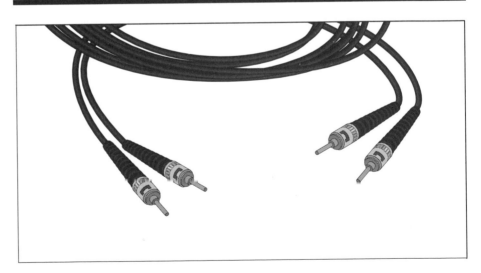

Those of you looking for ways to connect networks together or to connect remote and portable PCs into a LAN should seriously consider using modems and *remote-control software*. The ability to remotely control one PC from another effectively integrates distant computers into a local area network.

Chapter 7 covers the subject of communications servers, and the companies marketing these products are listed under "Communications Servers" in the Appendix.

■ LAN-Management Tools

LAN administrators in large and small organizations are coming under increasing pressure to back up their budgets, to monitor LAN operations in real time, and to safeguard against network abuse. Network management is a high-priority topic for anyone responsible for the tens of thousands of dollars invested in the typical network. Several categories of network-management software provide administrators with strong tools to prevent abuse, collect statistics, and provide reports on network operations. Chapter 9 contains more information on these products, and they are listed in the Appendix near the back of this book.

Traffic Monitoring

If you answer yes to the question about being the network troubleshooter, then you need some special tools. Network troubleshooters can use two types of traffic-monitoring systems. *Media-monitoring software* gathers statistical data from a centralized wiring hub and provides second-by-second control over the connections that servers and client stations make to the network. *LAN protocol analyzers* capture the packets of data flying across a network and decode them into more-or-less plain English.

Application-Metering Software

The question "Need to limit the number of application users?" refers to the need to keep the number of people simultaneously using an application within the limits of the software license. LAN *application-metering software* controls the number of people who can simultaneously access a networked application. This type of software helps you buy only as many copies of an application as you really need while eliminating the danger of abusing software licenses. *LAN-management software suites* are products that roll many functions together. They produce printed reports that administrators can use to plan LAN growth and justify expenditures, and they offer additional capabilities such as virus protection and backup.

■ Making the Right Choices

The Connectivity Decision Tree won't replace a good consultant, but it will help you organize your ideas and make some important early decisions about the best approach to take. An investment in a media-sharing LAN can pay big dividends in workgroup productivity, but such a complex system requires a great deal of investment, planning, and management. Less complex alternatives and techniques might work fine for you. The Connectivity Decision Tree and the Appendix can help you manage the growth and operation of your network for years to come.

- *Simple Switches*

- *Zero-Slot LANs*

- *Media-Sharing LANs*

CHAPTER

Connecting PCs for Printer Sharing and File Exchange

TECHNICAL TALE

Marty was furious. The little sticky piece of paper that was on the border of the monitor had disappeared. Now, nobody could remember how to export the report file to a diskette. Frustration is the mother of inspiration, so Marty unplugged the printer from the computer and the wall socket, lifted it with a grunt, and shuffled over to the desk on the other side of the office.

"There must be a better way!" he thought. He now had three computers in his insurance office and he didn't have the space or money to attach a printer to each computer. Moving files between the computers on a diskette wasn't going to work for long, and one session of lugging the printer was quite enough.

"My daughter says that they share printers in her classroom," Bill the accountant observed. "They use a network—something with cables between the computers." Marty fished out the telephone book, looked under COMPUTERS-NETWORK, and dialed a number.

"O.K. Networks," Steve Rigney answered the phone. "How can I help you?"

Marty's voice had an edge. "Do you know about networks, and can I share a printer between three computers using a network?" he asked.

"Sure," Steve replied. "Networks are what we do. But if you just want to share printers, then there might be even easier solutions."

"Could we send faxes, too?" Marty asked. "We usually have to print out a letter so we can shove the paper into the fax machine. Then we get something in on the fax, and we have to type it into the computer. Can we get around that?"

"Sure," Steve said. "Through a network, everyone can send and receive faxes on a PC without ever going to paper. The cost might be less than the price of one new printer."

"Humph... Yeah, let's talk." Marty said. "Maybe networking is just what we need."

W HILE WE ARE SEEING EVIDENCE THAT NETWORKING CAN REDUCE COMMUT-ing, reduce corporate overhead, and reduce inventory, we don't see much evidence that it reduces the amount of paper we use. Except for specific applications such as forms handling, described in Chapter 10, the once longed-for "paperless office" remains a dream. The primary output of computers seems to be paper, so printing capabilities are both important and a major investment.

Sharing relatively expensive printers among several people has always been a primary objective of PC connectivity. In the mid-1980s, even dot-matrix printers with "near-letter quality" were expensive. As the cost of letter-quality printers declined, printers able to produce the special fonts needed for desktop publishing appeared on the horizon as high-cost items. Now, as the cost of printers suitable for basic desktop publishing declines, printers that can use large sheets of paper or print in color populate the high-end market. Similarly, large-format plotters carry high price tags. Since one person probably won't keep a modern printer busy, it makes sense to share printers among as many people as possible.

■ Simple Switches

To many people, printer sharing means having a box with a switch on the front and cables running to the PCs and printer. When you turn the knob, the switch establishes a connection to the printer from one of two or three PCs.

Manual printer switches (Figure 3.1), often called *A-B boxes* after the designation of the switch positions, are simple to operate, but you can only use a maximum of about 15 feet of parallel cable to each computer. Additionally, several printer manufacturers, including Hewlett-Packard, warn against using manual switches with shorting contacts that make one connection before they break the other, as this can cause an excessive voltage spike that might damage your printer when someone changes the switch setting. A commercial A-B box offers a simple and effective way to share a printer among as many as 3 or 4 users, but you trade the benefits of simplicity for the hassle of remembering to change the switch and coordinate with the other people using the system.

Printer-Sharing Buffers

Printer-sharing buffers automate the concept of the manual printer switch. Although printer-sharing buffers come in a variety of sizes and shapes, each device typically has a cabinet just big enough for all the connectors mounted on it and a separate power supply molded into the wall plug. As Figure 3.2 shows, the printer-sharing buffer uses the existing ports on the computers

Figure 3.1

An A-B box provides a simple way of sharing a printer between two PCs. Lights on the switch's front panel show the status of activity. The unit pictured is for serial printer connections, but units for parallel connections are also available.

and printers and makes shared connections that don't involve adding hardware or software to the PC. You can often fit a printer-sharing buffer inconspicuously next to the printer. As Figure 3.3 shows, some companies even design them to fit inside popular printers like the Hewlett-Packard LaserJet. These devices connect to each PC and printer and switch print jobs and connections from the PCs to the printers.

A printer-sharing buffer allows each person who shares the printer to send print jobs just as if the printer were attached directly to the PC. The device receives the jobs, checks the printer's availability, and either passes the job to the printer or stores it until the printer can accept it. The most sophisticated units can select from among several attached printers based on the print job's format and content. Once the buffer has the print job, the person who sent the job is free to turn to other tasks while the buffer works with the printer.

Because the buffer stores print jobs, it needs enough memory to hold the kinds of jobs you're sending. Documents containing graphics print slowly and occupy a lot of memory, so if people on your network create a lot of graphical documents, consider adding four or more megabytes of memory to the print buffer. Adding memory raises the cost, but also increases the speed while the operation stays simple.

Printer-sharing buffers come in models that can handle a wide number and variety of PCs, such as Intel and Macintosh systems, and different printing devices. Note that printer buffers are particularly well suited to the problem of sharing a plotter. Plotters are typically serial devices and the software

Figure 3.2

Printer sharing buffers provide the simplest method of connecting computers and a shared printer. These devices require little setup and no special hardware or software on the PCs.

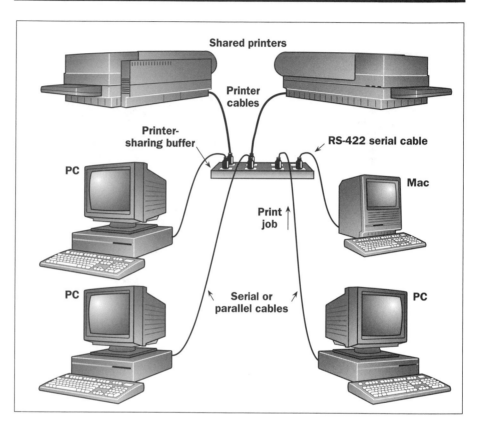

you use to create the plotted images often expects to directly address the PC's serial port hardware (particularly under DOS), so it's difficult to use these devices with LAN software and hardware. But since the printer buffer acts like a plotter connected to the serial port, all of the software works fine while you share the expensive plotting hardware.

You can find models of print buffers with up to 64 ports, but the price of these products typically stays at slightly more than $75 per port. Most modern printer-sharing buffers will also handle problems such as mismatched speed between the PC and printer serial ports, or the need to convert between PC serial connections and printer parallel connections.

The cables required for attaching PCs to printer-sharing buffers are limited in terms of the distance they can cover, particularly if you use a faster parallel-cable connection. You can count on a good connection using up to 50 feet of cable, but the distance between the printer and the most distant PC can't be much more than that. Several products in this market can carry serial-port connections to printers over several thousand feet of cable.

Figure 3.3

The ASP ServerJet is an interesting printer sharing product that slides into an I/O slot of an HP LaserJet and allows as many as 12 computers to share the printer without any other special software or adapters.

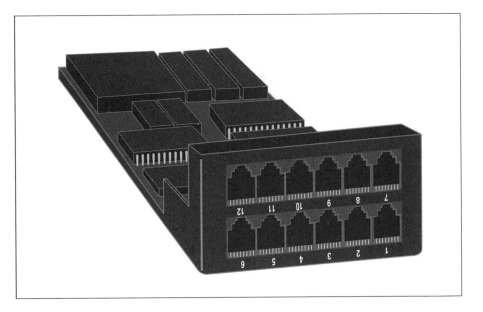

I've said that the print buffers don't need software loaded in each PC, but using a small piece of software in the client computers can improve flexibility. Typically, you can program a print buffer so it automatically sends print jobs to specific types of printers set up for envelopes, color, Postscript printing, or other special features. But if you want to manually select the printers, you can use terminate-and-stay resident (TSR) software under DOS or use a Windows program to select the printer you want to use for your print jobs.

Printer-sharing buffers are practical devices. They don't do anything more than move print jobs to the printer efficiently, but if that is all you need, your worries are over. Check the Appendix for the makers of printer-sharing buffers.

What to Consider when You Buy a Printer-Sharing Buffer

- How many PC and printer ports do you need?

- How much RAM is available for the print job queue?

- Do you want serial or parallel connections?

- Do the cables come with the unit?

- Does the unit allow PCs and printers operating at different speeds to be connected?

- What is the size of the unit and the type of cable connectors?

- Where will you get technical support?

Printer sharing is an important part of workgroup productivity. You should install a system that can provide all the capabilities you need, but don't pay for more than you require.

■ Zero-Slot LANs

I coined the phrase "zero-slot LANs" in a 1987 *PC Magazine* review of these low-cost but highly functional PC-connection products. To create a zero-slot LAN, you simply take two PCs, connect one cable between their serial or parallel ports, and load a small piece of software in each PC. The software lets the people using each PC share each other's printers, exchange files, and even simultaneously access the same data file. But the days of zero-slot LANs are over because the prices of shared media LANs have dipped so low. Any tiny cost advantage left to the zero-slot LAN doesn't outweigh its disadvantage in throughput, so I mention them here mainly as a historical note. The next section introduces media-sharing LANs, a very capable—perhaps overly capable—printer-sharing technique.

■ Media-Sharing LANs

The wide-ranging capabilities of media-sharing LANs are a major factor behind their popularity. Before we learn about lower-cost alternatives to media-sharing LANs, let's briefly examine how these popular connection systems function. Chapters 4 through 8 will provide more detailed information.

Media-sharing LANs carry messages simultaneously from multiple stations over a shared high-speed medium. The most common medium is coaxial copper cable, but advances in fiber-optic cable and twisted-pair copper wire continue to increase the popularity of these media alternatives. The media-sharing LANs use signaling and sharing schemes with names like ARCnet, Ethernet, and Token-Ring. *Adapter boards* for these networks occupy a slot in each PC and perform the data handling and precise timing chores that become necessary when the media are shared among hundreds of stations.

Because the shared-cable system moves data two to five times as fast as the rate at which a PC can accept it, network designers have enough headroom to create elegant network operating systems that fool DOS into thinking that distant disk drives and printers, residing on computers acting as servers, are really on the local computer. The redirection of DOS service requests to the network allows standard applications to use resources like the network server for file storage, but the special interface cards and sophisticated software these systems require also make them costly and challenging to install and maintain.

When you put together a card-carrying LAN, you need space in each PC and some technical skill to install the LAN adapter card, and you also need a good budget for the cabling and for special LAN software. The hardware and software for these networks have a minimum price of about $100 per station, and they can cost four or more times that amount. Managing a media-sharing network with a dozen stations or more can employ the talents of a PC support person full-time. You get what you pay for, because these LANs provide more functionality and speed than any other connectivity alternative, but then again you might not need all the functionality of a media-sharing LAN.

Print Servers

One or more PCs on a media-sharing LAN can take on the role of a *print server*. A print server makes its attached printers available to all other devices on the network. Software resident in each PC using the network intercepts the print jobs that standard applications create and sends them to a network print server.

The PC acting as a print server might simultaneously act as a file server or as a personal workstation. There are no special hardware requirements for the print server aside from having enough serial or parallel ports for the attached printers. An old cast-aside IBM PC with a slow 80286 processor works just fine as a dedicated network print server. Modern LAN operating systems provide ways for any PC attached to the network to fill this function.

The concept behind shared LAN printing is simple, but the administrative details involved in making everything work correctly are often complex. The print server accepts print jobs from client PCs on the network and queues these jobs until the attached printers can accept them. Utility software included in LAN packages gives network users and administrators control over the priority of jobs in the queue.

Sophisticated tasks, like downloading fonts to the printer for desktop publishing, often require several carefully executed steps. Because applications don't always reset the printer mode before and after executing a print job, people can find their text produced in compressed form, with strange fonts, or sideways because one of these attributes was used in a previous print job. If you use Novell's NetWare, see Chapter 8 for more information on NetWare printing.

On the Bottom Line of LAN Printing

You get the best value in a media-sharing LAN when you use it to provide simultaneous access to the same files for many people. Media-sharing LANs shine when you use them to provide accounting services, inventory control, and any other database applications. They also provide good value when you use them to share expensive communications links to distant locations or to different computer systems such as mainframes. But most people use these complex LANs just to share printers. If you merely want to share printers and similar peripherals such as plotters, print buffers offer economy, simplicity, and speed.

- *Networking's Necessary Hardware*
- *The Soft Side*
- *The Future*
- *Networking Acronyms and Buzzwords*
- *Now I Know My ABCs*

A Field Guide to LANs

TECHNICAL TALE

The airplane hit a pothole in the sky and Bill's laptop computer bounced against the seat in front of him. "A quick check on my mail and then I'll watch the movie," he thought.

Bill's modem connection was the tail end of of a nest of connections between corporate computers on desktops across the country. The system started with cables connected to adapters in desktop computers—a local area network— and extended across leased telephone lines spanning the continent. Within the system, devices called routers acted as automated portals, guiding the movement of digital zeros and ones collected into groups called packets. A management system reported the flow of traffic and recognized problems at many points. Bill thought of it primarily as a way to get his e-mail, but the network performed many storage, sharing, and data routing functions.

The first message Bill found in his inbox told him that the other company wasn't going to show up at the meeting he thought he was headed toward. He was belted in and cruising in a metal tube at 32,000 feet for no good reason.

Having nothing better to do, Bill pondered the efficiency of all this connectivity. He was sure that his voice mail held the same information about the meeting, but he hadn't checked it on the way to the airport. No one had called him at home to tell him of the cancellation because they had left him voice mail and e-mail. Electronic mail had partially replaced direct telephone contact and voice mail had displaced the rest. Almost no one talked voice-to-voice anymore.

No technology goes away completely, but they all evolve. Faxes displace surface mail, telephone conferences replace face-to-face meetings, but none of it goes away completely. Bill vowed to learn a lesson, so he ignored the movie and spent the rest of the flight trying to figure out how he could make money out of the next evolutionary slips of connectivity technology.

How ABOUT A HELICOPTER VIEW? LET'S LOOK OVER THE NETWORKING TERRI-
tory a little so you can find the areas you want to know more about and dip
down into them. I've written this chapter to give you an overview of the pieces
and parts in a media-sharing LAN system and to describe the important considerations in stringing together those pieces and parts. Later chapters deal
with the features and foibles of specific cabling schemes and operating systems
in more depth. This chapter gives you the strategic view, the buzzwords, and
the background you'll need to get the most out of the material in later chapters.

As a first step in explaining these systems, we'll divide them into hardware
and software. Even this seemingly simple division isn't clean, because some
hardware elements have software on board in read-only memory (ROM), but
it's a good way to start to examine the pieces of the LAN puzzle. After we examine the real pieces and parts, we'll move from the material to the ethereal
and introduce a number of networking acronyms and concepts.

■ Networking's Necessary Hardware

Servers, client PCs, adapter cards, and cables are the dry-bones hardware
into which networking and application software breathe life. Because modern hardware products follow international standards, you can often mix and
match hardware products from different vendors within the same network.
Similarly, the hardware you buy does not determine your selection of application software for the network. But the selection of the right hardware isn't
simple. You have to make up-front decisions with long-term consequences.

Servers and Clients

In a PC-based network, computers act in the functional roles of servers and
client stations. The servers make their attached disk drives, printers, modems,
and unique communications links (such as fax) available to the client stations.
Software running in the client PCs gives network users access to the data and
devices available on one or more servers. The networking software running
on a server determines whether the server is dedicated to its service role or
whether it also runs local application programs in what is termed a *peer-to-
peer network*.

Practically any 80386-, or 80486-based computer can act as a server, but
machines with 80286 processing power are better suited for use as print servers in modern network. Powerful LAN operating systems like Microsoft's
Windows NT Advanced Server and Novell's NetWare can use the power and
memory-addressing capabilities of 80486 and Pentium processors. An increasing number of new network applications run partly in the server, so an investment in a powerful processor today will pay future dividends. Considering
their reasonable prices, I recommend buying Pentium-based PCs as servers.

Many companies sell computers with multiple expansion slots and disk drive bays as servers, but simply designing a computer with a lot of internal space, a fast processor, and a vertical mounting pedestal doesn't make it a good server. In the real-estate business, they say the three most important things about a piece of property are location, location, and location. Similarly, the three most important things about a server are disk drive speed, disk drive speed, and disk drive speed. Spend your money on large, fast hard drives for your server. This is the most important investment you'll make in LAN hardware.

Here is my advice on servers in a nutshell: First, price a good set of hard drives with triple the capacity you think you'll ever need, plus a fast disk controller, and a PC with a processor in the Pentium class. Load it with a minimum of 16 megabytes of RAM and buy the RAM in a configuration that allows you to add more without throwing away what you already have.

Interface Cards

The most frequent investment you make in LAN hardware is in network interface adapters (generally called interface cards or adapter cards). Companies such as National Semiconductor Corp., Standard Microsystems Corp., and Texas Instruments market chip sets for Ethernet, ARCnet, and Token-Ring network interface cards. In 1987, a typical network interface card cost $600. Today, the increased availability of these chip sets has turned interface cards into commodity products, with current prices for no-frills Ethernet and ARCnet cards in the $100 range.

Every computer on the network needs one of these printed circuit boards to move the serial signals on the network cables, or media, into the parallel data stream inside the PCs. Figure 4.1 illustrates the process. These adapters can also change the format of the data from parallel to serial and amplify the signals so they can travel over the necessary distances. In some cases, you will put two or more adapters in a server to split the load, which helps overcome any limitation of the ISA bus.

These adapters also have the important job of controlling access to the media. This media-access control (MAC) function takes three general forms: listen-before-transmitting, sequential station number, and token-passing.

Media-Access Control

The listen-before-transmitting scheme, called carrier sense multiple access (CSMA), operates like a CB, police, or other two-way radio system. A station with a message to send listens to the LAN cable. If it doesn't hear the carrier or transmitted signal of another network node, the station broadcasts its message. Various techniques (detailed in Chapter 5) handle the problems

Figure 4.1

The network interface card changes the parallel signals inside the computer into serial signals that go over the network cable. The interface card determines what type of network cable system you will use.

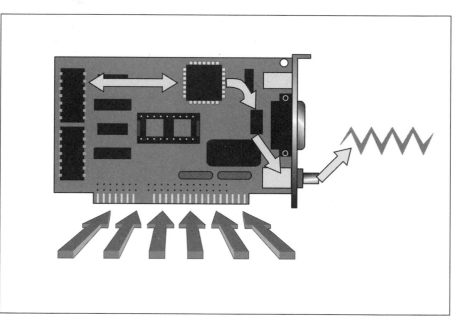

that arise when more than one station hears the empty channel and starts to transmit.

ARCnet uses a different media-access scheme, which assigns a station number (0 to 255) to each node on the network. The stations with messages to send simply wait for their number to come up in turn.

The other popular media-access control scheme, token-passing, involves a special message called a token, passed from node to node by active stations on the network. This token grants the receiving station permission to transmit.

LAN scientists and the people marketing LAN products can argue for days over the theoretical advantages of the CSMA, token-passing, and ARCnet media-access protocols. My advice is not to worry about the question. Other factors, such as the type of wire you want to pull in the walls, are much more important than the type of media-access protocol used by the adapters you choose. But you do need to know what people mean when they talk about the media-access scheme or MAC protocol.

Wire, Wire Everywhere, and Not an Inch to Link

The most important question associated with the adapter board is what kind of cable or wire to use for the network. Modern Ethernet and ARCnet adapters, and to some degree Token-Ring adapters, give you a wide variety of wiring choices. But remember, your network will never be any better than its cabling!

This is the link that ties everything together and poorly installed cabling is a sure prescription for frustration and failure.

The network interface card determines the type of cabling you'll need to connect the servers and the client stations. Choices include coaxial cable, fiber-optic cable, unshielded twisted-pair wire, and shielded twisted-pair. If one of these types of wire is already installed in your building, you'll want to select an interface card that can work with the existing wiring. Figure 4.2 shows some wiring examples.

Figure 4.2

The major types of network wiring are (from left to right) a thin coaxial cable with BNC connector, fiber-optic cable and connectors, shielded twisted-pair wire with an IBM Token-Ring connector attached, and unshielded twisted-pair wire with a modular connector attached.

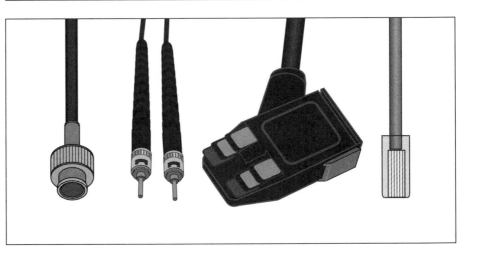

Electric Evils

Two electrical phenomena can disrupt your network: crosstalk and outside electrical noise. Crosstalk is caused by electrical fields in adjacent wires inducing false signals in each wire. Outside electrical noise comes from lights, motors, radio systems, and many other sources. The negative effects of crosstalk and noise only increase as the signaling speed of the network increases. The goal of all good wiring schemes is to keep crosstalk and noise to a minimum. If you're interested in the nitty-gritty of the cabling business, look for another book I've written, *Get a Grip on Network Cabling*, also published by Ziff-Davis Press (ISBN 1-56276-057-2).

Coaxial Cable

Coaxial cable, particularly the thin RG-58 or RG-62 type, provides good protection from crosstalk and outside electrical noise. A woven metal or foil braid surrounding the outside of a single conductor presents a formidable barrier to electrical noise. Originally, thin Ethernet and ARCnet schemes used only coaxial cable. One version of Ethernet uses a thick coaxial cable—particularly, for example, as a backbone between workgroups on different floors of a building. Thick Ethernet cable—known in the trade as "frozen orange garden hose" because it's stiff and carrot colored—is difficult to install, and its popularity is diminishing. Overall, because coaxial cable is more expensive and takes more space in wiring conduits, it is being superseded by unshielded twisted-pair wire.

Fiber-Optic Cable

Fiber-optic cable allows for greater distance between stations and provides total immunity to electrical noise. A fiber-optic link can run for several kilometers without the need for repeaters to regenerate the signal. Radio transmitters, arc welders, fluorescent lights, and other sources of electrical noise have no effect on the light pulses traveling inside this kind of cable. Many vendors offer versions of their network interface cards adapted for fiber-optic transmission.

However, fiber-optic cabling is expensive. Depending on local labor rates and building codes, installing this type of cable can cost as much as $500 per network node. At one time, we thought that fiber optic cabling would replace all copper, at least in heavy-duty commercial applications. But new developments in the engineering of cable schemes, particularly in the ability of unshielded twisted-pair wire to carry high-speed data, have reduced the technical advantages of fiber.

Unshielded Twisted-Pair Wire

The unshielded twisted-pair wire (UTP) used in networks can meet all of your networking needs. A number of organizations, including the Electronic Industries Association, the Telecommunications Industry Association (EIA/TIA), and Underwriter's Laboratories (UL), have standards for UTP wiring. The EIA/TIA 568 standards describe a UTP structured wiring scheme that can handle the fastest networks we forsee in this decade. See Chapters 5 and 6 for more detailed information on unshielded twisted-pair wiring and the EIA/TIA and UL specifications. For a list of companies marketing these products, refer to the Appendix.

Shielded Twisted-Pair Wire

Shielded twisted-pair wire has a name similar to the more widely used unshielded twisted-pair wiring, but it has a very different construction. Shielded twisted-pair wire is bound in an external aluminum-foil or woven-copper shield specifically designed to reduce electrical noise absorption. Different companies have their own specifications for such cables, although IEEE standards apply to systems like IBM's Token-Ring.

Shielded twisted-pair cables are expensive and difficult to work with, and because they are so thick they fill up wiring conduits. Still, IBM has successfully marketed a wiring plan that uses these cables for Token-Ring installations. The IBM plan adds reliability (and substantial cost) by using a separate run of cable between each server or workstation and a central wiring hub. This wiring plan significantly increases the amount of cable used, but it also ensures against the total failure of the network in the event that one cable is broken or shorted. See Chapter 5 and check the Appendix for more information on Token-Ring wiring.

Network Topology

Isn't *topology* a lovely word? Basically, in networking it means "the shape of things." A physical topology is a description of the route the network cables take as they link nodes. The logical topology describes how the messages flow to the stations. As Chapters 5 and 6 will explain, the physical form and the logical path can be two different things.

ARCnet typically uses a wiring plan or topology in which every station links directly into a central wiring hub, a scheme that reduces the vulnerability of the overall network. Token-Ring uses a similar hub in its physical topology. Thin Ethernet, on the other hand, uses a station-to-station wiring scheme that is economical because it uses less cable than a hub-type scheme, but runs the risk of total network failure if any one link is severed or shorted. The EIA/TIA and UL structured wiring plans use a wiring hub.

■ The Soft Side

Because of the current de facto standards and protocols, you can mix and match these pieces—servers, network interface cards, cables, and software—in myriads of ways to form an optimally productive and cost-effective network.

Many people worry more about network interface cards and cabling than about operating systems. While they can usually specify that they want a server with fast disk drives and a fast processor, they don't know how to quantify, describe, or select networking software. But software can make or break a network.

Networking operating systems make distant resources local. If you are interested in files residing on a computer down the hall, the networking software enables you to access those files as if they resided on disk drives in your own machine. It lets you use printers located thousands of feet away—or even miles away—as if they were snugly attached to your own LPT1 port. And it allows you to use network modems or minicomputers as if they were cabled to your own COM1 port.

Network operating systems have a multitasking and multiuser architecture; in that respect, they're more like minicomputer and mainframe-computer operating systems than like Microsoft's DOS for the PC. Your PC's DOS takes requests from application programs and translates them, one at a time, into actions to be performed by the video display, disk drives, and other peripheral devices. Network operating systems, on the other hand, take requests for services from many application programs at the same time and satisfy them with the network's resources—in effect, arbitrating requests for the same services from different users.

Invisible and Modular

Ideally, networking software is invisible to users. When you use it, you know you have additional resources available, but you usually don't care where the resources are or how you attach to them.

Structurally, networking software has many modules. Most of them reside in the machine that acts as the server for data, printer, or communications resources. But, as Figure 4.3 shows, several important program modules must be installed in every workstation, or sometimes in devices posed between the workstation and the network.

Figure 4.3 diagrams how the operating software interacts with the hardware and software on the workstation (left) and on the server (right). For both workstation and server, the hardware is the bottom level of the diagram; everything above that is software. Arrows represent the flow of messages—requests for services and data and responses to those requests.

The workstation is only a "client," with no capabilities for contributing resources to other network stations. It has the same PC hardware (disk drives, monitor, keyboard, and so forth), BIOS (Basic Input/Output System, the software that links the hardware to DOS), and operating system (DOS) that all PCs have, whether they are networked or not.

For LAN operation, several additional elements are necessary, both hardware (the interface cards and cables) and software (the redirector, NetBIOS, and driver software). The application program running on the workstation may have certain added network attributes, such as the ability to issue record- and file-lock commands automatically through DOS. (This software enhancement is not strictly necessary, since even application programs not designed with a LAN in mind can run on a network.)

The redirector module is added to intervene between the application program and DOS. It intercepts software calls from an application program asking DOS for services such as file access. Each PC's redirector is programmed to switch certain calls out through the network for service (for instance, requests for data from drives that don't exist in the local PC's hardware). Thanks to the

Figure 4.3

Network software/
hardware interaction

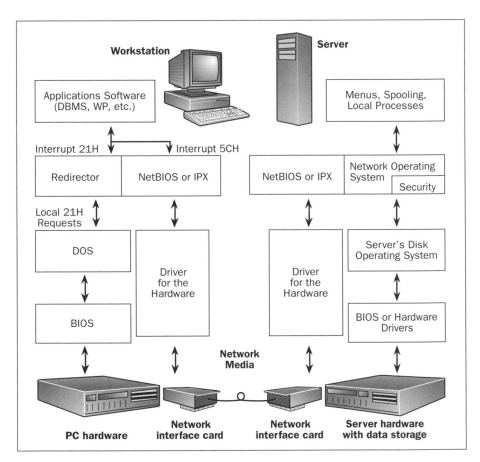

redirector, a PC application can easily use network resources just by addressing the correct disk drive.

Another added software module, the interface card driver, moves data between the redirector and the workstation's network interface card. This driver
software is specifically designed for network interface card hardware. Some
card vendors supply it in a format that, from the redirector's view, looks like
the NetBIOS program IBM and Sytek developed to link their network hardware and software. If the driver is wrapped in a NetBIOS interface, it fits the
Microsoft redirector supplied with Microsoft's Windows for Workgroups and
many other operating systems.

If the interface card driver doesn't perform the communications functions
associated with NetBIOS, another software module such as Novell's IPX must
perform those functions. Application programs are written to make a special

call for session-level communications services from the NetBIOS emulator or conforming NetBIOS software.

The network interface card sits in the expansion bus of the workstation. In modern networks, the wiring and media-access protocol are almost always independent of the networking software. The interface card includes programs in read-only memory that manage the creation and transmission of packets over the network.

At the other end of the cable from the workstation interface card is the server, with additional specialized LAN software and its own interface card. After the server's interface card does its job, a NetBIOS module or emulator watches for packets containing NetBIOS information. Other messages pass on to the security and multiuser software modules.

Like any other computer, the server runs an operating system—sometimes DOS, but often a unique system or one derived from the Unix operating system. If the system is DOS, you can almost always run local application programs and use your computer as a network terminal. But remember, all server software gobbles processing power, especially under DOS.

Finally, network utility programs run on the server, offering print spooling, auditing, and other LAN features.

Working together, these program modules perform the basic actions of networking software. In a nutshell, networking software recognizes users, associates their preprogrammed privileges with their identities, and then reroutes their DOS requests to the appropriate server for action. The operating-system software in the server frequently is not a variety of MS-DOS, but it must emulate DOS and respond properly to DOS requests routed from workstations.

Different Species

Darwin's method of categorizing strange critters according to species can also be applied to operating systems, which include two species, each having different ancestors and largely different attributes. One species is derived from MS-DOS; the other has roots in minicomputer operating systems like Unix.

The MS-DOS Species

MS-DOS is a weak basis for network operations because it was not designed to run multiple programs and satisfy many users simultaneously. Companies marketing DOS-based network software use patches and shell programs that intercept multiple requests, buffer them, and divide processor time among tasks. Some companies, such as Artisoft and Performance Technology, have developed their own programs to modify DOS and give stations network-client and file-server capabilities.

The largest number of DOS-derived operating systems are the work of Microsoft. That company developed a set of programs for DOS-based network operating systems called MS-Net, and many vendors license pieces of MS-Net for their own use. AT&T, Digital Equipment Corp. (DEC), and IBM, for example, have incorporated some part of the original MS-Net in their networking systems.

These DOS-based network operating systems share a number of characteristics. The most evident is peer-to-peer resource sharing—the ability to allow any PC on the network to contribute resources such as printers and disk drives. The DOS add-on programs that offer multifunction capabilities work in the background mode, so, for example, someone else on the network can use your disk drive or printer while you are running PC application programs on your machine.

The most significant advances in peer-to-peer networking have come from Microsoft. Windows for Workgroups set the stage for the highly integrated networking capabilities found in Microsoft's latest release of Windows. Under Windows for Workgroups, networking became an integrated feature of the computer's operating system. Electronic mail, scheduling, and even networked games are part of every package. Windows for Workgroups raised the stakes for all the players in the peer-to-peer networking game and firmly established Windows itself as a major network operating system.

Peer-to-peer resource sharing is both a capability and a limitation. On the positive side, it allows great flexibility and makes these systems economical in installations having as few as two PCs. Since the operating systems in question can run on any of the Intel processors used in the PC family, even PCs with 80286 processors can share their resources with other computers across the network cable. On the negative side, peer-to-peer resource sharing typically slows response times; it can stifle a network's growth and make the network more difficult to manage. When files and printers are spread among many machines acting as servers, administrative problems multiply.

The Unix Species

The other source of today's network operating systems is the minicomputer world. Minicomputer operating systems such as Unix were designed from the beginning with multitasking capabilities. Non-DOS operating systems for networked PCs don't need patches or added modules to do more than one thing at a time. But they still must respond appropriately to DOS calls for services.

LAN operating systems derived from minicomputer stock clearly include Banyan's VINES and Novell's NetWare. The link between Unix and OS/2 isn't as clear, but as OS/2 evolves, every new release makes it look more like Unix with a modern face.

VINES bears the greatest external resemblance to a minicomputer operating system. When you turn on a VINES server, the operating system describes step-by-step the programs it is initializing and running. Together, these programs constitute the network operating system on the server. The hard disk uses the Unix file structure, and Unix controls the server's I/O ports. While even the network administrator never directly addresses the Unix operating system underlying VINES, Unix is there performing the multiuser and multitasking functions so important to server operation.

In Novell's NetWare family of operating systems, the file structure of the server is unique to Novell, but the operating system incorporates many Unix structures, including an internal communications process called *streams*. MS-DOS limitations on memory space and I/O port limitations don't apply to a NetWare server. Novell's software runs the processor in its protected mode, allowing efficient internal processing and external memory addressing. The special techniques used in NetWare take advantage of the address space and internal processing capabilities of 80386 and 80486 processors.

Microsoft's Windows NT Advanced Server (NTAS) includes multitasking capabilities and a special high-performance file system that make an NTAS server powerful and fast. Since all Windows for Workgroups and Windows NT computers have both client and server capabilities, you get both flexibility and economy with this networking system.

All of these operating systems—VINES, NetWare, and Windows NT—use functionally similar software in the client stations. Software modules (NetWare calls them *shells*) running in each workstation communicate with the networking software on the server to pass along requests for service. Application programs or DOS command-line entries on the workstations generate the requests.

The server software accepts the requests, checks the identity and the authority of each requester, translates the requests into messages the server operating system understands, and passes them along to that operating system. The server software then sends back the requested data and issues appropriate error codes to the workstations.

The major differences between this Unix-based species of operating system and the MS-DOS–based species is that the server software in the Unix-based species takes care of mediating simultaneous requests for the same data and runs multiple programs. The result is typically much faster performance. In addition, workstations in these systems are not able to contribute resources to the network. Only one or a few dedicated computers perform the role of server—filing, printing, or running communications.

This type of network operating system is typically rich in accessories and management tools. You can expect to find network bridging, electronic mail, print spooling, remote-workstation support, and other software modules, either in the standard release of the software or in the form of inexpensive add-on modules supplied by the original manufacturer.

Operating-System Features

With the two broad species of networking operating systems in mind, you'll want to consider the following features when selecting a particular system.

- *Dedicated servers versus a shared solution.* MS-DOS–based network operating systems such as LANtastic, Personal NetWare, Windows for Workgroups, and PowerLAN, allow any workstation to contribute drives, printers, and other resources to the network. Microsoft's Windows NT has the same capabilities. Other operating systems, such as Novell's NetWare and Banyan's VINES, require a computer dedicated to the server role.

   The shared solution (also called *peer-to-peer resource sharing*) is appealing in small installations where the cost of a dedicated machine is a factor. Sharing a workstation's resources always slows the operation of local programs, while dedicated servers give faster network performance, but many PCs with 80386 and 80486 processors have enough power to support both server and local processing tasks.

- *Fault tolerance.* If critical business, security, or safety operations run on a network, the operating system software can help improve survivability. So-called "fault-tolerant" operating systems mirror the operation of a disk drive or even an entire server on a duplicate resource. If the first drive or server fails, the mirror image takes over. The dedicated server operating systems like NetWare and VINES provide a variety of options for system fault tolerance.

- *Server-based applications.* In the typical PC-based network, application programs run on the workstations, and the servers run special programs dealing only with security and resource sharing. This arrangement is usually efficient, but sometimes performing certain disk-intensive tasks on the network file server is more efficient; these tasks include indexing a database or compiling program source code. Some modern operating systems, like NetWare, Windows NT Advanced Server, and VINES can run appropriate application tasks on the server, increasing the efficiency (and complexity) of operation for installations that are busy with disk-intensive applications.

- *Server software memory.* The amount of RAM the server software uses is important if you want to use PCs as both workstations and servers in peer-to-peer networks.

- *Network administration.* Every successful network has someone who officially or unofficially acts as the system administrator. What kinds of information does your system administrator have to see in order to control who is using the network and what the workload is? Reporting system usage by user is standard in minicomputer systems but rare in LAN operating systems. Yet on a LAN with many stations, knowing who generates the heaviest workload could be important.

- *Diagnostic utilities.* Some network operating systems give the network supervisor certain utilities to use in finding problems and in configuring the server for optimum operation. These utilities can supply reports of bad packets and network errors, and include tools for the operation of disk-cache programs.

- *Security.* Security is usually provided through the use of passwords. The best systems have different levels of access giving users various privileges (including read, write, modify, create, and erase). Another form of security is the ability to provide password protection to facilities such as disk drives, subdirectories, or even selected files, and to regulate access based on the time of day or day of the week.

- *Electronic mail.* A good electronic-mail system alone might justify your investment in a LAN. But the simple e-mail systems of yesterday that focused on storing and forwarding messages have evolved into more sophisticated messaging systems. A messaging system provides an underlying architecture that allows many kinds of application programs to identify users across the network and move information between programs. Messaging systems, led by Microsoft's Messaging Application Program Interface (MAPI), are an important part of modern network operating systems.

- *Print spooling.* When several LAN stations use a printer attached to a central server, the print jobs are saved in a special file called a *spool.* The print jobs are then queued for printer access. Users should have a way to check the position of their jobs in the queue and to kill jobs sent there by mistake. The network administrator should be able to change the priorities of jobs in the print queue and assign specific priorities to certain users.

■ The Future

Interoperability is the key trend for the future of PC-based networks and their operating-system software. Computers running under DOS, Apple's Finder, OS/2, Unix, Xenix, and other operating systems such as DEC's VMS can all interact as peers on the network.

Another clear trend is improved tools for LAN administrators in new operating systems. Many companies offer improved reporting and better ways to manage security, costs, administration, and operational control of networks. Novell, Banyan, and Microsoft each provide a rich menu of statistical utilities and management tools in their latest operating systems. The importance of this area shows in the number of third-party companies marketing add-on products with even more capabilities.

Essentially, the future of networking is based on greater cooperation among computers. Tomorrow's *enterprise LAN* (a network serving an entire business group, organization, or enterprise) will have many servers running different operating systems. Specialized machines will perform specific I/O-intensive tasks, and powerful computers will split their resources in many ways. Multiple solutions will be available to handle every task. As is true today, no one solution will be perfect for every requirement, but every environment will have one ideal solution.

■ Networking Acronyms and Buzzwords

Before you can fully understand networking, you've got to speak the language. At the very least, the next time your boss asks whether you think the company should migrate to SAA, you should know that this doesn't mean moving corporate headquarters south of the border. The following guide will help demystify the acronyms and buzzwords that industry insiders toss around so glibly.

ISO's OSI Model

Since you need a structure to hang the acronyms and buzzwords on, you first have to know about the ISO and its OSI model. The International Standards Organization (ISO), based in Paris, develops standards for international and national data communications. The U.S. representative to the ISO is the American National Standards Institute, or ANSI. In the early 1970s, the ISO developed a standard model of a data communications system and called it the Open Systems Interconnection (OSI) model.

The OSI model, consisting of seven layers, describes what happens when a terminal talks to a computer or one computer talks to another. This model was designed to facilitate creating a system in which equipment from different vendors can communicate.

The other data communications models are IBM's Systems Network Architecture (SNA) and Digital Equipment Corp.'s DEC Network Architecture (DNA), which both predate the OSI model. These companies now more or less equate their systems with the OSI model (DEC more and IBM less), and both promise OSI compatibility.

Protocols

Most of the buzzwords we discuss here are protocols. Like the signals that a baseball catcher and pitcher exchange, *protocols* represent an agreement among different parts of the network on how data is to be transferred. Though you aren't supposed to see them and only a few people understand them, their effect on system performance can be spectacular. A poorly implemented protocol can slow data transfer, but software following standard protocols can make communications between dissimilar systems possible. For instance, the TCP/IP protocol allows you to transfer data between computers that have different architectures and operating systems.

The key elements of a protocol are syntax, semantics, and timing. The *syntax* specifies the signal levels to be used and the format in which the data is to be sent. *Semantics* encompasses the information structure needed for coordination among machines and for data handling. *Timing* includes speed matching (so a computer with a 9,600-bit-per-second port can talk to one with a 1,200-bit-per-second port) and the proper sequencing of data in case it arrives out of order.

Protocols describe all these functions. Since protocols are implemented in real products, though, they often don't fit the full description of the OSI model, either because a product predates the model or because its engineers couldn't resist adding that extra little tweak.

Layer Cake

Think of the OSI model as a layer cake like the one in Figure 4.4. At the bottom, holding everything else up, is the physical layer—the wiring or cables.

The Physical Layer

The physical layer furnishes electrical connections and signaling. Subsequent layers talk through this physical layer. Twisted-pair wiring, fiber-optic strands, and coaxial cable are all part of the physical layer.

Probably the most common standard in the physical layer is RS-232C, a wiring and signaling standard that defines which pin on the connectors does what, and when a voltage level on a wire represents a 1 or a 0. A new standard called RS-449 is supposed to replace RS-232C eventually. Europeans use an international standard called V.24, which is a lot like RS-232C. All of these are physical-layer standards.

The physical layer carries the signals for all the higher layers. Pull the plug and you won't communicate at all. But without the higher layers, you won't have anything to say. The higher in the OSI model you go, the more meaningful the communication is to the end user.

The Data-Link Layer

Once you've made the physical and electrical connections, you must control the data stream between your system and the one at the other end. The data-link layer of the OSI model works like the overseer of a railroad yard putting cars together to make up a train. This functional level strings characters

Figure 4.4

Layers of the OSI model

7) Application layer: At this level, software follows standards for look and feel. 6) Presentation layer: Here, data is formatted for viewing and use on specific equipment. 5) Session layer: This layer provides a standard way to move data between application programs. 4) Transport layer: This layer of software is particularly important to local area networks. Transport-layer software provides for reliable and transparent transfer of packets between stations. 3) Network layer: Software operating at this layer provides an interface between the physical and data-link levels and the higher-level software, which establishes and maintains connections. 2) Data-link layer: This layer provides for the reliable transfer of information across the physical link. It synchronizes the blocks of data, recognizes errors, and controls the flow of data. 1) Physical layer: The most fundamental layer is concerned with transmitting a stream of data over the physical cables and wires. Hardware and software operating at this level deal with the types of connectors, signaling, and media-sharing schemes used on the network.

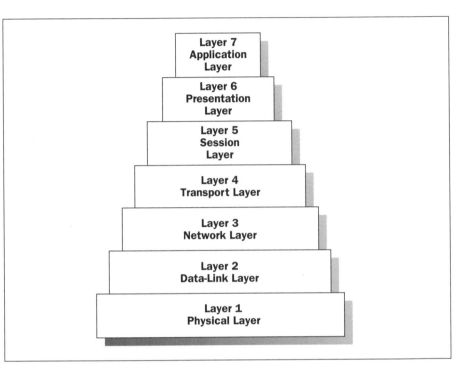

together into messages and then checks them before putting them on the tracks. It may also receive an "arrived safely" message from the overseer in the other yard, or work with the other yard to reconstitute a message when a data disaster strikes. Routing trains between yards is the job of the network layer.

The data-link layer uses many protocols, including High-level Data Link Control (HDLC), bisynchronous communications, and Advanced Data Communications Control Procedures (ADCCP). You don't need to know the details of any of these protocols; just picture them putting data trains on the right tracks and making sure they arrive safely. In PC-based communications systems, special integrated circuits on interface cards (instead of separate software programs) typically perform the functions of the data-link layer.

Certain programs in PC communications act like data-link-layer protocols. If you use Xmodem or Crosstalk's DART protocols for error detection and retransmission during a file exchange, you're using an application program that acts like a data-link-layer protocol while it is transferring a file.

The Network Layer

Larger wide-area networks typically offer a number of ways to move a string of characters (put together by the data-link layer) from one geographic point to another. The third layer of the OSI model—the network layer—decides which physical pathway the data should take, based on network conditions, priority of service, and other factors.

The network-layer software usually resides in switches out in the network, and the interface card inside your PC must put the train together in a way the network software can recognize and use in routing. In traditional PC-to-PC networks, the network layer isn't important. But if you use value-added carriers like Accunet, CompuServe, Telenet, or Tymnet, they provide such network-layer services for you.

The Transport Layer

The transport layer—layer 4 of the OSI model—does many of the same jobs as the network layer, but it does them locally. Drivers in the networking software perform the transport layer's tasks. This layer is the railroad yard dispatcher who takes over if there is a wreck out in the system. If the network goes down, the transport-layer software will look for alternative routes or perhaps save the transmitted data until the network connection is reestablished. It handles quality control by making sure that the data received is in the right format and in the right order. This formatting and ordering capability becomes important when transport-layer programs implement connections among dissimilar computers.

The data-link layer can count boxcars to see whether they are all there. The transport layer opens them up to see whether anything is missing or broken.

Networks of dissimilar computers can use several transport-layer protocols. One of the most common is the Transmission Control Protocol (TCP), developed by the Department of Defense and now adopted and marketed by many companies as part of the TCP/IP protocol suite. Because TCP does not exactly match the ISO model, companies are moving to a new ISO-compliant protocol called TP4.

Three commonly used software products that perform transport-layer functions in PC networks are NetBIOS, Named Pipes, and NetWare's Internetwork Protocol Exchange (IPX). We will describe these products later on; for now, all you need to know is that one or more pieces of software resides in every network station and passes calls between application programs on the network. The primary applications that make use of transport-layer communications are network gateway programs.

The Session Layer

Layer 5, the session layer, is often very important in PC-based systems. It performs the functions that enable two applications (or two pieces of the same application) to communicate across the network, performing security, name recognition, logging, administration, and other similar functions.

Programs like NetBIOS and Named Pipes often jump the ISO model and perform both transport-layer and session-layer functions, so I can't name a piece of commonly used software that is unique to this layer. But the ISO has developed ISO 8327, the Connection-Oriented Session Protocol Specification, so that companies will have separate software programs performing these functions.

The Presentation Layer

As soon as you see blinking characters, reverse video, special data-entry formats, graphics, and other features on the screen, you're in the presentation layer. This layer may also handle encryption and some special file formatting. It formats screens and files so that the final product looks the way the programmer intended.

The presentation layer is the home of control codes, special graphics, and character sets. Its software controls printers, plotters, and other peripherals. Microsoft Windows and IBM's Presentation Manager are two program environments that perform the presentation-layer functions.

The Application Layer

The top of the layer cake—the application layer—serves the user. It's where the network operating system and application programs reside—everything from file sharing, print-job spooling, and electronic mail to database management and accounting. The standards for this top layer are new, like IBM's Systems Application Architecture (SAA) and the X.400 Message Handling specification for electronic mail. In a way, this layer is the most important one, because the user controls it directly.

Some functions, such as file-transfer protocols, work from the application layer but do jobs assigned to a lower layer. This is something like the president of a railroad sometimes sweeping out boxcars.

That's it—the top of ISO's OSI model. The concepts are pretty simple, but dozens of committees are working to define standards for little pieces of each layer, and great political fights are being waged over whose ideas should prevail. Let's go on to hang some buzzwords on the model and see where they fit.

IEEE 802.X Standards

The Institute of Electrical and Electronics Engineers (IEEE) has developed a set of standards describing the cabling, physical topology, electrical topology, and access scheme of network products. The committee structure of the IEEE is numbered like the Dewey decimal system. The general committee working on these standards is 802. Various subcommittees, designated by decimal numbers, have worked on different versions of the standards.

These standards describe the protocols used in the lower two layers of the OSI model. They don't go above those layers; thus, using the common name of an IEEE standard (like Token-Ring) is an incomplete response to the question, "What network do you use?" Your reply should also specify the network interface, including the media and access protocol as well as the networking software.

IEEE 802.3 and 802.5

Let's look first at two IEEE 802 committee standards that relate to PC-based LANs: 802.3 and 802.5. I'll describe the work of the 802.6 committee a few paragraphs later.

IEEE standard 802.5 describes the Token-Ring architecture. The work of a committee that received a lot of attention and leadership from IBM, this standard describes a token-passing protocol used on a network of stations connected together in a special way, combining an electrical ring topology (where every station actively passes information on to the next one in the ring) with a physical hub topology.

IBM's Token-Ring system is important to corporate data-processing managers because IBM supports a number of mainframe-computer Token-Ring interfaces. Under IBM's Systems Application Architecture (SAA), mainframes and PCs share data as peers on networks.

An increasing number of vendors, like Proteon, make Token-Ring interface cards for popular minicomputers. These allow easy interaction without resorting to complex and expensive micro-to-mainframe links and gateways.

IEEE 802.3, on the other hand, describes a standard that owes a lot to the earlier Ethernet system. It uses carrier sense multiple access (CSMA) signaling on an electrical bus topology. The standard leaves room for several wiring options. The latest additions to the 802.3 standards include signaling at 100 megabits per second under what is commonly called the 100Base-X standard.

You can buy 802.3 interface cards for the PC from dozens of manufacturers. Similar cards designed for popular minicomputers are widely available. IBM even includes an optional Ethernet port on its mini/mainframe computer, the 9370.

IEEE 802.6

Metropolitan-area networks or MANs make up a subcategory of the IEEE 802 standards project called 802.6. Metropolitan networks can take many forms, but the term usually describes a backbone network of fiber-optic cables that could span hundreds of square miles. Local exchange carriers (the local telephone companies) provide a great deal of MAN connectivity, as do a growing number of cable television companies. While some organizations install their own microwave systems for MAN circuits, the majority lease circuits from local carriers. State utility commissions may regulate the tariffs for MAN services.

MAN carriers usually offer services in 1.544-megabit-per-second increments, and their backbone services provide throughput in the range of 80 megabits per second. The 802.6 MAN standard calls for a Distributed Queue Dual Bus topology with drops at each service location. This topology uses multiple fiber-optic cables with special equipment at each service location to interleave messages into the cable.

Wide-area networks (WANs) generally link cities. Specialized long-distance carriers lease circuits to organizations and communications companies to construct WANs. You can buy service at any speed, but speeds of 56 and 64 kilobits per second are the most economical, and 1.544-megabit-per-second service is common. The Federal Communications Commission has authority over the rates the long-distance carriers charge.

Eight-Oh-Two-Dot-Something

While the 802.X standards don't describe every popular network cabling and access protocol scheme (ARCnet, for instance, is not a perfect fit), "eight-oh-two-dot-something" is a frequently used expression that you should know.

IBM's Cable Plan

Another shorthand used by LAN writers and speakers is derived from IBM's cabling scheme. The major vendors—AT&T, DEC, Northern Telecom, and others—have their own wiring schemes. These vendors all want you to wire your buildings in certain ways that are advantageous for their equipment and will keep competing vendors away from your door.

The IBM cabling plan, like most things IBM, is comprehensive, capable, and expensive to install. IBM has developed standards for certain types of cables, and certifies certain manufacturers as meeting those standards. Here's a quick rundown:

- Type 1 Cable (Figure 4.5): Shielded cable with two twisted pairs made from solid wire (as opposed to the stranded wire used in Type 6, below). Used for data transmission, particularly with Token-Ring networks.

- Type 2 Cable (Figure 4.6): Four unshielded pairs of solid wire for voice telephone and two shielded data pairs in the same sheath.

- Type 3 Cable: Four unshielded, solid, twisted pairs of wire for voice or data. IBM's version of modern twisted-pair telephone wire.

- Type 4 Cable: No specification published.

- Type 5 Cable: Two fiber-optic strands.

Figure 4.5

Many companies sell cable that follows IBM's Type 1 specification. This cable combines two separately shielded pairs of solid twisted wire. PVC and Teflon jackets provide different degrees of fire resistance.

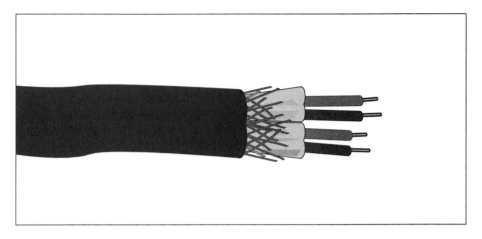

Figure 4.6

Cables that follow IBM's Type 2 cable specifications are used primarily to combine telephone and Token-Ring wiring within the same cable installation. Two pairs of shielded twisted-pair wiring are joined with four unshielded twisted pairs.

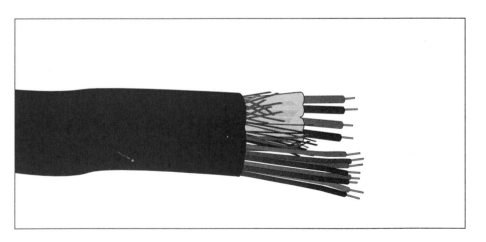

- Type 6 Cable: Shielded cable with two twisted pairs made from stranded wire. More flexible than Type 1 cable. Designed for data transmission; commonly used between a computer and a data jack in the wall.

- Type 7 Cable: No specification published.

- Type 8 Cable: A special "under-the-carpet" shielded twisted-pair cable designed to minimize the lump in the carpet that covers it.

- Type 9 Cable: Plenum cable. Two shielded, twisted pairs covered with a special flame-retardant coating for use between floors in a building.

Linking LAN Segments

Signals can travel only limited distances before losing power. For instance, on an Ethernet network, a signal can typically travel up to 1,000 feet; on a Token-Ring system, it can travel up to about 600 feet. Networks use repeaters, bridges, routers, and gateways to relay and regenerate signals traveling long distances and to talk to other LANs or wide-area networks.

Repeaters do what their name says: They repeat electrical signals between sections of networking cabling. You won't find many of these relatively simple devices in new networks. Repeaters relay signals in both directions with no discrimination. More modern devices, like bridges and routers, look at the messages the signals carry to determine whether they really need to pass each message to the next segment.

Bridges allow you to join two local area networks, and they allow stations on either network to access resources on the other. Bridges use media-access control (MAC) protocols in the physical layer of the network. They can link dissimilar types of media such as fiber-optic cable and thin 802.3 coaxial cable as long as both sides use the same MAC-layer protocol (such as Ethernet).

Routers operate at the network layer of the OSI model. They examine the address of each message and decide whether the addressee lies across the bridge. If the message doesn't need to go across the bridge and create traffic on the extended network, they don't send it. Routers can translate between a wide variety of cable and signaling schemes. For example, a router could take your messages from Ethernet and put them out on a packet-switched network operating through modems connected to high-speed leased telephone lines.

Gateways, which run on the OSI session layer, allow networks running totally incompatible protocols to communicate. In PC-based networks, gateways typically link PCs to host machines such as IBM mainframes. You'll find more information on bridges, routers, and gateways in Chapter 14.

Higher-Level Protocols

Moving up through the OSI model's layers, let's look at the techniques (and buzzwords) that different LAN software suppliers use for the transport-layer and session-layer protocols.

If you don't specify the transport-layer protocols you want to use, you'll get whatever the vendor includes in its standard "protocol stack." Those protocols may or may not be available for the various mainframes or minicomputers in your network. For managers of large corporate networks, selection of the proper higher-level protocols is a complex, important task.

TCP/IP

The earliest large network systems were fielded by the Department of Defense (DoD). The DoD financed the development of interactive network communications software for many different mainframes and minicomputers. The standard core of the DoD-specified software consists of programs that implement two protocols, Transmission Control Protocol (TCP) and Internet Protocol (IP). The availability of TCP/IP software and the DoD's continuing enforcement of the protocols (through software certification) make them attractive to managers who face the challenge of integrating dissimilar computer systems.

TCP and IP perform primarily what the OSI model terms layer-3 (network) and layer-4 (transport) functions. Particularly important is the ability to communicate and to order data among two or more different computer systems.

Companies like ftp Software and The Wollongong Group sell TCP/IP software customized for specific computers and controller cards. These software modules communicate through the network, recognize each other, and pass messages in a common format generated by the higher-level session-layer and application programs.

TCP/IP software is popular with managers of large networks because it works and is available for many computers. Artisoft, Microsoft, Banyan, Novell, Performance Technology, and other vendors of networking software offer various options, ranging from standalone interface boxes to TCP/IP LAN gateways.

NetBIOS

Another institutional solution whose grass-roots support is starting to slip is NetBIOS. NetBIOS started as an interface between the IBM PC Network Program (PCNP, superseded by PC LAN) and network interface cards provided by Sytek. When the IBM/Sytek team designed the interface, they also made it a programmable entryway into the network, allowing systems to communicate over network hardware without going through the networking software.

A grass-roots movement of large-network users has been pushing a combination of NetBIOS (operating at the OSI session layer) and TCP/IP. In this combination, application programs make calls to NetBIOS. Vendors like Banyan and Novell don't actually use NetBIOS to drive network interface cards, but their operating systems can run NetBIOS emulators to furnish the same session-layer communications services NetBIOS offers.

NetBIOS modules establish virtual communications sessions with each other across the network. But NetBIOS uses a simple naming scheme that doesn't work well between networks or in a wide variety of operating systems. The Internet Protocol portion of TCP/IP envelops the NetBIOS modules so that they travel intact through multiple levels of network names and addresses. However, since Microsoft now favors an implementation of Novell's IPX, NetBIOS is going to be less popular than it has been.

Layer 4 and Above

If you don't use TCP/IP and NetBIOS—or some rare layer-4 (network-layer) protocol complying with the ISO model—you enter a maze of vendor-specific protocols. If you use PCs only, working together in a network, or perhaps using a gateway for mainframe file sharing, you won't care what protocols the networking software uses. But if you want computers from DEC, HP, IBM, and other vendors to treat each other as peers on the network, and if you want to access files on the DEC from your PC's D: drive and files on the HP from your PC's H: drive, the network protocols you use become very important. (One caveat: These protocols don't make otherwise incompatible application files compatible; they just move them across the network and offer access to them.)

Each vendor engages other vendors to support its protocol in their products. What's important is that the set of vendors supporting a specific protocol matches the set of vendors whose equipment is used on your network.

IBM's SNA and APPC

IBM would like to wrap you in the Big Blue web called Systems Network Architecture. IBM's answer to the OSI model, SNA describes how IBM thinks a communications system should work.

Advanced Program-to-Program Communications (APPC) is a protocol within the SNA model that establishes the conditions enabling programs to communicate across the network. APPC is analogous to the session layer of the OSI model. According to IBM, APPC is the communications basis for all of the corporation's future applications and systems products. Two other hot buzzwords from IBM—APPC /PC and LU 6.2—are the names of products that actually implement the APPC specifications. These programs, however, are large and cumbersome and have not caught on quickly.

IBM's SAA

You can think of IBM's Systems Application Architecture (SAA) as a stack of documents describing how things should be done. SAA describes application program interfaces (that look just like OS/2's Presentation Manager), screen and keyboard standards, and protocols that govern communications to operating systems and to facilities like APPC.

DECnet

The other company that can drown you in a sea of acronyms is Digital Equipment Corp. DEC has developed its own protocol stack for interconnecting DEC systems, both locally and over wide-area networks. The DECnet protocols are supposed to be heading toward compatibility with the ISO standards. It seems likely that DEC will adopt certain ISO protocols (as will many other vendors) to beat the drum for their compatibility.

Apple

Apple Computer has its own set of protocols in the AppleTalk family. The AppleTalk Filing Protocol (AFP) is the one that allows distributed file sharing across the network. AFP is attached to the Hierarchical File System (HFS) in the Macintosh operating system.

Distributed File Systems

SMB, RFS, NFS, and XNS are acronyms for some of the contending distributed-file-system network protocols. *Distributed file systems*, which are a part of every network, allow one computer on a network to use the files and peripherals of another networked computer as if they were local. The two operating systems link so that a subdirectory made available on the host is seen as a disk drive or as a separate subdirectory on the user's computer. Thus, application programs running on the user's computer can access the files and resources on the host without requiring special programming.

These protocols operate in approximately the same way, but they are not interchangeable. Typically, a major vendor develops a protocol for use within a product line, and other vendors license it to achieve compatibility.

SMB stands for Server Message Block, a protocol developed by IBM and Microsoft for use in the PC LAN program and in Windows networking. AT&T, DEC, HP, Intel, Ungermann-Bass, and others all support or accommodate this protocol to some degree.

RFS is the Remote File Service developed by AT&T. Since RFS is integral to Unix V, Version 3 and later, vendors in the Unix market support it in their products. RFS is implemented in Unix System V.3 using the powerful streams facility, which allows applications to open a stream to or from a device (in Unix everything is a device: serial port, disk, and so forth) across any defined transport-level interface (TLI). The TLI can be the default Unix transport services, or TCP, or some other protocol.

NFS stands for Network File System, an architecture developed by Sun Microsystems. Sun's PC-NFS is a complete but no-frills network operating system for the PC. This memory-resident module gives you access to files stored on Unix-based minicomputers. Companies in the professional workstation market, including Harris Corp., HP, Texas Instruments, and many others, support the NFS architecture in their products.

Largely because of its leading role in selling Ethernet products, Xerox has been successful in promoting its own Xerox Network Services (XNS). 3Com uses XNS in its 3+Share software, and Novell uses a subset of XNS (called IPX) in its popular NetWare.

■ Now I Know My ABCs

Although this primer on buzzwords and acronyms just scratches the surface of networking terminology, it should help you gain a better understanding of the strange new language of connectivity.

- *Network Adapters*
- *LAN Cable Standards*
- *Cables for Network Connections*
- *Topologies*
- *Putting It All Together*

Cables and Adapters:
The Hardware Heart of the LAN

TECHNICAL TALE   *"So it's all in the twists, right?"*

Willy Barnett smiled slightly. "Well, there's more to it than that. The wire twists in unshielded twisted pair cable help to shield the cable from outside interference, but that's just the start. You have to use the right connectors and hubs, and you have to install the cables in such a way that you minimize the crosstalk between wire pairs and the outside electrical noise. Doesn't do any good to use the best stuff if you don't install it right."

He was sitting in the city manager's office, and they were discussing the new municipal building. He was into the second half hour of a question-and-answer session that had become a tutorial on network cabling.

"But let me ask you something," Willy said. "You'll have the police station and the county dispatcher along with the city office, right?" The manager nodded and Willy pressed ahead, "Will the police station holding cells have an extensive alarm system?"

After the city manager explained the alarm system, Willy said, "It will be slightly more expensive, but I think the city needs coaxial cable instead of unshielded twisted pair. Coax will give you better protection against interference from and into the radio systems, and it also keeps out possible interference from the radio frequency motion detectors in the alarm system."

"Do we lose any flexibility with the coaxial cable?" the manager asked.

"Yes. Unshielded twisted pair will work with Ethernet, Token-Ring, and even ARCnet LAN adapters. Coaxial cable is only good for Ethernet, but you already have an investment in Ethernet adapters, so that's no real limitation."

"Now, let me ask you something," the manager said. "I'm building a new house. What kind of cabling should I put in for my home network?"

A lightbulb went off in Willy's head. "Well, sir, let's see how we can help you."

IN THIS CHAPTER, I DESCRIBE THE SMALL PIECE OF HARDWARE REQUIRED TO link a computer to the LAN—the network adapter card. Then we follow the path of the network cables that link the computers in a local area network, and explore how to send signals using light. I've structured this information to help you buy the best adapters and make the right wiring choices for your installation. In Chapter 6 you'll learn about the big-three LAN cabling and signaling schemes—Ethernet, ARCnet, and Token-Ring—but here I'll explain the details of the pieces and parts all those schemes use.

■ Network Adapters

Inside a computer, the low-powered electrical signals representing digital data travel on 8, 16, or 32 thin, parallel conductors, which are collectively called a data bus. The data bus carries signals between the central processor, random access memory (RAM), and input/output (I/O) devices. Modern computer designs put I/O devices, such as serial and parallel ports, both on the main board of the computer and in the expansion interface slots connected to the data bus.

A local area network *adapter card* (Figure 5.1), also called a *network interface card* or *NIC*, fits into an expansion interface slot and changes the low-powered parallel signals on the data bus into a robust stream of electrical 0s and 1s marching in single file through a cable connecting the stations on the network.

Figure 5.1

Artisoft's LANtastic Ethernet adapter uses the 16-bit expansion slot in a PC AT and provides the interface between the network and the PC's internal data bus.

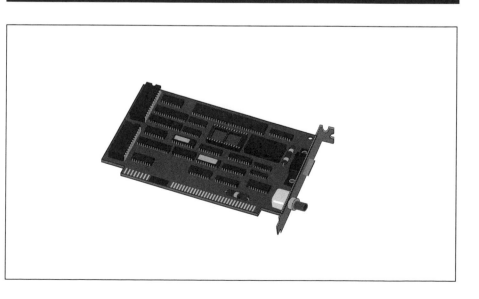

The concept of putting a special adapter inside the computer to communicate with devices outside the computer isn't new. In early personal computers, the serial and parallel port connections were always provided by separate extra-cost adapter cards. In the early 1980s, companies such as Zenith and Tandy began including serial and parallel ports in their computers to increase their value.

The industry-wide acceptance of PC serial ports configured according to the IEEE RS-232C standard, and of parallel ports following the de facto standard established by Centronics, encouraged manufacturers to include these ports in their PCs. Designers knew these standard ports would be compatible with a wide variety of products such as modems and printers.

You've probably heard the names Ethernet, Token-Ring, and ARCnet mentioned frequently. Until the past few years, each of these terms encompassed a family of products that included specific types of wiring, connectors, network communications software, and adapter cards, but now the products within these families have evolved beyond the original definitions. For all practical purposes, these terms currently define the techniques the adapters use to share the LAN wiring, the "media-access control" (MAC) protocols in LAN-talk, and the type of signals they send over the wiring. The adapters you choose determine what media-access control and signaling parameters you'll be using.

Linking the Adapter and the PC

Although I spend a large part of this chapter describing how the cables and other external LAN connections work, the most important network connections are inside the PC. The best cabling and signaling schemes won't be much use if data can't move quickly between the adapter and the PC. This is particularly true when the PC is acting as a file or communications server on the network. A bottleneck in a server slows the entire network's performance. Bottlenecks can occur both in the software that integrates the adapter into the computer and in the way the adapter and computer electrically exchange information.

A LAN adapter has two sides, the expansion bus side and the LAN cable side. Both sides offer several types of technical alternatives, and you have to find the right combination of alternatives in the system you buy.

Hot Drivers

Our tests at PC Magazine LAN Labs clearly show the importance of a small piece of software loaded into every networked computer called the network interface card *driver*. We'll discuss how this software integrates into the total networking software package in Chapters 7 and 8, but for now you should understand the driver's role in adapter performance.

A software company gains a significant market advantage by offering a network operating system that can work with hardware from many companies. Some LAN operating system developers include the integrating software, or drivers, for many adapters in their installation packages; for example, Novell provides drivers for many adapters in NetWare. But the operating system vendors typically can't keep up with every change and new-product release by the adapter vendors.

Hardware and software companies have taken several approaches to the problem of compatibility between the adapter and the operating system. Microsoft and 3Com developed the Network Driver Interface Specification (NDIS), which they hoped everyone would support. In theory, if the adapter company provides a diskette with NDIS drivers, any NDIS-compliant LAN operating system like Microsoft's LAN Manager, Banyan's VINES, or Hayes LANStep will run over those adapters. Microsoft's plan has been quite successful, and most LAN adapters come with NDIS-compliant driver software. In addition, Microsoft includes the NDIS drivers for dozens of popular LAN adapters in their Windows and Windows NT products.

Working from a position of market domination, Novell has proposed what it calls the Open Device Interface (ODI)—a specification similar to NDIS in general concept. ODI is now as widely supported by the market as NDIS, and Microsoft has adopted an ODI-compatible interface in its NDIS III description.

Some manufacturers of LAN adapters like Standard Microsystems and Intel try to insure compatibility by shipping a diskette full of drivers for different network operating systems with their adapters. Artisoft and D-Link tried the reverse approach: They cloned the operation of an adapter with a wide range of support, the NE2000, to take advantage of the large library of software already published for these boards.

When you shop for LAN adapters, make sure the adapters you buy have NDIS drivers as insurance against obsolescence. If you plan to use Novell's NetWare operating system, check for ODI drivers too.

Programmers use different techniques to create the driver software. Certain ways of moving data and using data storage buffers move the bits quickly between the adapter and the PC. Some programmers write small and efficient code using highly detailed assembly language, while others take the easier route and write less efficient drivers in the C programming language. Quite simply, some programmers write faster and more robust adapter-board drivers than others, and some companies spend more resources developing driver software than others.

While network adapter boards from different companies are alike in many ways, your safest bet is to buy adapters from name-brand companies. Typically, the drivers for these adapters are field-tested and incorporated in the installation packages of the major software vendors.

Some smart adapter-board vendors clone the adapter interface specifications of products known for their proven driver software. Artisoft, for example, sells excellent Ethernet adapters with interface characteristics identical to the popular NE1000 and NE2000 adapters originally marketed by Novell. You can pay less for the Artisoft adapters and run them using the carefully crafted drivers for the NE1000 or NE2000 contained in Novell's NetWare and other operating systems.

I/O Options

The PC and adapter can communicate across the data bus using several techniques. You need to understand the different input/output options in order to balance performance, complexity, and cost when you select adapters.

The designers of modern network adapters use one of four techniques to move data between the board and the PC's RAM: programmed I/O, direct memory access (DMA), shared memory, or bus-mastering DMA. Unfortunately, not every interface scheme works in every PC; for this reason, many adapters allow you to select between at least two schemes. In preparation for the challenge of interfacing adapters to PCs, I'll present the details of the four I/O techniques here.

Programmed I/O

A technique called programmed I/O provides an efficient way to move data between the PC and the adapter. In this technique, the special-purpose processor on the adapter board controls a shared 8K, 16K, or 32K block of memory. The adapter's processor communicates with the PC's central processor through this common I/O location.

Both devices move data quickly by reading and writing to the same block of memory, which functions like the window between the kitchen and the counter in a fast-food diner. As in the diner, the processor on either side of the shared window rings a bell to signal the presence of something in the window. In the case of programmed I/O, the bell is a signal called I/O Ready.

The programmed I/O technique uses less memory than some other data-transfer strategies. For this reason, many LAN adapters, such as Artisoft's AE-2, D-Link Systems DE-250, and Novel's NE1000 and NE2000 use programmed I/O as their primary operating mode.

On the downside, to use programmed I/O the host PC must have a processor more powerful than the Intel 8088 and 8086 used in the IBM PC and PC XT, because the processor must execute a specific command to read the memory address—a command that is unique to the 80286 and later chips. Also, older PCs generate a wait-state signal for each I/O operation, and this reduces throughput. If you have the correct processor, however, programmed I/O is the right choice for an adapter interface technique.

Direct Memory Access

Many adapters use a technique called direct memory access (DMA) to signal between the processor in the PC and the processor on the adapter. This alternative is particularly useful for older PCs with 8086 and 8088 processors. When it receives a DMA request from an adapter or interface card, the PC's processor halts other operations to handle the data transfer.

In early PCs, the DMA signaling channel used a 4.77-MHz timing clock. Newer PCs still use the same clock rate to maintain compatibility with older adapters, so DMA can be an inefficient data-transfer technique for modern PCs, and you should use it with care.

Shared Memory

Shared memory is a method devised to overcome the shortcomings of the programmed I/O and DMA techniques. A shared-memory adapter contains memory that the host PC's processor can access directly at full speed with no wait states. You can buy such adapters with both 8- and 16-bit-wide interfaces to the PC's data bus, but the 16-bit adapters often run into memory conflicts with other devices in the PC. Shared memory offers the fastest way to move data to and from an adapter, but installing a shared-memory adapter in a PC crowded with VGA video and other memory-hungry interfaces can be a frustrating job. You may run into memory conflicts that only manifest themselves when the LAN adapter and some other device try to use the same location at the same time.

Bus Mastering

Bus mastering, a special technique used primarily on Micro Channel Architecture (MCA) and Extended Industry Standard Architecture (EISA) computers, provides an adapter board that can send data to and receive data from the computer's memory without interrupting the processor. Bus-mastering DMA adapters take control of the data bus and move data directly between the network adapter and the PC's RAM while the processor continues its operations. Figure 5.2 shows a DCA Token-Ring adapter.

Only a few companies market bus-mastering adapters because they're difficult to develop, and carry high price tags. Typically, you would buy bus-mastering adapters only for LAN file servers, although their fast throughput might enhance some workstations used for computer-aided design because graphics workstations frequently move large files.

Features and Options of LAN Adapters

One option that's become almost a standard feature among LAN adapter manufacturers is an open socket for a remote-boot ROM. This special ROM forces

Figure 5.2

The IRMAtrac/16 is a unique 16-megabit-per-second Token-Ring adapter marketed by DCA. You can use the same board in a computer with an ISA expansion bus or in one with an MCA expansion bus. This product is one of a family of similar convertible Token-Ring LAN adapters using shielded, unshielded, and fiber-optic cabling.

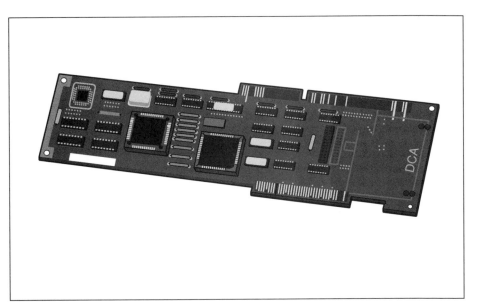

the host station to take its DOS start-up files from the server. PCs equipped with a remote-boot ROM don't need local floppy or hard disk drives. Diskless PCs eliminate the potential for theft of data files or programs stored on diskettes; this concept also cuts costs and reduces the minimum size of the computer. Other useful features include LEDs indicating operational status, dual in-line package (DIP) switches that make it easy to change the card configuration, and different kinds of connectors.

Some buyers will want to note whether their Ethernet adapters include an attachment unit interface (AUI) port. The AUI port connects to a device called a *transceiver*, with connections for thick and thin Ethernet coaxial cables and fiber-optic cables. Some companies call a transceiver a *medium attachment unit* (MAU), although the same acronym has other meanings. A board with an AUI gives you more flexibility and greater potential for reuse on other wiring schemes. These boards might cost a few dollars more, but they offer a wider variety of connection options.

Finding Space in Crowded PCs

PCs have a limited number of expansion interface slots, memory addresses, IRQ lines, and DMA channels. High-density video adapters, mouse ports, and other communications boards all consume these resources in their host PCs. Table 5.1 shows some of the IRQ lines and I/O addresses standard PC devices use; these lines and addresses commonly interfere with the operation of LAN adapters.

Table 5.1

Commonly Used IRQ
Lines and Memory
Addresses

IRQ LINE	MEMORY	DEVICE
2	–	Use with care in a PC AT
3	2F8h	COM2
3	2E8h	COM4
4	3F8h	COM1
4	2E8h	COM3
5	280h	Tape controller
5	3FOh	PC XT hard disk controller
5	278h	LPT2
6	3FOh	Floppy disk controller
7	378h	LPT1

Some professional installers consider the techniques they use to avoid interrupt and memory-address conflicts trade secrets, but the real secret is organization. Smart network administrators record the I/O and interrupt address of every device in every networked PC. You don't need a fancy database program—a three-ring binder works nicely—but having a quick reference to the I/O and interrupt addresses used in each machine can avoid frustration and save hours of installation time.

My first advice about network adapter installation is to use the defaults recommended by the manufacturer of your adapter. The company chose those defaults to avoid typical problems.

If the adapter doesn't work at the default memory and I/O address, its installation manual will typically list at least two alternatives. Adapters designed for the standard IBM PC AT expansion bus (the Industry Standard Architecture or ISA bus) usually use slide-on jumpers to determine the shared RAM address and IRQ line. Adapters designed for the Micro Channel Architecture (MCA) and Extended Industry Standard Architecture (EISA) change all parameters through special configuration programs provided on a diskette that is shipped with each adapter.

Remember, you must change the network driver software to match the memory address and IRQ line set on the board; the software can't find the adapter if it doesn't know where to look. The first installation trick you should be aware of concerns IRQ3. The COM2 serial port on all PCs uses this IRQ line. But many LAN adapters come with the same IRQ line set as the default. Most PCs use electrical techniques to avoid a conflict as long as both devices don't send signals on the same IRQ line at the same time. This means you can usually use a LAN adapter at IRQ3 even if a COM2 is in the machine, as long as you don't try to use the COM2 serial port and the network at the same time—as you might, for example, with a serially attached printer or modem.

Many manufacturers of PCs provide a method in either software or hardware to disable an on-board COM2 port, but there is no single standard technique. A smart LAN administrator asks how to disable COM2 whenever a new PC comes into the office. Getting this information early can save problems later.

Because so many computers come equipped with an internal COM2, installers often use IRQ5 whenever they put LAN adapters in these computers. But don't try this setting in an IBM PC XT, because its hard disk controller will conflict with IRQ5 every time. Similarly, the LPT2 port used in many PCs acting as network print servers also uses IRQ5.

Selecting IRQ2 for an 8-bit LAN adapter often works on AT-type machines. However, this IRQ is actually served by IRQ9, so you can encounter conflicts if any devices in the AT use this higher-numbered interrupt. IRQ2 conflicts often sneak up on you when you try to add an internal device to a PC AT that has been happily operating with a LAN adapter at IRQ2.

You'll have to set an I/O address for the general operation of the board and perhaps one for a special auto-boot ROM. Many adapters use I/O addresses at 2A0h and 300h with success. Auto-boot ROMs let you use diskless workstations to boot from the server. The auto-boot ROMs use higher addresses, and can conflict with the ROMs in modern video adapters. At the PC Magazine LAN Labs, we've successfully used CC00h as the boot ROM address in many computers with VGA video systems.

If you must install an adapter using a DMA channel, try DMA3 as the default on an AT-style machine. On an XT, slip down to DMA2 to avoid the XT's hard disk. All PCs use DMA2 for the floppy disk drive controller, however, so someone simultaneously trying to use the floppy disk drive and a LAN adapter set to DMA2 will experience problems.

You usually won't have a problem setting up a LAN adapter in a typical client workstation if you use the defaults. The challenge comes when you want to put a LAN adapter in a PC equipped with a special adapter for a mainframe connection or with a tape drive controller. These devices (and to a lesser extent, internal mouse adapters) often default to the same IRQ lines and memory locations used by LAN adapters. Some conflicts are insidious. You might not see a problem, for example, until you try to perform a tape backup and pull files across the network at the same time. In this case, one of the conflicting products must move—usually to IRQ5 with an I/O address of

320h in an AT. Figure 5.3 shows the jumpers used to select IRQ lines and memory locations, along with other important components of the adapter.

Figure 5.3

This diagram identifies the major components on a 10Net Ethernet network adapter board. This board is typical of modern adapter design.

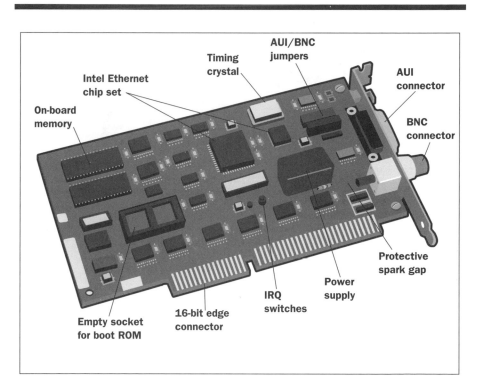

Getting multiple boards to work together in tricky installations is often a matter of experience and luck. That's why many system integrators support only products that have a proven ability to work together. The craft of LAN installation involves some art, but it is primarily a skill, with specific rules and a road map of the PC's architecture that you can follow.

External Adapters

A LAN adapter normally resides in one of the PC's expansion slots. But notebooks typically don't have standard expansion slots, and some PCs are already crowded with add-in options. If you don't have a spot for an internal adapter, or if you simply don't want to open up the PC, you can use an external adapter to link the PC to the LAN. Several companies, including D-Link Systems, Megahertz Corp., and Xircom, sell external network adapters that connect to your PC's parallel printer port. With special software, the parallel port—normally a one-way device—becomes a two-way path to the PC. These devices don't have the same fast throughput as an internal adapter, but they are adequate for 99 percent of all network client-station tasks. Figure 5.4 shows Xircom's popular external adapter.

Figure 5.4

The Xircom external adapter attaches to the parallel port of a PC card and provides connections for Ethernet or Token-Ring networks. This kind of product is particular useful for laptop PCs and those with limited internal expansion slots.

Xircom Corp. (the folks who developed the external LAN adapter in 1989) and Zenith Corp. have developed technology for a high-speed enhanced parallel port (EPP) that can achieve signaling rates as high as 2 megabytes (16 megabits) per second. Note that because they move data out the port in parallel as a single byte, parallel port speeds are traditionally listed in bytes per second, but the effective rate in megabits per second is really impressive.

When connected to older equipment, EPP hardware works at the typical 30- to 50-kilobyte-per-second speed of existing applications and ports, but when you connect one EPP device to another, they can move data at the higher rates. Obviously, Xircom sees this higher parallel port speed as critical to eliminating the constriction that chokes the practical throughput of external LAN adapters to well under a megabit per second, depending greatly on the type and speed of CPU in the system.

EPP has rolled into a more comprehensive IEEE standard called EEE 1284. This standard defines the EPP and another type of parallel port supported by HP and Microsoft, the Extended Capabilities Port (ECP). The IEEE standard also defines the electrical connectors and cables that can extend parallel port signals at speeds of up to 5 megabytes per second across cables up to 30 feet long.

EPP provides fine control over the data for interactive communications such as LAN adapters, CD-ROM drives, or tape drives. ECP moves data in bigger blocks and is especially useful as a high-speed interface to printers and scanners. Both types of ports are more useful than the simple parallel port available on most PCs. On the bottom line, IEEE 1284 will be an interesting alternative to PCMCIA (discussed in the next section) and to SCSI. Look for an emerging group of PCs and peripherals that advertise their compatible IEEE 1284 parallel ports.

I see the development of the EPP technology as a cue ball headed into a mass of elements that could rebound in every direction. Certainly, EPP will enhance the capability of external LAN adapters; however, it also has the potential to kill off the market for separate internal LAN expansion cards and simultaneously to drive vendors to install LAN adapters on PC motherboards. EPP ports might also be the gateway to much lower-cost ISDN services in PCs. If networking is important to you, you should consider the availability of an EPP technology parallel port in any new computer system you buy, just to keep your bets down on the future.

PCMCIA

A standard that emerged in 1991, PCMCIA, has a significant impact on LAN adapters in the mid-90s. The acronym PCMCIA stands for the Personal Computer Memory Card International Association and the PCMCIA standard describes several connection schemes for credit-card sized modules containing memory, modems, LAN cards, and other devices. While PCMCIA began as an interface used primarily on laptop computers, it has become popular for desktop computers, too. The PCMCIA specifications describe the physical size of these devices and, most importantly, they set the standards for how these devices interface with the computer. If you have the right interface software, you can simply slide the device into the slot and start to use it.

The PCMCIA standards describe three sizes of cards. All cards are about 3.3 inches long and 2.1 inches wide and have a 68-pin connector on the end. Type II cards, the type used for modems and LAN adapters, are slightly under one quarter of an inch thick.

The PCMCIA specifications describe two levels of interface between the device and the compute: socket services and card services. The socket services specification describes how the socket for the device interfaces with the computer. Software working at this level detects the insertion or removal of a PC Card while the system is on.

Card services describes how resources such as memory and interrupts interact with the device, and provides a way for higher levels of software, like the network redirector, to talk to the PCMCIA hardware. In theory, the combination of the PCMCIA hardware, card services software, and socket services software allows you to add and remove PCMCIA devices without turning the computer off. PCMCIA modems are easy to carry on the road, but the downside includes memory conflicts, frozen applications, and frustration. The situation is improving, though.

PCMCIA slots showed up in volume in laptop computers at the end of 1993. Early on, a lot of products didn't work in a lot of computers. The card and socket services software—actually as many as 3 or 4 programs that logically glue the device into the PC—needed a lot of work. The developers had to tweak buffers, timing loops, and other parameters to get 100 percent interoperability between products. In this respect, these programs are no different from LAN card drivers, SCSI drivers, and similar programs.

Your source for the interface software varies. Sometimes the computer comes equipped with these programs and often the programs come with the PCMCIA device. The best advice is always to get the newest version of the card and socket services software from the dealer or the vendor's BBS or forum. The PCMCIA product vendor typically offers better software and support than the computer vendor.

Here are some things to look for in PCMCIA devices:

Inside   Electrically, PCMCIA modems are similar to internal ISA bus modems and LAN adapters. Amazingly, the modems pack a UART, a data pump, a line transceiver, and all the other necessary parts inside a credit-card sized package. All of the manufacturers seem to have settled on 16550AU UARTS, so the PCMCIA modem provides a good way to work around the less capable 8550s occupying the serial ports in most laptop PCs. Also, it's handy to reset a hung modem; you can just pull it out and slide it back in.

Outside   The telephone or LAN cable connection is the only part of a PCMCIA device you see, and vendors are even competing over that. Megahertz Corp. pioneered the X-Jack, a telephone-cable connection device that retracts out of sight when not in use. Other vendors use special external connection cables, so if you misplace the cable you can't make a connection. However, these external cable systems are less fragile than the X-Jack, and they provide a link to the wall jack

Memory   Memory conflicts are still PCMCIA's biggest problem. The PCMCIA installation programs typically exclude blocks of memory from memory management programs, so if you're tight on Windows memory, adding PCMCIA makes things worse. But without these exclusions, the memory manager can load other drivers into the space, and then nothing works. You can work around some of these problems by using the [menu] function in CONFIG.SYS to selectively load the PCMCIA drivers and memory configuration when you need them. Check the [menu] function in you DOS manual for instructions on the use of this function.

Power   PCMCIA devices draw their power from the computer's battery. A modem draws about 7 watts in use, but drops to about 1 watt in sleep mode. A LAN adapter takes slightly less. In rough numbers, PCMCIA modem operation can be 10 to 30 percent of your laptop's total power requirement, so using this kind of modem can significantly reduce the run-time of your battery. However, PCMCIA still provides a great way for the screwdriver-phobic to install LAN or modem hardware painlessly. Our tests show that the average desktop or laptop computer doesn't pay a penalty in throughput for using PCMCIA. These devices are more expensive than internal expansion cards because they cost more to fabricate, but they do work well.

The Need for Speed

There are several possible choke points in any network. The speed of the file server's hard disk has the biggest influence on the server's response time, but once you've installed a fast hard disk drive and controller and sufficient RAM for caching, the server's LAN adapter card becomes the next most likely choke point. Busy client stations can ask the server to provide 3 to 7 megabits of data per second over a heavily loaded network, and this transfer rate taxes the whole data bus, driver software, and adapter system.

The easiest way to improve server performance on a busy network, after you're sure you have the best hard disk system you can afford, is to split the network load among two or more LAN adapters in the server, as shown in Figure 5.5. NetWare and VINES can host up to four adapters in the same server, while other operating systems can use at least two adapters at the same time. Although it often takes some juggling to find an open combination of IRQ line, memory address, and DMA channel for more than one adapter, it's worth the effort.

When you split the network load among adapters, you give each adapter interface a chance to make an orderly transfer of its data. This trick can allow you to postpone the installation of another server in a growing network, and can ensure fast response times in stable networks. As a side benefit, if one cable run or adapter fails, the stations on the other side of the network will still have the use of the server.

The First Things to Consider When You Buy Network Adapter Cards:

- What kind of bus is in the computer?
  8-bit Industry Standard Architecture (ISA) (PC bus)
  16-bit ISA (AT bus)
  Micro Channel Architecture (MCA)
  Extended Industry Standard Architecture (EISA)

Figure 5.5

This diagram shows how
the network load can be
split among two or more
adapters in the server.
Tests at PC Magazine
LAN Labs prove that
splitting the load in the
server among multiple
network adapters
significantly increases
the throughput on heavily
loaded networks,
providing the hard disk
subsystem can carry the
load.

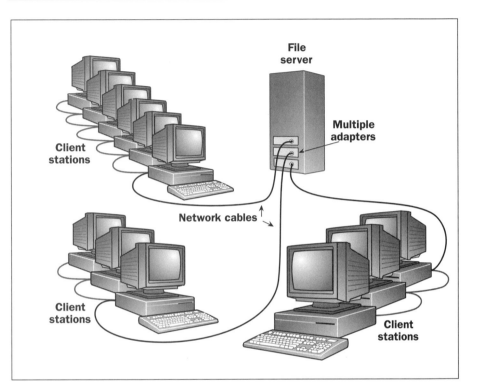

- Can you use bus mastering in the server? (Must be MCA or EISA)
- What other devices occupy memory and IRQ lines in the PCs?

■ LAN Cable Standards

Cable systems are described by many cable and wiring plant standards. You'll find it useful to understand these standards and specifications when you write a request-for proposal or select a network cable system. It's important to carefully plan your network's cable system because it is probably the most expensive, and certainly the longest lasting, part of any network. Overall, a network can't be any better than its cable system.

A long list of companies, organizations, and even government bodies regulate and specify the cables you use. Some companies, such as AT&T, Digital Equipment Corp., Hewlett-Packard, IBM and Northern Telecom, have volumes of detailed specifications that go beyond the cable to include the connectors, wiring and distribution centers, and installation techniques. These plans are called *premise distribution systems* (PDS).

National and international organizations such as the Institute of Electrical and Electronic Engineers (IEEE), the Electronic Industry Association, and the newer Telecommunications Industries Association (EIA/TIA), Underwriters Laboratories (UL), and government agencies at various levels that develop fire and building codes all issue specifications for cable material and installation. EIA/TIA has issued EIA/TIA 568 and 569 standards for technical performance and the EIA/TIA has an active program to extend their requirements. The IEEE includes minimal cable requirements in their 802.3 and 802.5 specifications for Ethernet and Token-Ring systems, but some of the IEEE's work is being overshadowed by the popularity of the unshielded twisted pair wire specified by the EIA/TIA and UL. The designations for coaxial cable had the benefit of being set in practice before most of the standards committees began their deliberations.

The National Electrical Code of the United States describes various types of cables and the materials used in them. The Underwriters Laboratory focuses on safety standards, but has expanded its certification program to evaluate twisted-pair LAN cables for performance according to IBM and EIA/TIA performance specifications as well as National Electrical Code safety specifications. UL has established a program to mark shielded and unshielded twisted-pair LAN cables that should simplify the complex task of making sure the materials used in an installation are up to specification.

National Electrical Code

During a building fire, a cable going between walls, up an elevator shaft, or through an air-handling plenum could become a torch that carries the flame from one floor or one part of the building to another. Since the coverings of cables and wires are typically a form of plastic, they can also create noxious smoke when they burn. Several organizations, including Underwriters Laboratories, have established standards for flame and smoke that apply to LAN cables. The standard most widely supported by local licensing and inspection officials is the *National Electrical Code* (NEC).

The National Electrical Code was established by the National Fire Protection Association (NFPA). The language of the code is designed so that it can be adopted through legislative procedure. In general terms, the NEC describes how a cable burns. Among other things, the standards limit the maximum amount of time a cable may burn after a flame is applied. Other standards, developed by the NFPA and adopted by the American National Standards Institute (ANSI) also describe the type and amount of smoke a burning cable may generate.

While the industry recognizes and generally acknowledges conformance to the NEC standards, every individual municipality, city, county, or state can decide whether or not to adopt the latest version of the NEC for local use. In other words, the NEC standards might or might not be a part of your local fire or building codes. In either case, we urge you to select cable that meets the NEC codes for your application.

You'll see NEC type codes listed in catalogs of cables and supplies. These codes classify specific categories of products for specific uses. Generally, you'll find LAN cables listed under type CM for communications or type MP for multipurpose. Some companies choose to run their cables through testing as remote control or power-limited circuit cable CL2 or CL3, class 2 and class 3, general tests, but the flame and smoke regulations for these categories are generally the same. The differences in these parts of the codes concern the amount of electrical power that could potentially run through the cable under the worst conditions. MP cable is subjected to tests that assume the most power-handling capability, with CM, CL3, and CL2 going through tests that assume decreasing levels of power handling. Type designations OFC and OFN cover fiber optic cables. Type OFC fiber-optic cable contains metal conductors, inserted for strength, type OFN cable contains no metal.

The cable types have an additional letter designating their use. The letter *P*, as in NEC Type CMP (Communications Plenum) cable, designates a cable that has passed tests showing a limited spread of flame and low smoke production. Plenum cable is typically coated with a special jacket material such as Teflon. The code defines a *plenum* as a channel or ductwork fabricated for handling air. A false ceiling or floor is not a plenum.

The letter *R*, as in NEC Type CMR (Communications Riser) cable, shows that the cable has passed similar but slightly different tests for the spread of flame and production of smoke. For example, riser cable is tested for its burning properties in a vertical position. According to the code, you must use cable rated for riser service whenever the cable penetrates a floor and a ceiling. Riser cables typically have a polyvinyl chloride (PVC) outer jacket.

Company Plans

AT&T, Digital Equipment Corporation, IBM and Northern Telecom, along with other companies, have developed and published complete architectures for premise distribution systems (PDS). AT&T calls their architecture the AT&T Systimax Premises Distribution System; Digital uses the name Open DECconnect; IBM calls their architecture simply the IBM Cabling System; and Northern Telecom has the Integrated Building Distribution Network (IBDN). IBM and AT&T fielded their systems in 1984 and 1985, and DEC-Connect came out in 1986. Northern Telecom's IBDN, which is quite similar to AT&T's Systimax, is a relative newcomer; it emerged in 1991.

Overall, the plans from IBM and AT&T have had the most profound effect on the industry. You'll often see cables in catalogs rated in terms of IBM or AT&T specifications. IBM's concept of cable *types* permeates the industry, while AT&T has influenced every cable and connector standard.

Other companies, particularly Amp, Anixter, and Mod-Tap market and sell specific equipment for structured wiring systems. Anixter particularly deserves praise for setting openly documented fair performance and electrical standards for twisted-pair wiring. Anixter's original concept of *levels* is used by EIA/TIA and UL in their standards.

AT&T Systimax

AT&T's Systimax PDS is deeply rooted in history. Before the breakup of the Bell System in the United States, the technical side of the telephone industry was controlled by a series of publications called the *Bell Standard Practices* (BSPs). Because it was largely a monopoly, the industry didn't need many standards beyond those in the BSPs. The BSPs described in detail how installers should cut, twist, and attach every wire and how to secure every cable span. The Systimax specifications are at least a spiritual and cultural offspring of the BSPs. They are detailed and, if followed, can give you a flexible, reliable, and expandable cable plant.

AT&T manufactures, sells, and installs the products in the Systimax family. The company also offers training, so you will find many installers in local companies who know how to work to Systimax specifications. The AT&T Systimax plan is based on unshielded twisted pair wire for the *horizontal* cable, the cable that runs from the wiring closet to the desktop, and on fiber-optic cabling for everything else. It takes about three inches of AT&T catalogs to describe all the products in the Systimax line, but the basic Systimax 100-ohm impedance cable for horizontal data wiring uses four pairs of unshielded twisted-pair 24 AWG copper wire, which provides two spare pairs in most installations. With an outside diameter of about .17 inch, these cables are easy to pull through conduits and inside walls. The Systimax specifications allow a cable run of 100 meters for data transmission at speeds of up to 16 megabits per second.

AT&T also specifies a cable combining copper and fiber-optic conductors. It provides a total of eight unshielded twisted-pairs and two fibers inside one jacket. This combination offers plenty of bandwidth for data and voice telephone connections to any desktop and the capability to add fiber connections for higher-speed data, video, or other applications. If you have a big budget and plan to own the building forever, we think this is the right stuff to install, but it is expensive and bulky.

AT&T offers a variety of fiber-optic cables to use as backbone cable linking wiring closets, and as horizontal wiring for special applications. Some products in this family group as many as 216 fibers together inside a protective jacket for the long trip up an elevator or air shaft. The AT&T fiber-optic standard calls for 62.5/125 micron multimode fiber operating at 850 nanometers (nm) and 1,300 nm and a bandwidth of 160 MHz and 500 MHz.

Cross connection and termination equipment give a PDS its flexibility; the cable system is no better than its connectors and terminators. The AT&T 110 Connector System has set the standard for the industry. This family of products includes several types of rack or wall-mounted connector hardware that typically goes into a wiring closet to terminate horizontal and backbone cable.

AT&T takes the wiring almost up to the desktop. The company offers a variety of wall outlets that terminate eight conductors for data and voice connections. The wiring sequence for these jacks—which wire goes to which terminal—is critical to the proper operation of the network. AT&T's Standard 258A is the most widely specified wiring sequence for four-pair plugs and jacks. It is also the same as the wiring sequence specified for ISDN and 10Base-T Ethernet over unshielded twisted-pair wiring. However, the AT&T 258A standard puts pairs 2 through 4 in a different sequence from the older Universal Service Order Code (USOC) sequence still used by many local telephone companies. This difference is a primary cause of problems when data networks are added to older wiring systems.

Amp and Mod-Tap

Many companies manufacture or sell PDS components, but two companies, Amp and Mod-Tap stand head and shoulders above their competition in providing consistent quality, training, and support of their products. These companies don't attempt to set PDS standards. Instead, they market cable and connection products that conform to popular standards, while also innovating and providing improved convenience and quality. Both Amp and Mod-Tap have training programs for installers.

Among its many products, Amp markets the Ampix cross-connect system, a distribution system for voice and data, with specially designed, high-quality wire terminations and printed circuit board connections between the wire termination and the RJ45 jack of the patch board system. Amp also offers a wide variety of fiber-optic cable splicing, terminating, and testing equipment.

Mod-Tap's product line stresses flexibility. The company markets products that meet the requirements of AT&T, IBM, Digital, and many other companies as well as standards committees. They also have an excellent line of fiber optic products that range from the cable itself to connectors and to splicing equipment and supplies. The company is a single source of supply for a wide variety of products ranging from wall plates and connectors to all the components of a distribution frame.

Anixter's Cable Model

Anixter is a worldwide distributor of wiring system products. The company's place in history is assured as the developer of the multilevel model of performance for cables. Anixter's model includes five levels that describe the performance and electrical characteristics of cabling ranging from the most common telephone cable used in residences to sophisticated twisted-pair cable capable of moving data at 100 megabits per second. The Underwriters Laboratories and EIA/TIA both developed new cable specification systems based on the Anixter cable model.

EIA/TIA

The *Electronic Industry Association/Telecommunications Industry Association* (EIA/TIA) is a U.S. standards body that has a long history of issuing standards for communications systems including, for example, EIA RS-232C and RS-232D for serial communications ports. The EIA/TIA tackled the problem of specifying LAN cables by starting with the Anixter five-level model, but the EIA/TIA calls the divisions "categories" instead of levels. Amp and other companies have worked in the EIA/TIA to expand the model to account for other categories of products including coaxial cable and fiber-optic cable. The result is the EIA/TIA 568 Standard for Commercial Building Telecommunications Wiring.

The primary advantage of EIA/TIA 568 is its publication as an open standard without the stamp of any single vendor. You can select and specify cable meeting a specific category of the EIA/TIA 568 standard and expect to get comparable bids from a variety of vendors. However, the EIA/TIA categories are not tied to the NEC specifications, and they don't deal with shielded twisted-pair wiring.

The EIA/TIA standard describes both the performance specifications of the cable and its installation; however, it still leaves the network system designer room for options and expansion. The standard calls for two cables—one for voice and one for data—to be run to each outlet. One of the two cables must be four-pair UTP for voice. You can choose to run the data on another UTP cable or on a coaxial cable. If you elect to run fiber to the desktop, it can't displace the copper data cable. Here is a capsule view of the EIA/TIA 568 standards:

- *Category 1*   Overall, EIA/TIA 568 says very little about the technical specifications in Category 1 or Category 2. The descriptions that follow are for general information. Level 1 cable is typically untwisted 22 AWG or 24 AWG wire with a wide range of impedance and attenuation values. It is not recommended for data in general, and certainly not for signaling speeds over 1 megabit per second.

- *Category 2* This category of cable is the same as the Anixter Level 2 cable specification, and is derived from the IBM Type 3 specification. This cable uses 22 or 24 AWG solid wire in twisted pairs. It is tested to a maximum bandwidth of 1 MHz and is not tested for near-end crosstalk. You can use this cable for IBM 3270 and AS/400 computer connections and for Apple LocalTalk.

- *Category 3* This category of cable is the same as the Anixter Level 3. Generally, it is the minimum level of cable quality you should allow in new installations. This cable uses 24 AWG solid wire in twisted pairs. It displays a typical impedance of 100 ohms and is tested for attenuation and near-end crosstalk through 16 MHz. This wire is useful for data transmission at speeds up to 16 megabits per second. It is the lowest level wire standard you should use for 10BaseT installations, and is sufficient for 4 megabit-per-second Token-Ring.

- *Category 4* This cable is the same as the Anixter Level 4 cable. It can have 22 AWG or 24 AWG solid wire in twisted pairs. This cable has a typical impedance of 100 ohms and is tested for performance at a bandwidth of 20 MHz. It is formally rated for a maximum signaling speed of 20 MHz. Although it was popular for a while, Category 4 cable has been superseded by Category 5 in most new installations.

- *Category 5* This is 22 or 24 AWG unshielded twisted-pair cable with a 100 ohm impedance. This cable is tested at a bandwidth of 100 MHz and can handle data signaling under specified conditions at 100 megabits per second. Category 5 cable is a high-quality media with growing applications for transmitting video, images, and very high-speed data. I recommend Category 5 cable for all new installations.

Trying to describe the EIA/TIA 568 standard and the category system is like trying to paint a moving train. The standard evolves through an interactive committee process and change—particularly expansion—is constant. For example, because IBM's 150 ohm shielded Type 1 and Type 9 cable are so important in the market, we expect to see them accommodated in the standard. There are also proposals that integrate Thinnet Ethernet coaxial cable, 62.5/125 micron multimode fiber, and single-mode fiber cable used for long distance connections into the specification.

Underwriters Laboratories

Local fire and building code regulators try to use standards like those of the National Electrical Code, but insurance groups and other regulators often specify the standards of the *Underwriters Laboratories*. UL has safety standards for cables similar to those of the NEC. UL 444 is the Standard for Safety for Communications Cable. UL 13 is the Standard for Safety for Power-Limited Circuit

Cable. Network cable might fall into either category. UL tests and evaluates samples of cable and then, after granting a UL listing, conducts follow-up tests and inspections. This organization's independent status makes the UL markings valuable tools for buyers.

In an interesting and unique action, the people at UL have tied safety and performance together in a program designed to make it easier to select or specify cable. UL's LAN Certification Program addresses both concerns. IBM authorizes UL to verify 150 ohm STP to IBM performance specifications, and UL has established a Data-Transmission Performance-Level Marking Program that covers 100 ohm twisted-pair cable. UL adopted the EIA/TIA 568 performance standard and, by evolution, the Anixter cable performance model. There is a small inconsistency: The UL program deal with both shielded and unshielded twisted-pair wire, while the EIA/TIA 568 standard focuses on unshielded wire.

The UL markings range from Level I through Level V. You can tell a UL level from an Anixter level because the UL uses Roman numerals. As we described, IBM's cable specifications range from Type 1 through Type 9, while the EIA/TIA has Categories 1 through 8. Of course, it's easy to become confused by the similarly numbered levels and types. The UL level markings deal with performance and safety, so products that merit a UL level also meet the appropriate NEC MP, CM, CL, or FP specifications along with the EIA/TIA standard for a specific category. Cables that earn these UL markings can have them printed on the outer jacket as, for example, Level I, LVL I, or LEV I.

Here is a quick summary of the UL markings:

- *UL Level I Marking*   Meets appropriate NEC and UL 444 safety requirements. No specific performance specifications.

- *UL Level II Marking*   Meets performance requirements of EIA/TIA 568 Category 2 and IBM Cable Plan Type 3 cable. Meets appropriate NEC and UL 444 safety requirements. Acceptable for 4 megabit Token-Ring, but not for higher-speed data applications such as 10BaseT.

- *UL Level III Marking*   Meets performance requirements of EIA/TIA 568 Category 3 and NEC and UL 444 safety requirements. Lowest acceptable marking for LAN applications.

- *UL Level IV Marking*   Meets performance requirements of EIA/TIA 568 Category 4 and NEC and UL 444 safety requirements.

- *UL Level V Marking*   Meets performance requirements of EIA/TIA 568 Category 5 and NEC and UL 444 safety requirements. This is the right choice for most modern LAN installations.

A Star to Steer By

As you navigate through the landscape of your network's cabling system, it's often difficult to see the forest for the trees. Structured architectures like a premise distribution system, the EIA/TIA guidelines, or the UL marking system provide some assurance that you can pick the right path to network success.

But simply using the right materials doesn't insure that a cable installation meets the performance specification. Many factors, including how much the wire is untwisted before it reaches a termination, the type of termination equipment, the electrical noise in various frequency bands, and the near-end crosstalk (NEXT) caused by wires in proximity to each other determine the quality of the total installation. You can get a good start on a high quality installation by using the correct cable, but good cable does not guarantee a good installation. The actions of the installer are critical to the overall quality of your cable plant.

■ Cables for Network Connections

The type of adapter you buy dictates the types of cable that will work in the network, the physical and electrical form of the network, the type of electrical signaling used on the network, and how the networked PCs share access to the connecting cable. People in the network business generally refer to the path of the cables as the *physical topology* and to the route of the messages on those cables as the *logical topology* of the network. There is no fancy turn of phrase to describe *electrical signaling*, but sharing the cable is known as *media-access control*.

In the remainder of this chapter, I discuss the general characteristics of cables, their physical topologies, and the signals they carry. In the next chapter we'll look at the logical topologies and media-access control schemes specifically associated with the Ethernet, Token-Ring, and ARCnet networking systems.

The larger the area your LAN covers, the more critical cabling design becomes. You must look at the issue of cabling first to determine whether it will drive your network budget and planning cycles or is only a minor consideration. The type of cabling you have installed or want to use might be a deciding factor in the design and layout of your network, or it might be a minor factor that you can handle quickly.

There are five possible cabling choices: unshielded twisted-pair, shielded twisted-pair, coaxial, fiber-optic, and no wiring at all. Wireless LANs, or at least wireless segments of LANs, provide a way out of difficult wiring problems in many installations, and we'll describe them later. First, let's focus on physical cabling.

You can have the wiring for your LAN installed by contractors as big as AT&T or GTE, by your local telephone company, by a local electrical contractor, or by your own employees, but be sure to consider the need for a final electrical inspection when you plan your installation.

Major vendors including AT&T, Digital Equipment Corp., IBM, Northern Telecom, and many smaller vendors have developed their own premise distribution system (PDS) plans. These cabling architectures provide for an integrated telephone and data cabling plant using hardware components from a single supplier. The advantage of having one source of supply is that there is only one place to point the finger of responsibility; the disadvantage is that you become wedded to that vendor. If you are planning a new building or major renovation, shop for a PDS, but plan for a long term relationship with the supplier you select.

If you start from scratch, the cost of LAN wiring is divided between the costs of material and labor. Prices vary with the amount of cable you buy, but here are some general estimates: When bought in reels of 1,000 feet or more, typical fiber-optic cable should cost just under $2 a foot; the shielded twisted-pair wiring used for Token-Ring networks runs about 40 cents a foot; the thin coaxial cable used for Ethernet costs about 15 cents a foot; and four-pair twisted wire costs 10 cents a foot. These prices skyrocket for shorter hunks of cable.

A lot of contractors know how to install twisted-pair wiring, and the cable television industry has taken the mystery out of installing coaxial cable. There are very few good fiber-optic contractors or people who know how to wire Token-Ring networks, however. Labor costs for cable installations vary widely, driven by locale and the availability of knowledgeable contractors, but expenses of $1,000 per networked PC are frequently reported in major metropolitan areas.

Companies often elect to have their own computer resource people plan and even install LAN cabling with the help of a licensed electrical contractor. Involving your own people in LAN wiring can save money, avoid mistakes, and facilitate expansion. Several companies, including AT&T, Cabletron Systems, Northern Telecom, and SynOptics Communications, provide courses in wiring techniques.

The Harmonics of Square Waves

The signals on LAN cables are electrical square waves. A signal that rises quickly to a level of 15 volts represents a binary 0, and one that falls rapidly to a negative 15 volts represents a binary 1. The voltage transition from 0 to the positive or negative level signals the transmission of the bit to the receivers on the network. This signaling scheme works well, but it has two problems: radiation and interference. The various network cables take different approaches to these problems.

The problem with radiation comes from the harmonics generated by the rising and falling voltages. A simple rule of physics states that the harmonics of square waves are infinite. This means that the square waves generate radio signals all the way up the radio-wave spectrum. The radio-frequency emissions generated by the data signals on a LAN cable can cause interference with a wide range of radio and television devices located miles away. So LAN cables and equipment must somehow prevent radiation of the unwanted harmonics. Government organizations set limits on the degree of allowable radiation for all computer products. The U.S. Federal Communications Commission sets two standards: Class A and Class B, for office and home use respectively. Class B requirements are more stringent than those for Class A.

Organizations engaged in commercial or international espionage can use the radiated electrical signals to intercept the data moving across LAN cables. Some cable systems meet a stringent set of specifications called the Transient Electromagnetic Emanations Standard, or TEMPEST, designed to make it very difficult for any unauthorized party to receive signals from the cable.

The second problem cable designers must deal with is outside interference. The effect of electrically radiated signals works in the other direction, too. Electrical signals from motors, power lines, fluorescent lights, radio transmitters, and many other sources can distort and override the desired signals on the LAN cable. LAN cables must somehow protect the signals they carry from disruption by such outside electrical interference. Fortunately, the same techniques that work to cut down unwanted radiation also reduce incoming interference.

Coaxial Cable

Coaxial cable consists of a core of copper wire—either solid or stranded—surrounded by an external shield of woven copper braid or metallic foil. The braid and central conductor have the same axis, and that's where the term coaxial cable comes from. Flexible plastic insulation separates the inner and outer conductors, and another layer of insulation covers the outer braid. Figure 5.6 shows the shielding on thin and thick Ethernet cabling.

The outer conductor shields the inner conductor from outside electrical signals and reduces the radiation of interior signals. The distance between the two conductors, the type of insulation, and other factors give each type of cable a specific electrical characteristic called *impedance*.

Different LAN signaling schemes, such as Ethernet, ARCnet, and IBM's 3270 cabling scheme, use cables with specific impedances, and they aren't interchangeable. You can't judge a coaxial cable's impedance by looking at it

Figure 5.6

These pieces of thick and
thin coaxial cable have
multiple layers of braid
and foil shielding.

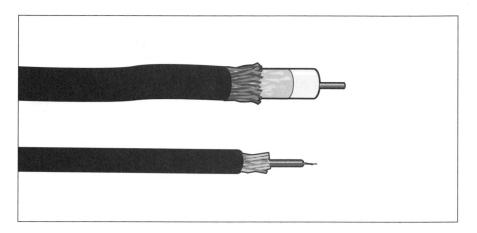

unless you read its type on the outside of the cable. The cables follow a letter
and numeric designation scheme. If you just remember that Ethernet uses a
cable called RG-58 and ARCnet uses a cable called RG-62, you'll have as
much knowledge as you're ever likely to need.

It takes a little experience and practice to install the connectors on coaxial cable, but the skill is important because one bad connection can halt the
operation of an entire network. It pays to invest in good connectors that are
plated with silver, not tin. It also pays to invest in a good crimping tool to install the connectors. Figure 5.7 shows a BNC connector attached to a piece of
coaxial cable. Watch particularly for cheap Ethernet T-connectors. Use only
connectors that meet military specification UG-274. If a T-connector meets
this specification, it will say so on the body of the barrel or on the lip of the
male connector; be sure to look for that mark before you accept or install
Ethernet T-connectors. I also recommend replacing unmarked generic connectors. With good connectors retailing for $6 to $10 each and crimping tools
selling for $150, you'll feel an urge to scrimp, but believe me, it's a bad gam-
ble. Figure 5.8 shows two T-connectors.

Similarly, don't scrimp on the cable itself. Markings on thin Ethernet
cable should identify it as RG-58/A-AU or as conforming to IEEE 802.3
specifications. Don't confuse 53-ohm-impedance RG-58/A-AU cable with
the 73-ohm RG-62/A-AU cable used in ARCnet, IBM's 3270, and other systems. The radio industry is plagued by low-quality coaxial cable that allows
unacceptable power losses at high frequencies. LAN cables aren't asked to
carry high frequencies, so this problem might not show up for a few years
until the insulation breaks down and the cable changes electrical characteristics. Always insist on brand-name cable that is clearly labeled with the standards

Figure 5.7

The connectors on the ends of this coaxial cable are typical of those used for thin Ethernet.

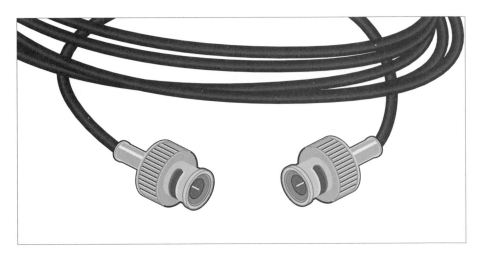

Figure 5.8

The quality of the T-connectors you use can have a major impact on the reliability and efficiency of your Ethernet network. The connector on the left shows it MIL SPEC numbers and has a reinforced junction at the center. Experience at PC Magazine LAN Labs shows that connectors like the one on the right fail at the junction due to mechanical stress from the cable, and such failures are often difficult to detect.

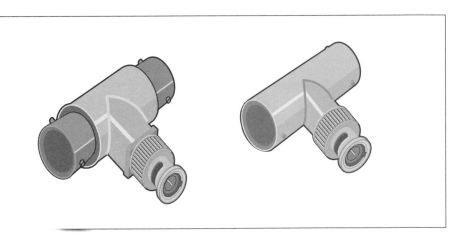

it meets. An investment in good connectors, tools, and cable pays dividends for years.

The thick backbone cable used in classical Ethernet networks requires some special handling. Known as "frozen yellow garden hose," thick Etherent cable has the distance markers on the outside of the jacket to show the quarter wavelength points. It's important to get the terminators installed exactly on a black mark at each end; then, when you tap into the cable at the points marked between, the transceiver sees the correct impedance. If you miss the point by more than a few inches, theoretically the impedance mismatch could set up reflections within the cable that might cause problems.

However, in practice people report that thick Ethernet works despite all types of mishandling. Instead of worrying about problems with the backbone cable, I'd watch out for smaller glitches, like a bad adapter or a transceiver with the Signal Quality Error (SQE) switch turned on. SQE is an old feature that causes more problems than it solves. Installers say that SQE has three letters just like OFF, and that tells you what to do with the switch.

Thick Ethernet is difficult to install because of the size of the cable and the complex hardware involved in making every connection, but once it is in the walls it should work until the building falls down.

Unshielded Twisted-Pair

As the name implies, twisted-pair wiring is made up of pairs of wires insulated from each other and twisted together within another insulating sheath. The twisting of the wire pairs produces a mutual shielding effect. Although this effect cuts down on the absorption and radiation of electrical energy, it is not as effective as an external wire braid or foil.

Unshielded Telephone Wire

People often associate the term *twisted-pair wiring* with telephone wiring, but not all telephone wiring is twisted-pair. The wires in each pair of a twisted pair cable are twisted together to reduce the electrical coupling between them and the amount of outside electrical noise they pick up. Figure 5.9 shows UTP wire pairs and Figure 5.10 shows the most typical type of UTP termination, the RJ-45 plug. But there are many types of telephone wire that are not twisted. *Quad*, the wiring found in residences, has four parallel wires in one cable. The telephone wiring plants in many older buildings were designed for a key system—one using phones with multiple line buttons and thick multiconductor cables. A few modern buildings are wired with something the industry calls *silver satin*. Silver satin cable is flat and typically has a silver vinyl jacket. None of these wiring systems—quad, multiconductor, or silver satin—is adequate for modern LAN data services.

Unshielded twisted-pair wiring is very popular with network buyers, but much of its popularity is based on misconceptions or outdated information. Before you decide to string along with UTP, see if your decision is based on any of these ideas:

• *UTP is cheap.* Maybe, but while the wire itself is low in cost, the cost of the labor used to pull the wiring is the major portion of the bill. Fiber can cost ten times the price of UTP, but even at slightly more than $1

Figure 5.9

Unshielded twisted-pair wire offers an economical alternative for both Ethernet and Token-Ring networks. The twist of the wire provides a degree of shielding from external electromagnetic currents.

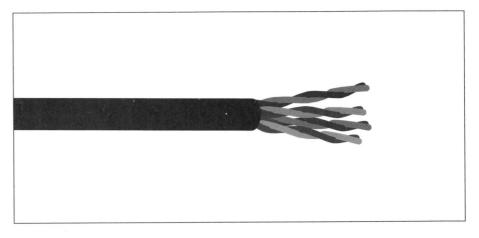

Figure 5.10

Unshielded twisted-pair wiring typically terminates in RJ-45 modular connectors like those shown here.

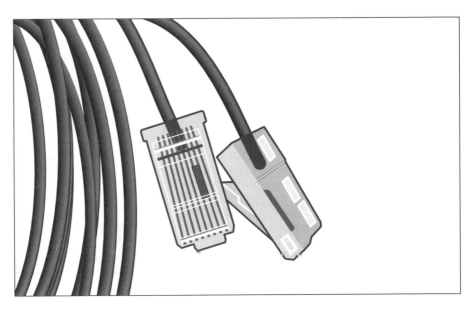

per foot, the cost of installation by a licensed electrical contractor can dwarf the cost of materials.

- *I can use the UTP that's already in the walls.* Again, maybe, but you need to analyze every wire run to be sure it meets the length, noise, and other electrical specifications for the networking architecture you want to use.

- *UTP gives me the reliability of the star wiring scheme.* Sure it does, but this arrangement is not unique to UTP. Modern wiring concentrators allow you to arrange any type of wire in a star physical topology.

The EIA/TIA and UL standards for UTP have made it practical for all network installations. My personal favorite wiring plan is still a system that uses thin coaxial cable in a star-wired configuration, but most organizations find UTP to be a more comfortable solution.

In all likelihood, even if you have UTP installed in your building for a telephone system, you will have to pull more wire for a new network installation. Expect to pay about 10 cents a foot, in bulk, for the wire—plus the cost of labor and parts such as connection blocks and wall jacks. Also, budget about $2,000 for a wiring hub that can accommodate 20 nodes. This $100-per-port hardware expenditure lays waste to arguments in favor of unshielded twisted-pair wiring based solely on installation cost.

By comparison, thin coaxial cable is about 15 cents a foot, but you can easily use less than half as much as you would if you were using twisted-pair, because thin Ethernet uses a point-to-point wiring scheme instead of the 10BaseT star wiring plan. Your hardware cost is about $5 per station for co-axial cable connectors, assuming the LAN card vendor supplies the needed T-connector for each card. On close inspection, low cost and the chance to use existing wiring aren't the major advantages of a twisted-pair setup. Let's examine its real benefits.

Even if you must pull additional twisted-pair wiring to install a LAN, at least the same wiring can be used for the telephone system (although I don't recommend running voice telephone and data signals on wire pairs in the same outside sheath because of crosstalk problems). The technology of twisted-pair wiring, unlike coaxial Ethernet alternatives and Token-Ring's shielded twisted-pair, is familiar to technicians you already have on staff or under contract. If an installer abides by a few rules (for example, keeping to a maximum wire length of 330 feet between computer and hub and avoiding sources of electrical noise), the installation is simple. Also, choosing un-shielded twisted-pair wiring doesn't introduce complex and ugly cabling, wall jacks, and desktop attachments into your office.

Avoiding Twisted-Pair Problems

Telephone system suppliers such as AT&T, Northern Telecom, the regional Bell operating companies, and other PBX companies have standards for tele-phone wiring systems. Their standards, and the resultant wiring systems, are not identical, but they are close enough that you can usually assume their wiring systems can carry your data—assuming there are enough vacant wire pairs in the cables.

The heart of all the systems is the same: a wiring closet with rows of punch-down blocks. Some companies call them *telco splice blocks*, and veterans know them from the old AT&T monopoly days as *Type 66 blocks*. Whatever their name, these central wiring points often become central failure points in wiring plants.

A punch-down block gets its name from the act of using a special hand tool to punch a wire down between the jaws of a retaining clip. The clip slices through the wire's PVC insulation and makes electrical contact. Punch-down blocks make installations and modifications simple while avoiding the major problem of telephone system short circuits; however, the quality of the electrical connection made by the punch-down process varies considerably. The contact area between the clip and the wire is small, and moisture, crystallization, electrolysis, and corrosion can all degrade the electrical connection. On a voice system, a bad connection manifests itself in lower volume and perhaps frying or popping sounds. The human ear and brain deal with those problems admirably—unfortunately, computer data systems have less-than-human flexibility.

AT&T and other companies have new wire-splice blocks. AT&T calls its design the *Type 100*; it uses wire-wrap techniques and gold contacts for better connections. If you have transmission problems using unshielded twisted-pair wire and repunching or wiggling the wires on the existing splice block changes the condition, you should consider retiring the old punch-down blocks in favor of more modern (and higher-priced) wire connection alternatives.

I've devoted a lot of space to unshielded twisted-pair wire as a LAN connection scheme because this method of connecting network nodes is becoming increasingly important; however, another twist on twisted-pair is making some important inroads of its own. Shielded twisted-pair wiring is growing in popularity because it is IBM's choice for its Token-Ring network system.

Shielded Twisted-Pair

Telephone twisted-pair wiring has no external shield. By contrast, data-grade twisted-pair wire carries an external aluminum-foil or woven-copper shield specifically designed to reduce electrical noise absorption. Thus, it combines the shielding properties of both coaxial cable and telephone twisted-pair wire. Different companies have their own specifications for such cables; the IEEE standards apply to systems like IBM's Token-Ring. Figure 5.11 shows the foil and braid shielding on shielded twisted-pair wire.

Shielded twisted-pair cables are relatively expensive and difficult to work with, and they require custom installation. Nonetheless, IBM has successfully marketed a wiring plan using these cables for Token-Ring installations. The IBM plan adds reliability (and substantial cost) by using a separate run of cable between every server or client station and a central wiring hub. This wiring plan

Figure 5.11

Shielded twisted-pair wiring combines the shielding of coaxial cable with the twisting of unshielded twisted-pair wire. On the other hand, this kind of wiring is bulky, expensive, and tricky to install properly.

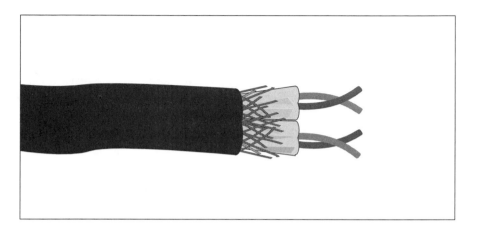

significantly increases the amount of cable used, but it also insures against the total failure of the network in the event one cable is broken or shorted. IBM uses special connectors, shown in Figure 5.12, for connection to the central wiring hub.

Figure 5.12

The D-shell connector shown here connects the cable to the Token-Ring adapter card. The larger, darker connector is an IBM Data Connector, which attaches the two twisted pairs of wire and shielding to an IBM medium attachment unit.

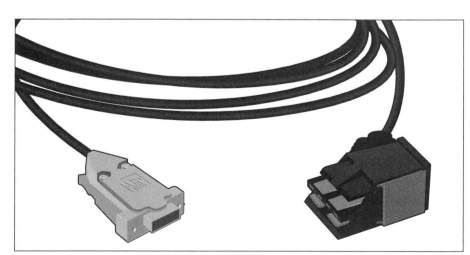

Coaxial cable, particularly the thin RG-59 or RG-62 type, is easier to install than shielded, data-grade, twisted-pair cable, and it has many of the same noise-resistance advantages. But if you want real data security and immunity from noise, you can't beat signals sent with light.

Fiber-Optic Cables

Fiber-optic cables, shown in Figure 5.13, are made of glass fibers rather than wire. These lightweight cables run many channels of stereo sound to airline passengers' seats, eliminating hundreds of pounds of wiring. Certain automobiles (such as Chevrolet's Corvette) rely on fiber-optic strands to route light from exterior lights to the dashboard so drivers can monitor safety conditions. Now even PC-based local area networks can use fiber-optic cables.

Figure 5.13

Fiber-optic cable consists of a glass fiber surrounded by a Teflon coating. Kevlar or even stainless steel fibers often surround the Teflon for added strength. The lower illustration shows two types of connectors attached to fiber cables.

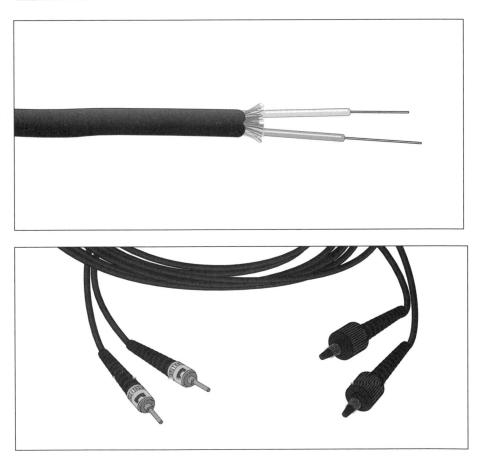

Fiber-optic cabling is made of a hair-thin strand of glass surrounded by strengthening material such as Kevlar. Small lasers or light-emitting diodes send pulses of light representing the 0s and 1s of the digital message through the fiber.

Fiber-optic cable has many advantages over copper wire including complete freedom from electrical interference, a small diameter so you can reclaim your building's conduits, and the potential for carrying large amounts of data at high speeds over longer distances.

Practically all fiber LAN technologies use two strands of fiber going to each node, so some of the size advantage of fiber cable over small copper coaxial cable is lost in real installations. Each strand carries data in one direction for full-time, two-way communications.

A couple of years ago, the big promise of fiber-optic systems came from their bandwidth. Hundreds of simultaneous telephone conversations or high-speed data transmissions can travel down a single fiber of glass a couple of times the diameter of a human hair. The telephone companies are making good use of fiber technology in this way as they expand and replace their systems.

Most people imagine data moving through fiber-optic cables at never-before-possible speeds. But speed is not one of the major advantages of PC-based, fiber-optic local area networks. EIA/TIA Level 5 UTP installations can carry data at 155 megabites per second. The biggest advantage of fiber comes from increased distance. Fiber allows longer connections without requiring the installation of devices to repeat the signals, and also provides total immunity from interference in noisy electrical environments, but it doesn't move data any faster. Fiber systems that replace copper cable use a star wiring pattern from a wiring center to each node, or they only connect wiring centers that are located in different parts of a building or campus. Codenoll Technology Corp., Proteon Inc., and PureData, Inc. sell PC LAN adapters that use fiber in place of typical LAN cables.

Distance and reliability are the primary assets most people value in fiber-optic cable; however, security is equally important to many users.

Distance

Although signals on a copper cable and light in a glass fiber travel at approximately the same speed, the light meets less resistance as it moves along; therefore, light signals go farther with less attenuation. Fiber-optic links from simple PC-based LAN systems can run without a repeater to distances of more than 3.5 kilometers. This is more than 11 times the maximum distance for coaxial cable, and 15 times the distance for twisted-pair systems such as StarLAN. (Architectural criteria other than the media limit Ethernet networks to 2.5 kilometers overall.)

Reliability

The primary reason for the reliability of fiber systems is that they don't pick up electrical signals and impulses. Despite shielding, bypassing, and grounding, copper cables become antennas. The longer they are, the more energy they absorb from sparking motors, radio transmitters, power wires, and other electrical devices. Additionally, metal cables can develop different voltage potentials to the electrical ground, leading to electrical ground loops that can induce interference and even sparking from metal cables. The energy from all these sources modifies and smothers the data signals in the metal cable, causing bad packets and sometimes transient unreliability. Fiber cables are immune to all electrical fields, so they carry clean signals and never spark or arc.

The physical topology of fiber LANs also adds to their reliability. All fiber-optic LAN systems use a physical hub topology. This means that cables run from each workstation to a central hub, like the one shown in Figure 5.14, so if one cable breaks, the network remains operational. This setup is in contrast to station-to-station wiring schemes or even some coaxial hub systems, where the entire network fails if one cable is shorted or one connector is open. In addition, the hub serves as a point for translation between fiber and copper cable links.

Figure 5.14

Products like this fiber-optic hub and adapter break the typical mold by increasing the signaling speed to 100 megabits per second.

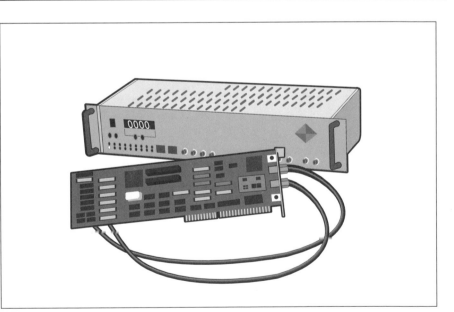

All fiber is not alike. AT&T favors a fiber with a core diameter of 62.5 microns (a micron is $1/25,000$ of an inch), while IBM specifies a 100-micron core. You must match the equipment and the fiber, but if you install fiber before you buy the equipment you'll be safe specifying the 62.5 micron size. Expect to pay about $1,100 for a 1,000-foot roll of cable with two fiber strands.

Security

Fiber LANs offer improved security because they carry light, and that light is precisely controlled. If I can get my hands on a coaxial cable LAN, I can tap into it and read all the data passing over it, including unencrypted passwords. Some coupling techniques let me intercept the signals without even piercing the cable; this is because copper cables radiate signals as well as picking them up. Fiber-optic cables often play a major role in voice and data communications systems approved under TEMPEST criteria because they radiate their light only at the ends of connectors.

If the amount of light going through the cable is precisely adjusted, the insertion of an unauthorized device to tap off some of the light causes the entire link to fail. System failure indicates that something unusual has happened to the cable. Since they don't leak, and it's difficult or impossible to insert a physical tap, fiber-based systems are practically immune to interception.

Who's Buying Fiber Optics

The people buying fiber-optic LANs, or fiber-optic links for their LANs, aren't necessarily computer scientists and engineers with huge amounts of data to send. Instead, they are likely to be stockbrokers, bankers, medical technicians, and people in the fields of security or intelligence who need extended-distance coverage, absolute reliability, and perhaps confidentiality for their networks.

Fiber optics has moved quickly from a young technology with great promise to a set of mature, practical products that have significant advantages over other methods of connecting computers. At the same time, fiber systems bring some unique installation problems, and cost more than alternative systems using copper cables.

The price of connectors and the skill needed to install connectors on fiber-optic cable is much less of a problem than it once was. In the late 1980s, installers needed special equipment and expensive training to properly attach a connector to a piece of fiber, but now AMP Inc. offers their LightCrimp system at a cost of approximately $6 to $7 per connector. Installation takes about two minutes per connector and installers can quickly learn to use the simple installation tools.

FDDI

You have probably heard the acronym FDDI, which stands for *Fiber Distributed Data Interface*. FDDI is a standard specified by ANSI, the American National Standards Institute, as ANSI X3T9.5 for transmission at 100 million bits per second. Don't assume that all LANs using fiber conform to the FDDI standard, because actually very few of them do.

FDDI is something completely different. The FDDI standard defines two physical rings that simultaneously send data in different directions. The configuration is designed for reliability and flexibility as well as high throughput.

The robust FDDI architecture is so appealing that companies like Crescendo Communications, Digital Equipment Corp., and Microdyne have announced products that use the 100-megabit-per-second FDDI architecture over different types of copper wiring—thus the standard becomes CDDI instead of FDDI.

The high prices of devices like LAN adapters make fiber-optic cable and FDDI in general 10 to 20 times more expensive than copper cabling alternatives right now. These prices will come down slowly, but it will be at least several years before FDDI becomes as economical as copper LAN alternatives—assuming it ever does—so fiber links aren't likely to reach every desktop soon.

Wireless LANs

The name is misleading. Wireless LANs typically aren't totally wireless, but instead use either radio or infrared technology to connect a node or group of nodes into the main body of the network. It's difficult to categorize wireless LAN systems because they have many different architectures. Some products work only with Ethernet or only with Token-Ring cabling, while others replace the cabling on certain segments. *Wireless* may be the hottest word in networking, but nobody owns the term and it means very different things to different people. There are at least five major types of wireless network connectivity:

- Conference room

- Building/campus

- City/region

- Nationwide (U.S.)

- Worldwide

Each type of wireless networking involves a different group of companies and, to make things even more confusing, there are overlaps between the categories. But before we get too far into this topic we want to make one point clear: *Wireless networks in every category are always an extension of cabled networks, not a replacement of them.* If any totally wireless networks actually do exist, they are rare exceptions.

The rules of physics apply to wireless connections just as they do to cable, but they are more confining in the wireless environment. Radio waves traveling through space face a much more hostile environment than electrons traveling through copper. You can have long distance connections, fast connections, and inexpensive connections over wireless, but not all three. Distance and signaling speed always work against each other and raising either of those parameters while keeping the other one steady always raises the cost. This relationship makes it very difficult to field a wireless system that is less expensive or faster than one based on copper cables.

Remember, with wireless LANs, you can have it fast, over a long distance, or inexpensive; pick any two.

So, for wireless systems to succeed, they must be deployed in niche situations where copper is at some disadvantage. The two most fruitful applications for wireless are in areas where it is difficult to install copper cables and where people need or are willing to pay for, mobility.

Any number of situations can arise that make it difficult to install copper cable. For example, you mght want to extend the network out to a lone PC in a warehouse or in some other part of the building, but find that the distance limitations exceed a single span of LAN cable. A repeater would solve the problem, but would also substantially increase the cost of connecting that single node. In this case, a wireless link could be less expensive than copper and a lot easier to install.

You might also run into situations where the type of building construction or the inability to get a construction right-of-way blocks the cable installation. Wireless connections work in these cases too.

Companies such as Motorola, AT&T, Proxim, Xircom, and Travelling Software all market useful wireless products. It seems that the primary use for these products will be linking portable computers into a campuswide network.

Cabling Recommendations

My advice about fiber is clear and conservative. First, if you have a large installation, always use fiber between wiring closets in the building and around the campus regardless of what cabling you run between the wiring closets and the desktops.

Second, if you are planning a new building or doing a major rewiring and plan to install Category 5 unshielded twisted-pair wire, pull as much fiber with it as you can afford and let the fiber sit dark and unused in the walls until the prices of the adapters come within reach. If you install coaxial cable or shielded twisted-pair wiring to each desktop, it isn't necessary to back it up with fiber.

If you haven't yet begun to install a LAN, you must decide between a reasonable up-front investment or a low-cost entry point with a balloon payment some time in the future. If you invest in STP, coax, or a fiber backup to UTP in a star wiring scheme today, you'll be set for the future.

■ Topologies

You can't always tell how messages flow by looking at the physical layout of the cables in a LAN—the physical and logical topologies of a network are relatively independent; however, both can affect your network's reliability, economy, and resistance to interruption.

Logical Topologies

The nodes on a LAN handle messages in one of two logical ways: Either they relay messages from node to node in a *sequential* logical topology, or they send messages to all stations simultaneously in a *broadcast*. Ethernet and ARCnet use a broadcast topology, while Token-Ring uses a sequential technique.

Physical Topologies

Theoretically, there are several ways to arrange the cables connecting a group of computers, but in the real world, you can only buy products that conform to one of two physical topologies: the *daisy chain* and the *star*. Figure 5.15 shows how fiber-optic cables are laid out in a typical installation.

Figure 5.15

Fiber-optic systems always use a physical star topology. Some adapters connect directly to the fiber-optic cables, while others use an external transciever or medicum attachment unit (MAU). Many manufacturers market fiber-optic wiring hubs that can accept fiber, coaxial, and twisted-pair wire at the same time.

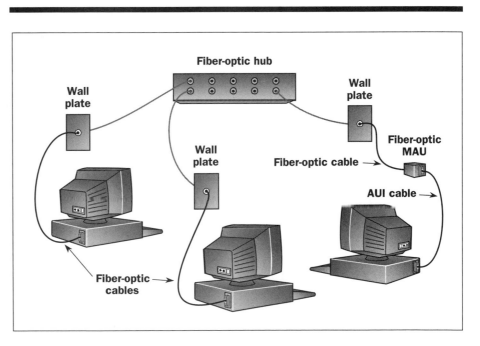

The Daisy-Chain Topology

In a physical daisy-chain topology, the cable takes the shortest path from one network node to the next. Another common name for this arrangement is *bus* topology, presumably because the cable follows a direct route from stop to stop. This topology is typically associated with Ethernet, a complete signaling and media-sharing scheme that is described in the next chapter. A version of ARCnet that's marketed by several companies also uses this general node-to-node cable topology.

The cable goes from PC to PC in a daisy-chain topology, but it doesn't go into each PC and come back out again. Instead, a coaxial T-connector provides a tap into the cable at each network node; thus, the cable has many connection points. Unfortunately, because of the electrical characteristics of a daisy-chain topology, a bad connection at any point spells failure for the entire network.

Daisy-chain cable installations are often messy because two cables run from the CPU to the back panel of each computer and then go off along the floor in separate directions. You can make a neater installation by using an interesting product called the LAN-Line Thinnet Tap from Amp, Inc., a well-known connector manufacturer. This system, shown in Figure 5.16, costs about $9 when purchased in large quantities. It terminates the two cables in a single wall connector and eliminates the twin-cable clutter of typical thin Ethernet installations.

Figure 5.16

The LAN-Line Thinnet Tap system from Amp, Inc. provides an answer to the difficult task of making a neat installation with thin Ethernet cabling (LAN-Line is a trademark of Amp. Inc.)

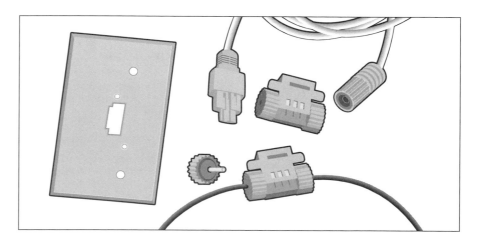

The Star Topology

The second physical arrangement for cables is the star or *hub* topology. In this topology, the network wires run between the network nodes and a central wiring hub, usually located in the building's wiring closet. Figure 5.17 shows a wiring hub for combining 10BaseT, Token-Ring, and fiber-optic systems.

Figure 5.17

SynOptics LattisNet Model 3000 concentrator allows you to configure a combination of wiring schemes in a physical star topology. This combines fiber-optic cable, 10BaseT wiring, and Token-Ring cabling. (Technical support courtesy of SynOptics Communications, Inc.)

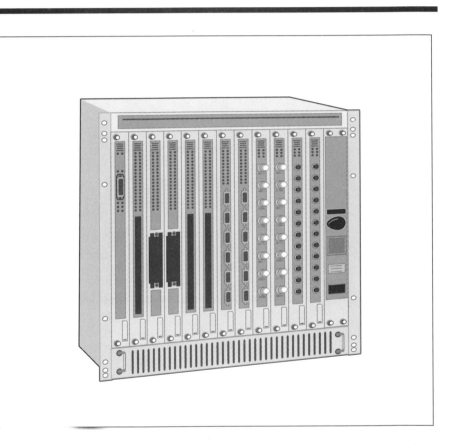

As indicated previously, the primary advantage of the star wiring topology is operational survivability, because the wiring hub isolates the runs of network cabling from each other. Even if a wire between a station and the wiring hub breaks or develops a bad connection, the rest of the network remains operational.

Because the wire in a star topology runs from the wall plates to a central point, like telephone wiring, it is typically easier to install than cable that runs from point to point. The overall installation is usually neater too, because fewer wires run to each node. This topology also makes it easier to move PCs and change connections. On the down side, the star topology uses more wire than the daisy chain. In addition, you have to pay for the wiring hub or for a concentrator, and these can be complex and expensive devices.

Although you'll often see the term *wiring center* used as a generic reference for both hubs and concentrators, the two devices are not identical; while the differences between them aren't engraved in stone, they are very real. A hub is typically a simple device contained in one cabinet, which has little flexibility but a reasonable price—assuming you consider $400 to $800 for eight connections reasonable. A hub usually connects only to nodes with one specific type of cabling, although it isn't unusual to have a separate coaxial cable or fiber-optic cable connector for hub-to-hub links.

A concentrator has many pieces, parts, and options including a cabinet, a power supply, and various connection modules. Each module, which is about the size of a hardback novel, slides into the cabinet and connects to a data bus. You can typically insert modules with different cable connectors into the cabinet and add devices like bridges and routers. You might select options like dual power supplies for reliability and add management modules and even LAN-to-LAN options like an interface to a high-speed, long-distance telephone circuit. A fully loaded concentrator able to handle 48 ports with sophisticated management and some fiber-optic connections could top $50,000.

One thing you don't have to worry about is compatibility between the brand of hub or concentrator and the brand of LAN adapter cards you buy. It's perfectly okay to mix cards and wiring centers from different vendors, as long as they use the same media-access scheme and cabling.

As your network grows, the management capabilities of your cabling system become increasingly important. Hubs and concentrators often have their own microprocessors in the 80186 class and programming in ROM. These processors can count the packets of data as they fly by, recognize errors in the data stream, and generate reports. They hold data in a "management information base" (MIB) until it is polled by a computer running management software. These processors can protect the network by automatically disconnecting nodes generating bad data and, in some cases, they can even enhance security by restricting the day of the week and time of day specific nodes may enter the network. They can also send special messages, called *alerts*, to computers running network management software.

A signaling and reporting scheme called the Simple Network Management Protocol (SNMP) provides an architecture for network reporting and management that includes "agent" devices which gather data in wiring centers and other network devices, and computers that act as management stations. The management computers can be PCs, typically running Windows, or they can be other platforms like Sun workstations running Unix.

Formally, SNMP uses the TCP/IP network communications protocol set to move alerts and MIB information between the agents and the management computers, although many companies now offer the option of using SNMP over the popular NetWare IPX protocols. While SNMP is the most popular and widely supported management scheme, IBM's NetVIEW and the Common Management Information Protocol (CMIP) developed by the International Standards Organization are evolving to compete with SNMP. I'll describe these management features more thoroughly in Chapter 9.

You usually install these wiring centers in a telephone wiring "closet." The term *closet* survives, even though these may be large rooms with their own air conditioning and power systems. Whether your wires come together in a special room, in a real closet, or under someone's desk, I urge you to provide backup power for the wiring center—it won't do much good to have backup power for the server and client PCs if the wiring center fails.

In late 1991 some companies, including Novell and Artisoft, made provisions for the installation of wiring hubs in PCs acting as file servers. That's an interesting approach for a small office LAN, but it's only practical in large LANs when you're doing a new installation and can create a combined "server room" and wiring closet. Overall, the wiring hubs and servers remain separate in most installations.

In the Token-Ring arena, the names of the products change a little. IBM calls their Token-Ring wiring center a "Multistation Access Unit" or MAU, so this term is often used when referring to Token-Ring wiring center products. As with Ethernet, you can buy simple Token-Ring wiring hubs or much more complex management systems.

ARCnet wiring centers typically carry much lower price tags than those for Ethernet or Token-Ring. PureData, Standard Microsystems, and Thomas-Conrad Corp. are among the dozens of companies selling ARCnet wiring centers.

I recommend a star wiring system for all but the smallest network installations. When you grow to a couple of dozen nodes, or anytime the network is running "bet the business," mission-critical applications like order taking, I also recommend buying wiring centers with management capabilities.

Here are some of the advantages of each physical topology:

Star	**Daisy chain**
Provides a neater installation	Uses less cable
Does not allow total outages to occur because of a break or short at any one point in the cable—one bad connection takes a whole daisy-chain network down	Does not require space or power for a wiring hub, as the star configuration does

■ Putting It All Together

The next chapter describes the combinations of physical topologies, cables, and adapters used in three standard network architectures. As you'll see, these architectures continue to evolve and expand to include a variety of alternatives with a solid grasp of the features underlying each of these systems, you'll be able to master the array of options each alternative provides.

- *How the Standards Got That Way*

- *Ethernet the Elder*

- *Token-Ring: The IBM Way*

- *ARCnet: Low-Cost Performance*

- *100 Megabits per Second Plus*

- *Networking Alternatives*

The Big Three LAN Standards: Ethernet, Token-Ring, and ARCnet

TECHNICAL TALE

The cloaked space cruiser 'Ion Storm' approached the third planet from the sun. The cruiser's mission was to monitor the planet's powerful transmissions that filled the spectrum from sound to light.

The ship's biological computer translated and interpreted the incoming data while it monitored and communicated with the ship's sole inhabitant. "There is a major increase in the number of intelligent transmission systems since the last survey," the computer informed the being known simply as Pilot. Pilot inclined its head in acknowledgment, so the computer continued, "Digitized patterns now make up more than three-quarters of the signals we are receiving. The most common are very weak signals coming from cables within buildings—obviously designed for local network communications."

"Any sign of telepathy between beings, or personal-wave communications?" Pilot asked.

"There is a small amount of wireless digital connectivity, but the majority of information travels over cable and is difficult to intercept. The most common transmission scheme, designated as Ethernet, moves data in a fashion that assumes polite interaction such as that found among beings in a civilized culture. In Ethernet, each node waits for silence and tries to transmit into the empty ether, but there are data collisions. After a collision, retransmissions take place in patterns I have not yet divined. Two other transmission schemes, apparently designated as Token-Ring and ARCnet, are much more orderly, but complex. Packages of digital bits travel in specific patterns with high reliability. These systems are less common."

"It seems the entities of this planet are becoming increasingly intelligent and technologically sophisticated," Pilot observed.

"Oh yes," the computer agreed, "but the role of the biped biologicals identified as 'humans' is still puzzling. They are apparently swelling their own ranks so they can better serve and improve the intelligent entities of the planet."

"Evolution is an interesting process," Pilot observed to his biological helper. "It works in many strange ways."

THE PHYSICAL ELEMENTS OF LAN CABLING—THE ADAPTERS, CABLES, AND CON-nectors—are defined by sets of standards that have evolved since the early 1970s. These standards, which have undergone many revisions, ensure the inter-operability and compatibility of network devices. Committees established by such organizations as the Institute of Electrical and Electronics Engineers (IEEE), the Electronic Industries Association (EIA), and the International Telecommunications Union typically labor for years to develop agreements and adopt standards on how electronic devices should signal, exchange data, and handle problems; however, it's companies that develop products conforming to those standards. Some companies, particularly IBM, used to establish their own proprietary standards and products (at least partly because they wanted to lock customers into their technology), but today, "open systems" built around standards established by national and international committees prevail.

In theory, if any company develops a product that operates according to a standard, it will work with products from all other vendors meeting the same standard. In practice, companies often implement the standards in such different ways that the products don't work together without a lot of adjust-ment on both sides. Nonetheless, the concept is sound, and constant efforts to improve compatibility among LAN products are succeeding.

Three standard protocols for LAN cabling and media-access control should interest you: Ethernet, Token-Ring, and ARCnet. A few companies, usually in the low-cost-LAN market, still sell adapters following protocols that aren't approved or even de facto standards. Generally, I urge you not to buy nonstandard LAN adapters or cabling systems. The small cost savings put you at risk of owning an orphan system without support or the ability to expand.

Each LAN standard combines physical and logical topologies, signaling, and media-access control techniques in different ways. I'll describe the im-portant features of each one in this chapter.

■ How the Standards Got That Way

The IEEE assigns numbers to its active committees. Committee 802 is a very large organization that includes members from industry and academia inter-ested in a broad range of wide-area and local-area network systems. Subcom-mittees of Committee 802 develop and maintain standards for several LAN topologies. The subcommittees use decimal numbers to identify their work. The glossary describes many 802 committee standards in addition to 802.5 and 802.3, which I will discuss here.

IEEE standard 802.5 covers the Token-Ring architecture. This standard describes a token-passing protocol used on a network of stations connected in a special way, combining a logical ring topology (where every station actively passes information to the next one in the ring) with a physical star topology.

IEEE 802.3 describes a standard that owes a lot to the earlier Ethernet system. Networks conforming to IEEE standard 802.3 use a carrier sense multiple access (CSMA) media-access control scheme on an electrical bus topology. This standard leaves room for several wiring options, including thin coaxial cable and unshielded twisted-pair wiring.

ARCnet is not an IEEE standard, but is nonetheless an accepted industry standard. So many companies sell equipment meeting the ARCnet specification developed by Datapoint Corp. that you can install ARCnet adapters with full assurance of continued support and interoperability.

■ Ethernet the Elder

Ethernet was one of the first LAN architectures. This network cabling and signaling scheme entered the market in the late 1970s and is still a respected standard. The reason for Ethernet's longevity is simple: The standard provides high-speed transmission at an economical price, offering a broad base of support for a variety of LAN and micro-to-mainframe applications. Companies marketing Ethernet adapters have kept their products up to date, and Ethernet is still a wise network choice. There is a clear and reasonably economical migration path from 10-megabit-per-second Ethernet to systems with faster throughput such as Ethernet switching and 100-megabit-per-second networks.

These days you can buy an adapter card that will let you plug your PC into an Ethernet network for as little as $50, although retail prices are usually slightly over $100. Figure 6.1 shows an Ethernet adapter for laptop PCs. Over 20 companies market comparable adapters for other computers. Since most adapters are made from the same set of function-specific chips—usually from National Semiconductor Corporporation—you'll find them quite similar; however, some are better for plugging into a server than into a PC workstation, and there are other important differences in features, performance, and cost.

Definitive Ethernet

People often associate Ethernet with network elements beyond the scope encompassed by the cabling and signaling scheme coinvented by Robert Metcalfe and David Boggs at Xerox's Palo Alto Research Center (PARC). According to Metcalfe, the name "Ethernet" derives from "the luminiferous ether thought to pervade all of space for the propagation of light" (a.k.a. electromagnetic waves).

Actually, Ethernet is a specification describing a method for computers and data systems to connect and share cabling. Ethernet encompasses what the International Standards Organization calls the physical and data-link layers of data communications. (See "Networking Acronyms and Buzzwords" in Chapter 4 for a more detailed explanation of the ISO's OSI architecture.)

Figure 6.1

This Ethernet adapter fits inside a variety of Toshiba laptop computers and gives them the ability to connect directly to thin Ethernet cable. On some models the T-connector is a tight fit!

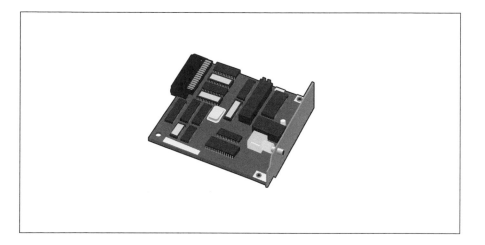

The IEEE 802.3 family of standards includes the specifications of the older Ethernet protocols, but the committee's work also includes changes to the basic structure of the data packets, so technically the term *Ethernet* doesn't include all of the options outlined under 802.3. "Eight-oh-two-dot-three" is a more complete description of the standard, but more people understand the term *Ethernet*.

The primary characteristics of the physical Ethernet link include a data rate of 10 megabits per second, a maximum station separation of 2.8 kilometers, a shielded coaxial cable connecting the stations, and a specific kind of electrical signaling on the cable called *Manchester-encoded digital baseband*. The latter specification describes the electrical signals that make up the digital 0s and 1s that are constantly passing over the network.

The major part of the data-link layer specification for Ethernet describes the way stations share access to coaxial cable through a process called *carrier sense multiple access with collision detection* (CSMA/CD). CSMA/CD is the kind of operational scheme that modern standards committees call a *media-access control* (MAC) protocol. The medium is the coaxial cable connecting the network nodes, and the MAC protocol determines how nodes on the network share access to the cable.

Ethernet the Perennial

For many years Ethernet was the fastest-growing network system and the first choice of many data managers and system integrators. But many people now buying networks choose IBM's Token-Ring cabling and media-sharing plan instead. Token-Ring performs well, and IBM continually dangles new ways of using it to connect PC and mainframe computers as bait for prospective buyers.

Token-Ring installations are very expensive compared with those of Ethernet, however, and Ethernet offers efficient ways to connect to DEC, Hewlett-Packard, IBM, Xerox, and many other computer systems.

As befitting a network scheme with its tenure, Ethernet has many offspring. Ethernet adapters using fiber-optic cable are available from Codenoll Technology Corp. and Optical Data Systems. The latest growth area is in Ethernet adapters operating over unshielded twisted-pair wire at data rates of 100 megabits per second.

The "coax" cabling scheme found in PC-based networks installed during the late 1980s and early 1990s, uses a thin, 52-ohm coaxial cable between each pair of network stations. This cable, commonly called thin Ethernet and sometimes "cheapernet," is typically limited to 305 meters (1,000 feet) between repeaters, although an IEEE specification limits it to 600 feet. The network interface card in each station usually attaches to this cable through a T-connector, which facilitates connecting and disconnecting stations on the network without breaking the continuity of the cable (see Figure 6.2).

Figure 6.2

The thin Ethernet coaxial cable runs from PC to PC in a physical daisy-chain topology. The cable connects to each node through a coaxial T-connector. The terminating resistors at each end of the cable are critical to proper operation. You should use only Ethernet T-connectors that meet military specificaton UG-274.

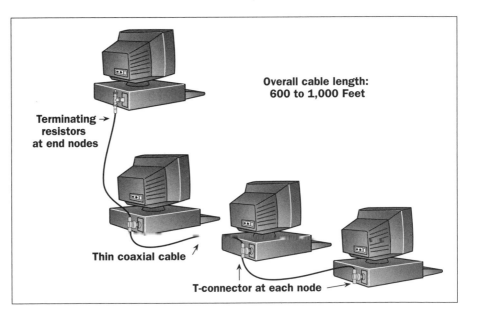

The oldest Ethernet cabling scheme is more frequently found in installations with larger computers. This scheme uses heavily shielded coaxial cable (informally named "frozen orange garden hose," which aptly describes its size, color, and ease of installation) to serve as a backbone among the clusters of nodes scattered around a building. Here the maximum length of cable between repeaters is 500 meters (1,640 feet), and the cable attaches to devices called *transceivers*, which transform the cable's connections into something more suitable for a PC or terminal. A flexible transceiver cable made up of a shielded twisted-pair wire runs between the transceiver and the AUI port on the network adapter. Transceiver cables can be up to 15 meters (45 feet) long; they connect to the network card through a 15-pin D-connector (see Figure 6.3).

Figure 6.3

Standard Ethernet cable is thick coaxial cable that usually remains hidden behind walls. Transceivers connect directly at the cable and then extend the connection to each node through AUI cable.

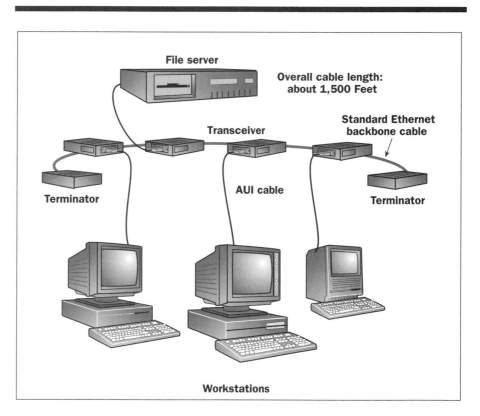

Packaging and Moving Data: The Ethernet Way

Ethernet uses a communications concept called *datagrams* to get messages across the network. The CSMA/CD media-access technique makes sure that two datagrams aren't sent out at the same time, and serves as a method of arbitration if they are.

Ethernet's datagram concept is based on the simple premise that a communicating node will make its best effort to get a message across. The datagram concept does not include a guarantee that a message will arrive at any specific time or will be free of errors or duplications, however—it does not even guarantee that delivery will occur. If you want any of these assurances, you have to implement them in higher-level software.

The Ethernet datagrams take the form of self-contained packets of information. These packets have fields that contain information about their destination and origin and the sort of data they contain, not to mention the data itself. Because the data field in each packet can be no larger than 1,500 bytes, large messages must traverse the network in multiple packets. (Articles statistically describing the efficiency of packet-transmission systems have been the favorite filler of professional journals since Bob Metcalfe published his Harvard Ph.D. thesis, "Packet Communications," back in 1973.)

One element of the Ethernet packet structure, shown in Figure 6.4, differs from that codified by the IEEE 802.3 committee. The committee saw a need for a user ID in the packet; thus, its specification trades the byte count field for a user ID field. Fortunately, the network interface cards don't care. They take their data from higher-level software that sets up the packets. Ethernet and 802.3 packets can traverse the same network, but nodes operating under one format can't exchange data with nodes designed for the other without software translation at some level.

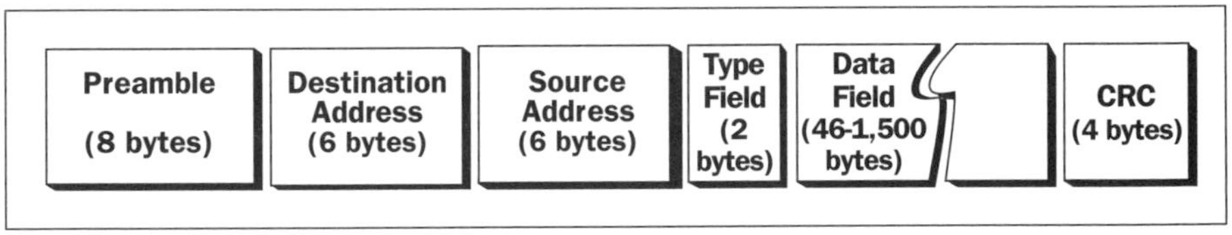

Figure 6.4

In the Ethernet protocol, messages are sent between workstation nodes in the form of "packets," or frames. Each packet measures 72 to 1,526 bytes long and contains six fields, five of which are of fixed length. The preamble field allows the receiving station to synchronize with the transmitted message. The destination and source address fields contain the network ID of the nodes receiving and initiating the message. The type field indicates the type of data in the data field that contains the actual data. The CRC field helps the receiving node perform a cyclical redundancy check—an error-checking analysis of the total packet.

| Preamble (8 bytes) | Destination Address (6 bytes) | Source Address (6 bytes) | Type Field (2 bytes) | Data Field (46-1,500 bytes) | CRC (4 bytes) |

Listen before Transmitting

Before packets can traverse the coaxial cable of the Ethernet network as datagrams, they must deal with CSMA/CD, the media-access protocol that determines how nodes on the network share access to the cable. CSMA/CD works in a listen-before-transmitting mode: If the network adapter receives data to send from higher-level software, it checks to see whether any other station is broadcasting on the cable. Only when the cable is quiet does the network adapter broadcast its message.

CSMA/CD also mediates when the inevitable happens—when two or more nodes simultaneously start to transmit on an idle cable and the transmissions collide. The adapters can detect such collisions because of the higher electrical-signal level that simultaneous transmissions produce. When they detect a collision, the network adapter cards begin transmitting what is called a *jam signal* to ensure that all the conflicting nodes notice the collision. Then each adapter stops transmitting and turns to its internal programming to determine a randomly selected time for retransmission. This "back-off" period ensures that the stations don't continue to send out colliding signals every time the cable grows quiet.

IEEE 10BaseT

In late 1990, after three years of meetings, proposals, and compromises, an IEEE committee finalized a specification for running Ethernet-type signaling over unshielded twisted-pair wiring.

The IEEE calls the 10 megabit UTP 802.3 standard 10BaseT. The IEEE 802.3 family of standards generally describes carrier sense multiple access signaling, like Ethernet, used over various wiring systems. The name 10BaseT indicates a signaling speed of 10 megabits per second, a baseband signaling scheme, and twisted-pair wiring in a physical star topology (see Figure 6.5).

Figure 6.5

10BaseT is the IEEE designation for Ethernet running on unshielded twisted-pair (UTP) wire in a physical star topology. The UTP can run directly to the adapters in each node or to an unshielded twisted-pair medicum attachment unit (MAU) connected to the node through the AUI cable.

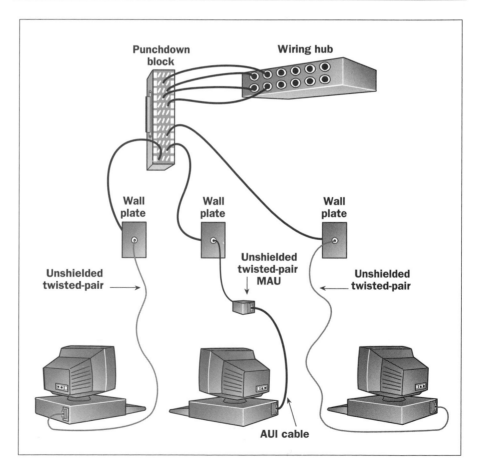

The theoretical—and widely touted—appeal of the 10BaseT standard is that it gives LAN managers the option of using installed telephone wiring, thus saving installation costs and problems. Many organizations don't have enough existing high-quality wiring to support a network installation, however, so LAN planners often find they must pull more wire anyway. On the other hand, the technology of twisted-pair wiring, unlike coaxial Ethernet alternatives and Token-Ring's shielded twisted-pair, is familiar to technicians you probably have on staff or under contract already. Importantly, the "home run" wiring scheme of 10BaseT—running a single wire from the central wiring hub to the desktop—improves the reliability of the system over the daisy-chain wiring scheme. As we found during testing at PC Magazine LAN Labs, the strong practical appeal of 10BaseT products is in their commonality. You can safely mix and match 10BaseT adapter cards and wiring hubs from many companies and use them together on the same network. This commonality assures you of multiple sources of supply, competitive pricing, and confidence in long-term support.

Our tests also proved that you don't pay a performance penalty for using 10BaseT twisted-pair. Our throughput tests showed consistent performance, on a par with that of coaxial-cable Ethernet wiring.

For a network manager, the biggest potential advantage of a 10BaseT wiring installation comes from the star wiring scheme, which provides both reliability and centralized management. Like the spokes of a wheel, the wires radiate from a central wiring hub, like the one shown in Figure 6.6, out to each node. If one wire run is broken or shorted, that node is out of commission but the network remains operational. In Token-Ring or thin Ethernet wiring schemes, one bad connection at any point takes down the entire network.

The central wiring hub is also an ideal place to install a monitoring microprocessor and network management software. I'll discuss that management facility more fully in Chapter 9.

Commodity Products

I'll probably make a few companies angry by sticking the label "commodity products" on the 10BaseT market. I don't mean to imply that there are no technical differences, but the differences between 10BaseT adapters won't matter much to most buyers. After weighing a few technical considerations, you can safely buy 10BaseT adapters based on price, availability, brand name, and the other factors that usually influence commodity purchases.

In keeping with the commodity label, the prices of these products continue to fall as companies maneuver for position. The products on the market vary in terms of a few technical points, such as the number and types of diagnostic lights on each adapter and whether it sets communications parameters using jumpers or software. The diagnostic lights are valuable (we avoided several

Figure 6.6

The 10BaseT twisted-pair wiring system gains reliability and flexibility through the use of a wiring hub. Note that such 10BaseT hubs require AC power.

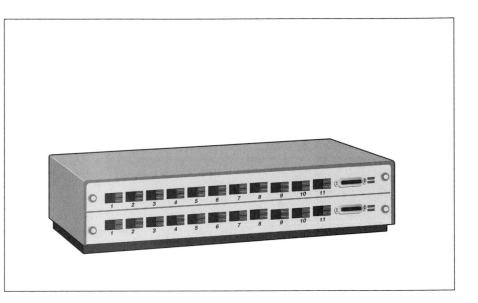

time-consuming troubleshooting sessions during our testing just by looking at the lights showing connection status and activity), but most people will focus on two factors that differentiate among these adapters.

The first factor is the availability of the right software driver interface for whatever LAN file-server software you use. Practically all companies now support the Network Driver Interface Specification (NDIS), a Microsoft specification for writing hardware-independent drivers; this provides compatibility with all versions of LAN Manager and certain other operating systems, including VINES and LANtastic.

Standard Microsystems has an excellent set of adapter card interfaces, including a good implementation of NetBIOS. If you're buying LAN hardware for an organization that uses a variety of different LAN file-server systems, you should look at SMC's adapters first. Using its adapters lets you standardize on one type of hardware, but if you need only an interface to NetWare or Microsoft's Windows, 10BaseT is a commodity market for you.

The second important consideration in selecting a 10BaseT product is the availability of appropriate adapters for a server, such as 16-bit ISA, 32-bit Micro Channel, bus-mastering, or 32-bit EISA devices. You can mix and match 10BaseT and other standard adapters though, so you don't have to use adapters from the same vendors for the servers and workstations.

Note that the designers of these products seem to have faith in their quality. Warranties of three years are common, and many companies cover their boards for as long as five years.

Installing a wiring system according to the 10BaseT standards might not save you money up front in comparison with other LAN wiring alternatives, but 10BaseT's LAN management advantages and ability to stay operational despite physical wire problems make it a good option for any modern network installation.

10BaseT Installations

10BaseT uses only two pairs of wires. That's all you need, but equipping your wall jacks with the full capacity of four pairs is a smart move, as long as you don't use those spare pairs for anything else (like voice telephone systems).

The 10BaseT standard uses pins 1 and 2 for the first pair and pins 3 and 6 for the second pair. There is never any need for transposed pairs or cross-wiring in 10BaseT standard data systems. In fact, you should take care to make sure that the connections are straight-through all the way; otherwise, you'll lose the effectiveness of the electrical shielding generated by the twisting of the wires in each pair.

Eight wire sequences are commonly used for wiring an RJ-45 jack in the U.S. Among those sequences the Preferred Commercial Building Cabling Specification of the Electronic Industries Association (thankfully referred to in the trade as the EIA standard), AT&T 258A, AT&T 356A, and the 10BaseT standard are now the most popular. These standards are all very similar and you won't run into problems if you follow any one of them. However, an older Universal Service Order Code (USOC) was once the most popular wiring sequence, and it is not compatible with 10BaseT. You can quickly identify a USOC sequence because the pairs work their way in to the center, 1-8, 2-7, and so on, instead of using the 1-2 sequence of 10BaseT.

It is very difficult to do a good wiring job with a poor tool, so The best advice I can give you is to invest in a good RJ-45 plug presser. This device aligns the plug and applies the correct pressure to seal the contacts. Also, make sure that you buy and use the proper RJ-45 plugs for the specific wiring segments. You'll need plugs for solid wire on the main runs and plugs for stranded wire on the jumper cables and the cables that run between the wall and the PC. Using the incorrect type of plug practically guarantees intermittent operation as the system ages.

Finally, keep the twists in the wires. It's tempting to untwist them to make a neat connection, but don't do it! Keep the twists in each pair all the way to the plug or jack in order to retain as much shielding capability as possible.

Logical Topology

IEEE 802.3 Ethernet can have either of the two common physical topologies: the daisy chain or the star. Regardless of how the wires run, the logical topology remains the same. This is a broadcast system—each station broadcasts data into the network for all other stations to hear. The CSMA/CD media-access control plan is based on the assumption that all stations on the cable will receive some part of the packet at the same instant, so no station starts sending its own packet while other stations are still receiving an older packet.

How Fast Does It Go?

The fact that Ethernet's 10-megabit-per-second throughput specification is much faster than either IBM's original Token-Ring specification (4 megabits per second) or ARCnet's (2.5 megabits per second) can be misleading, because these figures describe the transmission rate over the cable. What they fail to reflect are the factors that limit effective throughput on a PC-based LAN—things like the data transfer rate of a hard disk, the transfer rate of the computer's data bus, and the efficiency of the networking software. Ethernet was designed to handle traffic in bursts, and that is exactly what it gets in real-world, PC-based LANs.

To share access to the coaxial or twisted-pair cable effectively, Ethernet adapter cards must follow the CSMA/CD protocol. The "back-off" algorithm that CSMA/CD generates in the event of packet collisions has a tiny, practically immeasurable, effect on the performance of any one client PC on the network.

Adapter Chip Sets

All Ethernet adapters on the market are designed using chip sets that contain the basics of the Ethernet protocols. Currently, the majority of the cards use the set created by National Semiconductor Corp., although some use Fujitsu and Intel chip sets.

The Ethernet adapter cards available from various manufacturers differ in the way they use the chip set and in the features the designers add. Although companies have designed different implementations to improve performance and incorporate value-added features, the adapters remain very similar.

On the cable side of the network, these adapter cards are interchangeable. Adapters from 3Com will happily exchange packets over a shared cable with an adapter from Intel or any other vendor. All of these cards conform to the same electrical signaling, physical connection, and media-access protocol specifications.

Ethernet Switching

Ethernet's CSMA/CD media-access control scheme is both its weakness and its strength. In most networks, particularly those that transmit in short bursts, CSMA works well. But some modern applications like video conferencing and transferring of very large multimedia files result in an extremely high average traffic load and many CSMA collisions, which degenerate the throughput of the network.

A technique called Ethernet switching can improve the network throughput enjoyed by individual nodes without forcing you to change the LAN adapters installed in the PC or the cabling system. Switching hubs don't provide faster signaling, but they do provide greater bandwidth so you achieve faster throughput and the results are the same as you'd obtain by providing faster signaling. You keep your present Ethernet LAN adapters and they still work at 10 megabits per second, but each adapter performs as though it were the only one on the network. Unlike all of the other networking alternatives described in this chapter, switching hubs don't divide the network bandwidth between all of the active nodes. Instead, a fast processor in the hub moves the packets across a backplane operating at hundreds of megabits per second. This is called a *collapsed-backbone architecture* because it acts as a series of individual wiring hubs connected by a fast backbone link.

In practice, most computers can't take advantage of the full 10-megabit Ethernet channel, so most companies offer Ethernet switching products in versions that allow you to share 10 megabits of bandwidth between one to eight nodes.

Generally, you can install switching hubs in one of four configurations: server front end, back end to a group of hubs, high-speed wiring concentrator, and FDDI concentrator.

- As a server front end, a switching hub is the only connection point for one or more servers. Each server gets the maximum bandwidth it can use while the client computers compete for more limited bandwidths.

- As a back end to a group of nonswitching wiring hubs, a switching hub acts as a very fast, yet economical, backbone. As many as a dozen hubs can have 10-megabit bandwidth with no competition for the channel.

- As a high-speed wiring concentrator, a switching hub allows the administator to give each node the necessary amount of bandwidth. This is the classic collapsed-backbone architecture.

- As a concentrator for a high-speed system, a switching hub can feed an FDDI link or other type of backbone technology. At this time Kalpana's Etherswitch does not offer FDDI connectivity.

Switching hubs are now available and affordable. You don't need to worry about changes in emerging standards or losing an investment you've already made. They don't meet every requirement for fast networking, but they can offer the equivalent of hundreds of megabits per second of connectivity over an area as wide as any Ethernet network using existing adapters and cabling.

■ Token-Ring: The IBM Way

The IEEE 802.5 subcommittee, with a firm lead from IBM's representatives, developed a set of standards describing a token-passing network in a logical ring topology. IBM also put identical standards into place within the structure of the European Computer Manufacturers' Association. The original implementation of the standard used 4-megabit-per-second signaling, but faster 16-megabit signaling is also part of the standard.

The Token-Ring network is to networks what the Boeing 747 is to airplanes. It makes strange noises and requires special handling, but it can carry heavy loads; it offers power and flexibility, but demands skilled management and control; it is one of the fastest things flying—but not one of the prettiest. In 1989 IBM introduced a supersonic 747 when they adopted the 16-megabit-per-second signaling scheme for Token-Ring. The higher signaling speed moves data more quickly, but also requires more careful installation. The basic techniques of 4- and 16-megabit-per-second Token-Ring operation are the same.

The Token-Ring structure is the keystone of IBM's wide-area and local area network architecture. IBM provides optional Token-Ring connections on its mainframe computer hardware and software to make PCs and mainframes act as peers on the same network. Don't assume that you must use only IBM hardware and software on networks with Token-Ring adapters, though. Madge Networks, Thomas-Conrad, 3Com, and many other companies sell Token-Ring adapters. You can use networking software from Banyan, Microsoft, Novell, and other companies on adapters from IBM or from the other Token-Ring hardware manufacturers.

IBM didn't invent the concept of tokens or the idea of the ring configuration. Indeed, IBM paid a fee—allegedly in the area of $5 million—to clear a patent on Token-Ring networking filed by Olof Soderblom of the Netherlands. Other companies in the Token-Ring business have to decide whether to fight or accommodate Soderblom's claim of proprietary rights.

The multiple standards and IBM backing have apparently nurtured the faith of the semiconductor companies. Texas Instruments leads a pack of companies who sell relatively inexpensive chip sets like the TMS 380 that can perform all the functions of the 802.5 standard. Companies such as Madge, Olicom, and Ungermann-Bass use these chips to market network adapters that follow the 802.5 standard.

Token Technique

In a token-passing ring network, a stream of data called a *token* circulates like a freight train through the network stations when they are idle. This technique defines both the sequential logical topology and the media-access control protocol. A station with a message to transmit waits until it receives a free token. It then changes the free token to a busy token, and transmits a block of data called a *frame* immediately following the busy token. The frame contains all or part of the message the station has to send. The system does not operate by having one station accept a token, read it, and then pass it on. Instead, the stream of bits that make up a token or a message might pass through as many as three stations simultaneously.

When a station transmits a message, there is no free token on the network, so other stations wishing to transmit must wait. The receiving station copies the data in the frame, and the frame continues around the ring, making a complete round trip back to the transmitting station. The transmitting station purges the busy token and inserts a new free token on the ring. The use of the token-passing media-access control system prevents messages from interfering with one another by guaranteeing that only one station at a time transmits.

This streaming of data makes Token-Ring networks better suited to fiber-optic media than are broadcast-type systems like Ethernet or ARCnet. Optical media typically carry one-way transmission, and the token travels in only one direction around the ring, so there is no need for optical mixers that divide power, or for expensive active repeaters.

Ring around a Star

The physical topology of a Token-Ring network isn't what you might expect. Although the tokens and messages travel from node to node (client station, gateway, or server) in a sequential logical topology, the cables actually use a physical star topology, as shown in Figure 6.7.

Token-Ring systems use a wire center (hub) that houses electromechanical relays to make the physical star into a logical ring. (Note that IBM's name for the Token-Ring wiring hub is Multistation Access Unit, or MAU. Don't confuse this MAU with the medium attachment unit—a transceiver connecting to the AUI port on an Ethernet adapter.)

When a station tries to join the ring, a voltage passes from the adapter board, through the cable, to the hub, where it activates the relay for that wire run in the hub. The action of the relay reconfigures the ring in milliseconds and adds the new station. Token-Ring networks are the only networks you can hear operating, because there is an audible click from the relay in the wire center whenever a station joins the ring.

If the cable from the station breaks, or the wires in the cables short together, or the station loses power, the relay opens and the station drops out of the ring. This arrangement prevents one bad cable from taking the entire system down (a major selling point for Token-Ring, ARCnet, and 10BaseT systems using a physical hub topology).

Figure 6.7

Token-Ring uses shielded wire to connect each node to a central Multistation Access Unit (MAU). This diagram also shows two-port hubs, used to reduce wiring costs. Wiring hubs can connect through optional fiber-optic cable links.

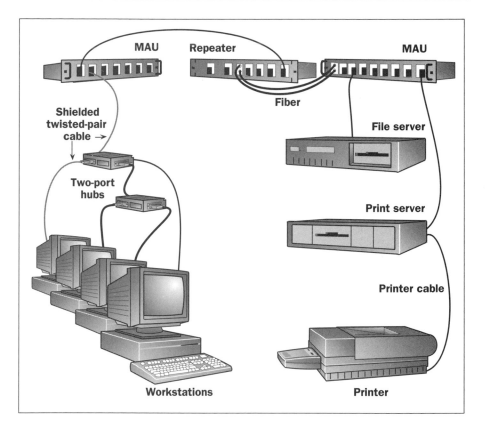

The typical Token-Ring wiring hub (Figure 6.8) accommodates eight nodes. The hubs stack on top of one another in a rack, and are connected by patch cords running from one hub's "out" port to the next hub's "in" port. These cables extend the logical ring from one hub to another, so nodes are on the same ring even if they are attached to different wiring hubs. Provisions are also available for linking the hubs through fiber-optic cable. Figure 6.9 shows a hub for small workgroups that can extend connections to other hubs.

When the Ring Stops

While the hub topology improves the network's chances of surviving a disrupted cable, the token-passing media-access protocol has its own unique survivability problem. If one adapter fails in an Ethernet or ARCnet system, only that node loses network access. But the malfunction of one adapter in a Token-Ring network can bring the whole network down because every node

Figure 6.8

This illustration shows an unshielded twisted-pair wire Token-Ring wiring hub on top of a wiring hub for shielded twisted-pair wire. The RING-IN and RING-OUT connectors used to link hubs together are clearly visible.

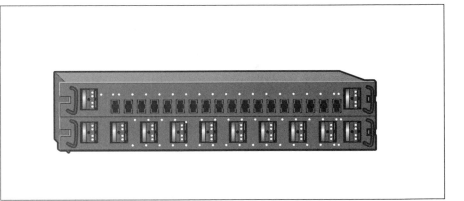

Figure 6.9

This Token-Ring wiring hub economically connects four nodes together using unshielded twisted-pair wiring. Its RI and RO jacks can be used to make connections to other hubs located several hundred feet away.

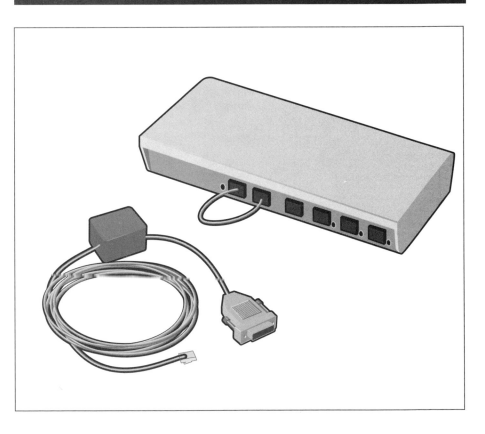

in the ring must actively pass every token and message. If the receiver or transmitter in one Token-Ring adapter fails, the token stops there.

While this type of failure is not common, it is catastrophic. For this reason, and because active management at the network hub makes sense, many companies (including Cabletron, Proteon, SynOptics,and Thomas-Conrad) market Token-Ring hubs with active management capability and controlling software for a monitoring PC. These products immediately alert a manager to problems such as malfunctioning adapters, and provide a way of forcibly disconnecting nodes from the ring. Management hubs cost more—in the vicinity of $1,100 each, as opposed to $600 dollars for an eight-port hub with no management capabilities—but each management hub can also report on activities in less capable units.

IBM's basic MAU has no management/control capabilities, but then it doesn't require primary and backup 120-volt AC power in the wiring closet as the management hubs do.

Cables for the Ring

The typical cable recommended for Token-Ring installations contains two pairs of twisted wire covered by a foil shield. The maximum length of cable between the Token-Ring hub and the attachment point for the network node can't exceed 150 feet (45 meters). You can have another 8 feet of cable between the attachment point (for example, a jack in a wall plate) and the node itself. The cables are connected to the hub using a special data connector that requires some experience to attach to the cable.

It is possible to install a special device in the cable coming from the LAN adapter that allows the use of unshielded twisted-pair wiring or to use adapters configured for this wiring. But these techniques require careful installation, and I don't recommend them. I've heard too many stories of problems caused by electrical interference absorbed through the unshielded twisted-pair cable. Because the token must circulate through each station, a single noise problem on one leg of the network cable can halt the entire operation.

Ring Speed

The original IBM Token-Ring product uses a 4-megabit-per-second signaling speed on the network cable. In 1989, IBM released a Token-Ring version using 16-megabit-per-second signaling. The 16-megabit adapters also work at 4 megabits on networks with the slower adapters. Other companies tried to follow IBM's high-speed lead, but they took over a year to get their products to market.

Although the signals representing 0's and 1's move faster across the wire, don't assume that 16-megabit-per-second Token-Ring will provide faster responses on your network than the 4-megabit-per-second variety. On the other hand, don't assume that 4-megabit-per-second Token-Ring will give slower responses than 10-megabit-per-second Ethernet. Many factors other than the network signaling rate limit throughput—particularly the speed of the server's hard disk and the interface between the adapter and the server's data bus. Few organizations will see an improvement in overall network throughput by changing from 4- to 16-megabit-per-second Token-Ring systems, but if your network plans include hundreds of nodes, multiple servers, and mainframe equipment on the LAN, an investment in a 16-megabit-per-second Token-Ring network makes good sense. Note, however, that installing 16-megabit Token-Ring over unshielded twisted-pair wire introduces new problems. The allowable cable lengths and number of nodes on each ring are determined by a complex chart. The faster signals are much more difficult to decode and more easily masked by cumulative noise on the cable system. Microtest markets a device called the Next Scanner that measures your wiring system and reports on its ability to support 4- and 16-megabit Token-Ring.

Caught in the Ring

Many companies, spurred by IBM's sponsorship, choose Token-Ring as their wiring and media-access control architecture. While the operational benefits of Token-Ring over Ethernet are still the subject of esoteric debate, you need to look for the real benefits—particularly the potential for direct mainframe attachments—and weigh them against the cost of installing Token-Ring adapters, cables, and wiring hubs. As I explain in Chapter 12, there are effective ways to interface with mainframe computers that don't require a Token-Ring installation.

■ ARCnet: Low-Cost Performance

Using tokens or messages to regulate when a station can transmit over a shared wire isn't unique to IEEE 802.5. The ARCnet system, originated by Datapoint and fostered in the microcomputer world by Standard Microsystems, uses "transmission permission" messages addressed to specific stations to regulate traffic. The acronym ARC stands for Datapoint's Attached Resource Computing architecture.

ARCnet Topologies

ARCnet uses a broadcast-type logical topology, which means that all stations receive all messages broadcast into the cable at approximately the same time.

The ARCnet scheme traditionally uses RG-62 coaxial cable in a physical star topology that allows for a hierarchy of hubs. Small two- or four-port wiring hubs can feed other large and small hubs in an economical wiring scheme that retains the resistance to total outage inherent in a star topology. Modern versions of ARCnet can also use coaxial cable or unshielded twisted-pair wire in a station-to-station physical topology. Figure 6.10 shows a variety of ARCnet products.

Figure 6.10

ARCnet adapters and wiring hubs are available for both coaxial cable and unshielded twisted-pair wiring. Interchangeable modules in the Thomas-Conrad Smart hub provide the needed connections. These adapters are intended for 8- and 16-bit ISA and MCA computers.

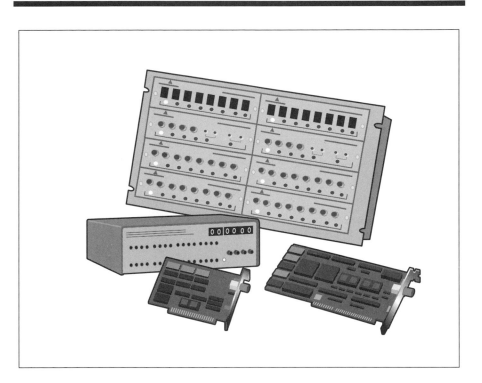

A complex set of rules regulates how big an ARCnet network can be. Generally, the maximum length of cable from one end of the network to the other is 20,000 feet. The maximum cable length between powered or "active" hubs that can regenerate signals is 2,000 feet. The length between a powered hub and a network node is also 2,000 feet. Unpowered "passive" hubs can connect to nodes over 100 feet of cable. As you can see, ARCnet systems can cover a large geographical area.

The RG-62 cable specified for ARCnet is the same cable IBM uses in its 3270 wiring plan, which links terminals to mainframe terminal controllers. Since this plan also uses a physical star topology, many companies find it easy to install ARCnet when they downsize their computer systems from IBM mainframes to networks of PCs.

High-impedance ARCnet adapters allow a physical daisy-chain topology identical to that of thin Ethernet networks. The daisy-chained nodes can also connect to active powered hubs, for an overall network of 20,000 feet of cable.

Several companies, including PureData and Standard Microcomputer Systems, offer fiber-optic versions of ARCnet systems. These systems have the typical fiber-optic characteristics of low electrical emissions, low absorption of electrical noise, and extended distance.

ARCnet Access Control

The technical literature describes ARCnet as a token-passing system, but ARCnet operates very differently from IEEE 802.5 Token-Ring. Instead of passing a token from station to station, it has one station broadcast the transmission permission message to the others on the network.

Each Ethernet and Token-Ring adapter has a unique adapter identifier assigned by the manufacturer and drawn from a common pool established by industry associations. ARCnet adapters don't come with identification numbers assigned, however; you set an identification number, from 1 to 255, using switches located on each adapter. The identification numbers have no relationship to the position of the nodes on the cable or to other physical relationships.

When activated, the adapters broadcast their numbers, and the lowest-numbered active station becomes the controller for the network. This controller sends a token to each active station granting permission to transmit. When each station receives the permission token, it either sends its waiting message or remains silent. Then the controlling station sends a permission token to the next station in numeric sequence.

When a new station enters the network, the stations all rebroadcast their station numbers in what is called a reconfiguration or "recon." Like the collisions in Ethernet, the concept of a recon bothers people who worry about esoteric matters of network efficiency. In reality, a recon takes no longer than 65 milliseconds, at worst, and scarcely disturbs the flow of traffic on a network.

Here are a couple of practical hints for all ARCnet installers:

- There are two things you can't afford to lose: the instruction manual telling you how to set the adapter numbers and the list of adapter numbers active on the network. If you know what station numbers have been assigned, it's easy to add more stations. If you don't know what station numbers are active, you face a frustrating session of research or trial-and-error installation.

- Keep your assigned station numbers close together, and put PCs with the most powerful CPUs in the low-numbered slots. The polling task takes a tiny bit of CPU power, so position your husky servers and other fast PCs to take on that role.

Speed

Traditional ARCnet operates at a signaling speed of 2.5 megabits per second. While many installations will never find this speed a limitation, it doesn't keep up with the capability of modern servers to deliver data. There is an economical solution to this problem that also improves overall network reliability, however: You can divide the ARCnet network into sections by installing several adapters in the server and splitting the output into multiple channels.

ARCnet Futures

Two things are happening on the ARCnet front: First, in October, 1992, the American National Standards Institute (ANSI) specified the ARCnet protocol as the "ATA/ANSI 878.1 Local Area Network Standard." There is no IEEE committee working on ARCnet because the formal role of the IEEE is to design a standard; ANSI standardizes an existing specification, and the ARCnet specification is now about 15 years old. Similarly, FDDI is not an IEEE standard, but it is a widely accepted ANSI standard. Organizations with a policy of buying products that follow open standards can finally refer to the ANSI ARCnet standard in their requests for bids.

The second interesting happening in the ARCnet world is Datapoint's introduction of ARCNETPLUS. ARCNETPLUS provides signaling at 20 megabits per second, but you can intermix it with existing 2.5-megabit-per-second ARCnet wiring systems, hubs, and adapters. Thus, you can put ARC-NETPLUS in the nodes that can benefit from faster service, while leaving the rest of the network unchanged.

For example, you could replace the old-style ARCnet adapter you presently have in a file server with a Datapoint ARCNETPLUS LAN adapter and it would service intermixed requests from both 2.5- megabit and 20-megabit adapters. If you equipped the few fast PCs that need high-speed network access with 20-megabit adapters, you woudn't need to touch the rest of the nodes. You must upgrade any ARCnet wiring hub that is the first point of contact for a 20-megabit adapter, but you don't have to upgrade intervening hubs. Datapoint sells a hub card that fits into a PC, providing four ports and also serving as the host PC's ARCNETPLUS LAN connection.

I still like ARCnet. It works reliably and the 2.5-megabit-per-second signaling speed is not a limitation in typical office installations—few PCs can move data faster than 1.2 megabits per second under ideal but demanding conditions. The adoption of the ANSI standard and the introduction of 20-megabit service that you can intermix with existing nodes adds greatly to the appeal of this proven technology.

■ 100 Megabits per Second Plus

"Faster is better!" is an American credo. In networking, the increased use of audio and full-motion video in applications is driving some of the push toward faster networking. Even if you don't currently need faster network signaling, you'd better understand the emerging options for fast local area networking because it's virtually certain you'll be ordering a testbed or a trial system within a year or so, and doing an operational installation within three years. But right now the options are confusing and surprises are likely, so it's a little early for most organizations to make major strategic investments.

Still, there are already some valid uses for network signaling in the range of 100 megabits per second. Fast and accurate transmission of digitized x-ray images from the treatment facility to a consulting room requires high through-put, as does mirroring two servers using NetWare's SFT III operating system. One channel of broadcast-quality video requires about 8 megabits of band-width using the best available compression techniques, and audio takes just under 1 megabit per second, so companies planning multimedia and network teleconferencing projects will need LAN connections in the 100-megabit range.

If you do need higher speed throughput than 10-megabit Ethernet or 16-megabit Token-Ring provide today, I advise placing a bet on switching hubs. With these devices you can give a dozen nodes access to a full 10-megabit bandwidth without contention and still keep your existing network interface cards, cable, and hubs.

In general, though computers and application programs have a way to grow—particularly in the acceptance of multimedia and television in the PC—before the need for 100-plus megabit-per-second signaling is widespread. That's good, because a lot of dust needs to settle before we can clearly see the styles and strengths of the contenders.

The present leaders in the 100-plus race include four architectures that can run over unshielded twisted-pair wire: 100BaseT "fast Ethernet," 100BaseVG (sponsored by HP and AT&T, to name two notable backers), FDDI over copper, and Asynchronous Transfer Mode (ATM). The dark horse in this race is FDDI over fiber; many people thought this option was out to pasture, but now it's making a run for the money on the inside rail.

Two opposing teams are pushing their proposals for technology that will eclipse today's 10-megabit-per-second CSMA signaling. It's easy to predict the outcome: both teams will win some level of acceptance because there is seldom a shutout in the networking business. On the one side, Hewlett-Packard and AT&T are spearheading a group supporting the 10BaseVG signaling and media access control scheme. More than a dozen companies, including Microsoft, Novell, and Ungermann-Bass have announced plans to field 100BaseVG products. On the other side, Grand Junction Networks is heading a group that's backing the 100BaseT plan.

Fast Internet

In very simple terms, 100BaseT is Ethernet brought up to date, so it is commonly called fast Ethernet. Companies such as Intel, National Semiconductor, 3Com, Sun Microsystems, Synoptics and many others have a significant investment in Ethernet technology and are ready to support fast Ethernet.

A 100BaseT installation will look exactly like today's 10BaseT. The connections are made over EIA/TIA 568 Level 5 cable, presently the highest grade of unshielded twisted-pair cable, with runs of up to 100 meters in length between a hub and node. Fast Ethernet retains the carrier sense multiple access with collision detection (CSMA/CD) media access control technique of the 1973 Ethernet invention.

The original Ethernet and the follow-on work by the IEEE 802.3 committee resulted in a standard that is speed independent. Except for the gap between packets, CSMA/CD works at any speed. On a practical level, this means vendors will be able to market economical dual-speed Ethernet LAN adapters and hubs. Many vendors have the Ethernet chip technology, so competition in the fast Ethernet market will keep prices down. Finally, Ethernet-to-fast Ethernet bridging is relatively simple, so linking old and new LANs isn't a problem.

Fast Ethernet has a lot of appeal and only one potential drawback: It requires a good-quality wiring plant. While many organizations have installed Level 5 cabling, the quality of the cable doesn't guarantee the quality of the installation. Installers have to dress the wire scarefully and use patch panels and cross-connection blocks that sustain the low crosstalk requirements of Level 5. Many, if not most, organizations will have to go through a cable certification process before they can install fast Ethernet adapters.

100 Megabits on Voice Grade

The 100BaseVG proposal is radically different from CSMA/CD Ethernet. The VG suffix stands for voice grade, and the major appeal of 100BaseVG—as well as AT&T's support—rests on its ability to run over voice-grade, unshielded twisted-pair wiring; that is, EIA/TIA Level 3 cable, instead of the Level 5 cable required for 100BaseX. The voice-grade cabling used by 100BaseVG exists in many walls, but Level 5 cable often requires a new installation by trained workers.

Actually, the "100Base" label is a misnomer—if not a pure marketing ploy—because HP's proposal is not Ethernet and doesn't deserve an Ethernet-type label. The HP proposal uses a completely different media access control scheme called *Demand Priority Access Method* (DPAM). Under this architecture, the administrator, user, or developer assigns priorities to specific message packets. The node sends the packet to the hub in a broadcast, without contention, using four pairs of wires simultaneously. The hub has a small storage capacity. It services the highest priority packets first and holds the rest. The priority system provides a way for time-sensitive traffic such as full motion video or sound to use the bandwidth while less critical packets wait.

The trick to getting faster signaling over Category 3 cabling is to use twice the number of pairs of wires. Both the 100VG and the fast Ethernet groups have to abide by FCC limitations on the amount of radio frequency energy their systems broadcast, because a LAN cable system can make a fine broadcast antenna. But they must also keep the signals strong enough to overcome electrical noise so the system maintains acceptably low levels of errors. With a cap of 30MHz on their transmission spectrum, the companies had to develop clever signaling schemes that used the the two extra pair of Type 3 wires most organizations installed in their 10BaseT system as spares.

Products from the 100VG vendors incorporate a technique called *Quartet Signaling* that sends data and access signals in parallel over all four pairs at rates of 30 megabits per second per pair. Since the real data is split up into 5-bit words encoded onto the the wire as 6-bit data words, the effective data transfer rate is 100 megabits per second.

Both fast Ethernet and 100VG borrow physical level signaling and encoding techniques from FDDI to operate on Category 3 cabling. Fast Ethernet uses the 4bit/5bit coding technique called ANSI PMD X3T9.5. While the designers of fast Ethernet originally planned for the more hospitable Category 5, fiber, and IBM Type 1 shielded cabling, they responded to the marketing challenge of the 100VG-Anylan group with their own plan for signaling over Category 3 cable, 4T+. This technique still uses four pairs of wire in the Category 3 cable, but instead of running data over four pairs it uses three pairs for data and one pair for the CSMA/CD media access control process. Fast Ethernet also has a standard that uses only two pairs of Category 5 wire.

While the attempt to use exisiting Level 3 wire sounds appealing, it's worth remembering that PBX installers traditionally run four wire pairs to each wall jack because one or two wires in this kind of installation are often unusable. The 100VG system is limited to 100 meters, the same as the formal 10BaseT standard, but while system integrators know that 10BaseT cable runs can often be as long as 175 meters and still work fine, that isn't the case with 100VG. The acceptable fast Ethernet cable lengths vary with the type of cable. So, you need to know the length of each cable from the hub to the wall plate. As a minimumn, you'll certainly need a cable survey and you might need a new installation before you can use even the multipair signaling schemes designed to replace 10BaseT.

People who want to install 100BaseVG will still need to make careful checks and improvements to their wiring system.

FDDI

The major competitor to the fast signaling schemes under consideration by the IEEE is the Fiber Distributed Data Interface (FDDI). The term FDDI is misleading. Under the latest definition of the American National Standards Institute, it can include fiber-optic, shielded twisted-pair, or unshielded twisted-pair cable—so FDDI doesn't necessarily imply fiber-optic cable.

FDDI is a networking scheme that gains high reliability through redundancy and sophisticated data-handling protocols. The fiber-optic cable alternative in FDDI provides signaling out to 2 kilometers, but the relatively high cost of fiber has limited its popularity. The FDDI protocols can run over copper cable if you accept distances limited to 100 meters and the need for a Level 5 UTP installation.

An ANSI committee has approved a plan for signaling using two pairs of Level 5 UTP. The ANSI standard uses a transmission scheme called called *Multi-Level Transmission-3* (MLT-3); it is a specific scheme for randomizing data to reduce emissions, and a method of equalizing signal levels.

In addition, IBM and other vendors are pushing for the use of FDDI protocols over shielded twisted-pair wire, a proposal that goes by the name *SDDI*. IBM, Network Peripherals, and Synoptics are among the companies shipping SDDI modules for their chassis-based wiring hubs.

Crescendo Communications uses the term *Copper Distributed Data Interface* (CDDI) to describe its products that use the FDDI techniques over unshielded twisted-pair. Crescendo markets a 32-bit MCA CDDI adapter designed for the IBM RS/6000 workstation. Other companies like Network Peripherals use the term *FDDI over UTP* to describe products that conform to the ANSI standard.

FDDI over Fiber

So what's wrong with fiber? Why do so many companies go to the trouble of putting the FDDI protocols over copper when fiber offers longer distance, resistance to outside electrical noise, better security from tapping, and additional bandwidth for growth? The initial answer is cost, but that isn't the total explanation.

Today, fiber FDDI adapters cost about $500 more than copper FDDI adapters because the fiber-optic parts cost that much more, but recently two big companies, Motorola and HP, have thrown down the gauntlet on price. Motorola has announced significantly lower prices for its next generation of FDDI chip sets—which will affect all types of FDDI products—and HP claims their new chips will reduce the costs of the fiber optic transceivers by 75 percent over the next few years.

Despite its benefits, fiber isn't a comfortable technology for many managers. It takes a day of specialized training and about $1,800 worth of tools to equip one employee to install and repair optical-fiber cables. Many managers believe that it takes only a few minutes of on-the-job training and $20 worth of tools to equip someone to install unshielded twisted wire. In truth, people need as much or more training to be able to install and certify a Level 5 UTP cable plant, as they do to become competent at installing fiber-optic cable. Still, the notion persists that there's less time and money involved in preparing people to install wire.

Staff people are typically more comfortable installing and repairing UTP than they are handling fiber. This is particularly true because the component that receives the most stress and is most likely to fail, the end connector, is difficult to install in a fiber optic system and relatively easy to install with any category of UTP or STP. Managers resist a technology that they can't handle with staff people because they feel it puts them at the mercy of outside service providers.

ATM

Another network buzzword—a technology that isn't ready for prime time but gets a lot of attention—is *asynchronous transfer mode* (ATM). ATM is a packet-switching scheme that divides a stream of data into 48-byte cells. A 5-byte header provides routing information for a series of network cell switches. This architecture reduces the overhead in the switches and allows organizations to use the same ATM data cells between desktops as they do between cities.

Because the cells are small, time-sensitive data like voice and video can mix with other data without suffering much delay. If a few cells get out of sequence, a little buffering takes care of the tiny interruption. The first commercial use of ATM is in the city-wide Switched Multimegabit Data Communications System (SMDS). Bellcore defined SMDS based on IEEE 802.6 standards and 45-megabit-per-second SMDS services are being installed by telephone companies around the U.S.

ATM's next step toward the desktop will be as a backbone connection between wiring hubs. A list of companies including Ungermann-Bass, Synoptics, and Cabletron market wiring hubs with ATM capability. SMDS services offered by the local telephone company will appeal to many network managers as an ideal way to link LANs. But as ATM technology gets closer to the desktop, higher speeds are possible. ATM adapters for PCs with 32-bit expansion slots like the Intel PCI or IBM MCA will operate at 155 megabits per second over copper twisted-pair and fiber-optic cable. There are specifications for running at that speed over UTP, but the cable distances are limited and it takes a very good installation.

It's redundant, but accurate, to say that ATM's broad appeal stems primarily comes from it's broad appeal. Huge and tiny companies are lining up to support ATM in every niche. Standards are in place at many levels and ATM will expand from the WAN into the LAN throughout the 1990s.

■ Networking Alternatives

To a large degree, the type of network adapter you choose dictates the logical and physical topologies, the type of media, and the access protocol scheme your network uses. These choices do not, however, dictate the type of networking software you use. The LAN hardware and the network operating-system software are important but separate decisions. The next two chapters describe the operation and selection of LAN operating-system software.

- *LAN Software Functions*
- *Software in the Client PC*
- *Types of Servers*
- *The Structure of Server Software*
- *The Network Operating System Is a System*

The Structure of Network
Operating Systems

TECHNICAL TALE

"We can check it out like a book from the library, right?" Cindy Harms gestured with a shiny silver CD-ROM as she asked the question. "Only one reader at a time."

"That's what this license agreement says," Steve Rigney replied, "but many CD-ROMs are different. Most infobase publishers (an infobase is the stuff on the CD-ROM) require you to get a special license if you want to install the CD-ROM on a network."

"Okay, what do we need to network the CD-ROM drive on this PC so we can share this infobase?" Cindy wanted to show that she could use the acronyms as well as anyone. "This is a catalog of products that we order from once or twice a day, and the six of us can use the infobase one at a time, but each person needs to use it from his or her own desktop PC."

"Networking a CD-ROM drive is fairly simple," Steve replied. "First, we put a LAN adapter card in every PC. Those adapters connect to cables we can run along the wall between the partitions. Then, we load a module of server software into the PC with the CD-ROM drive attached. The server software makes the CD-ROM drive available for sharing across the network cable. Finally, we load software called a redirector in each PC. That redirector software acts as a client to the server software. Each person sees the CD-ROM drive as a new DOS disk drive letter. That's all there is to it!"

Cindy, who didn't want to appear in awe of technology, observed, "That doesn't seem very hard."

Steve mentally kicked himself. Selecting the right IRQ and memory address, resolving conflicts with other devices, properly attaching the cable connectors, loading the network drivers, and assigning sharing rights were all learned skills. He had made it sound too easy.

Steve smiled uneasily and said, "Changing the brake pads on your car and writing your own will don't seem difficult either, but if you need to be sure that the thing is done right, you get an expert to do the job."

T HIS CHAPTER REVIEWS AND ELABORATES ON THE CONCEPTS BEHIND NETWORK operating-system software described in Chapter 4. There, we'll explore the functions of server software, client workstation software, and the underlying communications protocols.

Chapters 5 and 6 detailed the basic hardware portions of a local area network: the cabling scheme and network adapters. There are other pieces you might think of as hardware—primarily servers, bridges, and gateways—but these are usually PCs acting in particular functional roles rather than unique pieces of hardware designed for networks.

One interesting and useful feature of LAN hardware like the Ethernet, ARCnet, and Token-Ring systems described in the previous chapters is its complete independence from the networking software. If you stick with IEEE- and industry-standard hardware and avoid proprietary cable and signaling schemes, you can choose practically any network operating system for your client workstations, servers, and other functional elements. Your decision on cabling and your decision on LAN software are separate.

■ LAN Software Functions

Three concepts you've encountered in earlier chapters are worth repeating here:

- The primary purpose of networking software is to let you share resources such as printers, hard disks, and communications links among client stations.

- The primary function of networking software is to make distant resources appear local.

- Networking software performs the same functions, regardless of whether it's contained within the computer's operating system—as in Macintosh computers and in PCs running Novell's DOS 7 and Microsoft's Windows NT—or sold as a separate product.

A network operating system is not one program, but rather a series of programs. Some of these programs run in the PCs acting as servers of various types, and others run in PCs acting as client workstations. The networking software in servers provides and controls multiple simultaneous access to disk drives, printers, and other devices such as modems and facsimile boards. The networking software in client stations intercepts and redirects the requests for service that application programs generate and sends each of them to the appropriate server for action.

Terms like *server* and *client station* describe the *function* of a computer on the network; they don't tell you anything about the power or capacity of the PC acting in that role. Also, they aren't mutually exclusive terms; a PC will often act as a server of some kind—particularly as a print server—and as a client workstation at the same time.

■ Software in the Client PC

We call computers using a network's resources *clients*. A client PC uses hard disks, communications lines, and printers on a server as if these things were part of each user's own workstation. That redirection capability is the prime power of networks. Under some network operating systems, client stations can also act as servers, but most computers on the LAN typically serve only as clients.

Here are some important concepts to understand about how networking software does its job:

- Client PCs use shared resources provided by servers.

- You don't always need special applications on client PCs.

- Redirection software routes requests to servers.

- Transport-layer software carries data across the cable.

- There are many kinds of servers.

The following sections explain these points in greater detail.

The Redirector

The redirection software in each client computer makes the resources available on the network look like local DOS or OS/2 devices to the programs and people using them. Commands sent from the keyboard and from programs to drives with names like D:, E:, and F: are redirected over the network to the appropriate file servers. Similarly, programs sending output to a network printer address a local LPT port just as they normally would. The print jobs are redirected to the shared printer and queued on the PC acting as a print server until the printer is ready to take the job.

Operating-system modules in the client stations include the redirector and the software elements that carry the redirector's output through the network. The redirector modifies the DOS or OS/2 operating system in the client stations so that certain requests made by applications go out through the network adapter for action instead of going to local disk drives or I/O ports. The network administrator programs the redirector through a menu or a command-line prompt to route all requests addressed to a specific drive letter or I/O port to a selected network resource.

For example, in a network using Novell's NetWare you would enter the following command to route requests sent to the F: drive out to a subdirectory called ACCOUNTS in a disk volume called VOLUME1 residing on a server named SERVER1:

```
MAP F: = SERVER1/VOLUME1: ACCOUNTS
```

Commands like this are usually part of the log-on script for an individual user, giving each person a customized view of the network resources. Network administrators have the important task of creating and maintaining customized log-on scripts and batch files for each user.

Transport-Layer Software

Additional layers of networking software in the client move an application's request for service from the redirector to the network adapter and onto the network cable. This software has three parts:

- An application program interface (API)

- A network communications section that follows a specific protocol

- Drivers customized for the LAN adapter

Figure 7.1 shows the relationship of the redirector and transport-layer software.

An application program interface (API) is actually a specification describing how application programs, ranging from word processing packages to graphics and spreadsheet programs, interact and request services from the disk or network operating system. The specification describes the *software interrupt* a program issues to identify a request for service, along with the format of the data contained in the request.

For example, when application programs want to access a file on a disk drive, they build a block of data containing the parameters for the request and pass it to DOS by putting its address in a register and generating an *interrupt 21 hexadecimal*. In response to the interrupt, DOS reads the address register and then the data block. All "well-behaved" programs follow this process. Only "ill-behaved" programs go around the DOS services to interrogate the disk-drive hardware directly.

In the case of the transport-layer software, the standard API provides the redirector (and certain classes of application programs that make direct calls to the transport-layer software) with a way to send and receive requests to and from the network.

Some operating systems provide only one API for the session-layer software, typically the NetBIOS API using software interrupt 5C hex.

Figure 7.1

Novell calls its redirection software a "shell" to indicate that it wraps around the MS-DOS operating system and intercepts all data requests and commands coming from application programs and the keyboard. The Microsoft redirector, licensed by IBM and many other companies, modifies MS-DOS so that it routes appropriate requests to the redirector. The NetWare shell and the Microsoft redirector move the messages they receive to the network adapter card through transport-layer software such as NetBIOS or Novell's SPX/IPX. Each driver is configured specifically for the brand and model of LAN adapter.

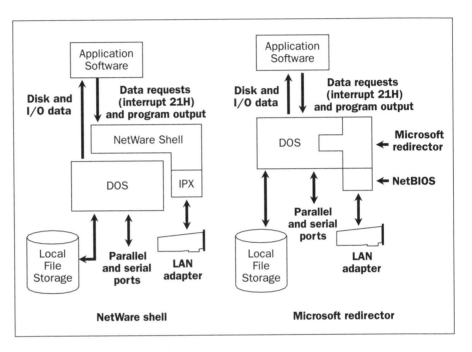

- Novell has a unique API for its SPX (Sequenced Packet Exchange). SPX is an enhanced set of commands implemented on top of IPX (Inter-network Packet Exchange) transport-layer software that allows more functions, one of which is guaranteed delivery. An optional Novell module accepts calls from application programs using the NetBIOS 5C hex interrupts and translates them to IPX.

- Microsoft LAN Manager networks can use another API called Named Pipes for special node-to-node applications, and particularly for access to communications and database servers.

The communications portion of the transport-layer software follows a standard protocol—perhaps NetBIOS, TCP, or Novell's SPX—to move information from one network node to another. Some products, such as LAN Manager, can load instructions conforming to different network protocols on demand, so that the application program can take advantage of transport-layer software using one of two or three protocols depending on the source or destination of a particular packet of information.

Some programs, such as QEMM from Quarterdeck Office Systems, Net-Room from Helix Software, and Microsoft's EMM386 provide ways to place network redirector and driver software into memory locations outside of those used by DOS. In addition, in mid-1990 Novell released versions of its network shell that can load and run outside of the RAM used by DOS applications.

Application Programs

Because the redirector routes requests for standard operating-system services from local devices to remote devices on the network, application programs don't have to be "the network version" to be able to save and retrieve data files on dedicated subdirectories in a network file server. The programs exchange data with DOS or OS/2 just as they would if the PC didn't have a network connection.

When a file is shared by several people at once, some level of software must arbitrate simultaneous demands for the same data. Having several applications read the same data at the same time is all right, but reading data while another application is trying to write it can lead to inaccuracy at best and a crashed program at worst. If multiple programs attempt to write to the same portion of a data file at the same time, the resulting data corruption can ruin an entire file.

Before the release of DOS Version 3.0 in 1984, local area network software designers had to put routines in each network operating system to control data access. Unfortunately, manufacturers didn't agree on standards for these routines or their use. You had to buy a customized version of a database product to work with a specific LAN operating system. Often, the database management system (DBMS) you wanted was not available for the network operating system you chose.

Microsoft helped alleviate this situation with the introduction of DOS 3.0 and the version that quickly superseded it, DOS 3.1. DOS 3.0 introduced these special commands for multiuser applications:

- ATTRIB makes files read-only to protect them from being changed or erased.

- LASTDRIVE is a CONFIG.SYS statement that tells DOS to make more drive designations available for use. These drive designations are linked to resources on a server.

- SHARE invokes the DOS file- and data-locking capabilities described later in this chapter.

When Microsoft added these capabilities to DOS, companies that don't use DOS on the network file server, like Novell and Banyan, added emulation of the DOS data-locking services into their operating systems to stay compatible. When DOS on a workstation locks data on a Novell or Banyan server, the unique operating system in the server responds just as if it were DOS.

Normally, the easiest way to use a program on a network is to use ATTRIB to make the program's .COM, .EXE, and .OVL files read-only and to give each user a private subdirectory in which to store data files. In this way, all parties can use the application program and keep their own separate data files. If they want to exchange files, it is easy and fast to copy the files from one subdirectory on the server's hard disk to another.

Licensing limitations usually prohibit multiple stations from running the same copy of a program, so be sure you don't let more than one person use the same program at the same time, even in private subdirectories, unless you own enough licensed copies of the program. In Chapter 9 I'll introduce a category of software *PC Magazine* has tagged "LAN metering programs." These programs regulate the number of client stations that can access programs and files at the same time.

Data Sharing

When you want to share data files among many people at the same time, matters get more difficult. Let's first consider the case where files are shared like library books—one user at a time.

When an application program opens a data file, the program can set certain restrictions on the simultaneous use of the file by other application programs. The options enabled under the DOS 3.0 SHARE function give programmers the ability to open a file for exclusive use (denying any other application the ability to read or write to the file simultaneously) or in other modes that allow reading or writing (or both) by other applications under certain conditions. Application programs can open data files under a condition called Deny None, which makes the file available to all applications for all functions at all times.

Many application programs designed before the introduction of DOS 3.0 open data files using what is now termed the Compatibility mode. This mode, originally designed to give DOS 2.0 backward compatibility, provides no protection against simultaneous users overwriting each other's data in files. That's why the safest way to install an application on a network is to give each user a private subdirectory for data files.

More modern applications use one of the DOS 3.0 SHARE modes to open a file. These are the sharing-mode options available to a programmer:

0 Compatibility

1 Deny Read/Write

2 Deny Write

3 Deny Read

4 Deny None

Programmers can open a file under any of these conditions. Option 2, Deny Write, is a common sharing mode for network operations because it allows one client PC to change the file while others can only read it. If all PCs need the ability to modify files, then all programs use option 4, and the programmers use special techniques to avoid data corruption.

If an application is not designed to create shared data files, the programmer should write the code to open data files in a mode that denies all access to a second program trying to get into a file. This means that the files created by the application are available to stations on a network on a first-come-first-served, one-at-a-time basis, like a book in a library.

Multiple Simultaneous Access

A database management system is the most common example of multiple simultaneous file access on a LAN. A database is made up of files containing records. Programs running in client PCs often must open several files at the same time in order to read records in each file. Simultaneously, programs on other PCs might have one of the same files open to write records. Obviously, if one station tries reading a record while another is writing it, some kind of problem will occur.

The DOS SHARE feature allows an application program to lock a range of bytes in a file for exclusive use. When an application program issues a DOS 21 hex *interrupt* and a 5C hex function call (don't confuse this with the 5C hex *interrupt*, which calls NetBIOS), it can then tell DOS how many bytes to lock for exclusive use. When DOS locks these bytes, no other program can write or read them. DOS sends an error message back to any application trying to access a locked data segment.

DBMS packages with their own programming languages—such as dBASE IV, for example—let programmers use this DOS data-locking function by providing an internal command called RLOCK. Typically, database programmers invoke the RLOCK command to tell the application program to lock one or more specific records before they are rewritten, but the DBMS converts this into a command telling DOS to lock a range of bytes.

If you are a database programmer writing applications for a multiuser system, either you or the database program must tell DOS which bytes to lock to prevent one application from reading a file while another application writes to it. If you have to remember to issue an RLOCK command (as in dBASE III), the program is said to have *explicit* record locking. If the DBMS is "smart" enough that it will automatically tell DOS to lock a range of bytes while the program writes a record, the program is said to have *implicit* record locking.

In a multiuser system, you also have to do something about the application that tries to access a range of bytes when it is locked by another program. Some database management programs will return a "Record locked" message to the application program when they run into locked bytes. The application programmer must anticipate getting this message and find a way to handle it.

The options for handling a "Record locked" return vary. A programmer can decide to build a loop that tells the application to wait a short time and try again, to abort the application, or to send a message to the screen asking the user what to do. Some database programs automate this process by automatically retrying the access. This feature is usually combined with a limit on the amount of time the record may be locked.

So a real application, such as a networked database management system allowing several operators to access and update a warehouse inventory, must contain lines of code directing DOS to lock a range of bytes in a file designated as a record or field while it is in use. The creator of the DBMS application also has to put in routines responding to the "locked" signal from DOS and informing an operator who tries to change a field that it is already in use and cannot be modified. Opening files for shared or exclusive use and handling conflicts over simultaneous access to a given range of bytes in a file are problems faced by people writing networked applications.

The most complex situation takes place when several applications have several files open at the same time. Since records in the different files are indexed to each other in some way, you can get into a situation where two applications simultaneously lock data that both of them need to finish their tasks. This is called a *deadlock* or "deadly embrace" in the classic computer literature. Many techniques (such as time-outs) can break a deadlock, but all of them slow processing.

Some database management programs—Paradox, for example—don't use the DOS file- and byte-locking options. They do the job for DOS in a more elegant way that is also designed to avoid deadlocks. A Paradox application leaves a message in a special log file while it creates or changes a portion of a data file; when it is finished, it erases the message in the log file.

Other applications check this log file. If one application needs to read a record being written by another application, it will wait. If the wait is too long, the person using the second application receives a message indicating which user has the record locked. At this point, it is up to the people using the data to resolve the problem.

This log-file architecture is a more elegant method of sharing data than the one DOS provides. It is much easier on the person writing applications, but it also puts a greater load on the network and the server. Each application accesses the log file before every access to the data file. Applications writing to a data file write an entry in the log file before each data file access and erase it afterwards. Thus, there are more packets on the network and many more disk access requests for the server to satisfy than there are under DOS data protection.

Neither method of protecting data is perfect. You should know the advantages and drawbacks of both architectures. But now, at least, networks of PCs have mature methods that allow many people to use the same data at the same time.

The best advice for the average person acting as a network or database administrator is to choose application programs with good technical-support options. You will often need to talk to an expert on the phone or in person to solve problems. The cost of LAN hardware, network software, and installation is just the opening gambit in the network game. You need good support to install, configure, and manage networked applications.

■ Types of Servers

A network can have up to three generic types of servers: file servers, print servers, and communications servers. Any particular network might have several servers of various types. Remember, I'm using the term *server* in a functional sense as a device playing a role in the network. Here is a list of the types and subtypes of network servers:

File servers:

Database servers

CD-ROM servers

Print servers:

On a PC

Special devices

Communications servers:

Gateways to mainframes

Facsimile servers

Electronic-mail gateways

Sometimes file, print, and communications services reside in one computer on the network, and sometimes the tasks are spread among many PCs. In networks designed by companies such as Novell and Banyan, one PC makes lots of services available to others. On a network using Banyan's VINES, one server can provide shared file access, communication links to a mainframe, and long-distance links between servers using X.25 technology. Figure 7.2 provides a generic view of the servers and client stations in a practical network.

Figure 7.2

PCs can act in multiple roles on a network. This diagram shows a network with three servers: a file server doubling as a print server, a communications server with a shared modem, and a remote print server. The communications server can also run standard applications as a personal computer, though there is always a trade-off when a computer simultaneously runs applications and provides network services. MS-DOS and OS/2 client stations share the resources.

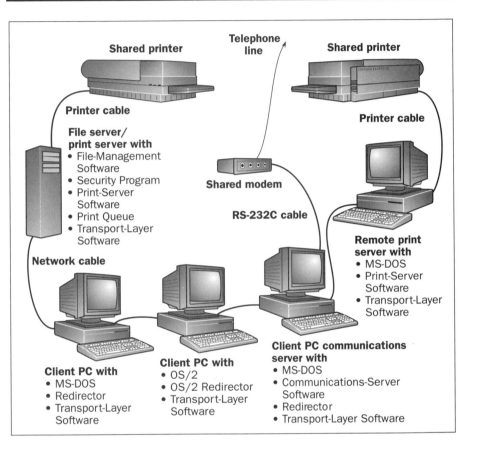

Companies like Microsoft and Artisoft design their network operating systems so that many PCs can act as servers of various types, even while people are using them to run standard applications. In a network using Novell's NetWare, the PC's acting as servers are typically dedicated to that task

The File-Server Functions

A *file server* makes hard disk storage space (up to a gigabyte or more) available to the client PCs. The file server answers requests for data read and write actions, routed from application programs by the redirector software in each client PC, and mediates simultaneous requests for access to the same data.

Database servers, a subset of the file-server category, include servers that make expensive hardware such as CD-ROM or optical disk drives available, as well as "back-end" database processors. These back-end database servers are the basis of the client/server computing model that has gained a great deal of popularity in recent years. The phrase *client/server* actually has several meanings. The oldest definition is simply a network technology that uses a dedicated server, as NetWare does. The opposite of this technology is a *peer-to-peer* network such as Windows for Workgroups. Two more recent definitions of *client/server* are based on differing network architectures: the database server architecture mentioned earlier, which uses a back-end database processor, and the application server architecture.

A database server architecture is arranged so that the client PCs send requests for data to a program called a database "engine," which runs a PC acting as a file server. Database engine vendors include Oracle, Gupta, Sybase, and Microsoft. In this architecture, the file server acts as a powerful database processor that executes special commands—often in IBM's Structured Query Language (SQL)—from database query programs running on networked PCs. The database processor receives simple requests for reports from the client stations and executes the complex code needed to extract and compile the information from a raw database. Because the database-engine software runs on a PC acting as a file server, the query programs don't have to pull files over the network cable for sorting and matching in the client PCs. This architecture reduces the communications load on the network but puts a heavy processing load on the PC that handles the database.

This architecture is in contrast to the older database technology, still used by most programs, in which the database program running on each client draws the information across the network and sorts it locally on each desktop computer. While the older technology is much less efficient, it is also less complex and has a lower up-front cost than running a database engine in the server.

Application server architecture is in itself a term with several meanings. As a client/server computing scheme, it means that one powerful PC runs some portion of the application, perhaps a database or a graphical processing program like X-Windows on request from programs running in client PCs. The two programs use a technique called *remote procedure calls* (RPCs) to communicate. RPCs are, in effect, prearranged shorthand requests for action.

IBM pioneered the database server and application server architectures through their development of an architecture called *Advanced Program to Program communications* (APPC). They developed APPC so that PC programs could use mainframe programs and hardware in client/server roles. As the role of mainframes diminished, IBM moved APPC to APPN (*Advanced Peer-to-Peer Networking*). So, the client/server technology originated as a way to prolong the life of mainframe hardware, but has now become a way to sell high-end PC hardware and AS-400s.

A twist on the application server is *distributed applications*. In common usage, distributed applications are those that cross the boundaries between different types of computer hardware and operating systems. The Open Software Federation, led by IBM, HP, and Digital, has established standards for the *Distributed Computing Environment* (DCE). DCE products provide standard program calls used between applications so they can share the available processing power. DCE includes security and administrative protocols that allow DCE programs to recognize and communicate with each other. DCE is a complex architecture, and there are many players in the game. Microsoft links into DCE with their *Object Linking and Embedding* (OLE) architecture—a set of programming tools designed to allow programs to share specific types of information modules called *objects*.

Another organization, the *Object Management Group,* has developed a set of specifications similar to DCE called the *Common Object Request Broker Architecture* (COBRA). These specifications accomplish about the same thing as DCE, but rely even more heavily on visual programming objects.

Novell rides their own wagon off in the same direction with their AppWare suites of programming tools, which supposedly make it easy to develop applications that will run on and share processing tasks across different computers running different operating systems.

On the bottom line, client/server means many things to many people. Strategists at IBM, Microsoft, and Novell think client/server computing is an important part of their future, but each organization views the technology involved from a slightly different angle. As client/server technology evolves, it's a safe bet HP and Digital won't be left behind either.

The Print-Server Functions

Computers acting as *print servers* make printers available for shared use—in some cases up to five for each print server. The print server accepts print jobs from application programs running on the client stations and stores them as files in a special subdirectory called a *print spool* on a hard disk drive. When the full print job has arrived in the print spool, its file waits in a queue for the first available printer (or for a specially designated printer).

The drive that holds the print spool could be on another PC acting as a file server, but this arrangement puts a lot of traffic on the network as print jobs move from the PC running the application to the print server, from there to the spool on the file server, and eventually back to the print server for printing. In common practice, either the print-server function is located together with the file-server software or the PC acting as a print server has its own hard disk.

Networking software products such as Artisoft's LANtastic allow any networked PC running DOS to act as a file or print server, or both, and still run application programs. Microsoft's NT gives the same server abilities to Windows-based PCs. Novell's NetWare lets you combine file- and print-server functions in the same PC or establish separate print servers. PCs acting as NetWare file servers can't run applications, but the print-server software can reside in a PC used to run application programs.

The biggest advantage in designing a network with separate print servers is the ability to arrange the geography of the network to suit the users. If you combine the print-server and file-server functions, you must locate the shared printers close to the server hardware, primarily because of distance limitations on parallel-port connections. Since the PC acting as a file server for a robust network has many noisy hard disk drives, powerful fans, and probably a bulky uninterruptible power supply, it's usually consigned to a remote location— perhaps even behind a locked door for security. You'll have to plan carefully or have a lot of luck to find a location suitable for the file-server hardware and convenient for people trying to retrieve finished print jobs.

Sharing printers through conveniently located personal workstations acting as print servers seems like a good way to overcome the problem of where to locate printers. While the idea of using a PC simultaneously as a print server and a personal workstation has appeal, it also has practical limitations. You can only slice a PC so many ways until the people at client stations and the person using the machine for local applications all receive slow service. Hardware interrupts generated by serial- and parallel-port activity and concurrent requests for access to the hard disk can slow down even the fastest PC when it operates as both a server and a personal workstation.

The decision of whether to make a print server part of a file server, part of a client PC, or a dedicated node hinges mainly on how much printing the client PCs will do. If your organization prints no more than 30 to 50 pages of plain text an hour, then combining the print server and file server makes sense. But heavier printing loads and considerations about the printers' physical location might dictate using separate print servers or print servers combined with client workstations.

As the number of print jobs coming from the client stations builds, and as the complexity of application programs increases, only people running lightweight applications find it practical to contribute printer services to the network through their PCs. The common practice is to set up dedicated PCs as network print servers in convenient locations around the office. This architecture takes space and requires the full resources of a PC, complete with hard disk, monitor, and keyboard, for each print server.

Special Print Servers

In late 1990, a new category of products showed up at PC Magazine LAN Labs. At first, we called them *Ethernet peripheral-sharing devices*. This mouthful of words describes their function, but it isn't a phrase likely to stick in the minds of buyers. After much brainstorming, we decided to call them what they are: *special-function servers* (see Figure 7.3).

These products from Castelle, Hewlett-Packard, Intel, and Digital Products attach to a network cable and make printers available to the client PCs using Novell software, without the need for any other hardware.

Figure 7.3

This print server for Novell and Ethernet allows users to locate printers anywhere along the network.

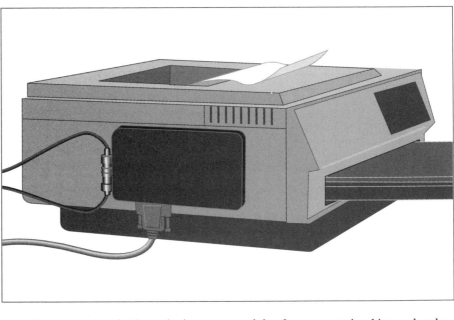

The processors in these devices use special software contained in read-only memory. They don't need attached monitors, drives, or keyboards. Special-function servers typically use print-server software running on a NetWare file server to receive and store print jobs, but then they take those jobs from the queue, over the network cabling, and send them to the printer. This architecture moves the print job over the cable at least twice—something purists will moan about—but no one can deny the practicality and value of these special-function servers.

While the initial versions of these products worked only on the IEEE 802.3 Ethernet cabling scheme under NetWare, later versions allow various Token-Ring and LAN Manager combinations. These products will not work with DOS-based LAN operating systems.

The Communications-Server Functions

The phrase *communications server* covers a variety of tasks. Communications servers can act as gateways to mainframe computers, allowing client PCs to share a costly mainframe communications channel. They can make pools of expensive high-speed modems available for sharing on a first-come-first-served basis. And they can run software such as Action Technologies' Message Handling Service (MHS), which is able to link different electronic-mail systems.

Unlike print servers, the major consideration for communications servers isn't geometry; you can set them anywhere you have a phone line. The major consideration is CPU power. While a print server buffers the print jobs going to the printers, communications servers must provide real-time connections between client PCs and communications channels. This puts a heavy load on the PC acting as a communications server.

Handling the hardware interrupts generated by the serial and parallel ports keeps the CPU in a communications server very busy. Few people will enjoy running application programs on a PC that simultaneously functions as a communications server. So in today's typical network, communications-server software usually runs on a separate PC dedicated to the task. I'll talk a lot more about communications servers in all their forms in Chapter 12.

Fax Servers

Fax servers provide everyone on the network with the ability to share the hardware for incoming and outgoing facsimile transmissions. PCs acting as communications servers are usually dedicated to this task.

Fax servers are great at sharing modems for outgoing calls, but there are problems in handling incoming faxes. When the fax hits the server, where should it go? At one time, someone had to read every incoming fax, but the technology continued to improve and there are now five good techniques for internally routing faxes: "read" a line of text, read DTMF tones, recognize the incoming line, recognize the incoming fax machine, and recognize distinctive rings. Some products, like Alcom's LanFax, can use any or all of these techniques.

Routing incoming faxes by reading a line of text involves using OCR software to look for a specifically formatted line containing the name of an addressee, but callers must know how to format the fax. Devices that read DTMF tones allow the sender to generate touch tone signals to designate the receiver after the connection is made. This technique is useful because it can accommodate many recipients, but it requires special actions on the part of the sender. If your fax server uses a multiline adapter, it can route faxes to individuals or to workgroups based on the incoming line. Recognizing the number, or *Customer Subscriber Identification* (CSID), of the incoming fax machine a useful trick because the sender doesn't need to take any special actions; however, this technique limits the sender to a specific fax machine.

Distinctive ringing is a useful option offered by your local telephone company. The telephone company sends calls directed to different phone numbers over the same incoming line using different ringing patterns. Just as some modems and fax machines can use distinctive ringing to determine when they should answer, some fax servers can use the distinctive ring to route incoming faxes to specific mailboxes. This technique doesn't require any knowledge or action on the part of the caller, and the caller can use any machine to place the call.

Finally, *Direct Inward Dial* is a technique that uses the signaling between the telephone company's central office and your private branch exchange telephone system to ring specific lines. The fax server interprets these incoming calls and properly routes the received documents.

■ The Structure of Server Software

Servers make possible the applications that provide the functional and economic rationale for installing a network; the ability to share information and the efficiencies provided by electronic-mail or workgroup-scheduling programs can all justify a LAN. Of course, servers need special software—the LAN operating system—to handle the many tasks involved in sharing resources.

The sharing software in file, print, and communications servers comes in many different modules. Communications servers run software that translates between the network and whatever communications speeds, data alphabets, and protocols the external connections use. File-server software includes sophisticated queues for requests and usually some kind of disk cache. Disk caching loads large segments of the data from the hard disk into RAM to satisfy requests from fast memory instead of from the slower hard disk.

Servers have the same kinds of transport-layer software as workstations. The server also runs software that buffers and queues requests for service from the network stations. The server software typically includes some kind of security protection based on either a password attached to each resource or a table of rights assigned to each named user.

File servers might use DOS to access their files, but only for the sake of simplicity and economy. DOS is not a multitasking operating system, so it must queue requests for service arriving from several clients, and it doesn't provide the fastest access to files. High-performance LAN file-server operating systems, like those from AT&T, Banyan, Digital Equipment Corp., IBM, DSC Communications, Microsoft, and Novell, handle multiple tasks at once, and they have very efficient hard-disk file formats that are capable of handling gigabytes of storage.

The choice between DOS and a multitasking operating system as the underpinning of the file server marks a significant difference between two kinds of LAN operating-system products. PCs running a file-server operating system based on DOS keep their ability to run standard applications at the same time. Since it is possible to share files or printers with the network and still run local applications, all PCs on the network can act as combination server/workstation "peers." We call these *peer-to-peer networks*. Multitasking file servers typically are not also used as client PCs, although some—particularly Windows and Windows NT—technically can run both file-server software and normal applications.

File-server software in DOS peer-to-peer networks resides in the individual PC's memory and divides or "slices" the processor's time between file services and the standard applications. The RAM left for applications is typically about 400K, and the programs run more slowly than normal, but many people happily share drives and printers on multiple networked PCs using peer-to-peer systems.

Network operating systems have many component modules, but today's software isn't difficult to install, and the default installation parameters usually provide excellent operation. LANs based on multitasking operating systems often have more features and options, so configuring their software is more difficult. Yet with careful attention to the manuals, anyone comfortable with DOS can install and manage these systems.

The Elements of File-Server Software

You can break file-server software down into three major elements:

- The *file-management system* writes and reads data on one or more hard disk drives.

- The *disk cache system* gathers incoming and outgoing data into a cache in RAM memory for faster handling than the physical capabilities of a hard disk would allow.

- The *access system* controls who may use the data and how multiple applications simultaneously access files.

The multitasking LAN operating systems—those able to let hundreds of nodes access gigabytes of data on a single server—set the pace and direction of the industry and determine how people will connect to, across, and out of their network environments.

Multitasking operating systems like NetWare, OS/2, Windows NT, and Unix provide important options for flexible, secure, and reliable connections. A network of PCs running with one of these operating systems can shove minicomputers out the back door in many organizations.

File-Management Functions

Regardless of whether the file management system is DOS, OS/2, Windows NT, Unix, or the highly specialized system underlying NetWare, its basic function is to move the heads of the hard disk drive and deliver data to the client stations through the network. Specialized programs, however, use techniques for fast and orderly movement far beyond what DOS can handle. Products like Novell's NetWare and Microsoft's Windows NT use all of these techniques in an attempt to gain maximum efficiency and throughput.

A technique called *elevator seeking* makes operation of the hard disks more efficient. The heads on a hard disk drive must move in and out on the spinning disk to read and write data. Each large movement takes milliseconds of time. The elevator-seeking software improves efficiency by queuing and ordering requests requiring head movement into orderly steps in the same direction. The order of the requests' arrival doesn't matter; each request is satisfied in the most logical fashion. This allows the drive heads to operate in a sweeping motion, from one edge of the disk to the other. Elevator seeking improves disk drive performance by significantly reducing disk head thrashing and by minimizing head seek time.

A *directory-hashing* technique indexes directory entries according to a mathematical formula for fastest retrieval. Two types of directory hashing expedite directory access. The first hashing algorithm indexes the volume directories, while the second indexes the files by volume and subdirectory. Directory hashing reduces the number of directory reads after the server starts operation. NetWare and other file systems take good advantage of directory hashing.

Server operating systems typically cache entire directory structures of volumes attached to the server. During initialization, the operating system reads entire volume directories into memory and continually updates them. First the copy in server RAM is updated; then the operating system updates the physical volume as time permits between servicing user requests. The technique provides fast response, but it carries a potential danger. If a power failure or other problem takes down the server before the volume is updated, the file can be damaged.

Disk Caching

Disk caching, the process of using server RAM to hold the most recent and frequently requested blocks of data from server storage, greatly enhances retrieval times. Hard disk drives can retrieve data in times measured in terms of hundredths of a second. Solid-state RAM can deliver the same data in thousandths of a second. When modern computers handle thousands of requests a second, people using client stations can perceive the difference a disk cache makes in delivering data to the screen.

Application programs typically request data in blocks of less than 1K. Caching file systems, however, will typically pick up at least 4K of data surrounding the requested bytes and place them in RAM. Network administrators can often tune the caching software to use different sizes of data blocks.

Caching doesn't help speed processing of the initial requests for data, but when the responses to subsequent requests for related data can come from the cache, they move more quickly than when they come from the hard disk. In many operations, the cache hit rate—the number of data requests satisfied from the cache—will exceed 80 percent.

File caching also speeds up user writes to network files. Requested writes are cached in flagged file-cache blocks. These blocks are systematically written to disk between the handling of other user requests. But caching file-write actions is usually an option that network administrators must turn on, because a write cache has one significant drawback. If the hard disk or server system suffers a catastrophic failure or power outage, the data waiting in cache to be written is lost. You must balance the potential efficiency improvement in a busy network against the potential loss of data due to a malfunction.

High-Reliability File-System Options

Fault tolerance, the ability to continue operation despite the failure of significant subsystems, is a relatively new factor in local area networking. As more users put their most valuable applications onto networks, fault tolerance has become increasingly important. Some network operating systems, notably the System Fault Tolerant (SFT) versions of NetWare, include capabilities to store data simultaneously on more than one drive for improved survivability.

Novell has offered SFT versions of NetWare for several years with such features as bad-block revectoring, disk mirroring, and disk duplexing. SFT NetWare is complex and significantly more expensive than the standard version.

In *bad-block revectoring*, a technique Novell refers to as *HotFix*, a small piece of software monitors the hard disk drive to detect malfunctions caused by a bad section of magnetic media on the drive. When it detects this problem, the software attempts to recover any available data and to revector the file address map to point to its new location. The software also marks the block of media as bad so that it isn't used again.

The *disk-mirroring* technique requires two disk drives: a primary and a secondary one. Ideally, the secondary disk is identical to the primary one; if it is not exactly the same, it must at least be of the same type and larger than the primary disk, although the extra space will not be utilized. All data copied to the primary disk is also sent to the "mirror" disk, although not necessarily to the same physical location. If the primary disk fails, the secondary disk immediately takes up the current task with no loss of data.

Another basic feature of disk mirroring is that data can be read from the mirror disk if a read error occurs on the primary disk. Read-after-write verification and HotFix are active on both disks. Therefore, the bad block on the primary disk will be marked, and the correct data from the mirror disk will be written to a good location on the primary disk. This completes a loop allowing full recovery from read and write errors.

Disk mirroring becomes *disk duplexing* through the addition of a completely separate hard disk controller card. This redundant configuration further improves reliability. Disk duplexing also benefits LAN throughput by allowing a technique called *split seeks*. When simultaneous multiple read requests occur, both drives receive and process them immediately, effectively doubling disk drive throughput and overall system performance. In the case of a single read request, the operating system looks at both disk drives to determine which can respond best. If both are equally occupied, NetWare will send the request to the drive whose current head position is closest to the desired data.

In summary, disk mirroring requires only one controller card and uses a second disk, which can immediately pick up a failed operation with no loss of data. Disk duplexing, with a controller card for each drive, enhances system performance by sending simultaneous writes and read requests to both disks through separate disk channels. It also allows continued operation if a disk controller fails. Disk mirroring and duplexing both provide additional levels of system survivability.

Security Systems

The concept of sharing resources and files carries a lot of appeal in terms of both economy and improved productivity. But too much sharing can become too much of a good thing. Server software must provide some way to differentiate the requests coming from different client stations and to determine whether each person or station has the right to receive the requested data or service. No one wants an unauthorized employee reading personnel or payroll records. You often need to limit the activity of network users to certain files to prevent both mischief and inadvertent damage.

A LAN software package typically uses one of two types of file security plans The first plan gives each shared resource on the network a "network name"; a single name can designate a whole shared drive, a subdirectory, or even a file. You can associate a password with a network name and limit the read/write/create capabilities associated with that password. This scheme, used by DOS-based networks, makes it easy to shift the shared resources, but one user might have to keep track of several passwords. Security is easily compromised when password management is a constant headache.

The other security architecture uses the concept of groups: Each person belongs to one or more groups, and each group has specific access rights. This architecture, used by NetWare and VINES, makes each person responsible only for one personal password. The LAN administrator can easily move people into different groups as they change jobs or leave the organization.

Both types of security architecture typically enable an administrator to allow or deny individuals or groups of users the ability to read, write, create, delete, search, and modify files. For example, you might want to give data-entry clerks only the ability to modify accounting files in order to prevent people from copying your financial files for their own purposes. A few operating systems even include a capability called "execute-only." This function allows a person only to run a program, which can't be copied or accessed in any other way. Appropriate use of various security options safeguards your important information.

The encryption of passwords, both when stored on-disk and during transmission, is an important feature in high-security applications. Where previously a technician could easily attach a network analyzer to the cable and capture passwords and data files as they crossed the network, NetWare 3.X now includes encrypted passwords to thwart anyone tapping into the cable.

A final note for the security-conscious: DOS-based networks have uniformly poor physical security for the server. Anyone who can get at the server's keyboard can access files on its hard disk.

■ The Network Operating System Is a System

Network operating systems contain many pieces and parts. Often, you can select options and configurations—such as transport-layer software or application program interfaces—that are uniquely suited to your organization. But such interactive systems need careful management. In the next chapter, we'll consider the most popular network operating systems and give some emphasis to their practical capabilities and limitations.

- *Industry Trends and Evolution*

- *The NetWare Family*

- *VINES*

- *Microsoft's Networking Strategy: Networking Everywhere*

- *Digital and AT&T*

- *POWERLan*

- *LANtastic*

- *Network Scalability*

- *Choosing Server Hardware*

- *Choosing Networking-Software Products*

C H A P T E R

The Best LAN Operating Systems

TECHNICAL TALE

"So how can you compete?" Willy Barnett asked Steve Rigney. "If Microsoft and Novell build networking into every computer's operating system, why will people need networking consultants? I'll still pull plenty of cable, but won't you be in trouble when setting up a network is just a matter of point and click?"

Willy and Steve, representing the O.K. Cable and O.K. Networks business units in O.K. Industries, were having their weekly business lunch.

"Things will change," Steve admitted. "As Windows and Windows NT become more widely used, we'll install less LANtastic and NetWare and spend more time integrating client/server applications, remote network entry, and long distance LAN-to-LAN connections."

"So are Artisoft, Performance Technology, and Novell going out of business?" Willy asked.

"Oh no, but they are adapting, too. Artisoft and Performance Technology are trying to be the universal clients. The client software from those companies will work with darn near any network operating system. On the server side, Artisoft is literally hiding in the shadow of the Novell giant by licensing part of the NetWare technology. Novell is moving up by trying to become the cross-platform enterprise-wide basis for client/server applications, but Microsoft's Windows NT might get there first," Steve explained.

"So you think you can make a good living even if the networking software becomes a commodity product, eh?" Willy observed.

"Well," Steve replied, "let me put it this way. I noticed that Mod-Tap has a nice do-it-yourself wiring system that people can use to put in their own level 5 cable systems. So I guess you're pretty worried, eh?"

"Oh come on!" Willy bridled. "A handful of cables and connectors does not make a certified cable system. You have to understand the structure of the network, carefully connect the resources, and then integrate all the pieces of the installation."

"Ahhh," Steve observed, "now you understand why simply having networking in the operating system isn't all there is to the problem."

IN THIS CHAPTER WE PROVIDE DETAILED OVERVIEWS OF THE BEST-SELLING and most technologically advanced network operating systems. We describe Novell's NetWare in its various flavors and pay special attention to Microsoft's networking strategy in Windows NT and Windows 4.0. We also discuss Banyan's VINES, Performance Technology's POWERlan, and Artisoft's LANtastic. Let's begin with a quick look at industry trends and the impact of competition on the various LAN operating systems.

■ Industry Trends and Evolution

Here are some things you should know:

- The major LAN operating systems are all fast enough for practically any organization's needs. Speed is only a minor factor in selecting a network operating system.

- Operating systems are becoming increasingly compatible and interoperable.

- NetWare has by far the largest market share.

- Microsoft's Wndows NT is a worthy challenger to NetWare.

- DOS-based products, such as LANtastic and POWERlan, have a cloudy future because of the networking built into Microsoft's Windows.

The size of the market and the potential for profit make for hot competition among LAN operating-system vendors. Novell, which enjoyed as much as 70 percent of the market share in PC-based networks, is no longer the only game in town. Although the current crop of network operating-system companies has not yet taken over much of Novell's market share, all of them are sinking more marketing and development dollars into their products, with Microsoft leading the way.

In 1989, network operating-system companies fueled the growth of networks by announcing and delivering products conforming to open standards instead of proprietary protocols. AT&T, Digital, and 3Com led the industry in providing interoperable products for open standards. Instead of trying to lock-in and control each account with unique communications standards, they lured buyers with software that worked according to nationally and internationally accepted standards.

In the 1990s, the companies in this market have continued to provide buyers with increased compatibility and interoperability. This trend has gone so far that now companies not only support open standards, they also deliver software for each other's proprietary protocols. Microsoft has adopted Novell's

IPX protocols as the default networking protocol for Windows NT; Performance Technology and Artisoft have become the universal clients for all network operating systems; and Novell is pursuing high-end Unix connections.

In the practical sense, support for multiple protocols means that an administrator can configure a networked PC so that the DOS F: drive is a VINES file server, the G: drive is a NetWare file server, and the H: drive is a Windows NT server. The person using this PC needn't know anything about any of these operating systems to access the data on each server. This capability is available today, but the pieces and parts must be carefully integrated so they mesh without binding.

Improved interoperability and flexibility are prime marketing and technology goals for networking software companies in the mid mid-1990s. Just as you can mix and match Ethernet adapters from different vendors, you'll be able to combine elements of network operating systems and linking servers running different operating systems on the same network, all of them supplying services to the same clients.

Performance and Other Important Factors

We learned a lot about network performance in four years of testing at PC Magazine LAN Labs, but we have also learned that some other important factors are more difficult to measure. To the average user, reliability, technical support, compatibility, and management features are more important than throughput. In terms of speed, all the operating systems described in this chapter perform well enough to meet almost anyone's computing needs.

Under a heavy network load equaling the activity of 100 client PCs, a typical file server delivers a 50K file to a client PC in 1.4 seconds—about the same performance a PC AT's hard disk supplies. Under a lighter network load, you'll get better file retrieval times from these systems than you will from a hard disk of the type usually found in 80286-based desktop machines of the late 1980s.

Another conclusion I've drawn from our testing is that a PC acting as a file server is an interactive and relatively homogeneous system, which makes it difficult to comment on the importance of one part of the system without commenting on other system parameters. For example, with today's drives, disk controllers, software, and LAN adapters, once you get to a 66 MHz 486, the speed and type of processor used in a machine acting as a file server don't seem to make much difference. The picture changes, however, when you take advantage of a modern network operating system's ability to run network management, communications, or database server programs in the same PC that is acting as a file server. These server-based applications can rapidly bog down the server's processor.

While investing in a server with a Pentium PCI or Extended Industry Standard Architecture expansion bus is generally a good idea, it won't help much if your hard disk drive system isn't adequate. However, the amount of processing power and type of interface bus you buy will make a difference in the coming years if you run more tasks in the server and install fast hard disk systems.

Modern file servers do much more than simply provide networked PCs with multiple simultaneous access to shared files and subdirectories. They have become the host for database engines that provide simple responses to complex queries from application programs. They also host other types of client/server applications such as messaging engines like Microsoft's Messaging API. Today's servers communicate with uninterruptable power supplies and take appropriate actions when the power goes out. In addition, they run network management and monitoring programs, and even hold wiring hubs for 10BaseT unshielded twisted-pair wiring systems.

RAM, RAM, and More RAM

Network operating systems consume RAM both in the client PCs and in every PC that acts as a server. On the client side, many companies have created compact programs and found ways to put the redirector and driver software elements into memory above the 640K block of RAM used by DOS.

Even as the RAM requirements for client PCs shrink, servers need more memory than ever. For example, NetWare 3.X works in a server with 2.5MB of RAM, but prefers 4MB or more, and while Windows NT operates with 8MB, Microsoft suggested we use 16MB when we installed it on our computers. The size of the hard disk drives in the server impacts the amount of memory you need. Larger drives benefit from more RAM for disk caching. If you plan to run other programs in the PC that is acting as a file server, each of them will have its own substantial memory requirements.

Client/Server Computing

The hot buzzword in the LAN operating-system market is *client/server computing*. In the client/server architecture, certain disk-intensive tasks, such as database and message services, stay on the file server. As explained in the previous chapter, this technique lowers network traffic congestion, but increases the load on the server's processor.

As you load more jobs onto the file server, it requires more RAM and processing power. As you gain power in the server, you can add more features in the LAN operating systems—and so the cycle repeats itself. New software, usually chasing the power of the latest hardware, will increase the importance of network operating systems in a growing web of computer interconnections.

My bottom-line advice on servers is simple: Buy the fastest and biggest SCSI hard disk drive system you can afford, and have it installed in a motherboard with a 486 or Pentium processor, four to six usable slots (after the video, memory, and hard disk controller are in), at least 16MB of RAM, and a power supply with at least a 300-watt rating. If you're planning to run a non-DOS operating system like NetWare, Windows NT, or Banyan VINES, consider using 32MB of memory. If the server will have more than a few dozen active clients, specify the EISA, PCI, or MCA architecture for the expansion slots, and don't forget to include an uninterruptable power supply for the server.

Networking Protocols

If you hang around with network people, you'll frequently hear the phrase "network protocols." We explain the phrase several times in this book, but the explanation bears repeating in different contexts. *Network protocols* are agreements on how data will be packaged, accounted for, and transmitted across the network. Vendors and industry committees develop the agreements, and then individual companies try to write software that conforms to them. Some initial attempts at developing conforming software are more successful than others, but after a few months of trial-and-error (often with end-users performing the trials and suffering the errors) companies usually manage to get the software right.

I bring this topic up here because specific network protocols are typically associated with each network operating system. Today, unless you are living in a world of only IBM or Digital Equipment Corporation midframe computers, you'll be concerned primarily with the IPX and TCP/IP protocols.

One of many great ideas to fall to the axe of individuality is the single protocol, keep-it-simple network. Most organizations with over a few dozen networked computers have a mix of computer and network operating systems that has evolved in response to unforseen mergers and reorganizations rather than careful planning. As networks become increasingly heterogenous, the job of networking and managing the different systems gets tougher. While there are tried-and-proven standards, managing one of these hybrid networks is still a complicated process.

Networks depend on protocols—agreements describing how things work—to reliably handle data. Although network protocols are invisible to users, the protocol architecture is one of the most important pieces you must choose when you plan and build a LAN or WAN. Except for single-vendor networks where protocols like IBM's SNA and Digital's DECnet prevail, your decision will probably come down to using Novell's SPX/IPX (Sequenced Packet Exchange/Internet Packet Exchange) or the TCP/IP (Transmission Control

Protocol/Internet Protocol) suite. Figure 8.1 shows how application data is encapsulated in TCP/IP packets.

Figure 8.1

TCP/IP data
encapsulation

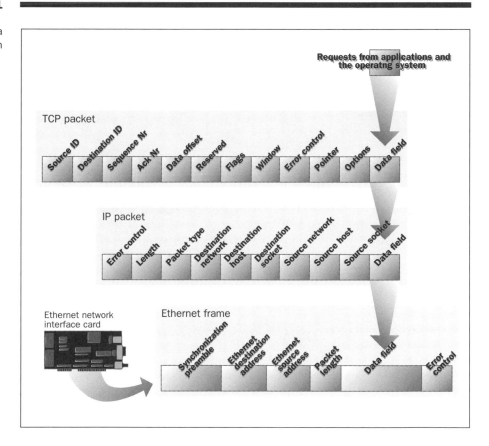

Novell's huge share of the networking market has given SPX/IPX a large installed base. Since the 1980's, Novell NetWare has based all network transport-layer communications on the SPX/IPX protocols. NetWare's success and power have drawn many other manufacturers to SPX/IPX, so you can buy everything from sophisticated analyzers to special communications programs for these protocols. At least the IPX portion of SPX/IPX is bundled with most major network operating systems including Windows, Windows NT, Artisoft's LANtastic, and Performance Technology's POWERlan.

Like other network communications protocols, SPX/IPX is not a single protocol, but a suite of standard procedures for connecting computers. In practice, each set of protocols formats a message or *packet* with specific characteristics such as addressing, receipt, or routing information. Packets are often nested three to four layers deep, so there may be a packet within a packet within a packet, each having a specific function.

The IPX part of the protocol is responsible for addressing the packets between the NetWare nodes, but it doesn't account or receipt for them. When it is used, SPX encapsulates IPX packets and receipts for the data at its destination. A few applications needing guaranteed delivery, such as network file transfers or electronic mail, can address their blocks of data through SPX. But most applications, particularly those that can monitor the success of communications for themselves, use IPX because it's more efficient and introduces less overhead into the network.

Novell's IPX is fast and efficient, particularly with the relatively small data packets—in the range of 512 bytes—usually requested by DOS or Windows applications. But small data packets aren't desirable on wide area networks with slower, expensive internetwork links because they add overhead. To hold onto its place at the top of the network world, Novell is working to enhance SPX/IPX so it performs better in an enterprise environment.

Until late 1994, Microsoft's networking products used a networking protocol called NetBIOS to carry data betwen LAN adapters. While NetBIOS is fast across small networks, the NetBIOS packets don't carry enough information for routing across inter-LAN links. Consequently, the latest versions of Windows NT and the networking capabilities in Windows use Microsoft's implementation of Novell's IPX as a primary networking protocol. Microsoft's products also work well with TCP/IP, but as I'll explain in a minute, IPX is more efficient than TCP/IP on local networks, and Microsoft backed the most efficient protocol.

The TCP/IP protocol is an open standard that was developed by the U.S. Department of Defense (DOD) to link thousands of dissimilar computers. The DOD's Defense Advanced Research Projects Agency (DARPA) developed a standard set of nonproprietary protocols that could provide communications between computers connected to a large WAN. Like SPX/IPX, TCP/IP is not a single protocol, but a suite of protocols designed to control communications services. Unlike SPX/IPX, TCP/IP is designed to provide communications between different types of computers in a truly heterogenous network.

The IP portion of the TCP/IP protocol handles the addressing between network nodes. Both IPX and IP provide the delivery mechanism for sending and receiving data. Like IPX, IP cannot guarantee the delivery of an application's data. A very simple, but important, benefit of IP is its ability to carry larger blocks of data across an internetwork link for greater efficiency. An IP packet can grow to 65,535 8-bit bytes—more than a hundred times the size of an IPX packet. That's like the difference between carrying your furniture across country on a motorcycle or in an 18-wheeler.

TCP packets encapsulate IP packets and provide the connection information services. TCP also provides the deliverability guarantee that IP lacks. Other TCP/IP services or utilities such as FTP, Telnet, and SMTP all address their requests for data transport to TCP. Unlike SPX, which is used very little in NetWare LANs, TCP is used by most applications in the TCP/IP environment because their creators anticipated running over less reliable connections.

TCP improves efficiency by a technique called *windowing*. It can transmit a number of packets while watching for acknowledgment of all packets in the window. The number of packets in the window varies with the degree of transmission success. NetWare includes a similar feature called *packet burst*, which uses the same general principle; however, packet burst is part of the higher-level NetWare Core Protocol, and not of SPX or IPX.

TCP/IP's most significant advantage over SPX/IPX is its ability to network millions of heterogenous computers over a global network. The Internet, which currently includes approximately three million networked computers, is the best example of TCP/IP's robustness across different networks and computers. Unlike SPX/IPX, which uses a broadcast technique to keep track of all the computers and services on the network, TCP/IP relies on a series of unique 32-bit addresses. Every node on a TCP/IP network must have an unique address and someone must keep track of the assignments in any organization.

This quick look at the SPX/IPX and TCP/IP protocol suites highlights their differences and drawbacks. In practice, SPX/IPX is a proven standard for PC-based LANs or WANs connected by high-speed, reliable communications devices. TCP/IP is the preferred protocol for connecting disparate computer systems over extended networks that have lower throughput and reliability.

If you only use PCs running DOS and Windows with a few Macs or OS/2 PCs on a LAN, you are certainly better off sticking with NetWare and SPX/IPX as your network communications protocol suite. The adoption of SPX/IPX by companies such as Artisoft and Microsoft makes it even easier to integrate the computers in your organization into a single network. SPX/IPX does not rely on manually assigned, independent network addresses and is much easier to install and manage than TCP/IP on a LAN or WAN. Novell also offers several solutions, including NetWare NFS and NetWare for SAA, that allow you to connect to other operating systems and computers such as mainframe and midrange systems over IPX.

Novell has taken great pains to enhance SPX/IPX services and to offer optional products for flexibility. While Novell's SPX/IPX support is flexible and customer-driven, TCP/IP is supported by a committee and by companies with many different, and possibly incompatible, interpretations of the standard. It's difficult for a customer with a TCP/IP problem to find out who to call for help.

The most appealing feature of TCP/IP is its ability to connect all of your systems together. Almost every combination of computer hardware and operating system has a driver available for the TCP/IP network protocol. If a particular company does not include a driver for TCP/IP, a third-party vendor probably makes one. SPX/IPX is widely, but not as universally, available.

Another important factor to consider is the type of software you are using. As a rule, software dictates hardware. If the software that runs your company does not work with a certain protocol stack, you are going to have to be flexible in your decisions. Most applications do not care about the protocol you are using, but certain network management utilities require a particular network driver to gather information.

Network communication protocols are becoming a commodity. Thanks to network interface card standards like NDIS and ODI, it's relatively easy to load software conforming to both protocol architectures in one PC, so they aren't mutually exclusive. Figure 8.2 illustrates how two protocol stacks can load over the same network adapter. When you are building a network, you need to decide on the protocol that offers the best performance and flexibility with the least amount of intervention and network maintenance. While hundreds of programs are available from third parties that will allow you to connect all your different computer systems using almost any network protocol, if possible, it's best to use the same protocol on your entire network.

With such factors as interoperability, compatibility, and manageability in mind, let's turn to the specific operating systems you can buy today. We'll start with the winner of many acquisition decisions, Novell's NetWare. If you are interested in the practical details of setting up and using a NetWare network, I suggest you consider the *PC Magazine Guide to Using NetWare*, ISBN 1-56276-022-X (Ziff-Davis Press, 1991), which I wrote with NetWare expert Les Freed.

■ The NetWare Family

In 1982, in a small office by the steel plant in Orem, Utah, Ray Noorda, Judith Clarke, Craig Burton, and programmers from a company called Superset foresaw what PC networking could become. At the time, their competition was from companies mainly interested in selling hard disks, like Corvus Systems, but from the beginning Novell has been directed toward providing software for integrated computing systems.

When times were tough and financial backers put pressure on Noorda to turn a quick profit, he kept Novell headed toward the longer-term goals of providing software, systems tools, and support. NetWare is now in at least its eighth major revision of a product that services more than four million people on over 400,000 LANs.

Figure 8.2

Two protocol stacks

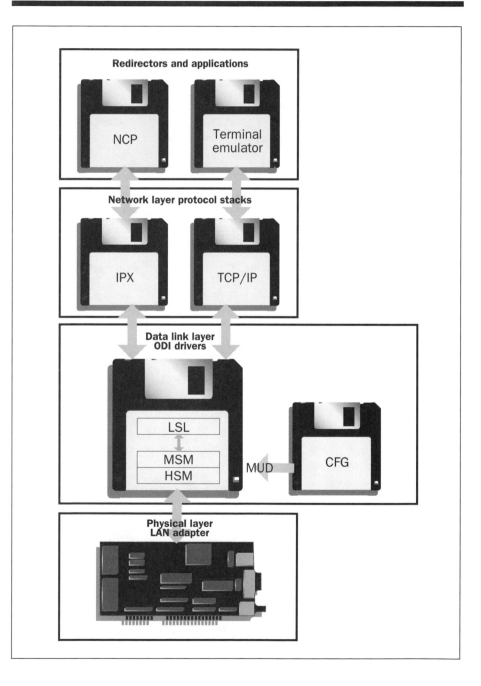

Novell's product strategy has been crystal clear and consistent: Market an operating system that offers good features and performance, and do everything possible to create the environment it needs to run. Novell is primarily a software company, but it has entered the hardware market several times to develop new products or drive down hardware prices through competition. Novell has never overtly used the "account control" strategy—raised to a fine art by IBM—to capture business. Instead, it has gone to great lengths to build outside support and even to stimulate competition. Its philosophy of "NetWare Open Systems" is in step with the current trend toward standards.

The NetWare product family has set four milestones for PC-based network operating systems:

- Novell was the first company to introduce a network operating system for true file-sharing, as opposed to simply writing private, unshared files to a shared hard disk.

- Novell led the way to hardware independence by providing NetWare with the ability to run on more than 30 brands of networks and over 100 network adapters.

- Novell reached companies needing reliability with System Fault Tolerant (SFT) NetWare. SFT NetWare ensures data integrity by including the Transaction Tracking System (TTS), disk mirroring, and disk duplexing.

- Novell introduced Open Protocol Technology (OPT). By providing a protocol-independent architecture for all NetWare services, NetWare supports heterogeneous connectivity.

Until early 1991, Novell's Entry Level System (ELS) NetWare products provided solutions for organizations in need of a small network. At that time, the company discontinued ELS NetWare and, a few months later, released a new, totally different, product called NetWare Lite. Lite was replaced in 1993 with Personal NetWare. Personal NetWare is a modern networking product that works over DOS or Windows and allows peer-to-peer file and printer sharing.

NetWare 2.X, previously known as Advanced NetWare 286, provides support for medium-sized networks (up to 100 users) and for internetwork routing services. Although it is still installed on thousands of servers around the world, Novell no longer directly supports the NetWare 2.X series. With NetWare 3.X, previously known as NetWare 386, Novell provides the industry with the necessary platform for building networked applications, in addition to incorporating all the features of previous NetWare versions. NetWare 2.X and 3.X share features such as high-performance disk caching (with elevator seeking and other techniques), strong security, and the ability to use a wide variety of network adapters.

NetWare 4.X and other products, such as versions of NetWare for Unix, represent a departure for the company. Despite statistics showing that most NetWare installations have only a dozen or so nodes, Novell is planning for upscale growth. NetWare 4.X includes a number of attributes designed for big networks with hundreds of servers spread across international boundaries.

Novell is a serious company that sets goals and maintains a good track record for meeting them. That's important to keep in mind, because a lot of NetWare's appeal stems from the promise of continued support and integrated products.

Personal NetWare

It's difficult to pin the right labels on Personal NetWare. It's a package of networking software that you can call an operating system utility because it ships as part of Novell DOS 7, but you also have to recognize it as a stand-alone product that works fine with Microsoft or IBM DOS. Personal NetWare is its own peer-to-peer network operating system—any PC can act as a file or print server across the LAN—but it's also a smooth ramp to the dedicated server versions of NetWare and, in fact, it ships as the client software in the NetWare 4.01 package. Although you can call Personal NetWare the successor to NetWare Lite, it has almost nothing in common with that earlier product.

Personal NetWare has first-class features. It allows any PC to share files, CD-ROM drives, and printers across the LAN. The software works over practically any brand of Ethernet, Token-Ring, or ARCnet networking hardware. Its design allows anyone designated as a member of a workgroup—Accounting, for example—to log in only once and gain access to all servers. This is very different from the server-by-server logins required for most peer-to-peer LAN systems. The use of SNMP network management also differentiates Personal NetWare from its peer-to-peer competitors.

Unlike the half-finished feel of the old NetWare Lite, Personal NetWare is fully integrated and interoperable. The Personal NetWare server module (SERVER.EXE) that runs under the memory management system in DOS 7 puts all but about 40K of the server software in high memory. The client software hides completely in extended memory, while other modules, such as those used to link to a NetWare 3.X server, load as needed. Unlike the highly competitive Windows 4.0 and Windows NT, Personal NetWare has excellent Windows and DOS interfaces.

On the bottom line, Personal NetWare is both an important stand-alone product and a good networking partner for Novell's DOS 7 operating system.

NetWare 2.X

In the late 1980s, shipments of NetWare 2.X accounted for much of Novell's $500 million annual revenue; however, by 1992 NetWare 3.X overtook the older operating system and in 1994 Novell stopped shipping 2.X in favor of the newer product. However, since there are still tens of thousands of NetWare 2.X installations around the world, I'll describe it briefly here. NetWare 2.X services medium-sized networks of up to 100 users. It can work with data files up to 255MB in size, which is a limitation in certain classes of applications. Theoretically, however, you can attach up to 32 gigabytes of data storage to a single server. The SFT version of NetWare 2.X adds disk mirroring and duplexing, providing networks with added reliability.

Under NetWare 2.X, one computer acts as the server that provides file and print services. The software does allow you to set up remote print servers around the network.

Novell bases all network transport-layer communications on its own IPX and SPX protocols. IPX, NetWare's native network communications protocol, moves data between server and/or workstation programs running on different network nodes. IPX usually exchanges data with the NetWare shell, but it also works with the NetBIOS emulator available in NetWare, and with programs such as terminal-emulation packages that exchange data with communications servers. SPX is an enhanced set of commands implemented on top of IPX that allow additional functions, one of which is guaranteed delivery.

Tests at PC Magazine LAN Labs have consistently shown the advantage of SPX/IPX for typical PC applications. Applications running on PCs generally request data in small blocks—often as small as 512 bytes. SPX/IPX is better suited to moving small blocks than are the transport protocols of competing operating systems such as Banyan's VINES and Microsoft's Windows NT. These products excel in tasks that use larger blocks, such as LAN-to-LAN communications.

If you need NetBIOS service for applications like 3270 terminal emulation, Novell provides an efficient NetBIOS API for SPX/IPX. You simply type "NetBIOS" on the PC that needs the NetBIOS service, and DOS loads a 40K program giving SPX/IPX the ability to use the NetBIOS application-program interface. Because NetWare 2.X is not a peer-to-peer operating system, the workstations on the network cannot share their resources without the addition of third-party products.

NetWare has an excellent security system that offers many options. The primary security structure assigns people to groups, each of which has specific rights. Of course, a group can consist of one person or hundreds of people. This structure works well in organizations of any size, and is particularly useful in companies that have high personnel turnover or where people move between jobs. The network administrator can easily add a person to or delete a person from a group such as Accounts Payable and be certain of effective security. Additionally, administrators can restrict the days and even the times when users can log onto the network. Forced periodic password changes require all users to adopt new passwords at selected time intervals.

The only drawback of NetWare's security system is that it requires you to create and update the data identifying groups, rights, and users on every file server separately. In large multiserver networks, this becomes an endless task for network administrators. As I describe later, Novell has come up with a response to this problem in NetWare Naming Service.

Overall, probably NetWare 286's biggest shortcoming is its print-spooling software, which is generally difficult to use and not as fast as that of competing products. Fortunately, printer-enhancement programs—notably PS-Print from Brightwork Development and LANSpool from Intel—can aid network printing by improving throughput and allowing client stations to make printers available across the network.

Electronic mail can be a tremendous asset to any organization. NetWare does not include e-mail, but Novell does include an important service that third-party e-mail systems can use. Message Handling Service (MHS) is a piece of software that runs on a single PC in the network and transmits users' messages between e-mail and other application packages.

Until the middle of 1989, Novell's NetWare 2.X was the standard of comparison for network operating systems. When the rest of the field started closing in on NetWare's speed and security, Novell released a new product, NetWare 386. NetWare 386 takes full advantage of the power in the Intel 80386 and 80486 processors. NetWare 386 and existing NetWare 2.X servers can coexist on the same network, and you don't have to make any changes to the client workstation's software to give them access to all NetWare servers.

NetWare 3.X

In NetWare 3.X, Novell provides the industry with a powerful platform for building client/server applications. NetWare 3.X is very fast; what's more, it doesn't degrade under heavy processing loads, and it provides huge amounts of storage. NetWare 3.X is a rich environment for the introduction of a new generation of applications.

Many of us can remember the days when people thought a 20MB hard disk would handle all their future storage requirements. Although it's tough to predict the future, you won't outgrow the RAM access and disk storage capability of NetWare 3.X anytime soon. By the same token, outfitting a PC with NetWare's theoretical maximums is not presently possible. You would find another alternative before sitting through a PC's memory check of 4 gigabytes of RAM (1G = 1,000MB).

Specifications

NetWare 3.X is a true 32-bit network operating system designed for use on Intel 80386, 80486, and Pentium processors. If NetWare 3.X detects the presence of a 486 or Pentium processor, it takes advantage of that chip's advanced features by executing longer instructions (more commands per CPU cycle). The file system in NetWare 3.X continues all the old tricks of elevator seeking, I/O queuing, and disk caching that it gained from NetWare 2.X , but it adds huge capacity. Sporting a maximum disk space of 32 terabytes (1TB = 1,000,000MB), NetWare 3.X can handle the largest organization's data load. Volumes can span multiple drives, and you can have files as big as 4 gigabytes. That means a single data file may be spread across several hard disks, and your application will never know the difference.

Gone are NetWare 2.X's limit of 100 users and 1,000 open files. NetWare 3.X allows each server up to 250 users and 100,000 open files. If a rare application requires 100 simultaneously open files (for example, multiple data tables, indexes, help files, and drivers), the old NetWare 286 can allow only 10 users simultaneous access to that application. Under NetWare 3.X, 250 users can run the same program with capacity to spare, and Novell has made provisions for adding still more users in subsequent releases.

The maturity of NetWare 3.X shows in the way it reports error messages. When I mistakenly left the cable from a NetWare 3.X server disconnected and tried to start the operating system, it responded with an on-screen message saying, "The network cable is not connected to the computer." That's a pretty clear error message! Another time, a NetWare 3.X server sent me a special message reporting that it was receiving an unusual number of bad packets from one of the client stations. When I inspected the network connection, I saw a small crack in the T-connector. These are good examples of how NetWare 3.X helps a network administrator succeed.

NetWare 3.X includes two security enhancements: security auditing and encrypted backups. A security auditing function keeps a nonmodifiable audit trail of all security changes occurring on the server. Moreover, as NetWare backs up files over the network, the data is sent and stored in encrypted form, and is unencrypted only when it returns to the server after a restore.

NLMs

NetWare Loadable Modules (NLMs) are applications—often developed by companies other than Novell—that run in the file server. This category includes simple programs like drivers for micro channel cards, complex but familiar products like SNA and electronic-mail gateways or network backup services, and products for network management, security, and workgroup productivity. NLMs allow the powerful server to replace the dedicated network machines you might be using today as SNA gateways, electronic-mail gateways, and communications servers—but not without some risk.

While NLMs offer great functionality, they run in the same machine and at the same time as the file-server software. If the file-server hardware malfunctions, you lose all the functions it contains. (In today's most common network configuration, with separate PCs acting as different kinds of servers, if the file server goes down you can still use SNA gateways and some other services operating on separate machines on the network.) What's more, if some task requires it, an NLM can access the kernel of the NetWare 3.X operating system. If the NLM crashes, it can potentially bring down the file server.

The remote-console NLM allows system administrators to monitor server information from their workstations. This feature is a network administrator's dream. An administrator can sit at any workstation and monitor any server on the network. In addition, the administrator's computer acts as though it actually is the server console, allowing an administrator to load and unload NLMs and completely control the server. An NLM called Aconsole allows dial-in modem access to the management functions.

The print-services NLM provides the spooling and queuing of print jobs for up to eight printers. It also allows authorized users to access and manipulate print jobs. The print-services NLM supports printers attached to local workstations, and manages up to 16 printers on the network. This flexibility lets organizations do high-volume printing at the most convenient and secure locations.

To keep just anyone from adding an NLM to the server, Novell includes the Secure Console option, restricting anyone but the system administrator from adding NLMs or server applications. Another feature that makes the system manager's life simpler is the new Workgroup Manager classification. As the name implies, a person with this description has supervisor privileges for the users assigned to a particular workgroup.

With add-on NLMs, NetWare 3.X also supports Network File System (NFS), a file-server program widely used in the Unix world. In addition, it gains better support for Macintosh computers acting as clients to the NetWare server. Servers running the optional NFS and Macintosh NLMs can store files from Unix and Macintosh computers in their native formats.

Programming for NetWare

The hefty NetWare 3.X shipping box includes diskettes with all the programming tools necessary to create distributed applications. The C Network Compiler comes complete with the Watcom C Compiler and Linker, a C graphics library, the Btrieve library, the Express C editor, the NetWare API Library, and a windowing debugger. Programmers can use these tools to create DOS-,

Windows-, and OS/2-based workstation front ends for accessing the server applications.

For creating NLMs, Novell provides the C Network Compiler/386, which has all the same functions as the regular compiler but is specific to the 80386 processor and NLMs. Along with these compiler packages, Novell includes NetWare Remote Procedural Calls and the NetWare Streams specification. Streams is AT&T's name for its method of handling many simultaneous tasks with the Unix operating system.

Since programmers can access the kernel of NetWare 3.X, a book, *NetWare Theory of Operations,* comes with the NetWare Programmer's Workbench to warn developers about the potential impact of actions inside the kernel, where the slightest mistake can bring down the server. To provide additional guidance, Novell also offers classes for NLM system developers.

Installation

You can install NetWare 3.X faster—and with less hassle—than you can Microsoft's Windows. To bring the server to life, the system administrator needs only to identify what types of network card and hard disk are installed. I've installed the operating system and had users logged on within about 15 minutes, not counting the time it took to prepare the hard disk. This is a far cry from the several hours required to bring up an early NetWare 286 file server.

Upgrading from NetWare 2.X to NetWare 3.X requires you to reformat your hard disk. NetWare 3.X boots from a DOS partition (or floppy disk) and then runs the SERVER.EXE program, which in turn accesses the Net-Ware partition.

On the client PC side, NetWare 3.X gives OS/2 client stations full IPX/SPX, NetBIOS, and Named Pipes support. The introduction of Named Pipes paves the way for applications using this powerful peer-to-peer communications architecture.

The memory-saving capabilities of the NetWare shell software please DOS users. By supporting expanded and extended memory, NetWare frees 34K of conventional memory for applications. Users of client PCs can unload NetBIOS and the workstation software to free memory when they don't need the network.

Novell provides companies moving from NetWare 2.X to NetWare 3.X a smooth transition. If you have extra hard-disk space available on another server, simply copy the entire server that is being upgraded to another one. After installing NetWare 3.X, run the MIGRATE program, which converts all of your NetWare 2.X system information, including passwords, user rights, and mappings, to the new format.

Functions

One useful feature of NetWare 3.X is Dynamic Resource Configuration (DRC). System administrators and users alike benefit from this artificial intelligence-type feature. NetWare 2.X requires the system manager to allocate specific amounts of memory for directory caching and routing buffers, and to bring the server down any time these values change. With NetWare 3.X, not only can these values change with the server up, but the operating system itself determines the optimal values and adjusts them on the fly.

A few other new or enhanced features are also of interest. The Multiple Name Spaces feature allows NetWare 3.X to handle files from different operating systems. NetWare 3.X associates different file names with the same file if it will be used by different operating systems. For example, a Microsoft Excel file used by both the DOS and Apple versions of Excel would have two file entries on the server.

NetWare 3.X provides added data security with file-salvaging and encryption features. One file-salvaging option automatically purges all deleted files, and another maintains all deleted files until NetWare runs out of disk space. When NetWare needs more disk space, it purges on a first-deleted basis, and the system manager can purge all recoverable files at any time. NetWare preserves security by letting only users with proper authorization undelete a file. In addition to encrypting passwords on the server, NetWare 3.X encrypts them on the wire, preventing network analyzers like Novell's LANalyzer from reading what the client PC sends to the server.

The system also includes NetWare Management Agent for NetVIEW. This group of NLMs enables a NetWare 3.X server with a Token-Ring adapter installed to forward NetVIEW-specific alerts to an IBM host running NetVIEW, which is an IBM network maintenance program.

A significant and useful feature in NetWare 3.X is TCP/IP support at the server. Transmission Control Protocol/Internet Protocol (TCP/IP) is a standard that provides connectivity across computer platforms ranging from mainframes to Macintoshes. These computers can exchange data when connected over a compatible network scheme, such as Ethernet or X.25.

The Multiprotocol Router

NetWare 3.X has a capability that can be invaluable to any manager of a modern network—the ability to establish a multiprotocol router in the server. *Routers*, described further in Chapter 13, are devices that move traffic between otherwise independent LAN segments based on the address of the destination station and on other information they read inside packets created by networking software conforming to protocols like IPX, IP, NetBIOS, or AppleTalk. Multiprotocol routers are often stand-alone devices with their own processing capabilities and price tags running to many thousands of dollars. However, each copy of NetWare provides the capability to establish a multiprotocol router in the NetWare file server.

For example, assume you have two LAN segments using Novell's IPX over Token-Ring, another segment using IP over Ethernet, and a fourth segment using IPX over Ethernet. In this example, each LAN segment has its own file and print servers for its client PCs (note that they could be NetWare servers but they don't have to be); however, the IPX over Ethernet LAN segment also has a PC that acts as a gateway to a mainframe computer, and some nodes on all of the LAN segments occasionally need to access the mainframe through that gateway. If you equip one NetWare server with two Token-Ring adapters and two Ethernet adapters with appropriate drivers for each LAN segment, you can run a multiprotocol router NLM that will move packets as needed between all the LAN segments. Client PCs can run mainframe terminal emulation software compatible with the shared gateway software and use the services of the gateway through the server acting as a router.

A NetWare 3.X server can even route among LocalTalk, EtherTalk, and TokenTalk in the same server, providing connectivity to several normally isolated LANs. LocalTalk is Apple's network hardware, while EtherTalk and TokenTalk are versions of AppleTalk that run over Ethernet and Token-Ring cabling. As the size of modern networks increases, so does their need to interconnect. Novell's multiprotocol router is an important tool in the LAN-to-LAN connectivity of modern organizations.

Packet Burst

One of the most useful and interesting networking features introduced in NetWare 3.X and carried into NetWare 4.X is *Packet Burst* mode. The Packet Burst software, which is implemented in the BNETX.COM file on a client PC and in PBURST.NLM on the server, lets your network go beyond NetWare's 512-byte packet limit so it can use expensive long-distance communications circuits more efficiently.

It has been widely, but incorrectly, reported that Novell's IPX protocol requires an acknowledgment for every packet. Actually, it's the higher-level NetWare Core Protocol (NCP) that imposes the SEND-ACK sequence on IPX. This sequence is a reasonable precaution on LAN cables that use signaling speeds of many megabits per second, but it becomes a burden on long-distance lines operating at ranges of 56 kilobits to just over one megabit per second.

According to Novell, IPX has always been capable of sending packets without acknowledgment using a technique called a *datagram protocol*. Novell's Packet Burst software allows a client PC to create IPX packets of up to 64K and to send those packets back-to-back without waiting for acknowledgment.

This type of transmission makes the most efficient use of an expensive long-distance, low-speed circuit.

The amount of throughput you gain using Burst mode instead of the traditional NetWare transmission scheme depends on factors such as how much data the client PCs write versus how much they read, the size of the files, and how applications handle the data. Writing is a one-way task, while reading demands a response, but if an application only handles data in small blocks, nothing the underlying network software does will be of benefit. You'll see a bigger cumulative improvement as you move bigger files.

The improvement figures range from as much as an ideal 400 percent gain to around 100 percent in typical applications. Clearly, by doubling your throughput you can avoid investing several thousand dollars a month in a higher-speed leased line, so it's a prudent step. Interestingly, Novell reports throughput gains of up to 50 percent using Burst mode on regular Ethernet and Token-Ring systems due to reduced overhead, but any gain you might see will vary widely.

You pay for using Burst mode in client PC RAM. The maximum size of the IPX packet you allow drives the amount of conventional memory used for buffers in the client PC. If you allow 64K packets, you might forfeit slightly more than 128K of conventional memory to the Burst mode software, although you can control the configuration. You don't have to use the Burst mode software in all the client PCs, just those that will benefit from it. Burst and non-burst clients can communicate with burst-equipped servers.

The NetWare 3.X Bottom Line

NetWare 3.X is everything users and application developers could ask for in a network OS. For users, the file system is fast, reliable, and spacious. System maintenance is simple, and you can expand your network in terms of both the number of users and the number of file servers. NetWare 3.X also provides programmers with a platform and all the necessary tools for creating next-generation server applications.

NetWare 4.X

"Where is SYSCON?" The absence of SYSCON, the comfortable management utility used by tens of thousands of NetWare administrators, underlines the difference between NetWare 4.X and its predecessors. NetWare 4.X isn't an upgrade to Novell's popular NetWare 3.X. It wraps the core NetWare file and print services with a new architecture aimed at the multiserver market. New utilities, which enable a new naming technology, replace SYSCON. Figure 8.3 sows the NetWare 4.X naming structure.

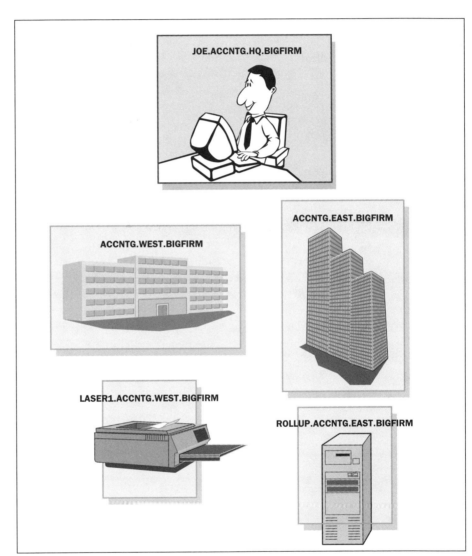

Here is my advice: If you have six active NetWare 3.X file servers, it's time
to consider the change to NetWare 4.X. If you have a dozen servers, the management benefits of 4.X are persuasive, but if you have only a few servers, are
happy with SYSCON, and have your login scripts working the way you want
them to, you don't have much reason to spend around $4,000 for a 25-user ver-
sion of NetWare 4.X.

The most obvious change in NetWare 4.X is its packaging. The standard price brings you a CD-ROM holding the software and documentation. If you need diskettes or printed documentation, there's an extra charge.

The major architectural changes to NetWare 4.X begin with a naming service that globally positions each user and resource in the network. In practical terms, this means each user logs in only once instead of logging into every server. NetWare 4.X includes file data compression so your server's drives can hold nearly twice as much data—a feature that can offset the price of the software by avoiding a hard disk upgrade. Upcoming versions of NetWare 4.X for Unix and OS/2 will complement the native version to meet corporate needs for servers running on different operating systems and computer hardware.

On the client side, the new NetWare shell, VLM.EXE, handles global naming requirements. VLM.EXE can look like NETX, so it works with NetWare 2.X and 3.X servers. A much needed innovation allows you to load and unload the client software under Windows. The client software comes with drivers for approximately 150 adapters and runs over Microsoft's NDIS if you have a rare adapter that doesn't use Novell's ODI. The client software also includes Novell's Burst mode client support, which improves throughput in some applications by streaming data without waiting for acknowledgment.

You can install the software in less than 15 minutes including the time it takes to read the documentation. During our evaluation, the upgrade utility built a 4.X server over our existing 3.12 server and kept the 3.12 user and resource names. If one person has accounts on several 3.12 servers, you'll have to give that person a single global name manually. You'll need a backup to restore the data files after an upgrade, so be certain your restore function works before you start the upgrade. If you select file compression, 4.X will immediately give you more disk space; the amount you'll gain depends on the nature of your files.

The installation is quick, but properly naming the server during setup can take days of study. The new NetWare Directory Services (NDS) replaces the server-by-server management process of earlier NetWare with a global naming scheme in which all servers know the rights of all users. When you answer the naming questions on any server you must have the whole structure in mind and understand how this particular server relates to all the others.

Planning the NDS naming structure is like planning the layout for all the directories and subdirectories on a hard disk drive before you load the data. NDS uses the same kind of root and tree organization, and you can make as many layers of branches as you need, but the top-level directories are key. The structure should have enough layers so you can add servers in a logical sequence, but you must limit the number of layers to reduce complexity. For example, the name LASER.ACCOUNTING.4THFLOOR might work for an organization that will never extend the network beyond one building, but another organizations might need a more specific name such as LASER.ACCNTG.4THFLOOR.NEWYORK.NAMERICA-.COMPANY.BIGFIRM for the same resource. Fortunately, NDS lets you designate aliases that represent the longer identification, so the same printer might be known by the alias NYLASER in this large organization's accounting departments around the world.

The global nature of the NDS drives other changes. For example, the servers recognize time zone changes when they update the time. Also, the NDS traffic is encrypted with a sophisticated public key encryption standard to keep security tight.

Although you can intermix NetWare version 3.X and 4.X servers on the same network, you have to manage them separately, so you're motivated to upgrade all the servers. In a mixed network, there is a tricky incompatibility in the underlying Etherent frames coming from a 4.X server. The drivers in early versions of NetWare conformed to an Ethernet protocol that has since changed. Unlike Netware 2.X and early versions of 3.X, version 4.X conforms to the current IEEE 802.2 standards. If you want the 4.X server to be compatible with earlier NetWare, you must make sure a "frame=" line in AUTOEXEC.NCF loads the 802.3 drivers.

Adopting NetWare 4.X is a strategic corporate decision. Installers and administrators will need training to learn how to set up and support the system, and changing the naming service will cause turmoil. Novell has announced other strategic options for 4.X, including the ability to run NetWare Loadable Modules (NLMs) on PCs, wiring hubs, and other devices across the network, and an imaging service for handling large image files. NetWare 4.X has memory management and protection features that make it more efficient at running NLMs. Adopting 4.X is a big step, but if you have a big network the product has a lot of appeal. Table 8.1 lists some of the differences between NetWare 4.X and NetWare 3.12.

Table 8.1 ▬▬▬▬▬▬▬▬▬▬▬▬▬▬▬▬▬▬▬▬▬▬▬▬▬▬▬▬▬▬▬

NetWare Comparison

VERSION 4.X	VERSION 3.12
Global naming	Server-by-server naming
Active security	Not available
Imaging option	Not available
Expanded Windows	Basic Windows
Packet Burst mode	Optional

■ VINES

Banyan System's VINES (VIrtual NEtworking Software) is a network operating system that delivers some of the complexity and features found in traditional minicomputer software. The VINES system is actually a series of applications running over a special version of AT&T's Unix operating system, but the Unix layer is hidden by VINES and is not available for other application programs. A PC running VINES typically performs all server functions, including acting as a communications server. This concentration of functions makes the system's multiprocessor capabilities particularly important.

The technical specifications for VINES put it in competition with Net-Ware 4.X and Windows NT, but both Novell and Microsoft have more agressive expansion and development plans in place than Banyan does. VINES' main claim to fame has been its ability to connect widely separated file servers efficiently through a variety of long-distance communications alternatives. For this reason, VINES finds its best acceptance in large network installations. However, Novell's NetWare 4.X is aimed directly at the same market.

Banyan pioneered the use of global naming services, a valuable feature for networks with many file servers, which has been emulated by Novell and Microsoft. Banyan calls its naming service StreetTalk. StreetTalk provides a way of naming resources and users located on various servers and nodes across the network. The VINES software lets you assign each resource a name in the form "Item@Group@Organization" and a password. Every server maintains and updates a universal Access Rights List (ARL) containing the StreetTalk names of the resources and the users allowed access to each resource. The administrator doesn't have to log onto each server and configure resources and user rights; one step does it all. This technique makes it easy to establish a high level of resource security and reduces the administrator's workload.

VINES also includes a feature called StreetTalk Directory Assistance (STDA). STDA replicates directory information on multiple servers throughout the network so users can find network resources faster. This feature is most useful for extremely large networks that have multiple servers.

One feature that sets VINES apart from the popular Novell and Microsoft LAN operating systems is the fact that StreetTalk allows users to access gateway services, mail systems, print queues, fax gateways, and host gateways with a single password. Another advantage Banyan has over the competition is its experience in client/server computing. VINES offered SQL database operations on the server years before other products did.

Banyan is also committed to supporting industry standards. In cooperation with Microsoft, Banyan has given VINES the ability to work with SMB, NDIS, NetBIOS, Named Pipes, mailslots, and Windows NT APIs. Because VINES can work with this acronym-laden list of interfaces, companies writing application software for networks have a common development environment that lets them master one technique for communicating between nodes on the network. Consequently there's a larger potential market for their products.

The VINES operating system uses a specially designed version of Unix V to run on computers that have multiple processors. Unlike other multiprocessor operating systems that assign specific types of tasks to specific processors, VINES divides tasks evenly among the processors by finely parsing the stream of work and assigning tasks to the available processors on a first-free-first-tasked basis. VINES can assign tasks to as many as eight 80386, 80486, or Pentium processors in a single PC.

VINES provides an all-in-one-box solution for connecting to remote servers and transferring data to other servers, SNA gateways, async services, database servers, and mail servers. Banyan also offers a host of communications products aimed at minicomputers and mainframes. These include products for server-to-server communication within the LAN, over a wide-area network, or through an X.25 network, as well as products for 3270/SNA terminal emulation, e-mail, and remote network management.

As a communications server, a computer running VINES has a variety of ways of connecting to IBM mainframes. For example, Banyan's 3174 Emulation/Token-Ring product allows a VINES server to communicate with an IBM computer using the SNA communications protocol over a Token-Ring network, or through an IBM 3174 controller or 3745/372X communications processor. This feature lets people use a single IBM Token-Ring network for both PC-to-host and PC-to-server traffic, and provides greater throughput when accessing the host.

Additional Token-Ring support comes through a feature called source-level routing. This technique allows VINES servers or clients to communicate across IBM Token-Ring bridges to remote VINES servers, so users gain flexibility in configuring Token-Ring networks. Another feature, Token-Ring bridge emulation, puts the bridge function inside the server and eliminates the need for dedicated PCs operating as Token-Ring bridges; however, this places some added load on the server's processor.

Overall, Banyan's VINES is a strong contender in the mainstream network operating system market. NetWare and Windows NT provide faster throughput than VINES file servers for PCs running typical applications, but VINES' throughput is good enough to support dozens of client PCs on one 386 PC acting as a file, print, and communications server.

■ Microsoft's Networking Strategy: Networking Everywhere

A psychologist coined the term "Aha! Phenomenon" to describe what takes place when developments click together and you see things from a new perspective. Microsoft's plan for networking is a set of developments that should set your "Aha! Phenomenon" in motion. The primary insight you'll discover is that networking is now everywhere in Microsoft's products, and nothing in the computing world will ever be the same. Microsoft started this trend in late 1992 by introducing a product called Windows for Workgroups. Windows for Workgroups was an advanced version of Windows that included both client and server software in every package. In the same time frame, a product called LAN Manager was supposed to carry the high-end server role for Microsoft. Windows for Workgroups and LAN Manager both had their ups and downs, but they became the root stock for the successful integration of networking into the lower-level versions of Windows and Windows NT. Now, networking is part of everything and other companies that make network operating systems, including Novell, must adapt, evolve, or die. Figure 8.4 shows how easy it is to connect to a networked drive.

Figure 8.4

Connecting to a network

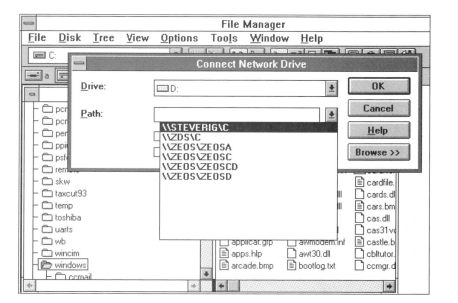

Starting with Windows 95, Microsoft's Windows comes with peer-to-peer networking built-in. With this product, any Windows PC can be a server or a client for any other Windows or DOS PC. While the availability of ubiquitous networking is interesting, in the long run, the most exciting development networked Windows brings to the market is its ability link not just computers, but Windows application programs across networks. Through these networked links, programs can automatically exchange and modify portions of files and documents. This feature allows you to link specific chunks of spreadsheets, drawings, text files, and other types of data objects into documents and presentations that are being constructed simultaneously on several networked machines. As one person changes a spreadsheet or drawing, it automatically updates its image wherever it has been pasted into documents and presentations. These behind-the-scenes links between programs will—in the long run—change the way end-users interact with networks and the way people work together.

Once we have ubiquitous and invisible networks with automated links between applications, a new picture of networking snaps into focus. Instead of simply sharing your C drive as the next person's D drive, you and your colleagues are suddenly doing cooperative, interactive work in real time. Now you can develop a document perspective instead of viewing your tasks according to the applications they require. You also have a completely new way of linking programs people use for online transaction processing—jobs like making reservations and taking orders; a new way to build process modeling and control programs ranging from war games to models of virus growth; and an excellent basis for interactive information services or games. Given nearly automatic installation of the networking software, the work of network managers shifts to linking applications and the activity of end-users becomes computer-aided, cooperative workgroup efforts.

No matter how much or how little you use Windows, you can't dispute its importance and popularity. In May 1992 Microsoft's monthly shipments of Windows began to surpass those of DOS, and the curve of Windows' use shoots practically straight up. Windows comes bundled with, and usually installed on, nine out of ten of the best-selling brands of PCs. Almost all new software development for PCs is being done under Windows.

Adding networking to Windows expands its power and appeal by giving PCs running Windows the ability to make disk drives, subdirectories, and devices like CD ROM drives and attached printers available to other DOS and Windows PCs across a wide variety of network adapters and cabling schemes. PCs running DOS can use Windows servers by loading the Microsoft Workgroup Connection or DOS client software from companies like Artisoft or Performance Technologies.

Windows NT

Windows NT (New Technology) is a separate branch of the Windows family. NT has full multithreaded and multitasking capabilities that Windows lacks. This means the computer can do several tasks, including communications, at one time without faltering. The NT server package also delivers better security than Windows. Both Windows and Windows NT make extensive use of 32-bit operations to quickly move data that's inside the computer.

The single biggest advantage of Windows NT is the increased speed gained from Microsoft's NT File System (NTFS), which is a departure from the original File Allocation Table (FAT)-based system developed for floppy disks well over ten years ago. At that time, hard disks for PCs were rare. In the early 1980s, their increasing popularity necessitated patches to DOS that did not manage large amounts of data efficiently. Like NetWare 3.X, Windows NT can handle gigabyte-sized files and heavy traffic loads.

Developers can use the WIN32 System Developer's Kit to write applications for both Windows and Windows NT. The SDK allows developers to create a single program that will run on both Windows 95 and Windows NT. Under Windows 95, these products can use a 32-bit flat memory model that allows developers to move data in bigger and more efficient blocks and take advantage of the 32-bit registers in 80386, 80486, and Pentium processors.

One unique attribute of Windows NT is designed to appeal to government and corporate users by providing data security meeting the U.S. government's C2 rating. But this architecture means NT must maintain total control, and cannot allow applications to take shortcuts by communicating directly with the hardware. This consideration also limits the compatibility of any application or driver that is not written according to specific guidelines.

Windows NT has the ability to use symmetrical multiprocessing—that is, to allocate tasks to two or more CPUs simultaneously—on hardware from NCR and other companies, and it includes TCP/IP network drivers. But on the bottom line, if you don't need the high security, extra reliability, or symmetrical multiprocessing of Windows NT, choose Windows 95 or later to run your modern applications and integrate your networking needs, because the overall cost of the software and equipment will be less.

Getting the Message

Windows and Windows NT now include a special version of Microsoft Mail 3.0. While this product lets you handle the usual electronic mail chores, it lacks many of the Post Office management features of the full Microsoft Mail package, and it can't use gateways. Importantly though, the mail program acts as an underlying engine to help link other workgroup applications. Overall, it is an excellent e-mail package for a workgroup in a single office, but if you want to add links to other mail systems or to remote callers you'll either need a full version of Microsoft Mail or you'll have to add an optional Microsoft program called the Mail Transfer Agent that completes connections to gateways.

The mail product enables another major application included in the Windows packages, Microsoft Schedule+. Schedule+, shown in Figure 8.5, is a full-strength networked scheduling program that allows you to maintain your local calendar while also coordinating appointments with others in your workgroup. The package shows conflicts in the calendars of people you want to invite to meetings, suggests free times, provides reminder alarms, and includes all the other expected functions. In short, Schedule+ is a full-power scheduling package that competes well with other stand-alone programs.

Figure 8.5

Microsoft Schedule+ provides a flexible way to schedule individual appointments and to coordinate them within a group.

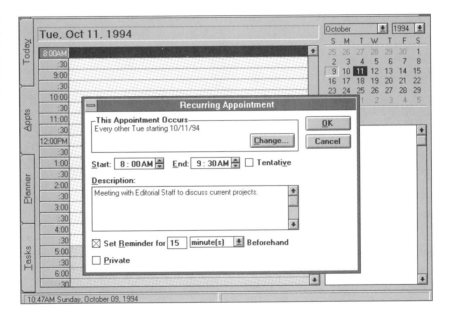

Schedule+ reads the list of authorized user names from the mail program and uses mail to communicate throughout the workgroup. Unfortunately, because Windows focuses on the names of computers instead of people, the mail program can't read user names from a central database as Microsoft Mail can from NetWare. Someone has to enter each user's name, mailbox name, and an optional password, and keeping this information current can add to the network administrator's chores.

The good news about the mail service is that it provides an underlying "engine" for new workgroup applications from Microsoft and other developers. These products use the concept of business forms to automate and manage interactive work between people in busy offices. The forms pass routing information to the mail system so that certain processes—accepting a credit application, for example—can be started by one person and routed automatically and simultaneously to the people responsible for collateral tasks, such as approval and notification.

Windows Protocols

Microsoft made a smart move by bundling network communications software for Novell's IPX protocol into Windows. The IPX protocol and ODI drivers are options you can load either during installation or at a later time. Under Windows you can simultaneously log into other Windows PCs and to NetWare servers. The NetWare server can even host the Microsoft Mail network mailbox, which is actually a file subdirectory on the server.

In effect, present users of NetWare can add the functions of Windows networking without losing the dedicated NetWare features. You can have both the shared links between applications offered by Windows networking and the elaborate server management, communications, and routing features of the higher powered NetWare server software at the same time. Some users on the network can elect to make disk drives, shared printers, or CD-ROM drives available through Windows while everyone continues to use the dedicated server for primary file operations.

If you don't want to contribute or use shared drives under Windows, you don't have to. But if you want to take advantage of available resources they simply appear as more DOS disk drive letters or LPT ports. The drag-and-drop file transfer feature is also available on all networked and local drives.

You can use Windows' ability to link programs today, but more specialized applications with built-in linking will soon appear. Figure 8.6 shows a present-day example. Assume three people have the job of generating a weekly report: One creates the text and a written document in Microsoft Word; the second juggles numbers in an Excel spreadsheet; and the third generates slides in PowerPoint. The people using Word and PowerPoint can paste and link specific segments (selected by the Clipboard COPY command) from the Excel spreadsheet into each application so their documents and slides always include the latest data and interpretation. For example, as the person using PowerPoint moves through the presentation, macros read-in linked elements created by the other programs. The other programs don't have to be active, but the files must be linked either automatically through macros or manually through the shared ClipBook.

Linking applications through macros is a task for someone with programming skills, but anyone can establish links through the menus. Once someone has practiced the steps, which aren't completely intuitive, using the ClipBook becomes simple. When one person copies an object—a piece of a picture,

Figure 8.6

A person working on the PC labeled "Source" creates a bar chart in a spreadsheet. Via menu commands contained in Windows for Workgroups, this chart is available for linking across the LAN. People using word processing and presentation software at the other PCs can link to the shared chart and integrate it into documents and presentations. There are various linking options, but in the most complex link-up as any one person changes the chart everyone sees the changes simultaneously.

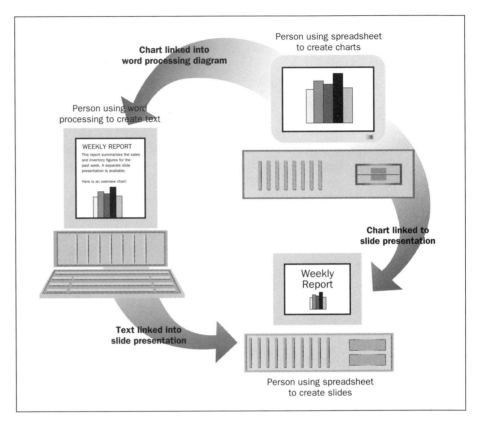

some text, or part of a spreadsheet—into a shared ClipBook, it can appear on all other Windows for Workgroups PCs as a selection in the ClipBook viewer, a new utility in the Windows Main menu. If you don't want everyone to have access, the shared ClipBook can be password protected.

While a few network managers will tackle writing the macros needed to integrate a weekly report, developers will provide many specialized applications. This architecture can challenge present-day database technology in many transaction processing applications; however, it provides an excellent way to track projects and manage work, and it's a great basis for building interactive games.

If invisible and ubiquitous networking is your goal, you've got to provide nearly automatic installation. The Windows networking software has the unique ability to recognize and automatically load drivers for nearly 200 makes and models of LAN adapters. If the adapter can be totally configured by software, as many products from Intel, 3Com, Madge, SMC, and other vendors can, the software takes care of everything. If the adapter has jumpers or switches, the software asks you to confirm the default settings or enter new ones. You'll only get truly automatic and seamless network installations in PCs equipped with fully programmable or on-the-motherboard LAN adapters, but the software will give you hints about IRQ and memory address combinations even for hardware-detectable adapters.

Automatic installation also means single-minded installation. If everything goes right the first time, installations are a snap. But in our tests, we sometimes made a mistake, particularly in naming people and mailboxes in the Microsoft Mail program, and then it was difficult to backtrack. It may often be easier to edit an .INI file with a DOS text editor or even to erase an entire .INI file, forcing the program to start over, than it would be to change a configuration through the program.

Use the Windows Main menu to set up the initial profile of drives and printers you want to make available to the network and the network resources you want to use. The program icons are the same as those in Windows, but the tool bar in each program has special share and connect icons and the pull-down menus include those functions. Once you make a selection, it is written into WIN.INI.

If anything, Microsoft might have made it a little too easy to stop sharing a subdirectory, drive, or printer. Although warnings caution you if other PCs are attached to a shared drive, with a few mouse clicks you can prevent someone from saving a file.

If you elect to load NetWare, you use the standard NetWare Map utility to select the resources that show up on NetWare servers. Of course, you have to avoid disk drive letters already used or potentially used by Windows for shared drives.

The question of how much processing power a machine needs to be a Windows server has one answer: "It depends." The only absolute requirement is that a PC must run Windows in enhanced mode on a 386 or better processor to act as a server.

If the person using a PC that will be acting as a server uses Windows applications heavily, keeps multiple applications open, and generates a large number of system interrupts by using a lot of keystrokes, and if other network users do a lot of writing to the shared hard drive, then the fastest available processor and something like 16MB of RAM are in order. But if the PC acting as a server sits idle much of the time and the network is lightly used, even a 486/33 with 8MB of memory will be sufficient for most installations.

The only hole in Microsoft's strategy—one that a company like Performance Technology is happy to exploit—is the lack of a viable DOS-based server alternative. The architecture of Performance Technology's POWERLan makes it an excellent DOS-based server for Windows clients. You can literally load a POWERLan server and share its resources with Windows clients with no changes on the Windows PCs. And these servers are noted for fast performance under DOS.

Interaction between Windows and IBM's LAN Server is limited by differing security concepts of these products. If your network includes both of them, you'll have to use names that follow the \\server\share model instead of the aliases that otherwise make the LAN Server so easy to manage.

Administrative Resources

Windows NT includes several administrative utilities that help users access shared resources and help the administrator regulate users. These menus conform to IBM's Systems Application Architecture, which means they are highly graphic; thus, many people will find it easier to work their way through them with a mouse than with a keyboard. You can control all the resources and make all the connections in a network using the menus, but in case you like to use batch files to control things, Windows NT has a command language too.

The popularity of IBM's PC LAN networking software and of the related MS-Net products marketed by other companies led to the industry's adoption of the MS-Net command language. This language contains commands such as Net Share, which makes a resource available; and Net Use, which links a workstation to the available resource. It also includes a concept called Sharenames. A *Sharename* is a handy way to refer to a resource. For example, it allows you to share files by calling them Accounts instead of SERVER1\D:\DBMS\ACCNTG\PAYABLE\JUNE, or something similar. While most of the time you'll establish links between the server and clients using graphical tools, if you want to, you can use the same command-language syntax with Windows NT that you use with PC LAN.

Windows NT's centralized management features make administering large networks much easier. Network managers can logically group a set of servers as one domain and administer it as a single server; thus, managers can change users' rights, passwords, and time restrictions for all servers at once instead of changing them for each server individually. Managers can also safely delegate certain types of management tasks, such as disk backup or print-queue management. Additionally, a complete set of security utilities allows fine control over end-user access to the system. Through the Remote Administration facility, network managers can do all of these things from any Windows workstation.

Other management tools include a network auditing facility, network statistics and error logging, and automatic event scheduling.

- The network auditing facility allows managers to monitor the use of any network resource.

- Windows NT logs error messages and network performance statistics that may be useful in fine-tuning the server. It includes a self-tuning memory-management facility like the one in NetWare 3.X. This artificially intelligent feature dynamically reallocates memory buffers, allowing the server to give the fastest possible response.

- Performing certain tasks at a specific time each day or month can be time consuming and monotonous. This is where auto-scheduling comes in. This feature can send messages and run programs at preset intervals, freeing the administrator for more thought-intensive tasks.

Windows NT supports diskless workstations better than NetWare 3.X does. Unlike NetWare, Windows NT lets each computer have its own AUTO-EXEC.BAT file, which allows system administrators more flexibility for configuring the users on the network. In addition, each user can have a unique log-on batch file. Conversely, NetWare's log-on scripts offer more functionality than normal DOS batch files.

Auto-reconnect is a great convenience for users. If the network goes down, the auto-reconnect feature establishes the network connection when the server comes back up. As long as a workstation wasn't expecting something from the server at the moment of failure, its user won't know the server has been down. This feature saves people the effort of logging on again and re-executing the Net Use command for all the resources they were using when the network went down.

Windows NT now offers built-in fault tolerance, including drive duplexing, disk mirroring, and a new file-replication system. These features match any offering on the market. File replication lets administrators automatically duplicate specified files across servers at predefined intervals. NTFS is similar to NetWare's HotFix—it manages bad disk space and reroutes the data to other sectors.

Windows NT protects the server from power failures with an uninterruptible power supply (UPS). The program communicates with the UPS through a standard RS-232 port. When the power goes out, the UPS signals Windows NT, which in turn sends a warning to everyone on the LAN. If the battery drops below "10 percent remaining life" before power is restored, the server is shut down safely.

Windows NT does an excellent job of handling shared printers through the OS/2 Print Manager. Microsoft's system designers obviously learned from some of the problems people had experienced with shared printing under early versions of MS-Net. Windows NT print-job-management capabilities include standard functions like prioritizing and managing jobs in the print queue. You can also control form feeds and set the system to hunt for available printers for certain kinds of jobs. In addition, Windows NT includes a PostScript despooler that makes it easy to use networked printers for desktop publishing. OS/2's Print Manager will not let anyone without the proper security level modify a print job.

Another interesting sharing feature allows serial devices like modems, scanners, and printers to be pooled and shared across the LAN. Thus, these serial devices can be addressed by an application program as if they were attached to a local serial port.

You can administer a Windows NT server from the server itself or from any workstation running OS/2 on the network. If your network has more than one Windows NT server, you can create a separate OS/2 management session for each server on the management workstation.

Windows NT has good capabilities for monitoring and troubleshooting network operations. A display screen called Net Statistics reports data such as the number of I/O actions, active sessions, and network errors, and even the average response time. Windows NT sends automatic messages to the administrator when certain problems arise, such as a malfunctioning printer or an excessive number of bad password attempts. A feature called the Alerter can forward alert messages to another user on the network.

The network administrator also has several tracking and recording tools. The Audit Trail service keeps track of who has used server resources and what kinds of actions they've taken. You can set up the audit log to record when users open files and access I/O ports. A real-time report on the active sessions that is available to the administrator shows who is connected to the server, how long the connection has been up, and how long the connection has been idle. To disconnect a user or free up resources, an administrator can force a session to close.

■ Digital and AT&T

I can't discuss serious network operating systems without describing the approaches taken by two important companies: Digital Equipment Corp. and AT&T. Digital has introduced or sponsored many networking concepts, most notably Ethernet.

AT&T doesn't have a big share of the LAN software market, but many important architectures and products, including Unix, have come from its laboratories, and it is a leader in the design of 10BaseT hardware. The company provides a wide range of services, and is an important integrator and installer of complete network solutions.

Digital and AT&T have many similarities beyond size and the ability to provide everything you need in networking products and services. Most notably, both have major LAN operating systems based on Unix—although Digital provides alternatives AT&T does not have—and both market their own versions of Microsoft's Windows NT. Both companies also back IEEE 802.3 Ethernet in competition with IBM's IEEE 802.5 Token-Ring as a favored network cabling and signaling system.

Digital's Networking History

Digital Equipment Corp. got its start in the 1950s in an old textile mill in Maynard, Massachusetts. Founder and CEO Kenneth Olsen saw a need for computers that could do things other than the accounting and payroll functions prevalent at the time. Olsen had a vision of computers that would be affordable to engineers and scientists and would not require a sterile environment to operate.

From its first minicomputer, the PDP-1, to its present-day VAX series of superminis, Digital has come a long way. The PDP-1, announced in 1959, was the first of its kind. It came with an unheard-of innovation, a CRT integrated into the console. The system was housed in a cabinet about the size of a refrigerator, but required only normal office power and air-conditioning.

The VAX 11/780 computer was introduced in October 1977, and was Digital's attempt to compete with the king of the hill—IBM. The idea was to provide a more powerful computer that would give current Digital users a way to migrate upwards without junking their existing investment in software and peripherals. The VAX 11/780 offered a "compatibility" mode in which software written for the PDP-11 series of minicomputers would run without modification. It also contained a compatible bus structure that would accommodate existing peripherals.

In May 1980 Digital made another significant announcement: Along with Xerox and Intel, they introduced the plans for Ethernet to the world. Ethernet provides a fast and economical way to connect computers in offices and across campuses. This capability let Digital set its sights squarely on becoming the largest computer company ever.

Along with the release of the first VAX computer, Digital also came out with its Virtual Memory System, or VMS. This operating system was written to take full advantage of the VAX hardware's 32-bit architecture. The VAX 11/780 with VMS was a true multitasking/multiuser, hardware/software system.

When it introduced the VAX 11/780, Digital also announced a networking product called DECnet, which became the basis of all Digital networks. DECnet is a network architecture implemented primarily in software that allows multiple computers to link using any of several kinds of connections and to share resources such as large disks and printers.

The original DECnet was designed for parallel interfaces and was intended to connect computers located within 20 to 30 feet of each other. Serial interfaces were available for longer distances, but they were much slower than the parallel connections. With Digital's announcement of its Ethernet plans in 1980, DECnet took on new significance—the DECnet protocol layers fit nicely over the Ethernet cable and signaling scheme. Today, DECnet over Ethernet cabling is Digital's preferred networking solution. Digital's customers represent a huge base of Ethernet connections, which they use to link terminals, minicomputers, and PCs in networks that are becoming increasingly integrated.

Digital recognizes that integrated multivendor systems are the rule today. In mid-1989, it began selling a full line of completely IBM-compatible PCs. Perhaps more importantly, the present system architecture has room for many non-Digital products. Technical-support people from Digital have been to Novell's schools, and can help you install NetWare, Novell's LAN operating system, on a VAX. The folks from Digital now know many ways to integrate PCs and VAX computers, and to link networks of these computers to IBM mainframes.

Digital's Pathworks

Several products on the market provide Digital's minicomputers with the ability to act as servers for networks of PCs running DOS. Digital's minicomputers run on one of two operating systems: VMS or Ultrix. VMS is the more widely used operating system, but Ultrix, a version of Unix, is growing in popularity. Digital markets a product that has gone through several name changes, but is now called Pathworks for VMS. Additionally, Novell markets a completely different product called NetWare for VMS.

The people at Digital Equipment Corp. once had very ambivalent feelings toward Unix. Throughout the 1970s and much of the 1980s, a lot of Digital's hardware ran versions of AT&T's Unix operating system instead of Digital's competing VMS. Now, seeking a more flexible stance, the people at Digital offer an implementation of Unix they call Ultrix for their hardware. In mid-1991, Digital released a version of Microsoft's LAN Manager called Pathworks for Ultrix and now Digital fully supports Windows NT.

Digital also includes support for electronic mail programs, including the Simple Message Transport Protocol and Digital's VAXmail. The client package also has TCP/IP capabilities, so applications and utilities using TCP/IP will work across the network to Ultrix software that also includes TCP/IP.

As one of the strongest proponents of Microsoft Windows, Digital's people believe in graphical user interfaces. Their Pathworks for DOS package includes a VT-320 terminal emulator designed to run under Windows. They have a version of the X Windows System called PC DEC Windows, which allows a person using a PC to execute and display an Ultrix DECwindows application in one window and a VMS DECwindows application in another.

People with networks of Digital's computers are likely to continue expanding the use of Digital's products while simultaneously linking them to other networking systems. Pathworks for Ultrix provides an excellent way to link PCs running DOS and OS/2 to Digital's RISC and VAX hardware, and to other computers running Windows NT and NFS.

Unix Networking

Unix is a multitasking operating system that enjoys widespread popularity. On one end of the spectrum, Unix runs on high-powered desktop computers called graphic workstations, used for computer-aided design work. By contrast, many organizations use Unix running on a computer with an 80486 processor as a very low-cost way to provide multiuser accounting and database services. Low-cost terminals connect to the computer running Unix and run special Unix application software in the shared processor.

These high- and low-level activities in the Unix market leave a lot of room in the middle, which will probably be occupied by Unix computers acting as file, print, and communications servers for networks of PCs.

I've been very impressed by releases of Unix from the Santa Cruz Operation (SCO). AT&T, Microsoft, and SCO have worked together to deliver "merged" versions of Unix that can use the same compilers and provide the same services; this gives people writing and rehosting applications a broad base of operating systems to shoot for.

The history of Unix involves both Digital and AT&T. For many years AT&T was the only company that could sell long-distance telephone service and high-speed communications circuits in the United States. Starting in the 1960s, the switches and control units AT&T used to deliver these services became computerized. As AT&T's engineers and computer scientists worked with the telephone switching systems, they determined that a program-development environment would make their efforts more productive. That's how the Unix operating system was born.

Initially, AT&T turned to companies like Digital Equipment Corp. for computer hardware. The Unix operating system was written for one of Digital's early machines, the DEC PDP-7. The initial work on Unix was done in 1969 and 1970, primarily by Dennis Ritchie and Ken Thompson at AT&T Bell Labs. In 1973, the Unix system was completely rewritten using the newly developed C programming language. AT&T made the operating system available at no cost to colleges and universities because the Federal Communications Commission prohibited them from selling computer products. This gave Unix a strong technical base, and computer scientists' early exposure to Unix has certainly contributed to its large and growing market.

Improvements to AT&T's Unix made at the University of California at Berkeley brought network support, support for many peripherals, and software-development tools. Specifically, the Berkeley Standard Distribution (BSD) version of Unix added an implementation of the TCP/IP protocols. In Unix System

V, Release 3.0, AT&T added networking capabilities and a high-level multitasking feature called Streams.

The increasing momentum of the Unix bandwagon has convinced many companies to offer application software that can run on a larger Unix-based minicomputer system as well as on DOS-based PCs. One example is the Informix database package, which lets you create data tables on a terminal through the minicomputer's multiuser operating system and update them from a PC. Common file areas can be created that look like DOS files to the PC and like Unix-type files to terminals attached to the host. This feature provides a means of creating a true distributed database system.

Similarly, there are several ways to turn a computer running Unix into a server for a network of PCs. An early favorite was a program called Network File System (NFS), first offered by Sun Microsystems. NFS gives client PCs running a program called PC NFS simultaneous multiple access to data files stored on a computer using the Unix filing system. Many companies marketing Unix products license NFS from Sun. AT&T included a similar program called Remote File Service (RFS) in AT&T Unix System V, Release 3 and later releases, but RFS has never gained the acceptance of NFS for PC networking.

In 1993, AT&T sold their proprietary interests in Unix to a division of Novell, so the future of Unix as a network operating system is now in the hands of Novell's managers. However, through its NCR hardware division, AT&T continues to play a role in networking. The company has also positioned itself to continue in another role (which it probably does best), acting as a long distance carrier providing circuits and services to link and extend local networks.

■ POWERLan

Founded in 1985 by the minds behind Datapoint's ARCnet, Performance Technology specializes in software but also offers some peripheral hardware products. POWERLan has top-end technical qualities and low-end pricing.

Performance Technology's POWERLan version 3.0 is ideal for medium to large organizations that need either a peer or client-server based network and room for growth. It offers added power in the form of a separate 32-bit server program and a user naming scheme configured with user names, group names, and a multiserver database of names. Its strong network printing system includes many features for busy offices. POWERLan's neat new Windows interface has a unique set of icons that make it easy to set up network connections. The POWERLan system delivers top performance and the 32-bit POWER-Serve program shows a significant performance edge compared to the nondedicated server program.

Performance Technology offers several pricing options for their POWER-Lan family of network products. The typical package includes a five-user license for POWERLan, a copy of the POWERServe 32-bit server, and a five-user copy of Lotus's cc:Mail for a retail price of $645. However, Performance Technology also offers other hardware and software bundles. The per-node cost of POWERLan is comparable to similar products such as LANtastic and Personal NetWare.

The POWERLan Windows interface, shown in Figure 8.7, is not only very intuitive, it's also fun to use. To a network resource such as a shared disk drive or printer, you simply drag a power cord that represents your local port or drive letter and plug it into a wall outlet that represents the network resource. Other features such as human-shaped icons that raise a hand when selected make the POWERLan Windows interface a joy to use.

Figure 8.7

POWERLan has an excellent graphical interface that makes it easy to attach to network resources.

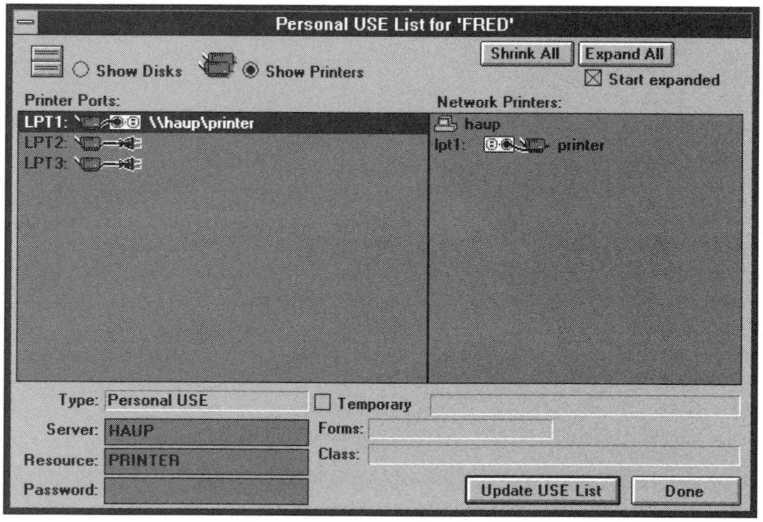

LANtastic and POWERLan support the SMB protocol and allow you to connect to a Windows for Workgroups or Windows NT server with no additional software, but POWERLan offers tighter integration and the ability to browse POWERLan server names from a PC running Microsoft's networking software. POWERLan also offers support for other protocols such as NDIS, IPXODI, and the Clarkson packet drivers. This feature insures support for most adapter cards for Ethernet, Token-Ring, or ARCnet networks.

POWERLan's printing system is slick. It is the only peer product that offers a feature called class-based network printing. Class printing allows you to set up a group of printers based on particular criteria such as having PostScript, using a specific paper type or size, or printing in color. When you're ready to print, you send your document with a request for a specific class, and POWERLan sends your job to a printer that has those capabilities. You can also use POWERLan to edit your printer's escape sequences and add header and trailer information. If you do not need class printing, you can select printers by assigned names as you do with the other network operating systems.

You can use the POWERLan floating-printer monitor to watch your print jobs and network printers from any application. Most other peer-based networks offer a print manager, but it is usually a separate program that requires its own window. The POWERLan print monitor can also alert you when your print job is complete or if the printer runs out of paper or goes off line.

POWERLan's user security system adds to the product's attractiveness. Like LANtastic, POWERLan lets you arrange users by specific names or group them into functional clusters. LANtastic offers more control of individual privileges, but POWERLan includes a user database that is maintained by all POWERLan login servers. With the user database, you don't have to know what server you are logging into; you can just provide your username and password.

The biggest advantages POWERLan offers are its ability to network both DOS and Windows clients, its excellent integration with NT, and the included 32-bit POWERServe program. If you need to network only two to four PCs, you should consider a less expensive solution such as Coactive Connector, but if you need security, several network printers, and room for growth, POWERLan is robust enough to meet the needs of a large network for many years to come.

■ LANtastic

Compared with a customized file-handling system such as NetWare's or a multitasking operating system such as Unix, LAN file-server software (see Figure 8.8) operating over DOS offers some significant advantages with only a few drawbacks. Servers that run over DOS can make resources available to the network and run normal applications at the same time. You can run your own word processor or spreadsheet on your PC while other people share your printer or hard disk through the network. You have less RAM for your applications, however, and they will run more slowly when the network software is loaded.

DOS-based servers typically don't retrieve files as fast as multitasking systems do, but they are less complex to set up and manage. PCs acting as file and print servers don't run applications as quickly as they might normally, but often the people using the machines don't notice the difference.

Figure 8.8

LANtastic is a small, fast operating system that works over DOS. The vendor, Artisoft, sells its own adapters using proprietary cabling as well as an excellent line of Ethernet adapters.

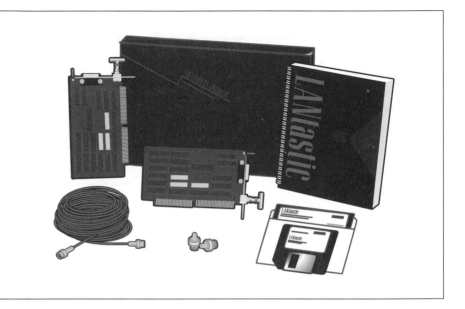

LANtastic Features

LANtastic uses a small amount of memory and provides fast throughput. A PC acting as a file and print server loses only 40K of RAM to the operating-system software, and the redirector in client stations takes only 13K. You can load the operating system into expanded memory or place the disk-caching program into either extended or expanded memory. This ability to load into the memory not used by DOS frees up enough room for large applications that require more RAM.

LANtastic's Quick-Install program automatically assigns network re-sources, account files, and privileges. It modifies the CONFIG.SYS file with the appropriate files, buffers, file-control blocks, and Lastdrive designation, and creates a batch file that activates the network in one command. If you have any difficulties using the Quick-Install program, an online help menu stands ready to aid you; it even scrolls automatically to the section in which you're working.

LANtastic has excellent print-server software, which includes the ability to feed jobs to multiple printers simultaneously. You can print specific jobs with a high-priced laser printer while the spooler searches the queue for files that can be printed by one of the network's lower-end devices.

You can also increase the size of the network printer buffers and specify the location of spooled files on the disk. Both of these improvements help make the printing process more practical. Another feature, global clearing of the print queue, allows you to delete the entire contents of the queue at once, rather than one file at a time. This comes in handy when someone doesn't understand the delays inherent in network printing and repeatedly submits the same job for printing.

In LANtastic 6.0, Artisoft stretched out to head off Microsoft Windows as the ultimate client for mixed networks of NetWare, Windows, Windows NT, and LANtastic servers. Version 6.0 introduced the concept of including all the software you need to interact with a NetWare server using Novell's NCP and IPX and with Windows servers using SMB over NetBEUI. The LANtastic 6.0 universal redirector supplies all the communications tools. For example, you can use the Artisoft redirector in place of the Novell NETX shell program. The LANtastic redirector loads only the specific protocols it needs for the servers it finds on the LAN when it loads. If the NetWare server is turned off when you log on, the LANtastic redirector will not waste your conventional memory by loading the NCP drivers.

The installation program automatically determines whether you have Windows and DOS installed on your PC and then brings in the correct LANtastic 6.0 program elements. You can use either the DOS or Windows interface to create network connections to disk drives, CD-ROMs, and printers.

LANtastic 6.0 includes powerful security options for users and groups, and it allows you to assign access to individual files and directories. You can also limit access to the network based on time and date. A network print-queue manager allows you to monitor and control print jobs. and can service up to eight printers per print server.

LANtastic 6.0 includes a version of network DDE (previously found only in Windows for Workgroups) that allows you to dynamically share and link information between two Windows applications across the network. You can cut and paste data from your client PC to another client on the LAN, and both PCs will reflect any changes made to that data.

In addition to its improved connectivity features, LANtastic also includes integrated network e-mail and scheduling applications for your Windows-based network clients. The Artisoft Exchange Mail program allows you to send electronic messages and binary attachments to anyone on your LANtastic LAN or WAN via a mail gateway such as MHS. Like the Microsoft Mail package included with Windows, Exchange Mail provides nested folders, address lists, and several delivery options.

You can use your Exchange Mail server in conjunction with a compatible fax card to send and receive faxes through Exchange Mail or through any Windows application using the fax printer driver. In addition to sending faxes, you can also use the Exchange Mail server and a modem to contact digital or alphanumeric pagers using e-mail.

The Artisoft Exchange Scheduler allows you to set up group and personal meetings. Exchange Scheduler includes a Windows interface for keeping up with your day-to-day tasks and appointments. The network scheduler can alert you if you schedule a conflicting group or personal appointment and you can set up an alarm to remind you of impending appointments.

Network printing is another area where LANtastic 6.0 offers several improvements. LANtastic allows you to set up any client PC as a print server for up to seven other network clients. In earlier versions of LANtastic, print servers had to run the same drivers as file servers. Optionally, you can automatically despool print jobs before the entire job is sent to the queue—a useful feature if you frequently print large jobs. I liked the print server configuration utility that allowed me to balance the amount of time the CPU spent servicing print jobs and running applications.

Version 6.0 includes a technology designed to increase the performance of your LANtastic network. LANtastic's Burst mode network file-transfer technique is similar to NetWare's Burst mode; it allows you to send several packets across the network cable without receiving an acknowledgment. Without Burst mode technology, each packet you send over the network must be answered by an acknowledgment before your network adapter can send the next packet. We found that the speed increase with Burst mode is proportional to the size of the files you transfer, so it's primarily valuable for jobs like backups across the LAN.

You can use LANtastic's network management utility to monitor configuration information, status, and performance statistics for all your network file servers. The network management utility helps you determine any changes that may be necessary to increase a particular file server's performance, such as adding memory or disk space.

LANtastic 6.0 is designed for expandability and ease of use. With powerful new features such as e-mail, scheduling, and connectivity, LANtastic will easily grow with the needs of your network.

Artisoft CorStream: LANtastic and NetWare Rolled into One

It is a network administrator's unwritten rule that once you outgrow peer-to-peer file sharing you either dedicate a PC as a server using the peer software or you switch to a client/server network. In an effort to break the rules, Artisoft's CorStream dedicated server combines the ease-of-use of LANtastic's peer-to-peer network operating system with the power of Novell's dedicated NetWare software. LANtastic's CorStream version 1.0 is a NetWare Loadable Module (NLM) that runs on top of NetWare 4.X and, in effect, creates a LANtastic file server inside a NetWare file server while taking advantage of NetWare's 32-bit multitasking file and print services of NetWare.

At first glance, CorStream seems like an ideal way to upgrade existing LANtastic LANs. But, because of performance limitations and cost, it is really best suited to merging existing NetWare and LANtastic LANs. CorStream is available in 5-, 10-, 25-, 50-, and 100-user licenses, and pricing starts at $949 for a stand-alone, five-user version, and $1,149 for the network bundle that includes a five-user license for CorStream and LANtastic 6.0. CorStream is bundled with a two-user license for NetWare 4.01, but you can load the CorStream software on any NetWare 4.X server. In comparison, Novell NetWare 3.12 retails for $1,095 for a five-user license and provides the same file and print services along with better performance, but minus the easy-to-use LANtastic front-end. For reasons we'll detail later, a few third-party NLMs will not run on the CorStream system.

The idea behind CorStream's operation is straightforward. The CorStream software intercepts the Artisoft Server Message Block packets from the LANtastic clients and converts the packets into NetWare service requests. The Artisoft software builds a LANtastic "curtain" around all the NetWare 4.X file and print services. While all the NetWare drives and printers appear to LANtastic clients as LANtastic drives and printers, NetWare handles all network requests in its normal fashion. Since it necessitates conversion, the CorStream server can't be as fast as the native NetWare server; in our tests CorStream came close to being as fast as NetWare. NetWare services are still available to clients using Novell's software.

Because CorStream runs on top of NetWare 4.X, you gain all the features found in NetWare, such as disk compression, disk mirroring and duplexing, and CD-ROM support, plus you have the ability to use hundreds of third-party NetWare NLMs for tape backup, network management, and virus scanning. In sum, CorStream enhances the features of NetWare 4.X with the LANtastic 6.0 interface.

Some NLMs such as Cheyenne's ARCServe backup system look for your NetWare user license and will not work with the two-user run-time version of NetWare shipped with the CorStream product. Other NLMs that require the Novell Netx driver on the client or IPX to communicate with the client will not work with LANtastic CorStream clients.

Each CorStream package contains a full two-user license of NetWare 4.X on a CD-ROM and eight diskettes containing a scaled down, run-time version of NetWare and the CorStream program. If you are not concerned with disk space and have a CD-ROM, you will definitely want to use the CD-ROM to install NetWare. It took us almost three hours to install the NetWare and CorStream files from the diskettes. As with any NetWare installation, you need to have drivers for your server's disk drive and network adapter card.

CorStream is targeted at LANtastic network users who are comfortable with the menus and features of LANtastic, but need the power and performance of a 32-bit multitasking operating system. In addition, LANtastic 6.0 offers network scheduling and e-mail, centralized management, powerful security, a Windows and DOS-based front end and many other features not included in NetWare 3.X or 4.X.

The combination of Artisoft's LANtastic 6.0 and CorStream gives you some interesting choices. Artisoft tried to make LANtastic 6.0 the perfect network client software, even giving it Novell's standard NetWare Core Protocol and IPX capability. Because NetWare 3.12 was approximately twice as fast as CorStream in our tests, users of LANtastic 6.0 might be better off using Novell's interface to a NetWare server without CorStream. However, the complexities of logging into different server security systems and the memory problems associated with loading two protocol stacks in the client computers include all the ingredients of a network manager's nightmare. Such nightmares will vanish if you load CorStream into the NetWare server and give users one interface and one set of protocols.

CorStream's primary value is as a tool to integrate NetWare and LANtastic networks. It gives LANtastic users access to files stored on a NetWare server without the trauma of encountering NetWare directly. As an upgrade, CorStream allows network managers to enjoy the benefits of NetWare management and NLMs while keeping things simple out on the client computers.

Central Station

Artisoft dubs their Central Station a "connectivity processor." The LAN Central Station helps your networked PC in a variety of ways and also works pretty well on its own.

The Central Station, shown in Figure 8.9, is a complete external CPU in a box 2 inches high by 12 inches wide by 5½ inches deep. It has its own power supply and programming that handles input/output tasks, particularly for laptop and notebook computers, even when those computers aren't present. Although it comes from Artisoft, the LAN Central Station isn't limited to LANtastic networks. You can add software that allows it to work on NetWare too.

Basically, the Central Station is a docking station in its purest sense, connecting to the parallel port of any PC and giving that machine a full complement of one parallel and two serial ports along with a third serial port used for configuration management and future features. This device also functions in several other modes, however: It's an external LAN adapter that works like a Xircom external adapter, providing any attached PC with a high-quality Ethernet connection. The Central Station has its own internal adapter—Artisoft's AE-3 circuitry—that emulates a Novell NE-2000 and includes both thin coax and 10BaseT RJ45 connectors.

Figure 8.9

Artisoft dubs their Central Station as a "connectivity processor." It is a complete CPU in a box that acts as an external LAN adapter for an attached PC, a print server, and a communications server for incoming and outgoing calls. This versatile and unique device works on LANtastic, NetWare, and other operating systems using Ethernet adapters.

With the addition of a modem, the LAN Central Station becomes an access server. People can load the modified LANtastic networking software on their laptops, run applications and environments like Windows locally, and dial into the LAN Central Station to gain full access to all networked drives. A slightly different twist of this flexible product allows callers to remotely control the LAN Central Station and run applications on their own NEC V50 processors and 520K of RAM. In addition, people on the network can dial out through a modem attached to the LAN Central Station, so it also acts as an asynchronous communications server.

Last, but certainly not least, the LAN Central Station can act as a print server like the Intel NetPort. You can attach a printer to the Central Station and allow any other PC to send it print jobs across the LAN. Interestingly, though, when it's acting in these remote control and print server roles, the Central Station doesn't need a PC attached. You can be on the road with your only PC tucked into your briefcase while the Central Station stays behind and performs all of its network server duties!

The LAN Central Station has a relatively simple CPU and operating system, so it can't do everything at once. Specifically, it can give only one application at a time access to the Ethernet adapter, so if you are using the LAN Central Station as an external LAN adapter, it won't be able to perform its other tricks. By taking advantage of its 32K (expandable to 64K) Electrically Erasable Programmable Read Only Memory (EEPROM), you can read specific pieces of software into the Central Station from your PC's floppy or hard disk drive, set it up for operation, and let it work with or without the PC, depending on the job.

The Central Station attaches to the PC's parallel port, so the client PC's LAN throughput is limited by that port to well under a megabit per second, depending on the type of CPU in the client PC and its speed. Connecting the Central Station doesn't eliminate the ability to print, as it does with external adapters, because the Central Station has its own parallel port for a printer connection. However, when you try to print and use the network at the same time, print jobs halt for the network traffic.

Artisoft is busy developing many types of applications for the Central Station. In concept, this external CPU could run all your TSR programs, leaving a maximum amount of low RAM available in your PC. The Central Station also brings the concept of parallel processing to simple computers. It will work with any computer, even the oldest PC, to carry the burden of network and other I/O tasks.

CD-ROM Support

Many interesting information sources, including maps, statistical summaries, and compilations of publications, are available on CD-ROM disks. But one person seldom needs sole and prolonged access to all the information contained on a CD-ROM. CD-ROM information bases beg to be shared through a network. In fact, in terms of productivity, sharing CD-ROM resources is one of the best reasons I know for installing a LAN in the first place. It's possible to add a third-party CD-ROM server (a type of file server) to a LAN running Novell, Banyan, or Microsoft networking software, but LANtastic includes the ability to share CD-ROM drives across the network as a built-in feature.

Artisoft's menu-driven installation program copies the files from the distribution disk to their proper place in the directory structure. Your next step is to install a CD-ROM drive with the proper device driver, along with a copy of a special program called Microsoft CD-ROM Extensions that modifies DOS to accommodate the large file sizes used in a CD-ROM. Fortunately, the PC does not have to be dedicated to the task of acting as a CD-ROM server. As the Microsoft CD-ROM device driver loads, the next available logical-drive letters are assigned to the CD-ROM drives.

Once LANtastic is installed, the program's menu lets you initiate an automatic broadcast to the network telling each station which drive letter is assigned to the CD-ROM device. You then assign a network resource name to the shared drive and inform LANtastic that the resource is a CD-ROM drive, whereupon the operating system channels any relevant service requests it receives from application programs to Microsoft CD-ROM Extensions. LANtastic also supports multiple CD-ROM drives by letting you give each drive a different network resource name.

When you want to access a particular drive on a CD-ROM server, you have LANtastic link one of your unused drive letters to the named server and drive. Thus, if you wanted your D drive mapped to a drive named DATABASE on a CD-ROM server named CDSERVER, you would enter the command

```
NET USE D: \\CDSERVER\DATABASE
```

on the DOS command line. The networking software would then make the link and direct the database retrieval software to your D drive.

LANtastic's CD-ROM capability is easy to install, use, and manage; it adds a significant and unique value to this program. On the bottom line, LANtastic's interoperability features, CD-ROM compatibility, good security, disk caching, high performance, and very reasonable price combine to make this package appealing to anyone seeking a high-quality LAN for 2 to 100 users.

■ Network Scalability

What do puppies, plants, children, and LANs have in common? They all grow! But while puppies, plants, and children can grow by ten times or more without changing their basic form, if you simply try to double the size of a LAN you often have to start from scratch. LAN systems typically lack "scalability"—the ability to expand smoothly, without disruption. Today, you might think you're investing in a network that will always remain small, but wouldn't it be nice to know that you won't have to throw everything away and start all over if you ever do want to expand?

If you ask most LAN people what "scalability" means, the first reply you'll get will be, "Adding more users!" because adding users is the most visible component of growth. But DOS-based servers falter under heavy loads, so scalable server software must be based on sterner stuff than DOS.

In many organizations, scalability means evolving from a LAN for just the front office into a widespread production network. This means expanding from front office word processing and check writing functions that support the business to the order entry, lead tracking, and manufacturing programs that *are* the business. Above everything, bet-the-business networks need reliable operation.

Scalability also means geographical expansion or reach. Communicating through and out of a modern network is a complex business. A fully capable network should be able to provide LAN-to-LAN links and remote access services. Often, this means using networking protocols like IPX or TCP/IP that can be routed across internetwork links.

In mainframe days, vendors self-servingly defined scalability as the ability to extend within a product line. In PC products, scalability means cooperation among vendors to support each other's products. You can't grow a LAN without using products from different companies, so interoperability with third-party products is important.

You can look at the scalability of a network operating system in several ways. First, you can compare how many active nodes a dedicated server can support under benchmark test conditions. Then you can examine one of the key underpinnings of scalability: the ability to use the widely supported and easily routable TCP/IP network protocols. Finally, you must consider server reliability as an important aspect of scalability.

Growing Nodes

Growth means adding nodes, but adding nodes to the LAN affects performance both on the cable and in the server. As the LAN grows, the best way to reduce congestion on the network cable is to segment the cable so you split the load. The best way to handle the load on the server is to dedicate it to networking.

Cable segmentation makes sense even if you have only one server because a modern server can deliver more data than a single 10MB span can accept. Many people are familiar with NetWare's ability to use multiple LAN adapter cards in the server with each card attached to a separate cable segment, and to route packets between the segments. None of the products in this review can route between adapters internally as NetWare can, so you'll need to use an external device like a switching hub to reduce cable congestion. A switching hub can clear the network path to the server.

In a peer network, a PC acting as a server shares its processing power between running applications and servicing requests for file and print actions. When the load created by the clients increases, you can improve server performance somewhat by not running applications on the PC that's acting as a server. But when it comes to supporting more users, you can't beat the performance of a dedicated server with 32-bit multitasking processing power. DOS simply can't do a good job of ordering and managing numerous calls for service, so scaling-up calls for better server software.

Each of the major low-cost networking products has a logical server upgrade path. Performance Technology's POWERServe comes bundled with POWERLan. NetWare 3.12 is the clear, but costly, growth path for Personal NetWare. Microsoft's Windows NT Advanced Server provides more power for Windows for Workgroups. Artisoft's LANtastic 6.0 has strong expansion capabilities using server software licensed partially from Novell.

During our benchmark tests at PC Magazine Labs Performance Technology's POWERServe performed beautifully—even compared to the ever-popular NetWare 3.12. It is an excellent low-cost alternative to more expensive server products like NetWare 3.X and Windows NT Server. The Windows server module allows you to set up 32-bit memory and disk addressing and to use a sliding bar control to give network services a higher percentage of the processor's time, but even the sliding bar can't create an operating system that is totally dedicated to networking. As you go beyond one or two dozen clients using Windows, you'll want a server that's capable of true multitasking, and the most logical choice is Windows NT Advanced Server. The NT operating system adds multitasking and NT Server brings in a more sophisticated multiserver naming system. The Windows network client software programs immediately recognize a new NT server as another LAN resource.

If you want to add more capability by using NetWare, the structure of Windows networking makes it very easy to slide software for Novell's NetWare Core Protocol and IPX into the client computers next to the Microsoft protocols, so putting a dedicated NetWare server on the LAN is only a little more work than adding an NT server. The users simply see another DOS disk drive; they don't know whether the network access through that drive letter uses Microsoft's SMB over NetBEUI or Novell's NCP over IPX. In this measure of scalability, Windows networking excels.

Performance Technology ships a dedicated 32-bit server program called POWERServe in the POWERLan box at no additional cost. POWERServe performs well and includes a sophisticated naming scheme that replicates a database of names and privileges across login servers, giving POWERLan the best native ability to manage a multiserver network among all the peer products. If you want to take a different route, POWERLan also interoperates nicely with Windows and Windows NT Advanced Server. As with Windows, you simply add an NT server to the network and all the POWERLan nodes can use its resoures immediately.

Novell's NetWare 3.X provides an obvious extension path for Personal NetWare; Personal NetWare nodes are ready to use the full NetWare server. A NetWare 3.12 server carries a high up-front cost, about $5000 retail for a 50-user version of the software plus the cost of the PC hardware, but it provides good performance and many features including internal routing for up to four adapters, management services, and the ability to run any of the hundreds of third-party NetWare Loadable Modules.

Doing Business

If you are going to install or create unique business applications on your LAN, you need reliability even more than performance. Total system reliability comes from a variety of features including some means of monitoring server performance, a way to mirror disk drives, and other capabilities such as the ability to use the status messages sent from an uninterruptable power supply.

As you would expect, high-level server products such as Windows NT and NetWare 3.X include monitoring and mirroring functions along with a UPS interface. But you might not expect to find almost the same capabilities in POWERServe. In fact, Performance Technology includes excellent monitoring and management capabilities along with a good UPS interface. POWER-Mirror, a very flexible disk mirroring program, is an affordable $249 add-on.

Because Windows for Workgroups is, in fact, Windows, it can use a variety of third-party mirroring, backup, troubleshooting, and UPS interface programs. You can be sure that companies developing Windows add-in products will strive to be compatible with Widows because of its popularity. Other network operating systems such as LANtastic and Personal NetWare can also use third-party add-in products to add growth features, but every revision of DOS, Windows, or the network operating system has the potential for new incompatibilities.

The Immunity program from Unitrol Data Systems, Inc. is a useful $249 product that works with different LAN operating systems and performs disk mirroring between dissimilar drives. We tried Immunity with each of the network operating systems we evaluated for scalability, and if we didn't use a disk compression it worked fine.

An interface to an uninterruptable power supply is another small but valuable contribution to server reliability. This interface is a piece of software that monitors a serial port on the server for signals coming from a UPS connection. Typically, the software warns users that the server is running on emergency power and, after a preprogrammed period of time, gracefully disconnects users and closes their files.

Overall, both Windows and POWERLan are good rootstock for building a scalable network. Artisoft has strong offerings, but I prefer POWERLan because of its modular approach. Personal NetWare, with its built-in NetWare compatability, provides an open but more costly path to growth. Scalability isn't hard to understand—its major components are flexibility and processing power. However, scalability requires a modular design and development work that pays close attention to standards and interoperability.

■ Choosing Server Hardware

Throughout this chapter, I've provided information on the amount of processing power and memory needed to run the various network operating systems. Several companies, including Compaq Computer Corp. and NetFrame Systems, market a class of computers designed specifically to act as file servers. These machines typically have room for many hard disks, and ports to connect printers and plotters. The newest feature of these specialized servers is their ability to make multiple CPUs available to the network operating system. These "super servers" typically carry a significantly higher price tag than machines with slightly more humble, but still very substantial, capabilities.

Very few organizations need super servers today. A properly configured computer with an 80486 processor operating at 50 MHz or beter can act as a file and print server under NetWare, VINES, Windows NT, or Unix for 100 to 200 client PCs running typical office applications. I recommend splitting the job of servicing client PCs between several servers instead of putting all your processing power in one cabinet. The separate-PC approach has some significant advantages in terms of system reliability and performance. In my opinion, the best approach is to build your network modularly. Use separate computers acting as servers to deliver the capacity and throughput you need where you need it. Modern networking software products make it easier than it used to be to manage separate servers, and the advantages of reliability and scalability inherent in a modular approach are considerable.

It's easy to tick off the elements of a good multipurpose server: the biggest and fastest hard disk system you can afford, a fast data bus, four to six usable expansion slots, enough RAM for the size of the drive and the number of users, and a sufficiently powerful CPU. The most important element is a fast hard disk drive. Modern disk-caching software can overcome the negative impact of a slow drive on subsequent requests for the same or related data, but common functions like loading application programs from the server ask for the data only once, and they get the best service from a fast hard disk drive.

Obtaining good support for the hardware is another key element in the successful operation of a network. The leading hardware companies offer at least a one-year warranty on parts and labor for their systems. Consider buying from companies that provide on-site support for your server.

RAIDs and SLEDs

When discussing serious server hardware, the contention is between advocates of redundant arrays of inexpensive disks (RAIDs) and single large expensive drives (SLEDs). Arrays combine multiple drives into one unit that can move data into storage in a parallel bit stream, provide varying degrees of added reliability depending on the number of drives and the sophistication of the controller, and achieve highly efficient read and write actions. However, single large drives are fast, very reliable, and getting cheaper. To provide a high degree of reliability through redundancy, it is possible to mirror large hard-disk drives within the same server or even in separate servers.

To add confusion to the issue of RAIDs versus SLEDs, you may think you have an array but actually have a single large drive team instead. If you elect to configure an array so that each drive can independently seek—as you can, for example, in the Dell PowerLine family of computers—you forfeit the reliability of the array, but gain faster responses to read requests. You can also set up several SLEDs to perform split disk seeks. Since disk systems can receive a four-to-one or better ratio of read to write requests from typical PC applications, anything you can do to improve the servicing of read requests will directly improve network performance. Many companies, including ALR, Compaq, Dell, and IBM, offer disk arrays. It's also relatively simple to add an array like the Core CPR series through a SCSI adapter and cable.

As a tip, if you have an active database file that exceeds 100MB, you can often improve performance by using the capability of an operating system like NetWare to span several drives as a single volume. Several small, fast drives can respond separately and quickly to read and write requests on the same very large file.

The subject of disk controllers with built-in caching is another area of confusion and contention in the server world. Modern server software does an excellent job of caching both reads and writes, and the PCs you are likely to use as a server can carry over 16MB of low-cost RAM. There aren't many technical or practical reasons to pay more for a caching controller which will simply cache the data that comes from or goes to the cache in RAM. The main theoretical advantage of a caching controller is that it is on the disk-drive side of the data bus; if the bus is a bottleneck, a caching controller can help.

Slots and Watts

Once the drive and disk cache are providing fast access to stored data, it's important to avoid a bottleneck where the network meets the server. Since a single 386/20 networked PC can pump data onto the cable at a rate exceeding a megabit per second, it doesn't take many active nodes to saturate the media-access control system of Ethernet, ARCnet, or Token-Ring. The best way to avoid cable saturation is to split the network and use multiple LAN adapters in the node that is the center of traffic—that is, the server.

Highly sophisticated LAN operating systems like NetWare, can route data between four active LAN adapters in the server, so the PC acting as the server needs plenty of expansion slots. Considering the potential need for four LAN adapters, a communications adapter, an internal modem for trouble calls, and perhaps a separate adapter for a file backup device, it isn't unreasonable to ask for six free expansion slots in a fully functional PC that you intend to use as a server. On a high-performance server, at least four of those slots should have 32-bit addressing.

In addition to the slots, you need a power supply that can deliver the current needed (particularly on the +5 volt line) and that has enough connectors for the storage devices you want to install. A server should have a power supply rated for at least 300 watts, and supplies of more than 400 watts are available. In addition to the amount of power, you might also need to know how many connectors for peripherals such as CD-ROM drives and tape drives each power supply has.

Finally, even the best PC power supply can't run your server if there is no power coming from the wall socket or if the main AC lines are subject to voltage surges and sags. You should equip every computer acting as a server with an uninterruptable power supply. All the operating systems I've described in this chapter have the ability to exchange signals with a UPS and gracefully shut down before the UPS runs out of battery power.

As a practical estimate, four Ethernet LAN adapters can deliver an aggregate of up to 30 megabits per second of data to a server. Each adapter has to unload fast and get back to the busy job of servicing the cable, so the ideal server needs an internal bus that can move data in 32-bit-wide blocks and yield control to bus-mastering adapters.

How Much RAM Is Enough?

ALR offers the ability to to load a whopping 256MB of RAM into the PowerPro. Computers like the Blackship 486/33 and Dell PowerLine can hold up to 96MB of RAM, and many other systems can hold as much as 64MB. The obvious question is, how much RAM is enough? The answer depends on what you want to do.

As a rule of thumb, a NetWare file server with a 600MB hard disk drive needs a minimum of about 4MB of RAM. By comparison, Microsoft's Windows NT, needs a minimum of 16MB, but 32MB is better. Network operating systems will allocate all remaining memory for disk caching. The amount of memory actually used for caching will depend on how people and applications use the server. In real NetWare or Windows NT installations with large hard disk drives, you should plan on installing 16 to 32 megabytes of RAM as a minimum.

The picture changes dramatically if you want to run a program in the server like the ORACLE Server for NetWare or Microsoft's SQL Server. The ORACLE program, a NetWare Loadable Module, needs 9MB of RAM to run, but the maximum amount of memory it requires depends on how the applications are written and on the number of active users. The SQL Server can address up to 28MB of RAM. Obviously, even a 32MB system can be restrictive if you have many active users on a database server.

CPU Power

Finally, after clearing out all other potential bottlenecks like hard disk drives and LAN adapter cards, the server workload falls on the CPU. The functions of a file server operating system don't put much of a burden on the file server's CPU, but when you run a few server-based applications such as network management programs, UPS monitors, and communications programs, it doesn't take long to overload the CPU. While there are many servers efficiently running 80386 processors under heavy loads, the modest cost of stepping up to a Pentium with at least a 90 MHz clock speed is a good investment in future growth.

Error Correction Code Memory

In many ads for computers sold as servers, you'll see a line about error correction code (ECC) memory. You probably assumed that ECC was good, but did you ever ask why? Did you ever ask how you use this ECC stuff or what it costs?

On the bottom line, ECC memory detects and corrects data errors on-the-fly and tells you about them later. The detection part is easy, but the correction part is tricky because it involves deriving the correct data from the incorrect data through the interpretation of a stored checksum. In 486-based computers, ECC probably costs more than it is worth, but in Pentium-based machines it is a tremendous and practically free benefit. And—just so we don't sound biased toward Intel—ECC also provides value in computers powered by several models of processors from Digital, IBM, PowerPC, and Sun.

As more Windows NT and NetWare servers use Pentium, Alpha, PowerPC, and SPARC processors, the presence of ECC becomes an important factor in deciding which server to buy. ECC is particularly valuable when it is linked to a management system for reporting errors, but it's useful in any computer that uses large blocks of RAM and a fast processor.

How Big Is the Problem?

Vendors of computer systems agree that the types of data storage errors caught and corrected by ECC—those in memory and on tape—are not the biggest source of malfunctions in servers. Hard disk drives top every vendor's list of server problem spots, followed by power and cabling problems that are often external to the computer. However, many memory problems can be caught and fixed on-the-fly, so it is useful to include some circuitry to handle them. In servers, the major causes of memory problems stem from different timing characteristics within memory chips. Differences measured in less than a microsecond can lead to broken bytes.

I asked experts in computer architecture and design at Compaq, Distributed Processing Technology, Digital Equipment Corporation, Hewlett-Packard, and IBM about the scope of the problems ECC can solve. In general, they responded that the more you use the computer, the more you need ECC. The industry typically offers DRAM (Dynamic Random Access Memory) chips that experience one error in a million hours of operation. According to Don

Smelser, a consulting computer hardware engineer at Digital Equipment Corporation, "If you have a PC with four megabytes of memory, that's about 100,000 operational hours between failures. If you run it only twelve hours a day, you could go for decades and never have an error. Now let's say you have a server with 256 megabytes of memory representing perhaps 500 DRAM chips that runs 24 hours a day. That's an error every three months or so."

Of course average failure rates operate over a normal curve and your computer may be anything but normal. Every flip of a bit is a new spin of the wheel. If you are betting your business on your server, then you want the intervals between downtime measured in terms of years, not months. If you need reliability at this level, you need ECC. So far, so good. But now, what is it?

Old and New Error Checking Systems

ECC is rooted in mathematics—polynomials to be exact. As each data word, typically an 8-bit or longer block, passes into storage, a processor mathematically derives an ECC code from the contents of the data word and tacks the code onto the end of the word. Then, when the word is read from storage, the processor checks the appended ECC code against a newly computed sum. The type of processor and the ECC formula it uses depend on whether the storage is on tape, on disk, in cache, or in RAM.

If you're familiar with parity checking you'll recognize the concept of computing a sum from the data word to catch an error. Parity checking systems typically count the number of ones in a byte and then tack on one bit, either a zero or a one, so that a count of the total number of ones, including the parity bit, comes out even. Anyone who has set up a serial port knows that odd parity—adding a bit so that the sum of all the ones is odd—is also an option in those systems. In communications software and in other products like tape backup software, a parity error will generate a retry. In computer memory there is no way to retry the access, so the parity detector is connected to the processor's nonmaskable interrupt (NMI) pin, which halts the processor. An incorrect parity sum in memory generates the dreaded NMI error and everything stops. By the way, there are many other causes of NMI errors; not all of them are memory errors.

Of course halting the system because there's an indication of a parity error isn't acceptable when businesses run their critical applications from network servers. Also, the relatively simple parity system can be fooled by an error that changes, for example, a one to a zero and a zero to a one in the same byte because the parity comes out the same even though the data word is wrong.

ECC computations address both of these problems. First, they find and correct errors without halting the system. Second, the ECC processor does binary addition of specific bits in the data word and repeats the process using different bit positions, as shown in Figure 8.10.

Figure 8.10

ECC's error checking is
far more sophisticated
than simple parity
checking.

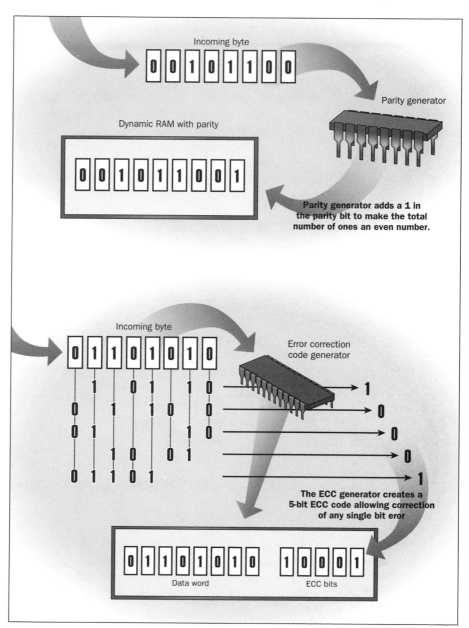

The resulting ECC addition to the data word is longer than a single parity bit—the exact length depends on the length of the data word and the size of the errors you want to catch—and it contains much more information. The ECC processor computes the ECC value of a newly read data word and loads both the new and the old ECC value stored with the word into a few gates that make up a device called a *comparator*. The comparator should come up with a match, represented by a string of zeros. If the result contains any ones, the positions of the ones tell the processor which segment of the word to correct and how to correct it.

The ability to both detect and correct errors in data words makes ECC a valuable feature in a server used in networks that are critical to a company's business. Price-conscious shoppers will never get ECC because the extra chips and processors it requires raise the cost of the systems. But value-conscious buyers, particularly those evaluating systems with high-end processors in the Pentium, Alpha, and PowerPC class, should keep ECC high on their checklists. Selecting ECC up-front could avoid a costly processor halt in the years to come.

Summing Up Servers

So what is a server? Obviously, it is a computer that has enough of the major elements like expansion slots, RAM, storage, and watts to meet your needs. Your definition of "enough" depends completely on how you want to use the network. If you have 2 to 20 PCs storing files from their word processing and spreadsheet programs on a server, you'll get enough of everything from a PC in the $2,000 to $4,000 price range—depending primarily on what hard disk subsystem you want—but if you need gigabytes of storage with backup subsystems on a database server, expect to spend $10,000 and up for your hardware.

■ Choosing Networking-Software Products

In some ways, finding the right server hardware is more difficult than finding the right networking software. Getting the right network software for your organization isn't as difficult as it might seem. Any of the products I've described in this chapter will serve you well.

Here's what you need to consider when you're making your networking choices:

- What is the maximum number of client PCs you're ever likely to have? If the number is less than 100, look closely at LANtastic.

- Do you need to integrate Apple Macintosh computers into your network? If so, NetWare, Windows NT, and Banyan VINES all offer excellent

Macintosh support. DOS-based networking products don't support the Mac as well.

- Do you need to integrate computers using the VMS or Unix operating system into the network? If so, consider the Windows NT products from Digital or AT&T.

- Do you need to link LANs across long-distance telephone lines? Banyan's VINES and the Windows NT family have excellent capabilities for LAN-to-LAN connections.

- Which product comes with the best local technical support? The success of your network operation is directly proportional to the technical support you receive.

- *Alarms and Acronyms*
- *Down-to-Earth Management*
- *Protocol Analyzers*
- *Gathering Statistics at the Server*
- *LAN Metering Software*
- *Network Management Brings Results*

Network Management and Control

TECHNICAL TALE

Walking back to your own desk after getting chewed out was worse than the chewing out itself. Tom Horton's job was a good news/bad news proposition. He started as a junior accountant with a side interest in computers. As the computers became more important to the company, so did he. But now the computer network was critical to the company, and Tom was in over his head. One more network outage, and he'd be out of a job. Most of the network problems were simple enough to fix, but avoiding them was his big worry.

His secretary Elaine (he had learned to call her an "assistant") was waiting in his doorway. "Look, Tom, here's some literature I picked up at that trade show you were too busy to go to. It's supposed to be an Early Warning Network for NetWare."

"Oh, I looked into that network management stuff. It's all based on TCP/IP and needs Unix computers. It's too much for us," Tom replied.

"No," Elaine persisted, "this stuff is just for NetWare, and it doesn't need special management stations. It can spot some problems before they happen, help with troubleshooting, and give you information you can use for budgeting."

Tom was still too shell-shocked to be sufficiently grateful, but at least he had some hope of keeping his job and had learned the real meaning of the term "assistant."

T HE PHRASE *MISSION-CRITICAL APPLICATIONS*—ALWAYS SPOKEN IN GRAVELY serious tones—is an overused part of marketing pitches for network products. It seems every company aiming to price its products at the high end of the scale touts their reliability and dependability for "mission-critical applications." Yet the amount of overuse this phrase receives actually signals an important fact: Organizations depend on their networks for productivity, and some companies start to lose money the second a network malfunctions.

Not only do networks represent an investment in wiring, computers, and software totaling thousands of dollars per node, the network is often the production equipment of the business. The local area network system of a modern organization rates as much management attention as the milling and welding machines in an automobile-manufacturing plant or the sales counters of a department store.

Good networks operate invisibly. The servers respond to requests from the client computers quickly and without any special actions on the part of the people using the network's resources. Because designers make these systems transparent, problems of wiring, configuration, design, and deterioration often don't appear or aren't reported until they result in catastrophic failures. The four words "Your network is down!" are guaranteed to flash-freeze the blood of any network administrator. My goal is to help you avoid unpleasant surprises from your network.

In this chapter, I describe the techniques and tools of network management and control. I'll deal with five somewhat overlapping levels of network-management systems:

- Management utilities

- Networkwide reporting and control

- Wiring-hub reporting and control

- Protocol analysis and traffic counting

- Statistical analysis

The field of network-management systems is confusing primarily because two major categories and several subcategories of products carry the "network management" title. The first category consists of suites of utilities aimed at easing the network manager's burden. These suites, marketed by several companies including Intel, McAfee Software, Saber Software, and Symantec, typically include networkwide virus protection, backup, server monitoring, software inventory control, and software distribution. The suite might also include features such as modem remote control and added security control. These suites of utilities are valuable, but they are only one side of the management story. The other side is networkwide reporting and control. We'll work from the top down, first examining the large-scale network reporting and control systems and then visiting some of the utility suites.

Network control and reporting activities take place at many levels throughout the network, providing readings on pulse points around the network in order to draw a picture of its total health. The largest networks have a hierarchy of devices and programs at several levels reporting status and problems upstream to a central data-gathering and reporting system. But you don't have to put this hierarchy in place all at once. Some products, such as wiring-hub traffic reporting and control systems, generate excellent reports on their own without any need to exchange information with other devices.

The lowest level of network reporting devices consists of hardware boxes with internal microprocessors and programs in ROM that report on the quantity and quality of data passing a particular point in the network. These internal reporting devices include LAN wiring hubs, bridges, routers, multiplexers, microwave radios, and telephone modems. Their internal processors and programs gather statistical information and send status reports to some intermediate level of management software that may be running on a PC practically anywhere in the network. These programs might provide all the analysis a particular network manager needs, or they might send specified items of information on to higher-level management programs for consolidation.

The LAN operating systems in print and file servers can also send special alert messages and periodic status messages on to higher-level management programs running on computers elsewhere in the network. At the highest level of network management activity, application programs complain to management programs about files they can't find or access. The reports from all these levels of hardware and software must be in some common format so that one top-level system can compile them and present them to people who use or respond to them.

Competing grand architectures for network management and control are marketed by such companies as AT&T, DEC, Hewlett-Packard, and IBM. But there is also an attempt to standardize network-management protocols and procedures within the International Standards Organization.

■ Alarms and Acronyms

The whole network management and control industry has two factors in common: reliance on the principle of alarms and the use of a bewildering blizzard of acronyms. The concept of alarms is easy to understand; the acronyms take a lot longer to master.

Using performance alarms means that you instruct the software to call for your attention only when something abnormal occurs. Typically, you can easily adjust the limits of abnormality. Abnormal events might be defined in terms of more than 30 consecutive Ethernet packet collisions, an unusually small or large number of packets sent within a period of time, or practically any other parameter you want to know about, from the temperature inside an equipment cabinet to the AC line voltage. The network management and control software packages offer responses to alarm situations that range from silently logging the event to calling the number of a pager and displaying special codes that describe the problem on the pager's screen.

Everybody's Talking ISO CMIP

The management structure everyone talks about, but few people use, is an emerging "open" architecture called the Common Management Information Protocol or CMIP (pronounced "SEE-mip"). CMIP is a proposal developed by the International Standards Organization (ISO). Major companies such as AT&T, DEC, HP, and Northern Telecom have released products that make up the various pieces of a full CMIP network.

The ISO proposals—evolving companion documents such as the standard developed by the U.S. National Institute of Standards and Technology—primarily define the functions of network-management software and describe how reports are formatted and transmitted. They also describe the format of the messages that are sent to devices trying to correct or isolate error conditions.

The functions the CMIP model defines include fault management, configuration management, performance management, security management, and accounting management. The other models agree with these definitions in general terms.

Fault management includes detecting problems and taking steps to isolate them. *Configuration management* provides messages describing active connections and equipment; it is closely tied to fault management because changing configurations is the primary technique used to isolate network faults. *Performance management* includes counting things like packets, disk access requests, and access to specific programs. *Security management* includes alerting managers to unauthorized access attempts at the cable, network, file-server, and resource levels. *Accounting management* involves billing people for what they use.

Digital Equipment Corp. and AT&T have the most complete implementations of CMIP. Digital calls its CMIP-compatible network-management system the Enterprise Management Architecture. AT&T calls its system the Unified Network Management Architecture (UNMA). The first product released under AT&T's UNMA—the first real CMIP product—was dubbed the Accumaster Integrator.

Everybody's Using SNMP

CMIP is a great idea, but as often happens, the ideal has been pretty much overcome by the practical. The control and reporting system used online today in many major networks is the Simple Network Management Protocol (SNMP). SNMP was developed and is used by the same federal-government and university community that gave us TCP/IP and its suite of protocols. Dr. Jeffrey Case at the University of Tennessee is a leader in the development and use of SNMP.

SNMP works well in the large DoD and commercial networks that use TCP/IP, and there are ways to use SNMP management on even the smallest PC-based LANs. VisiNet, from VisiSoft Corporation, is an excellent and affordable SNMP management platform that runs over Windows. Hewlett-Packard's OpenView SNMP management program for Windows (see Figure 9.1) is relabeled and marketed by many companies. Cabletron has an SNMP system called Spectrum that uses artificial-intelligence modules to apply complex rules and react to the reports of network events it receives. Even AT&T, a strong supporter of CMIP, has acknowledged the importance of SNMP and added support for this management architecture to the AT&T Systems Manager products.

Figure 9.1

This screen from Hewlett-Packard's OpenView SNMP program illustrates the wide-area nature of the program. However, the same management console can deliver detailed information down to the level of an individual wiring-hub port.

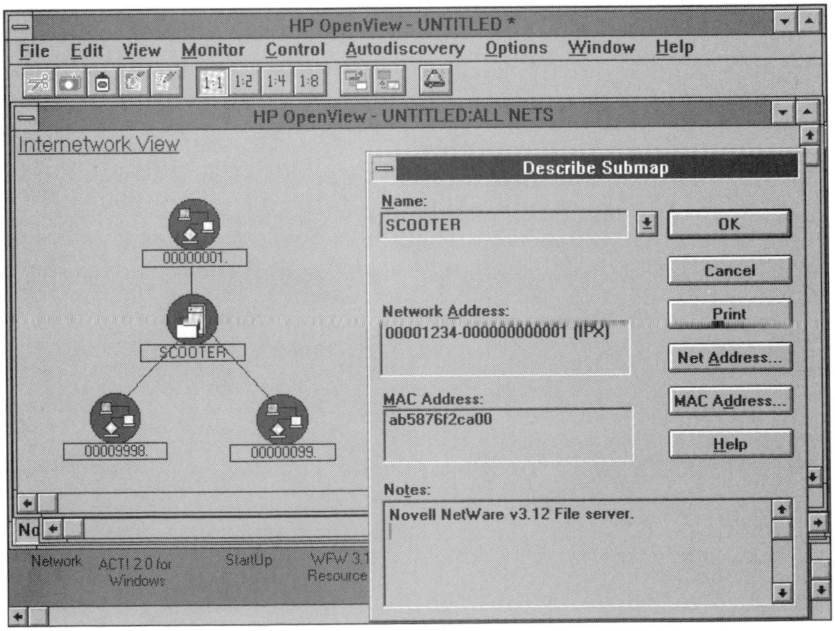

The devices in an SNMP-managed network consist of agents and management stations. *Agents* are devices that report to the management stations. The major requirement for an agent is that it gather statistical information and store it in a "management information base" or MIB. There are two standardized formats for the MIB, and some companies put even more information into what they term MIB extensions. Agents can be wiring hubs, routers, file servers, and any other type of network node. It isn't unusual for an agent like a wiring hub or router to have a separate special-purpose processor, typically in the 80186 class, with a megabyte of memory for gathering and holding statistical information.

The *management station* (there can be any number of these on the network) polls each agent and initiates a transmission of the MIB's contents to the management station. Management stations typically run Windows because of its graphical interface, or some version of Unix because Unix is commonly associated with the UDP and IP network protocols used to communicate between the agents and management stations. Sun workstations running Unix are often used as SNMP management stations.

SNMP's drawbacks center around its lack of security, the inconsistent quality of its documentation, and the tendency of some companies to create nonstandard configurations. In networks that don't use IP as their native transport layer protocol, such as those that use NetWare, you typically must create a computer that can communicate over IP to interrogate the agents. Despite these drawbacks, industry support for SNMP continues to grow because SNMP uses processing power and memory economically, is here today, and works well enough to meet the needs of even the largest network systems. If your network has more than a dozen active nodes or if its operation is critical to your business, you should consider installing wiring hubs and other devices with SNMP management.

VisiNet

VisiNet is an interesting, powerful, and economical SNMP management program that includes realtime monitoring of your network and an unlimited number of hierarchical defined VIEWs of your net. Background maps of the world, countries, and states are included in the bundled package. As a network manger, you can take this view further down to offices, floors, or whatever map best defines your LAN or WAN. The program uses the graphical multitasking environment of Microsoft Windows to set up and map your network easily. Using Dynamic Data Exchange (DDE) and Object Linking and Embedding (OLE) the network manager can send managed data to other Microsoft Windows applications that support DDE, such as Excel. OLE also allows for real-time reporting options and updates.

IBM's NetView

IBM unveiled its network-management products in early 1986; it calls its overall system NetView. While it started out as a proprietary management system centered on IBM's Systems Network Architecture (SNA), NetView is now one of the most ecclectic network management systems. NetView management stations can accept data from a variety of platforms ranging from PCs to mainframes and create a wide range of management reports. On the downside, the number of NetView products is bewildering and some of the acronyms and product names (is AIX NetView/6000 catchy enough?) are daunting. Despite its attempt to be all things to all people, NetView is clearly aimed at installations with IBM mainframe connections.

Down to the Desktop

NetView, CMIP, and SNMP are the grand strategies for management, but other organizations have smaller-scale plans. The Desktop Management Task Force (DMTF), an organization of more than 300 vendors, is completing its definition of a Desktop Management Interface (DMI) for network management systems. The DMI provides a sublayer of management integration below the grand strategies. The goal of the DMI is to define how an agent interacts with devices, components, and programs inside a PC to gather and report very detailed information. Companies that support DMI, such as Intel, use NetBIOS or IPX to bring this information to a central management station.

The Internet Engineering TaskForce also recognized the need for simplified management at the desktop level and has developed an SNMP Host Resources MIB. This MIB defines a common set of objects such as drives, adapters, and applications that a PC can manage.

While it would make sense to integrate the DMI with the Host Resources MIB, progress in this area has been slow. Early DMI programs, like Intel's LANDesk Gateway/SNMP, have consolidated DMI data and made it available to SNMP management consoles. Other vendors will follow the same path. For example, Microcom's LANlord has strong desktop management data-gathering capabilities and can, through the use of an optional proxy agent, relay the destop data to SNMP management consoles.

Novell's NMS

Novell's NetWare Management System (NMS) doesn't fit neatly into a specific network management category. In the minds of some people, NMS is an internetwork architecture that competes with and can replace both the SNMP architecture and products like SunNet Manager and HP OpenView. Some vendors—VisiNet, for example—regard NMS as a system of services and interaction points for their products. Yet others see NMS as another sublayer of

LAN management under the grand strategies of internetwork management. So there are products that interoperate and also compete with NMS. To evaluate these offerings, you'll have to scrutinize the extra management detail and functionality they bring to the system. In particulark, look for NetWare 2.X which NMS lacks.

■ Down-to-Earth Management

Since few people need the kind of network-management system NASA might use to control deep space probes, I'll narrow the focus of this chapter just a bit. Network operating systems like NetWare, VINES, and Windows NT include network management utilities, but these utilities don't tell you much, if anything, about the activities of remote printers, communications gateways, mail servers, database servers, routers, and other devices on the LAN. If you want a full picture of the network's activity and health, you have to go to the lowest common denominator: the physical layer of network cabling.

Reporting and Control from the Wiring Hub

As I pointed out in my discussions of 10BaseT and Token-Ring wiring topologies, a central wiring hub is a strong pulse point in the network. Since all the traffic goes through the hub—even traffic that bypasses the file server and moves directly between client stations and print or communications servers—a microprocessor in the hub can monitor and report on all network activity. The same processor can also give the network administrator certain levels of control over network connections.

Wiring-hub control and management systems, like the Proteon Token-VIEW Plus shown in Figure 9.2, provide a great deal of information. These packages are uniquely independent of the LAN operating-system software, and fit into most of the grand management-architecture schemes, or soon will.

From its central vantage point, a wiring hub sees every node. A hub can record events, measure the number and quality of packets each node sends, and provide information on network interfaces. The on-board processors in these hubs work with software running in a PC to report on all network nodes and control them when necessary, mainly by disconnecting them.

The leading companies marketing wiring-hub reporting and control software include 3COM, Cabletron, Fibermux, NetWorth, Proteon, SynOptics, Optical Data Systems, and Thomas-Conrad Corp. Figure 9.3 shows how the Fibermux SnapLAN system displays statistics.

The cable-hub data-gathering systems use a variety of wiring schemes. The systems from Cabletron, Fibermux, NetWorth, 3Com, and SynOptics can interconnect practically all types of cabling and adapters. Figure 9.4

Figure 9.2

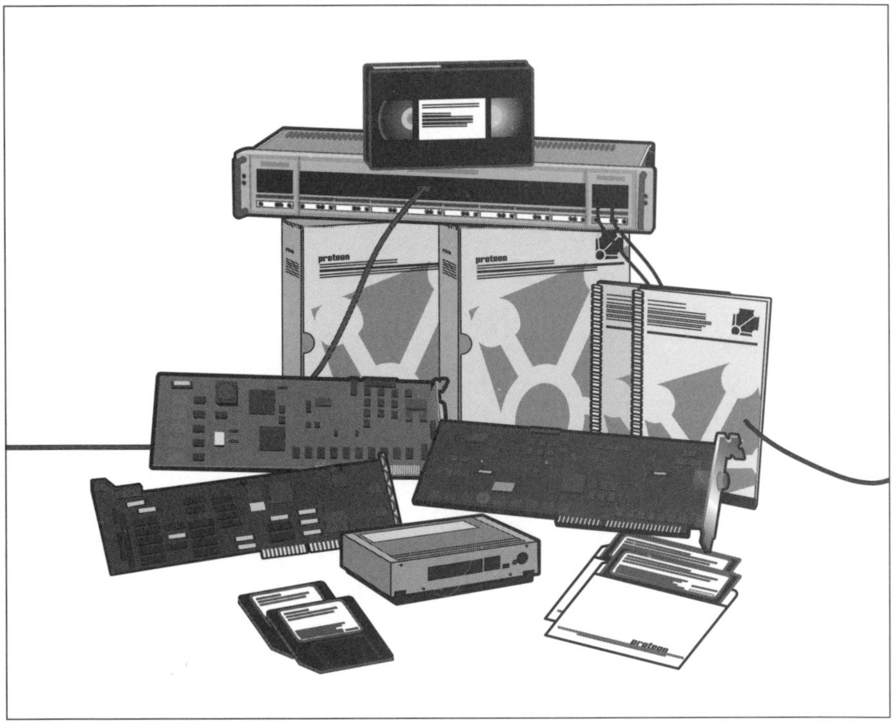

Proteon's TokenVIEW
Plus management
system includes a Series
70 Intelligent Wire
Center, TokenVIEW
Manager software, and
interconnecting system
boards.

shows another statistical view of the SnapLAN system. If you want to run similar software on a Macintosh, Farallon Computing has a product called TrafficWatch that reports on and manages networks using Apple's LocalTalk architecture.

These products don't decode the traffic passing through the hubs. More complex devices called protocol analyzers, described later in this chapter, handle the complex decoding chore. Protocol analyzers that capture and decode packets provide some of the same information available through wiring-hub reporting and control systems, but you have to work a lot harder to get the information, and you don't get the "big picture" that wiring-hub systems provide.

The reporting and control systems that operate at the network cable level don't decode packets, so they present no risk to the security of data or passwords. Protocol analyzers have a role in organizations where people develop sophisticated software and network hardware, but reporting and control systems have a role in almost every network. People who use protocol analyzers in place of network reporting and control systems are using a telescope to view a football game from the sidelines. They can read the quarterback's lips, but they miss a lot of the action.

Figure 9.3

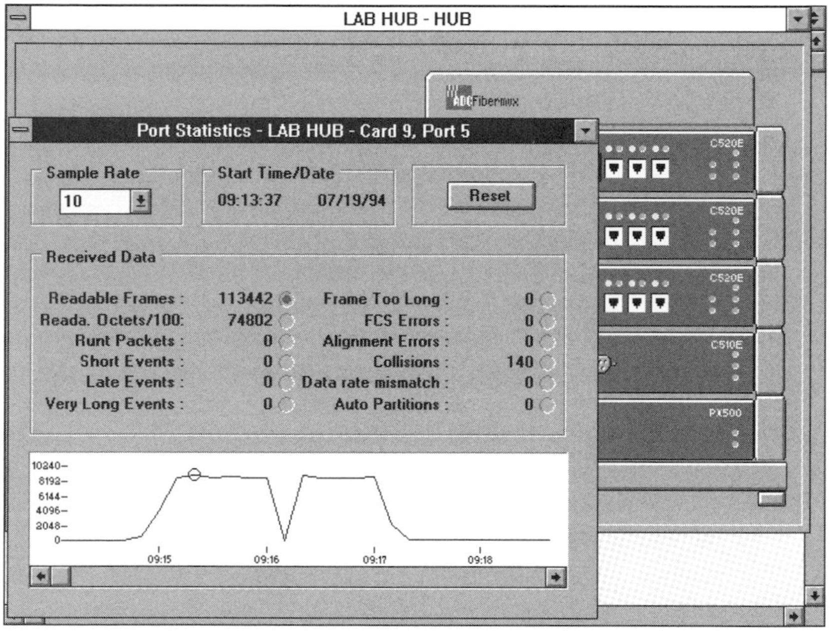

The Fibermux SnapLAN management software can graphically report a variety of problems and statistical information.

Figure 9.4

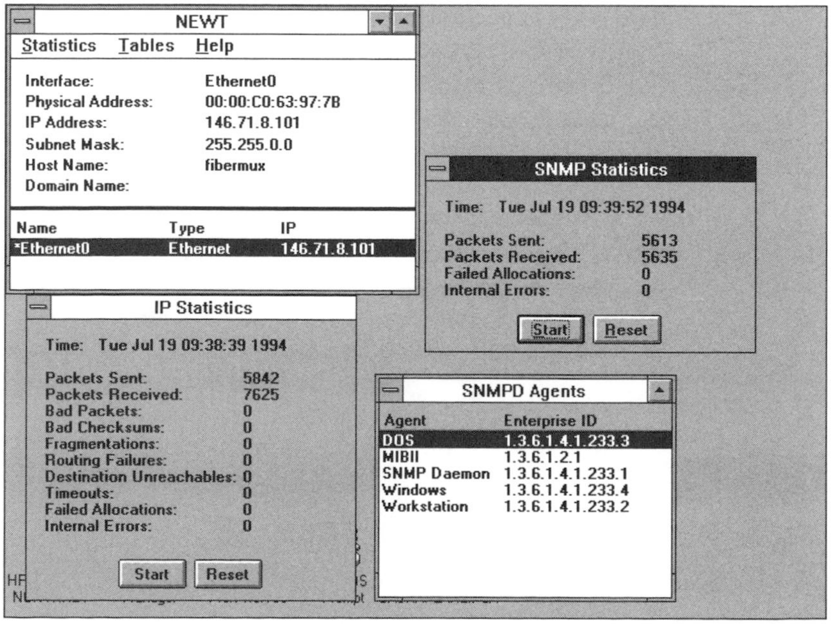

In this screen, the SnapLAN software provides a detailed analysis of the various protocols transiting through the hub.

It is difficult to break out the added incremental cost for the network reporting and control capabilities in wiring-hub systems. Wiring hubs or concentrators from Cabletron, SynOptics, and companies with similar products, include major elements of the network-management features. While the initial cost for software and hardware is usually several thousand dollars, that single outlay is amortized over all the nodes you have now and all that you will add in the future. Since larger networks usually benefit most from reporting and control, their per-node cost is typically very low.

By themselves, these products provide all the network reporting and control capabilities many organizations will ever need, but if you expect your network to grow with multiple servers, gateways, bridges, and wide-area connections, you may soon find yourself thinking about adding more layers of reporting. Looking for CMIP or SNMP compatibility in all your network components is a smart idea, but installing reporting and control now at the lowest hardware layer is the smartest move of all.

SynOptics LNMS

SynOptics Communications has been the leader in wiring-hub reporting and control systems, so I'll take a few paragraphs to describe this company's popular products. At the same time, Cabletron Systems leads a pack of aggressive challengers to SynOptics. Cabletron's LANview software, combined with its line of Multi Media Access Center intelligent wiring hubs, bridges, and network interface boards, makes this firm a powerful competitor.

SynOptics' LattisNet Network Management System (LNMS) runs in a PC under Microsoft Windows. It receives status and performance data, typically using the CMIP standards, from several models of network hubs called LattisNet concentrators.

Several pieces of hardware make up a concentrator. SynOptics provides a choice of cabinets, each containing a different number of slots and appropriate power supplies. A single Model 3000 Premises Concentrator can connect to as many as 132 nodes. Smaller units provide economical connections for department-size networks or subnetworks at a level price of about $75 to $150 per node.

Each concentrator cabinet accepts the same family of 10-by-14-by-2-inch slide-in modules, which provide connections for the nodes over twisted-pair or fiber-optic cable. Similar modules integrate thin Ethernet and fiber-optic cable with 10BaseT unshielded twisted-pair networks. SynOptics also has connections for the 100-megabit-per-second Fiber Distributed Data Interface (FDDI). These slide-in modules connect and translate between the different wiring and signaling schemes, so network planners can mix and match media to produce custom-tailored systems.

Each module in the LattisNet system has an array of status lights providing a visual presentation of the present activity that is echoed in the display of the LNMS software. The heart of the LattisNet Network Management System is a device called the Network Management Module. This module works in a concentrator and carries its own 80186 processor, which gathers data and sends packets to the special processor board and software running in the PC designated as the system-management console. Because the concentrator must maintain a connection to other concentrators and to the PC running LNMS even if the network is down, the Network Management Module can call those stations by using a modem and a telephone line if it can't make contact over the network. One version of the Network Management Module has an RS-232C port for an external modem, and another version has a built-in modem.

The display screen of the system-management PC running LNMS, created under Microsoft Windows, is certain to become a "must see" stop on every VIP tour of your facility. Even if people don't understand the details of what they are looking at, the LNMS screens are impressive.

For the network manager and troubleshooter, the LNMS screens are valuable tools. The primary system display shows a diagram of the network, portraying each LattisNet concentrator and every module and connection in it. You don't have to enter the details of the network into a database so the program can build the diagram. The software uses the network to interrogate each concentrator, gather its status on a second-by-second basis, and create the screen presentation from that current information base. If a person doing repairs on a concentrator across the campus changes a module or disconnects a cable to one node, you see the change on the screen within five seconds. You can supplement the database the program creates to add English names and other descriptive data to each node, but the program does most of the work.

An eye-catching part of the screen presentation is a histogram showing the activity flowing through each concentrator. This display is particularly useful for pinpointing very busy sections of the network that need more connections or perhaps require an intelligent bridge to isolate them from the rest of the system.

Other screens are even more spectacular. If you use a mouse or the cursor-control keys to select a particular concentrator on the network, the screen creates a complete diagram of the concentrator with all of its modules, plus a second-by-second update of the status lights on each module. If you make a similar cursor selection of a single port on the concentrator, you can choose displays showing the respective numbers of good, misaligned, undersized, late, and colliding packets. You can even display the activity on several nodes at the same time, so you can perform sophisticated tasks like checking the flow of data between a workstation and a gateway.

These screen displays give you a very detailed picture of the present status of the network and its subelements. For longer-term analysis, LNMS provides the ability to collect raw statistical data and the programming to create a predefined series of reports. The reports include half a dozen pie and bar charts showing throughput rates and out-of-tolerance operation. These data collections and reports are created as ASCII files, so you can pass them on to more sophisticated database programs.

In the area of control, none of these media-level systems can do anything more than disconnect a node from the network, but LNMS at least gives you the option of doing so politely. You can disconnect a node after a notification message or without notification, or arrange for automatic disconnection if certain criteria (such as a dozen packet collisions in a row) are reached.

SynOptics and Cabletron support the high-level NetView and CMIP protocol standards and also include reporting according to these protocols.

Adapters at Work

The key element in all protocol-analysis and traffic-counting tools is the network adapter card that links the computer into the network. The chip sets on such adapters alert the software to each passing packet, translate data formats, and move received data to RAM so the software can work on it. The chip sets also contain cable-testing functions.

The National Semiconductor chip set on a typical Ethernet adapter card can report 17 different errors pertaining to transmission control, reception, and packet format. Some of the most common errors include *runt* packets, which don't contain enough bits, and *dribble* packets, which contain enough bits but don't end on an even byte. The Hewlett-Packard LANProbe shown in Figure 9.5 shows a display waiting to report these types of errors.

When a transmitting Ethernet adapter detects a collision with another station's packet, it transmits a jam signal of 4 to 6 bytes of arbitrary data to ensure that all stations detect the collision. Any receiving adapter reports the jam signal as a collision to any monitoring software. The LAN traffic counters accept these reports from Ethernet adapters, or similar types of reports from ARCnet or Token-Ring adapters, and convert them into useful charts, graphs, and reports.

Some programs work with many brands of adapters, and some with only one brand. When the PC Magazine LAN Labs team tested these products, we found that the type of adapter in use significantly influenced each program's ability to report and capture data correctly under heavy loads.

Both wiring-hub traffic-management systems and traffic counters operating over LAN adapters provide a practical and broad view of the network. They measure the force and volume of the river of data coursing through your network. But sometimes you need to sample the quality of the water to

Figure 9.5

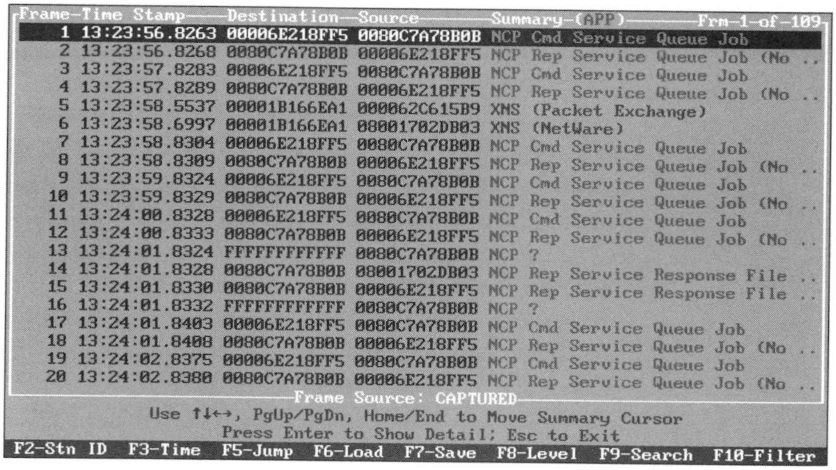

This screen from the NetWare LANalyzer program shows a string of 20 captured packets and describes their destination and source, and includes a brief description of function.

```
┌─Frame─Time Stamp───Destination──Source──────Summary─(APP)──────Frm─1─of─109─┐
│    1 13:23:56.8263 00006E218FF5 0080C7A78B0B NCP Cmd Service Queue Job       │
│    2 13:23:56.8268 0080C7A78B0B 00006E218FF5 NCP Rep Service Queue Job (No ..│
│    3 13:23:57.8283 00006E218FF5 0080C7A78B0B NCP Cmd Service Queue Job       │
│    4 13:23:57.8289 0080C7A78B0B 00006E218FF5 NCP Rep Service Queue Job (No ..│
│    5 13:23:58.5537 00001B166EA1 000062C615B9 XMS (Packet Exchange)           │
│    6 13:23:58.6997 00001B166EA1 08001702DB03 XMS (NetWare)                   │
│    7 13:23:58.8304 00006E218FF5 0080C7A78B0B NCP Cmd Service Queue Job       │
│    8 13:23:58.8309 0080C7A78B0B 00006E218FF5 NCP Rep Service Queue Job (No ..│
│    9 13:23:59.8324 00006E218FF5 0080C7A78B0B NCP Cmd Service Queue Job       │
│   10 13:23:59.8329 0080C7A78B0B 00006E218FF5 NCP Rep Service Queue Job (No ..│
│   11 13:24:00.8328 00006E218FF5 0080C7A78B0B NCP Cmd Service Queue Job       │
│   12 13:24:00.8333 0080C7A78B0B 00006E218FF5 NCP Rep Service Queue Job (No ..│
│   13 13:24:01.8324 FFFFFFFFFFFF 0080C7A78B0B NCP ?                           │
│   14 13:24:01.8328 0080C7A78B0B 08001702DB03 NCP Rep Service Response File ..│
│   15 13:24:01.8330 0080C7A78B0B 00006E218FF5 NCP Rep Service Response File ..│
│   16 13:24:01.8332 FFFFFFFFFFFF 0080C7A78B0B NCP ?                           │
│   17 13:24:01.8403 00006E218FF5 0080C7A78B0B NCP Cmd Service Queue Job       │
│   18 13:24:01.8408 0080C7A78B0B 00006E218FF5 NCP Rep Service Queue Job (No ..│
│   19 13:24:02.8375 00006E218FF5 0080C7A78B0B NCP Cmd Service Queue Job       │
│   20 13:24:02.8380 0080C7A78B0B 00006E218FF5 NCP Rep Service Queue Job (No ..│
│                       ─Frame Source: CAPTURED─                               │
│          Use ↑↓←→, PgUp/PgDn, Home/End to Move Summary Cursor                │
│                  Press Enter to Show Detail; Esc to Exit                     │
│ F2-Stn ID  F3-Time  F5-Jump  F6-Load  F7-Save  F8-Level  F9-Search  F10-Filter│
└──────────────────────────────────────────────────────────────────────────────┘
```

get a more detailed picture of what it carries. In networks, you sample the data stream with products called protocol analyzers.

■ Protocol Analyzers

"I'm not sure what it does, but I knew when I saw it that I just had to have one." That feeling, expressed by a fledgling network manager at a Manhattan bank, represents the feelings of many buyers of LAN diagnostic equipment. For some people, protocol analyzers are powerful tools, but for others they are merely talismans or amulets that confer status and just might ward off network miseries.

Protocol analyzers, like Network General's Sniffer and the SpiderAnalyzer shown in Figure 9.6, carry price tags of many thousands of dollars. They have growing competition from alternative products that are more economical and just as useful for typical network managers, so you'll want to find the right combination of price and capability for your installation. Let's start with a few simple definitions and explanations. What is a protocol, and why does it need analysis anyway?

Protocol = Agreement

A *protocol* is nothing more than a formal agreement about how computers should format and acknowledge information during a communications session. When products from different companies follow the same protocol, they have the ability to communicate—theoretically, at least.

Figure 9.6

Spider System's P320R is a portable protocol analyzer with a wide range of protocol-decoding and traffic-monitoring capabilities.

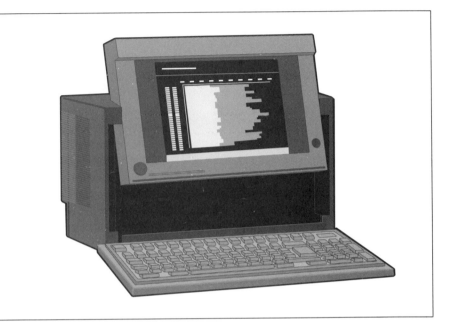

In operation, communications software wraps a data message inside leading and trailing data fields whose format is determined by the protocols that software follows. These data fields form an envelope for the message while it transits the communications link. Since the sending and receiving systems must use the same protocols, they know how to read an envelope's address, route it, deliver it, and even get a receipt, regardless of what it contains. If communications over the link break down, reading the leading and trailing fields and even opening the envelope and decoding the data in the message it frames might give you clues to the problem.

A *protocol analyzer* is the tool you use to read a protocol-configured packet. Different protocol analyzers exist for all types of communications circuits, including X.25, ISDN, and several specific types of local area network cabling, signaling, and protocol architectures. You can set up analyzers for ARCnet, Ethernet, and Token-Ring networks. These products typically look like laptop PCs. They have screens with flashing displays, and software that can produce graphs and printed reports.

Network protocol analyzers capture data packets flying across a network and use special software to decode them. All LAN protocol analyzers let you filter and sort incoming and captured data for easier processing, and the top units, such as Network General's Sniffer, provide an English-language identification of the protocols in use and an evaluation of any damage to or irregularities in the captured data.

You can use the protocol analyzer to display packets selectively in real time or to capture activity on the network for later study. You might set filter criteria so the analyzer displays only incoming packets going to or from certain stations, formatted according to specific protocols, or containing certain errors. Setting several filters simultaneously reduces the need for storage capacity in the analyzer. Alternatively, you can let the analyzer capture all the data it can hold—thousands of Ethernet packets—and then use the same filters to perform a careful analysis of the captured data. Some analyzer software contains an editor so you can delete unimportant data, enter comments, print reports, and even create files in common database formats. The ease of setting filters and reviewing data is an important criterion for protocol analyzers.

While their protocol-analysis capabilities are powerful, the function most people use these devices for is much less sophisticated. The screen display you usually see is a graph of current network activity. My experience is that people giving VIP tours of an organization love to bring visitors past the "network control center" so they can see the marching bar graphs showing network, and presumably corporate, activity. These screens, like the one shown in Figure 9.7, usually include other information as well, such as the number of bytes or bits per second moving across the network, the percentage of maximum network capacity, the number of bad packets, and some measurement of the peak load experienced since the monitor was activated.

Figure 9.7

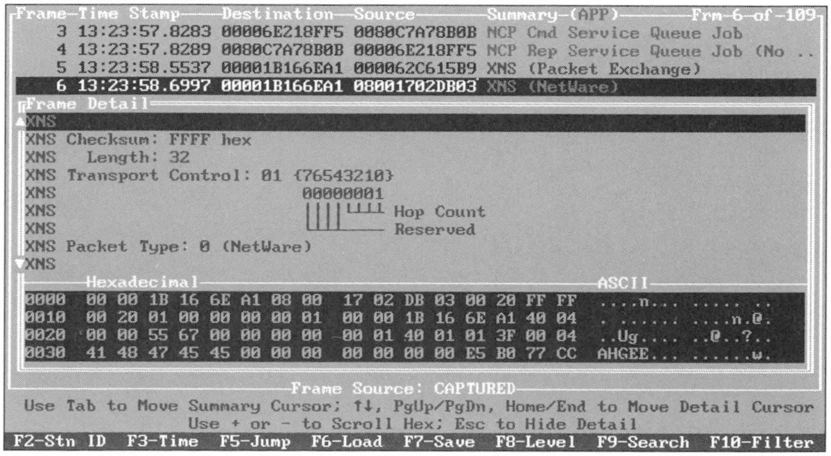

Another screen display from the NetWare LANalyzer provides a detailed breakdown of the contents of a specific portion of a packet coded in the XNS protocol.

Protocol analyzers also contain many other functions. Most have the ability to replace arcane hexadecimal station addresses with meaningful names, giving the whole process a friendlier face.

Most analyzers can also use a technique called *time domain reflectometry*, or TDR, to test cables for improperly terminated connections. This technique involves sending a signal out on the cable and then watching for and interpreting its echo. The systems can locate the position of open and shorted cable conditions with varying degrees of accuracy. At the PC Magazine Labs we've tested some products claiming to have TDR capabilities and found that you might be better off witching with a bent willow twig. Real TDRs are typically precision devices, often equipped with oscilloscope screens for exact measurement.

Protocol analyzers can generate network traffic too. Some systems, like Network General's Sniffer, contain a traffic generator that loads the network with a stream of good packets. This activity is useful for checking certain behaviors of adapters and routers, but not for much else.

An important troubleshooting capability, contained in Novell's LAN-alyzer, lets you rebroadcast a captured data stream onto the network. Imagine, for example, a network troubleshooter capturing an exchange between a client workstation and a server that contains errant responses from the server. The troubleshooter could enter the captured data file, edit out the bad responses, and send the same requests to the server over and over again while trying to isolate the problem. All of this could take place without interrupting activity at the client station. This capability has obvious security implications, which we'll address a little later, but it is certainly a useful troubleshooting tool.

LAN protocol analyzers aren't unique to any particular type of network operating system. You have to pick a product that works with the network adapters and cables in your system. Also, you should choose one that has decoders available for the protocols used by your networking software. For example, if you have a NetWare server, make sure the package has IPX/SPX decoding. If you have a LAN Manager server, select a product that can decode NetBIOS and SMB.

Security

As passive monitoring devices, analyzers don't log onto a server and aren't subject to server-software security. The ability to copy and decode packets as they cross the network means that anyone with a protocol analyzer can easily find and decode packets carrying passwords used as people sign onto servers; in fact, the protocol analyzer can capture any data sent across the network. NetWare 3.X encrypts passwords for transmission, but no operating system encrypts data files; this is typically the job of add-on encryption hardware or special-purpose software. When you give someone a protocol analyzer, that person gains a wide-open tap on the network.

Packet Decoding

A protocol analyzer can do one thing for you that no other product can: It can decode the contents of captured packets or tokens and display an English-language interpretation, in addition to the hexadecimal code. If you need that function, odds are you will lay out between $10,000 and $20,000 for the tools to do it.

Buy What You Need

The first consideration in purchasing these management products is value. Not only should you get what you pay for, you should use what you pay for, too. LAN protocol analyzers are impressive tools—if you need one, there is no substitute—but if you don't need all their power, wiring-hub reporting and control programs or LAN traffic counters can give you an excellent view into your network's operation for a lot less money.

■ Gathering Statistics at the Server

Mountains of statistics are nothing without interpretation and insight, but with those skills managers can use statistics to move mountains. Networks are dynamic operational systems. You can define their operation in terms of certain measurable parameters. Managers can use those measurements to plan for growth, determine a baseline for comparison, detect problems in early stages, and justify budgets.

A host of modern programs now provides statistical data in both raw and quantified form to LAN administrators. Careful analysis of the data helps administrators create a productive and efficient LAN environment. The products available range from those that check the LAN for circumstances exceeding certain limits to those that soak up every detail of operation they can wring from servers and network adapter cards.

The products creating statistical reports are typically software, although a few have specific hardware components. For the most part, these are third-party, add-on software packages for your LAN that complement any statistical-reporting and management-control capabilities your network operating system already has.

The factors these programs attempt to measure include

- The amount of disk storage space used by particular applications, persons, or cost centers

- The amount of activity in specific programs or files

- The connection time of specific people or client PCs

- The number of print jobs (expressed in several ways)

- Server workloads over a period of time

- Any of a few dozen other parameters

The statistical data you collect with such reporting programs constitutes a day-to-day assessment of your operation that serves as a baseline to assist in LAN troubleshooting and as a platform for planning growth. These programs allow you to compile and format your LAN information so you can see statistics before and after a problem or change. Such information is valuable for finding problems and for projecting requirements and budgets. In addition, programs that create data files in dBASE or comma-delimited ASCII formats lend themselves to financial-analysis tasks.

The newest word in network management is "suites." Suites of network-management programs are made up of many functional utilities that interact, more or less, and work together to present a comprehensive picture of a network's health. The elements of network-management software suites range in power from simple programs that monitor the CPU cycles on your network file server to software and hardware inventory programs that can report the interrupt numbers of every adapter in every client PC on your system. Integration within a suite of products can mean a common database of information, a common interface or management program, or even a single console program that ties the reports from isolated programs together.

The network management landscape includes upwards of 15 to 20 islands of utilities (some would argue more). But five basic areas that up the main mass of LAN management: inventory management (including software metering) , traffic monitoring, client PC monitoring, server monitoring, and application software distribution.

Some of the most popular and powerful network management utilities include Saber Software's Saber LAN Workstation and Saber Enterprise Application Manager (SEAM), Symantec's Norton Administrator for Networks, and Frye Computer System's Frye Utilities for Networks. These products are all different, but any of them can help you keep track of your network resources and, in turn, keep your costs in line.

Saber's LAN Workstation and SEAM, allow you to keep a full inventory of all of the hardware and software on your entire network. SEAM allows you to meter network software and ensure that no one in your company is breaking a license agreement. SEAM can also tell you if you have more user licenses of a particular product than you really need. Among the product's nicest features are the ability to meter software across a WAN and to loan different servers copies of an application. For example, if your server in California has a 50-user license of WordPerfect and another client needs access, that client can borrow a license of WordPerfect from another server on the network.

Norton Administrator is a collection of networking tools that allow you to edit network login scripts, monitor and control network printers and print queues, and keep a working inventory of your network software and hardware. The biggest selling point of the Norton Administrator is its graphical interface. All of Norton's tools are easy to access and use.

Frye's Utilities are designed as NetWare program replacements. With Frye Utilities for Networks, you can perform all the tasks of programs such as Syscon, Pconsole, and Fconsole, from a single menu-based program.

Like network applications, network utilities are designed to lighten the network administrator's load and to increase productivity by pinpointing problems on your network. Network utilities increase your network awareness. They can help you draw a map of your network, spot needed changes, and diagnose problems so you can eliminate trouble before it starts. Before we get into a description of a few specific management suites, let's examine the function of the most common suite component: metering software.

■ LAN Metering Software

LAN metering programs are a subset of general inventory programs, but the topic is worth addressing separately because it is the only area of networking that can keep you out of jail or help you to avoid legal fees and fines! Metering tools give you important information on how the network and network applications are used. If people abuse software licenses, you and your organization can face prosecution. Metering programs have the unique ability to regulate the number of simultaneous users for each application on your network and to establish better security on your LAN at the same time.

Marketing a networked application is a challenging task for many companies. The technology of file sharing isn't a problem anymore; any graduate of a one-semester programming course knows how to write applications that can have simultaneous multiple accesses to the same data file. But LAN piracy is a real threat to the survival of many software companies.

There are two forms of piracy: blatant and subtle. Blatant piracy takes place when someone copies a program from the LAN file server onto a floppy disk and walks out the door with it. LANs are often the scene of subtler piracy, however. When a network administrator buys one single-user copy of a spreadsheet program and lets twelve people access it simultaneously, the company selling that product has been pirated out of a lot of money!

Some software companies try to ignore networks and offer no site-licensing agreements. If you want to use their packages legally at multiple PCs, you need to own multiple copies of each program. Particularly in the case of several federal-government computer contracts, this has resulted in organizations with closets full of shrink-wrapped packages—one for each potential user—while one copy of the program is shared on the network.

Other program vendors have fought the LAN piracy problem with techniques like internal counters that lock out attempts to use more than the authorized number of copies and "bump disks" that increase the number of authorized users, but Network administrators hate these restrictions because they interfere with legitimate backups and server restorations.

Today, most vendors of applications that can work on networks have site-licensing agreements available. Because no one has a perfect solution, the most common licensing agreement is on a "per server" basis. Only the most inexperienced or corrupt administrator would violate this type of license.

Per-server site licenses are expensive for small LANs. Many administrators find that buying a supply of single-copy versions of each program is still the best alternative. But smart network managers also know that it isn't usually economical to have a separate copy of an application program for each person on the network. Seldom does everyone need to use any one application at the same time. Smart network planners and administrators attempt to buy only enough copies of an application to meet the peak demand—but demands have a way of changing.

Some products only audit and report on use; they don't lock people out. The reports show when the demand exceeds the legal supply, so you can take action to correct the situation before it becomes a serious problem. With metering-software tools, you can track the number of copies of an application in use and determine the number of copies you should buy for effective LAN management. You can also improve the overall network security and compile statistical data with these products.

Metering products vary in price from $100 to $800 and up, depending on the applications and nodes on your network. You can choose among simple packages that report LAN usage, menuing programs that control applications from behind customized screens, and auditing packages that create extensive reports on every type of network activity.

LAN administrators have a moral and legal responsibility to audit or meter the use of all licensed applications. Software companies lose money when people violate their software licenses by giving more than the allowed number of users access to the program.

Software companies have taken legal action against large corporate LAN pirates, although most cases are settled out of court. The vendors often learn about licensing violations from disgruntled employees looking for some way to strike at a former employer. Large organizations and independent auditing firms usually have software licensing on their internal audit checklists. If the application being audited is misused, there may be fines and discredit for the accused company. But with the audit and control measures established through metering software, license-abuse problems should never arise.

Because metering programs give you a full picture of who uses what resource when, they provide great support for budget requests and operations reports. You can wow the bean-counters by producing professional-looking reports from most of these programs. Add a few month-to-month statistics, put them on an overhead chart, and you may never again have to worry about your budget requests being rejected!

The Saber Software Suite

Saber Software's suite of network management applications includes Saber LAN Workstation, Server Manager, and the Saber Enterprise Applications Manager (SEAM). The $199 LAN Workstation is Saber's flagship program, and offers features including application metering, hardware and software inventory, software update and distribution, a DOS and Windows menu utility, and network remote control. SEAM is a $695 add-on to LAN Workstation that expands software metering across multiple file servers. The $695 Saber Server Manager allows you to monitor and tune your NetWare file servers. Figure 9.8 shows a Saber server manager screen. Together these programs offer an inexpensive but powerful way to monitor and control your local or enterprise-wide network.

Figure 9.8

Saber Server Manager provides a variety of graphs depicting many statistical functions within the server.

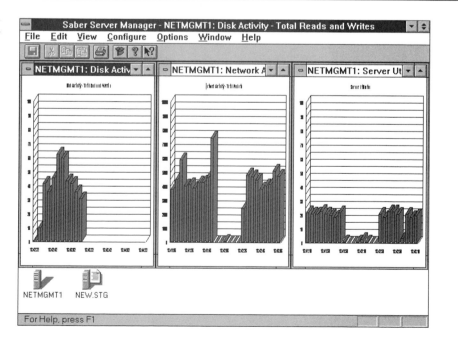

Saber LAN Workstation provides numerous useful utilities, and you should plan on spending a few days installing and configuring all these features. The LAN Workstation package includes five large manuals and requires approximately 21MB of disk space. LAN Workstation also requires you to edit your client and server configuration files manually, a task most other network utilities perform for you.

LAN Workstation allows you to produce an inventory of all of the hardware and software on your network clients. You can configure the inventory utility to perform a scan every time a user turns on their PC or at prescheduled times during the day. Unfortunately, LAN Workstation cannot produce an inventory of your file server hardware, only of the network clients. The hardware and software utility works with most major networks including Novell NetWare, Banyan VINES, and Microsoft networks.

The inventory utility is closely integrated with the software metering features found in LAN Workstation. The application meter uses the information from the software inventory scan to add metered application to the database. In fact, you cannot meter an application until it has been scanned and added to the Saber database. Unlike the Frye Utilities for Networks, which we'll discuss next, Saber allows you to meter applications on the file server and the client PCs. Figure 9.9 shows an inventory screen.

Figure 9.9

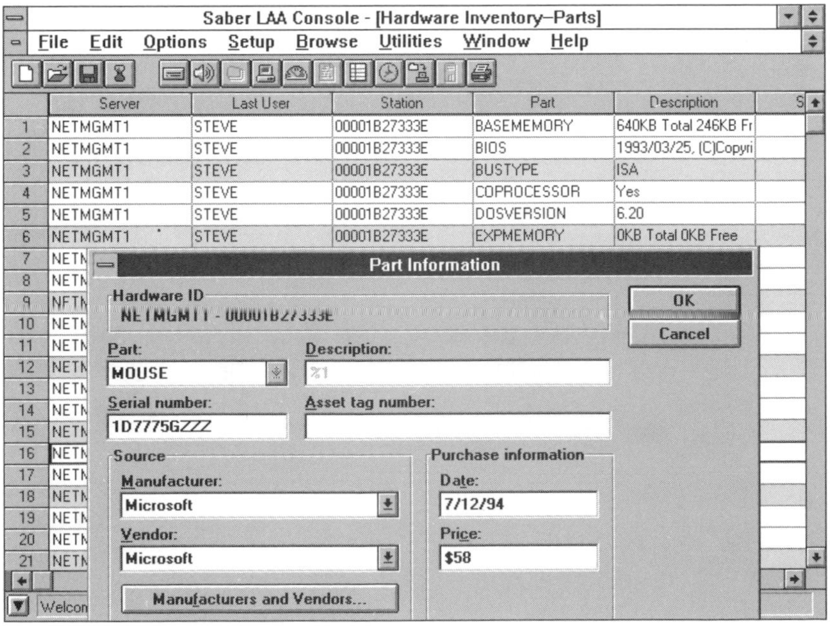

The Saber suite of management software can provide detailed inventory reports. This screen shows a mouse as part of a hardware inventory.

Saber offers four modes for application metering: Metering off, Audit only, Nonsecure, and Secure. Metering off disables software metering for all applications. Audit-only does not restrict people from accessing a licensed application, but keeps a log of all software usage. This mode is ideal for monitoring software usage before you invest in more user licenses. The Nonsecure mode allows you to run applications that are not metered, while the Secure mode requires you to meter every application on the server.

If you add SEAM, you gain the ability to meter applications over multiple file servers. SEAM runs as an NLM and includes additional features such as a queue for users waiting on a metered application and the ability to share licenses among servers.

Saber LAN Workstation offers a very powerful scripting language you can use to automate software updates and distribution. SaberBASIC is a Windows-based programming language that is very similar to Microsoft Basic. You can use SaberBASIC to create programs for distributing files, launching applications, and running reports. You can also create scripts that will automatically launch an application on remote network clients. Unlike the scripting language for Frye's FUN, SaberBASIC does not allow you to create a script for automatically loading and unloading NLMs on your server.

Although SaberBASIC is more powerful than the scripting languages found in Frye's FUN and McAfee's Sitemeter, Saber does not provide any canned scripts to use as examples. If you are not familiar with Basic, you will have to learn it before you can start creating even the most rudimentary scripts. (Saber does offer canned scripts on their BBS, however.) If you want a powerful scripting language use Saber; if you want one that's easy to use, look elsewhere.

The Server Manager allows you to fine-tune your NetWare server using NetWare set parameters. The Server Manager provides an easy-to-use menu for changing your server parameters and monitoring other server information such as I/O, disk usage, and cache statistics. Basically, Server Manager takes the raw data from NetWare and presents it in an easy-to-understand graph or report.

All of Saber's utilities offer excellent reporting tools. You can add comments and notes to your inventory information and create very detailed customized reports. For example, you can create a report showing how many hard drives you have and their total capacity, along with each one's manufacturer, warranty information, and price. You can also create a report on software usage for individual departments or by application.

Saber bundles Ocean Isle's Reachout Remote Control program for accessing network clients with its products. You can use Reachout to take control of another user's PC, and run applications or make configuration changes.

Saber's LAN Workstation, Server Manager, and SEAM provide a wealth of information and control over your network applications. Saber does not provide as much network traffic and server information as some other products, such as FUN, but if you want powerful application metering for your network, Saber's the way to go.

The Frye Utilities for Networks

Frye Computer Systems' Frye Utilities for Networks (FUN) is a suite of network management modules that provide hardware and software inventory, network traffic monitoring, software update and distribution, notification of network errors, NetWare server management, and network client tracking. The FUN modules range in price from $149 for the Node Tracker to $1,495 for the Software Update and Distribution System (SUDS) Wide Area Network Distribution Module.

By the time you combine several modules, FUN is more expensive than other network utilities, such as Norton Administrator for Networks or Saber LAN Workstation; however, the tight integration between individual modules and numerous features found in FUN make the product a bargain, especially for medium to large networks.

The LAN Directory module produces an inventory of all your network hardware and software. This program uses a utility to scan the network hardware and software of every client who connects to the network or turns on a PC. LAN Directory works with several network operating systems, including Novell NetWare, Banyan VINES, and Microsoft networks.

In addition to keeping track of the hardware on PCs, LAN Directory also inventories over 150 Macintosh hardware items. As well as recognizing different hardware items, it knows about 6,000 software programs and provides the name, vendor, and a description of each one. Naturally, you can use all of this information to create detailed reports. The LAN Directory is integrated with the Early Warning System, so you can configure it to alert the network administrator when hardware or software changes occur. The Software Metering and Resource Tracking (SMART) module allows you to control access to applications based on user licenses.

You can use the Node Tracker utility to monitor network traffic. The ability to monitor the number and status of the IPX packets moving across the cable is a handy way to find troublesome cable problems that sometimes masquerade as other complaints. Some other packages, such as McAfee's Bright-Works, lack the ability to monitor packets and collisions on the network. You can also use Node Tracker to create a map of all the nodes on your network and monitor each one individually.

Frye offers two Software Update Distribution (SUDS) packages: SUDS for a single network with one or two servers, and the SUDS WAN for enterprise wide networks. You can use either of Frye's SUDS products to distribute and update files and programs on every PC in your network; they allow you to collect files, edit them, and then send them back to network clients.

The SUDS model is based on procedures, criteria, and actions. *Procedures* are entire software update or distribution actions that you design. *Criteria* are lists of client PCs to be updated, and *actions* are the tasks themselves. Frye includes several canned scripts you can use to perform procedures such as updating every 486 PC with a new Windows video driver. While Frye's scripting language is not as powerful and versatile as that of some other products, such as Saber's SaberBASIC, it is easy to use and lets you create procedures quickly.

The Frye NetWare Management utilities allow you to perform every task found in NetWare programs such as Monitor, Syscon, Fconsole, and Pconsole from a single menu. NetWare Management provides information about your NetWare file server and lets you create users, control print queues, and change login scripts. The NetWare Management utilities integrate with the Early Warning System to alert the administrator if the file server has problems such as insufficient disk space or memory. Figure 9.10 shows server statistics.

Figure 9.10

This Frye utility provides numerical statistics about the server.

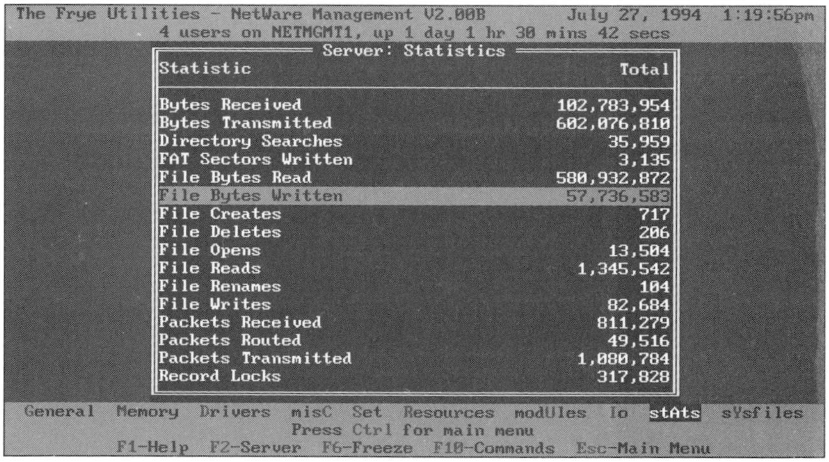

```
The Frye Utilities - NetWare Management V2.00B     July 27, 1994  1:19:56pm
              4 users on NETMGMT1, up 1 day 1 hr 30 mins 42 secs
                        ══ Server: Statistics ══
 Statistic                                        Total
 Bytes Received                              102,783,954
 Bytes Transmitted                           602,076,810
 Directory Searches                               35,959
 FAT Sectors Written                               3,135
 File Bytes Read                             580,932,872
 File Bytes Written                           57,736,583
 File Creates                                        717
 File Deletes                                        206
 File Opens                                       13,504
 File Reads                                    1,345,542
 File Renames                                        104
 File Writes                                      82,684
 Packets Received                                811,279
 Packets Routed                                   49,516
 Packets Transmitted                           1,080,784
 Record Locks                                    317,828

 General  Memory  Drivers  misC  Set  Resources  modUles  Io  stAts  sYsfiles
                         Press Ctrl for main menu
             F1-Help  F2-Server  F6-Freeze  F10-Commands  Esc-Main Menu
```

Another useful utility is the NetWare Console Commander (NCC), which allows you to schedule tasks on the file server. For example you could schedule your tape-backup NLMs to load at 2:00 A.M., perform a backup, and unload in the morning. This package is great for freeing up memory used by unnecessary NLMs.

This section provides only a glimpse of all of the features found in the FUN modules. Each module is a stand-alone application that you can add as needed, and Frye offers a utility for performing a majority of the procedures. If you want to control and monitor a large network from a single location and automate your network tasks, you should take a look at the suite of Frye Utilities.

■ Network Management Brings Results

Apart from a few dancing histograms and moving bar charts, LAN administrative software may look like pretty dull stuff. It can bury you under mountains of statistics and create deskwork when you might crave technical challenges. Yet these programs can not only save your job by spotting problems, abuses, and trends; they can also enhance your work by supporting your requests for money and people to help operate your LAN.

- *The Scheduling Dilemma*
- *Electronic-Mail Programs for Productivity*
- *Network Productivity Tools*
- *Get It Right the First Time*

Workgroup Productivity

TECHNICAL TALE

"Have you ever heard e-mail sing?"

The question stopped me in the middle of my familiar log-in keystrokes. "Singing, huh? I'd just be happy if I could read all the messages I get through different mail systems without having to cursor all over the screen. I'd settle for standard text formatting instead of standard harmony."

I didn't know the woman sitting next to me in the frequent flyer lounge, but we had the same model laptop computer, and we'd exchanged views on modems and battery life.

"Oh, we use Lotus Notes for everything," she explained. "I don't have formatting problems, but sometimes I run out of clip art."

"Huh?" was my witty response.

"Notes uses a rich-text format. That means you can do easy things like use bold face or italics or change font size for emphasis in your messages. But you can also embed sound clips and images. I keep clip art files on my laptop and try to include an image representing the city I'm in whenever I create a message."

"Show me," I replied.

"Well, I'm getting on a flight for San Francisco, so here's a little clip of the Golden Gate Bridge that I found in a clip art library. It's just a line drawing, so it's not a big file. I copy and paste it into my messages."

"That's nifty," I observed. "But I don't know what you'd use for the place I'm going."

"Oh?" she asked.

"I'm off to Borneo to work on the plans for a new communications system."

She thought for a minute and then pulled something up from a menu. When she turned the screen toward me I saw a picture of a cup of coffee.

"Oh, I get it!" I replied. "Java."

IT SEEMS THAT EVERYONE FROM SEMINAR SPEAKERS TO INDUSTRY WATCHERS and computer journalists has an opinion on the definition of *workgroup productivity software*. Obviously, the category includes software that runs on a LAN and makes people more productive as a group. But while some pundits define the category broadly enough to include any multiuser software, others defend only certain categories of software—such as project-management or document-control packages—as being true workgroup productivity programs. No matter where you draw the lines, these programs use the power of the network to help people work together more effectively, improve efficiency, and cut the time needed to perform some important, but often irritating, tasks.

As an editor of *PC Magazine*, I set a relatively strict definition of workgroup productivity software; in this context, the reviewers exclude standard applications running on a network and focus on packages unique to a network or multiuser environment. I don't think you get much group synergy from using a standard application program on the network, but you can broaden everyone's span of interaction, improve communications, and reduce repetitive tasks by using certain kinds of multiuser network programs. For example, I include group-scheduling or calendaring software in the category but exclude multiuser spreadsheet programs. Scheduling programs, group telephone directories, and electronic mail are an important part of the workgroup productivity category of software.

Among the programs that fit my definition of workgroup productivity software are Lotus Notes, Word Perfect GroupWise, DCA's Open Mind, and on the less expensive end, Futurus Team. These packages typically run with a wide variety of networking software and have no sensitivity to the network interface cards or cabling used in the LAN. As Figures 10.1 and 10.2 suggest, these packages typically offer many kinds of functions.

Programs that concentrate entirely on providing electronic-mail capabilities, such as cc:Mail, Da Vinci e-mail, and Microsoft Mail, are another key part of the network productivity category. Many of the programs that sport a variety of features can interact with these specialized electronic-mail packages and use their services to notify people of meetings, deadlines, and other important events.

■ The Scheduling Dilemma

In many organizations, scheduling three or more busy people for a meeting, along with arranging for such facilities as a conference room and slide projector, can be a frustrating and time-consuming task, requiring any number of phone calls. If one person or facility is not available when the other people or facilities are, a series of negotiations begins. Mathematicians refer to this method of simultaneously handling several unknown factors as "progressive

Figure 10.1

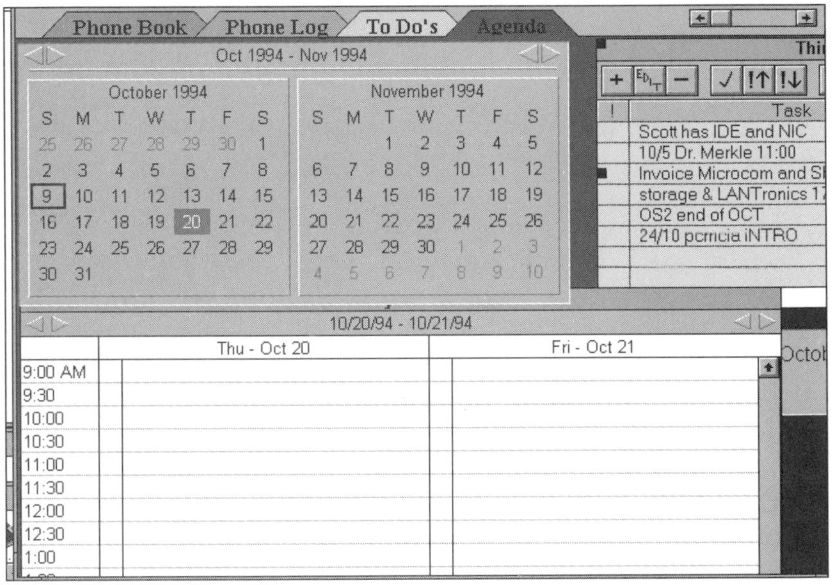

This main screen for the Packrat personal information manager shows its phone book, phone log, to-do list, and calendar. This program is powerful and flexible.

Figure 10.2

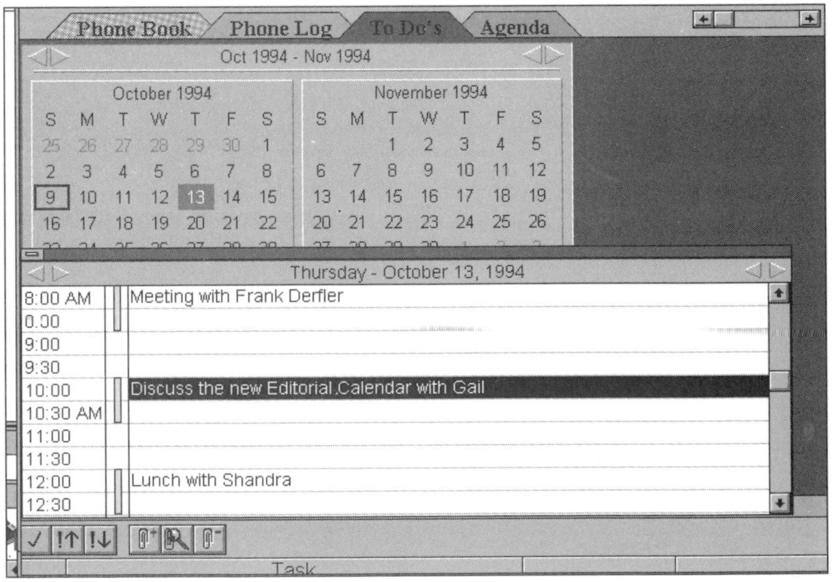

The Packrat to-do list combines a calendar with a "tickler" that reminds you about appointments and those little jobs you don't want to forget.

approximation," but whoever has to make all the contacts and coordinate the compromises will call it frustration.

LAN scheduling products simplify this task and often eliminate the frustration. If everyone in the organization uses the scheduling software, one person can access the public calendars of other people and the sign-up sheets for resources. It doesn't take long to determine when everyone involved is free to attend a meeting, and the process does not involve any invasion of privacy: The person planning the meeting doesn't see every detail on a personal calendar—just enough to find the free time.

Variations in Approach

Scheduling programs vary in how they present free time. Some packages display graphs of conflicting and open times. Futurus Team and several other programs use a representation of calendar pages, while a few programs use text explanations to outline the scheduling options. Powercore's Network Scheduler from CE Software offers a series of different views depicting how you and others in the workgroup spend your time.

Scheduling programs also vary in how they confirm the proposed events. The simpler packages assume that if the event fits on the calendar, the people scheduled to attend will be there. Other programs ask for confirmation, while some go as far as to tie into electronic-mail programs to create notification and confirmation messages.

Personal calendars are at the heart of the group-scheduling process. The best scheduling software is useless if people don't cooperate by keeping their personal calendars current. Calendars that aren't readily available and easy to use will never be maintained by group members. With this in mind, it seems imperative that these programs allow you to run the personal calendar as a TSR (terminate-and-stay-resident) module and make it easy to use under DOS. Windows programs must have good multitasking manners.

One problem common to all these packages is that they don't provide an easy way to schedule individual resources. Since a group of resources—like three conference rooms or three slide projectors—usually has only one manager, it's foolish to make that person repeatedly check into a separate personal-calendar module to confirm the scheduled use of each room or device. The person scheduling the meeting and the person managing the resources should not have to treat each identical projector, VCR, viewing screen, or meeting room as a separate entity.

Nice Utilities

The category of functions that are generally called personal information management or productivity management also benefit from being on a network.

For example, the names and telephone numbers of the people you do business with are a valuable resource for your organization.

When an organization publishes an internal telephone directory or a list of external telephone contacts on paper, a lot of resources are needed to prepare and update it. But the story is different when each user on a LAN contributes to and maintains an electronic telephone directory. The process is quick and simple, and the results are current. Looking up a listing in an electronic phone book certainly beats fumbling with business cards or photocopied lists of names.

Many people on networks in relatively large offices take advantage of multiuser chat programs. These programs substitute an on-screen real-time discussion for a face-to-face meeting or telephone conference call. When two or more people use one of these programs on the LAN, the screen on each PC divides horizontally into separate windows, one for each user. The text you type appears immediately in the window with your name. It's an ideal way for three or four people to conduct a fast exchange of ideas without getting up from their desks.

Chat programs are included in some integrated packages, such as Futurus Team.

Other shared resources available in productivity packages include document indexes and notepads. Many of these packages include personal productivity tools such as calculators and private telephone directories as well.

Workgroup productivity packages can effectively reduce the hassle of managing the daily activities of corporate employees. These packages alone don't provide sufficient justification for installing a network if you haven't already got one, but if you can also take advantage of a network's file- and printer-sharing capabilities, the increased productivity and reduced frustration these programs provide can be a welcome dividend from your LAN investment.

■ Electronic-Mail Programs for Productivity

The editors of *PC Magazine* are e-mail junkies. We make decisions, send magazine copy, and exchange information over electronic mail, and we provide electronic interaction with our readers through our online service, PC MagNet, shown in Figure 10.3.

On a practical level, the biggest benefits we get from using electronic mail are that it nearly eliminates telephone tag and that it allows our widespread staff to ignore time zones and office hours. These capabilities do a great deal to improve our individual and group productivity and to reduce frustration. The more people in an organization who use e-mail, with its ability to store information and deliver it when the recipient is ready to take it,

Figure 10.3

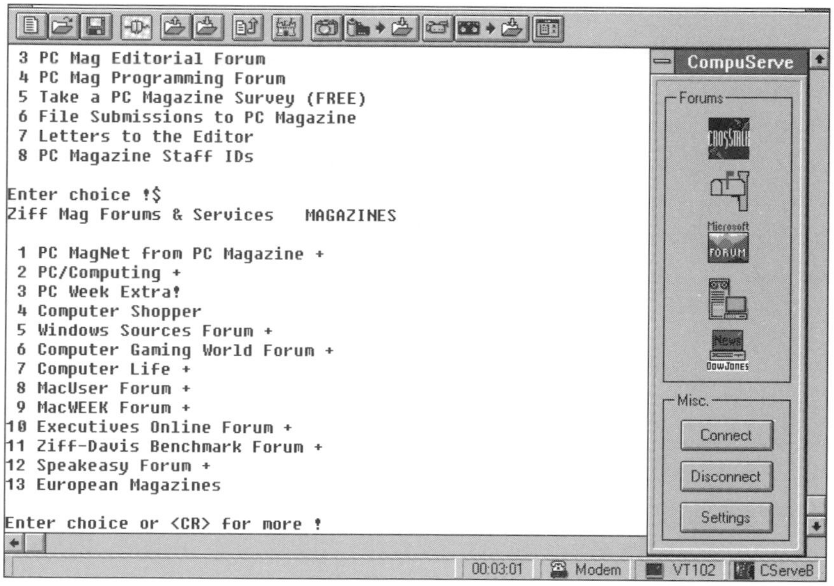

PC MagNet, an interactive online service that can be accessed via CompuServe, provides a way for the editors of *PC Magazine* to exchange information and views with readers. The menu system makes it easy for readers to download utilities and other useful programs and to participate in editorial forums.

the less they are controlled by the demands of that real-time communications device, the telephone.

Electronic-mail systems break the tyranny time holds over communications. For most of recorded history you couldn't engage in real-time communications farther than you could project your voice. The time required to communicate severely limited the quantity and quality of communications. The introduction of electronic devices, particularly the telephone, eliminated the time needed to move a message across distances, but telephone communications brought with them the new requirement of synchronicity—the need to beat the game of telephone tag. For most of this century, if no one answered the phone when it rang, the potentially fast-moving message wasn't delivered.

We work around the problem of synchronicity by using answering machines and facsimile machines. Additionally, many organizations have found relief from telephone tag and discovered a whole new way of communicating through electronic mail. Electronic mail breaks the tyranny of time by moving messages across long distances quickly and by storing messages and forwarding them to you where and when you're ready to receive them.

Our surveys of *PC Magazine* readers with local area networks continually show network e-mail as the third most common use of a network—after sharing printers and sharing access to mainframe computers. Once organizations develop the critical mass of users needed to make electronic mail effective, it becomes an indispensable and nearly addictive communications link.

The 80/20 rule of office correspondence says that 80 percent of the words you write are for internal consumption and 20 percent go outside your organization. E-mail makes it much easier to create and distribute the internal 80 percent, and it can invisibly handle distribution to the critically important external 20 percent, too.

Easy to Do, Hard to Do Well

It's easy to write an e-mail software package. The program simply writes files containing messages into specified shared subdirectories and retrieves them on request. You'll find e-mail capabilities in DOS-based LAN operating systems, such as Artisoft's LANtastic and in Microsoft's networking products for Windows.

The Basics of E-Mail and Beyond

The basic functions of electronic mail, illustrated by the menu shown in Figure 10.4, include creating, reading, forwarding, replying to, and issuing receipts for messages. All e-mail packages must do these jobs. Of course, e-mail programs vary significantly in the utilities, menus, and other amenities they provide for creating and receiving messages.

Figure 10.4

The Lotus cc:Mail client program uses icons to make it easy to compose, forward, and answer messages. You can file messages in appropriate folders arranged by subject, date, sender, or other category.

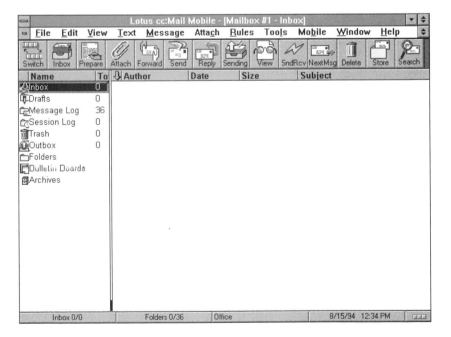

Here are some of the most useful features in an e-mail system:

- A TSR message-waiting notification module
- A pop-up window for reading messages
- The option of importing text files into messages
- The option of attaching binary files to outgoing messages
- The option of using standard word processing programs to prepare mail
- Return receipts for messages
- Electronic folders for special subjects
- Encryption during transmission
- Encryption of stored messages

Other important capabilities include the ability to set up special-interest bulletin boards where users can post messages pertaining to a specific topic, and the ability to attach binary files to e-mail messages. The best programs, like Higgins E-mail, Microsoft Mail, and cc:Mail, include extensive editing capabilities, special utilities to help you easily prepare text for transmission, and the option of using your own text editor to create mail.

Top-notch LAN e-mail programs also include the ability to connect across long distances and exchange messages with dissimilar systems. For the most part, these packages gain this ability through the actions of a program called the Message Handling Service (MHS).

Some packages, such as cc:Mail, Higgins, and Microsoft Mail, offer their own connections to different electronic-mail systems, to services like MCI Mail, and to fax devices. For example, Higgins offers a $995 add-on module called Higgins To:FAX that interfaces with the Intel Connection CoProcessor. This module sends facsimile copies of outgoing electronic mail, using the CoProcessor's modem for data exchanges with other CoProcessor-equipped machines. Even though some companies sell their own inter- and intranetwork e-mail links, MHS is the most flexible intermediary system.

Gateways to fax systems work well for sending fax messages from an e-mail system. The major drawback of e-mail/fax systems is the same one that plagues stand-alone PC/fax systems: an inadequate ability to receive incoming mail. There is no standard way to address a fax message to a particular recipient; someone must use special software to view each incoming fax and route it to the right person. What's more, incoming fax messages are saved as graphics images, which require a laser printer with a lot of memory to reproduce on paper.

The Purpose, Power, and Promise of MHS

MHS was one of the first messaging engines and it is still widely used in different forms. Although it was originally developed by Action, Novell manages development of the program. Some companies bundle it with their e-mail programs, and Novell makes it available at no additional charge to every purchaser of NetWare. Although MHS has been formally upgraded into NetWare Global Messaging, the old name endures.

MHS is easy to understand if you think of it as a communications program that runs on a networked PC and controls the serial ports while using extensive scripts and moving data in and out of shared files. The MHS server shares files with application programs such as cc:Mail and Da Vinci e-mail. These applications use MHS to connect with distant homogeneous LANs and as a gateway to dissimilar mail systems.

MHS can connect homogeneous LANs over telephone lines, but its real value lies in the MHS gateway interfaces that are available for Digital, IBM, and a growing number of other electronic-mail systems. Neither Action Technologies nor Novell makes the MHS gateway interface software. This comes from yet other companies that specialize in understanding the detailed actions needed to link dissimilar mail systems.

MHS servers on geographically separate networks can communicate over modems and dial-up telephone lines. They exchange e-mail messages according to the schedule you create.

Moving messages between applications inside the network is the major service MHS performs without adding other software. Its other important function involves moving messages between e-mail systems on the local network and those in completely different environments. You need to add gateway programs to link MHS to the external environment. MHS controls the operation of these gateways and runs them according to your script.

The gateways run in the same PC that acts as the MHS server. You must program each gateway with the appropriate telephone numbers, communications parameters, account numbers, and access codes. Of course, you must also provide modems or direct computer links between the MHS server and the external system. The designer of the gateway software has to understand the external mail system as well as the structure of the MHS-compatible files, and must create the code to translate between them.

X.400 for Intermail Communications

MHS and e-mail gateways sold by various companies provide workable ways to link different electronic-mail systems. Nonetheless, programmers must customize each gateway program. In an ideal world, each program would conform to specific standards spelling out how different products could exchange electronic mail.

The ITU-T has developed a set of rules for e-mail communications. This international committee's X.400 standard describes how to set up mail messages, name users, control access, and configure many other factors. The good news is that many companies have are developing new new products or interfaces for existing products that conform to the X.400 standard. The bad news is that implementing X.400 will probably take more time and money than most managers of PC-based LANs care to spend.

First adopted in 1984, the X.400 standard receives a lot of lip service, but only a few specialized products support it. In practice, its addressing scheme is burdensome and creates a great deal of processing overhead. Instead of including X.400 services in commercial programs, companies have delivered specialized X.400 gateways.

The first X.400 specification relied on X.25 as an underlying transmission protocol. X.25, the international standard for packet-switched, wide-area data communications, is more popular in the rest of the world than in the United States. In the U.S., the first gateway services were provided by X.25 value-added networks such as Tymnet and Telenet. A later evolution of the X.400 standard encourages building X.400 gateway products for use over local Ethernet links as well as long-distance X.25 networks.

At this time, only large organizations whose managers feel obliged to support international standards seem to make good use of X.400 systems. People with less stringent policies will find good ways to link e-mail systems using gateway options available from various companies and through MHS.

Making the Difficult Look Easy Isn't Easy

Once the system administrator gets all the e-mail packages, the MHS server, and the gateways set up properly, users can send mail to dissimilar systems by simply including the recipient's name in the mailing list and hitting the Enter key. Anyone on the LAN can use a few keystrokes to post the same message to people connected to mainframes, to the guy in the next office, to a colleague on MCI Mail, to a friend with a fax machine, and to someone who receives mail only in stamped paper envelopes. But our experience shows that setting up those mail programs and gateway programs can take a lot of consultation and experimentation.

The address strings hidden behind the seemingly innocent "recipient name" block in each application look like cartoon cuss words with strange groups of letters punctuated by @|#: and other symbols. The system administrator or savvy end user must create such an address string for each potential addressee. Each combination of application program, gateway program, and target system contains its own rules, hazards, and shortcuts. The only way to avoid wasted time and high levels of frustration is to make sure you can get good technical support from the e-mail and gateway companies. Once you learn the chants and incantations needed to link your particular combination of systems, you can work magic. Until then, you might as well try to transmute lead into gold.

If your organization plans to install a hundred or more electronic-mail nodes spread across more than one physical network, you'll probably need specialized help getting started. Unless you foresee expansion continuing for years, it isn't worth developing the expertise in-house, so buying the time of an experienced systems integrator or consultant is a smart idea.

E-Mail for Growth

An e-mail program simplifies information-sharing tasks for its users and moves information quickly without the annoyance of telephone tag. But large systems aren't simple to install and manage properly. Fortunately, links such as MHS and product-specific gateways allow you to mix and match e-mail systems throughout your organization to meet specific needs. Electronic mail is the foundation for a strong and practical information-sharing system in your LAN.

■ Network Productivity Tools

Everyone has heard the phrase "networks are for sharing," but what you share across the network is changing. Obviously networks are designed to allow you to share devices like an expensive laser printer or to trade word processing documents with a coworker, but modern network applications can do a lot more to increase your productivity and flexibility. In addition to networking hardware and operating systems, you'll also find several exciting products that can be called "true" network applications.

There are networked applications and network applications. It's a fine line, but what I call networked applications are those that simply share files and devices. In contrast, true network applications focus on sharing information in real time across local and wide area networks.

A concept called *messaging* is at the core of most network applications. Messaging systems use a transportation program, often called an *engine* or *service*, running on one or more messaging servers somewhere in the network. The messaging server transports blocks of data between applications running on client PCs. (This is part of the evolution of client/server computing you've heard so much about.) The most common network application to use messaging is electronic mail. Microsoft Mail is based on this model, and uses a service called the Messaging API or MAPI. Lotus has joined with IBM and other vendors to develop Vendor Independent Messaging or VIM.

Applications such as network scheduling, electronic forms distribution and tracking, and project tracking interact with the messaging engine. The messages they exchange might or might not be meant for direct human consumption, so messaging is not always the same thing as e-mail. The ability of applications to pass information about network users, rights, fonts, paths, and other details is increasingly vital to their usefulness.

While network applications are not new to the industry, they've now reached a level where companies have gone beyond testbeds and are implementing them in real "bet the business" environments. Let's take a few minutes to look at two established network applications, Lotus Notes and WordPerfect GroupWise (formerly Symmetry and, before that, WordPerfect Office), as well as some newer products, such as Microsoft Exchange and DCA's Open Mind.

Lotus Notes

Lotus released Notes as a network application in 1989, and it has since become a standard of comparison for other workgroup products. Notes is a client/server application that allows users to share information securely over a LAN, telephone line, or wide-area network connection. Lotus offers a Notes front end for most popular graphical operating systems, including Windows, OS/2, Macintosh, and Unix. Figure 10.5 shows Lotus Notes at work.

Figure 10.5

One of the strongest features of Lotus Notes is its ability to show a "threaded" discussion. This ability to arrange and display the interchange of ideas provides a powerful tool for discussion.

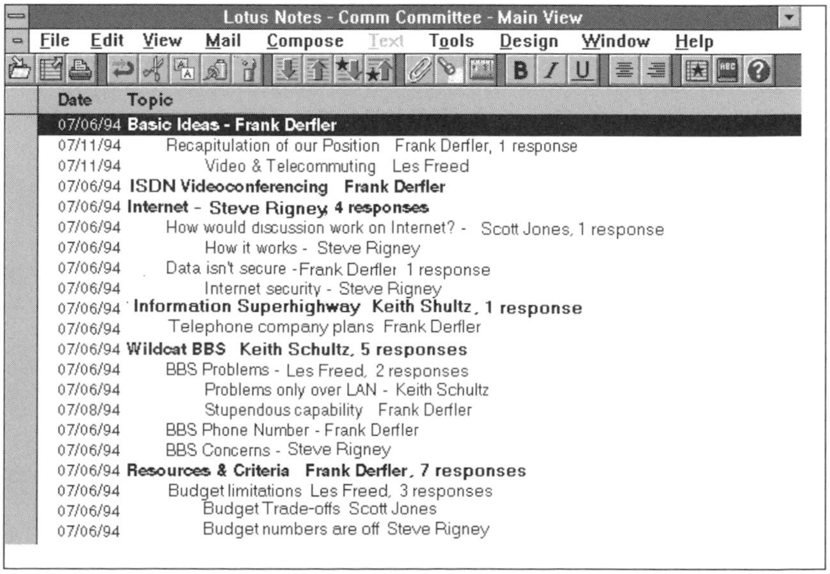

Replication, meaning to make a copy, is a busy word in the Notes architecture. Notes servers continually replicate databases among themselves and among users. Users can set rules describing what portions of a database they want to replicate locally. A Notes database is an object storage facility that users can use to access, track, and organize information on the network. Users connected to the same network, whether they are local network clients or mobile users who only occasionally connect to the network via a modem and a phone line, can replicate from the Notes database structure.

The word *database*, while technically correct, doesn't convey the actual uses of the Notes structure. The databases concerned go far beyond the typical concept of files and records to include sophisticated tools for making useful forms and adding and arranging information. News update services, online discussion groups with threading, lists of sales leads, and electronic mail are all services commonly based on Notes databases.

The E-Mail Connection, shown in Figure 10.6, is an integral part of Notes. Notes users can send any document to any Notes database, and all e-mail is stored in a Notes database. In addition to text, you can use Notes e-mail to send hypertext documents, OLE embedded documents, and various forms and applications. This flexibility means people can create messages that include graphics and enhanced text to add spark to their information. Because Lotus complies with the Vendor-Independent Messaging (VIM) standard, other e-mail systems on the network can easily exchange messages with Notes.

Figure 10.6

The E-Mail Connection program does an excellent job of integrating messages from many services, such as cc:Mail, CompuServe, and MCI Mail, into a single mailbox and a single address book. Heavy e-mail users need this kind of consolidated service so they don't have to remember the specific addressing quirks for each service.

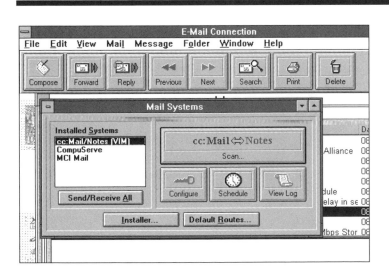

Notes is closely tied to other Lotus applications such as Lotus 1-2-3 for Windows. You can, for example, create a spreadsheet and store it in your Notes database so other Notes users can access it. This feature is ideal for people using different desktop operating systems and for those running over different network operating systems. Lotus plans to increase the links between Notes and other applications and continues to improve the tools for developing applications that can access Notes databases.

WordPerfect GroupWise

Not only does it sport a new name, WordPerfect's GroupWise also has more features than its earlier versions, which were known as WordPerfect Symmetry and Office. GroupWise is a messaging application that combines e-mail, personal and group scheduling, workflow routing, and rules-based message management, into a single application. Like Lotus, WordPerfect provides client software for Windows, Macintosh, and Unix-based computers. The GroupWise server platform will run on NetWare 3.X, OS/2, DOS, and on seven versions of Unix.

GroupWise allows you to send e-mail to local and remote users across heterogeneous mail systems using the Simple MAPI protocol. You can send and receive network fax messages using the e-mail front end. Under Windows, you can also create electronic messages and link them to certain applications so that an icon in the message will automatically launch a Windows application. This is a lot easier than attaching a binary file and hoping the recipient will figure out the file format and have the right application to run it.

Both Notes and GroupWise are designed to keep track of and access data no matter where it is stored on the network; however, Notes offers stronger database features for storing different file formats and information. With its replicating database structure, Notes delivers up-to-date information to every client, anywhere on the network.

Microsoft Exchange

It didn't take long for Microsoft to jump on the network application bandwagon. The Windows networking products include a feature known as network DDE that allows you to link an object in an application to another application on a separate PC anywhere on the network. For example, you can link your local spreadsheet to a document on another client PC, and every change you make to the spreadsheet will show up in real time on the linked document.

Microsoft Exchange combines messaging and information-sharing into a single product that ties directly to your operating system. Within Exchange, public folders allow people to create discussion groups and shared pools of information. Microsoft has produced "mail-enabled" applications, so you can send a message or attachment without switching to another e-mail application. Unlike GroupWise and Notes, Exchange is strongly tied to the Windows operating system and applications, especially to those developed by Microsoft.

DCA's Open Mind

Like all of the network applications, DCA's Open Mind is based on the idea that network users should be able to quickly access any type of information, on any server, anywhere on the network. While Open Mind is similar to Notes in many ways, its emphasis is more on group discussion and interaction than on large, shared reference files.

In addition to the standard e-mail functions, Open Mind includes a messaging and conferencing feature that allows you to communicate with your coworkers on the network in real time. These messages and conferences use the rich-text format so you can include graphics and fancy fonts to enhance your communications.

In DCA's model, the shared database is called the Mind. You can set up the hierarchical sections of the Mind to reflect the way your organization works. For example, you can have a section for each department, location, or task group. Open Mind servers replicate their databases, so users can have easy access to a local server across the network. The user software makes it easy to organize discussions and track tasks assigned across the Mind in many useful ways.

The Near Future

Network applications don't change an organization, but they do make change possible. When information is widely distributed and available to people at any level, corporate re-engineers can tear down old bureaucratic walls built on information control and slim down the organization, as shown in Figure 10.7. Extended communications links make it easy to form the virtual task groups and organizations that are needed to respond to constantly changing conditions.

As network programs mature, they will begin to disappear. Soon, as you work on a document the network environment will invisibly help you by retrieving information and references and then appropriately distributing your work without forcing you to change applications. That might sound like pie-in-the-sky, but the rate of change is increasing so rapidly that science fiction is quickly becoming reality. Network applications are already allowing new ways of doing business to develop and mature and they are critical to corporate success.

Figure 10.7

Improved information
distribution flattens the
structure of large
organizations.

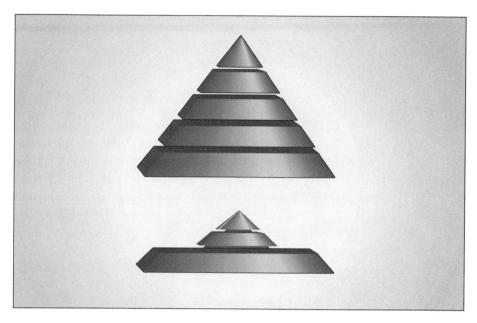

■ Get It Right the First Time

Individuals who use a network invest a lot of their own time and resources in workgroup productivity software. They come to depend on their scheduling programs to keep them on time, and on their electronic mail to keep them up to date. Their LAN-based telephone directories and lists of contacts become valuable corporate resources. Once they learn to use a system and trust it with their information, they won't want to move to new software merely because they've outgrown the old system or because it becomes unsupportable. You should put forth a lot of effort to make sure the workgroup productivity programs you buy will serve your needs for a long time.

I suggest you involve at least a representative sampling of the people who will use the workgroup productivity tools when selecting the software. In other chapters of this book, I've explained that you can safely shop for such products as Ethernet adapters and the computers you use as servers based on price. But cost should be a small consideration when you look for workgroup productivity software, because the investment you make can pay good dividends. Ease of use, room for growth, and support from a good company are the important factors to consider when you make this purchasing decision.

- *Modem Basics*
- *Communications Software*
- *Network Remote Access*
- *When Computers and Telephones Meet*

Telephone Modems and Network Remote Access

"The flood waters peaked last night and the sandbags are holding." The radio announcer went on, "Because of damage to the highway bridges, only emergency vehicles are allowed on the interstate."

"It will take me half a day to get into the city to go to work," Jill complained. "But I've got estimates to finish and budgets to prepare. The whole world can't just stop!"

When I lifted the phone, I heard a dial tone, so I punched a quick series of numbers and worked my way through the call routing system to Jerry Takata, the network manager in Jill's office.

"Jerry, do you have a remote access server on your LAN?" I asked without much introduction.

"No, we always thought it was too big a security risk. Hackers and all that," he replied.

"Keeping hackers out of the LAN isn't a problem, Jerry, but Jill and several other folks need to get into the LAN. Can we set something up?"

Takata was cautious. "How difficult is it to install?"

"Shiva makes a product that you install by plugging in the network cable and attaching four phone lines from your PBX. The callers must have special software, but we'll transfer that first with a regular modem file transfer program. You might also consider adding some more trunk lines to the PBX."

Three days later—the same day we learned that the bridges would be out for a month—my modem connected Jill to her office network, and she accessed the files she needed to complete her reports. "I guess every cloud does have a silver lining," she said. "I'm connected and productive without a long commute!"

"Now you know that you don't have to go to work in order to work," I said. What I didn't say was, "I wonder where I'll get another modem and computer so I can do some work, too."

Even when the topic of connectivity focuses on LANs, the discussion often includes modem communications. Today, people routinely extend the service area of local area networks by dialing into network communications servers through modems. As modems for standard, dial-up telephone lines have become faster, they've begun to challenge traditional, leased telephone lines as a way to link LANs. In this chapter I describe the latest developments in modem technology, provide tips on buying and using modems, and discuss some of the things to look for in modem communications software. Finally, I delve into the modem network remote access products that are so important in extending the network beyond the corporate office.

Even though this chapter provides quite a bit of detail on modems, it can only touch on the most important aspects of this subject. For more information on using modems to establish links between networks, see my book *PC Magazine Guide to Linking LANs* (Ziff-Davis Press, 1992). For details on how modems work and how to buy and use modems and communications software products to best advantage, see *PC Magazine Guide to Modem Communications* (Ziff-Davis Press, 1992), which I wrote with communications expert Les Freed.

■ Modem Basics

Because the dial-up telephone system was designed to pass the sounds of voices, it can't pass the electrical on-and-off signals computers use. The only way to pass computer data over conventional voice telephone lines is to convert it to audio tones that the lines can carry. Simply stated, a modem converts between audio tones on the telephone line and a serial data stream, typically connected to an RS-232 port.

In order to pass data in both directions at the same time, modem signaling schemes split the channel according to the frequency and phase of the signals. One modem uses an "originate" signal set and the other uses an "answer" signal set. Typically, the answering modem sends its signal out first when it picks up the line. This initial signal causes the calling modem to send its own tone set, and the two modems then negotiate a connection.

Sophisticated modems perform several actions during this negotiation phase, including adding electronic adaptation to account for different telephone line conditions and determining the fastest possible signaling rate the two modems can use. Unfortunately, while the procedures for these negotiations are set by international standards, people who design modems implement those procedures differently. Independent work leads to incompatibility, so whenever a new batch of modems emerges, vendors must spend several months working together to improve interoperability. The warning is clear: If you must be among the first to purchase a new breed of modem, buy all your modems from a single vendor. If you have to dial into modems whose identity you can't control, wait for the vendors to resolve any compatibility issues before you proceed.

Getting Modems Up to Speed

People want to move data quickly and reliably over telephone lines, but generally the lines don't cooperate. Modems convert the electrical signals from a computer into audio tones, but the bandwidth of the telephone line limits how fast the audio tones can change frequency to represent the zeros and ones of computer data. As modems developed, the drive for greater speed focused on two aspects of their operation: the way modems signal and what they say when they signal.

In the United States, early 300-baud and 1,200-bps modems used the Bell 103 and 212A modulation schemes, respectively. Other countries settled on similar signaling conventions described in the CCITT V.21 and V.22 standards. The former uses 0- to 300-bps, full-duplex modem transmission; the latter, 600-bps and 1,200-bps, half-duplex (two-way) modem transmission with a reverse channel of up to 75 bps. These early standards became the root of modem evolution around the world.

Modems have evolved on a regular and predictable schedule. On the average, technological developments double modem signaling speed every 18 months. The industry doesn't deliver a new species of modem that often, but the time lapse between modem products correlates closely to the newest product's gain in speed.

Lack of competition and the dearth of inexpensive modem chip sets were the major reasons for the relatively high cost of modem products in the 1970s and early 1980s. In the mid-1980s, Rockwell and other manufacturers made a modem chip that not only encompassed the V.22bis, 2,400-bps protocol but was also downward-compatible with the Bell and CCITT protocols for 300 bps and 1,200 bps. The availability and compatibility of such modem chips led to the introduction of a multitude of low-cost, high-quality 2,400-bps modems.

The combination of actions by the U.S. Federal Communications Commission that allowed the attachment of non-Bell System equipment to the telephone lines and the market pull of the PC industry spurred the evolutionary process in the 1980s. In 1987 vendors like Hayes Microcomputer Systems began offering modems with a 9,600-bps proprietary signaling scheme and data compression for under $1,000. In the same time frame, that company offered a modem with full-duplex, CCITT V.32, 9,600-bps signaling in the $2,000 price range.

In 1990, modem companies fielded affordable modems with V.32, 9,600-bps signaling and a new compression and error control scheme called V.42bis.

The V.42bis compression scheme offers as much as a four times improvement in throughput, depending on the compressibility of the data, so while they still signal at 9.6 kilobits per second over the phone line, under ideal conditions these products can theoretically move data at speeds as high as 38.4 kilobits per second. In practice, throughput of 20 to 25 kilobits per second is common when two modems use V.32-style, 9,600-bps signaling and V.42bis compression to move compressible data like spreadsheet files and some graphics files.

In late 1991, modem companies started delivering products that conform to a revised signaling standard called V.32bis. Modems that follow the V.32bis standard offer faster 14,000-bps signaling over telephone lines and smoother fallback to more choices of speeds than V.32 models. V.32 modems try to connect at 9,600 bps; if they experience errors, they drop back to 2,400 bps. The V.32bis modems do a more extensive analysis of the connection to immediately determine the best usable signaling speed, either 14.4, 9.6, 7.2, 4.8, or 2.4 kilobits per second.

In 1994, the CCITT approved a new modem standard called V.34. Because the standard took so long to emerge, a few companies fielded modems using an interim standard called V.Fast Class or V.FC. However, these modems did not provide a full implementation of the standard and, if possible, you should upgrade any V.FC modems in your inventory to V.34. Sometimes this upgrade is as simple as plugging a new chip into the modem board.

The V.34 modems push against a principle of physics called Shannon's Limit. In simple terms, this law says that the maximum signaling speed is governed by the bandwidth and the ratio of signal to noise on the line. Since the bandwidth of dialed-up telephone lines is set by technical standards and the modem output signal level is regulated by law, line noise effectively governs throughput. The V.34 modems should be able to signal as quickly as ideal lines theoretically allow.

At first, the modem designers thought that the telephone systems of North America would allow signaling at a maximum rate of 19.2 kilobits per second. But reexamination of the systems showed that fiber-optic cable and new equipment allow a signaling rate of at least 28.8 kilobits per second. V.34 modems will try to start signaling together at 28.8 kilobits per second and then move down.

In theory, the combination of V.34 signaling at 28.8 kilobits per second and V.42bis error control and compression could move highly compressible application data across the wire at an effective speed of over a megabit per second. As is true for so many top-end speeds, however, you only get something close to the theoretical maximum under ideal conditions on a closed track, and with a professional driver. As I'll explain later in this chapter, both the telephone lines and the PC hardware work against optimal performance.

ROM du Jour: Choosing Modems with Programmable ROMs

The most complex modem products use programmable digital signal processors, so they are what the programming in their ROMs tells them to be. This fact has important implications for anyone buying these modems. First, shop with an eye on the nameplate as well as the price and performance figures—you should choose a product from a company that will be in business long enough to refine their ROM programming. Second, don't expect to receive ROM upgrades automatically from any company except AT&T. The AT&T-Paradyne modem has a reprogrammable ROM that can take updates through a modem-to-modem telephone call to the AT&T support center, but many other companies typically require someone—usually someone at a maintenance facility—to replace chips.

It's true that most ROM updates make small changes that impact only a few users. One such example would be a ROM change that merely allowed a modem to recognize the busy signal or dial tone generated by a specific brand of PBX. Some changes certainly have a wider impact, however. My advice is straightforward: first, check the company's upgrade policy before you buy; and second, if you have trouble with one of these modems, contact your dealer or the company to see whether they've made any ROM changes to control the problem. The ROM tells the modem how to do its work, so don't hesitate to ask for new instructions if you think you need them.

Getting It Right: Error Control and Data Compression

As signaling speed increases, it's important to maintain—and ideally, to improve—accuracy. As communications systems have evolved, this has been accomplished through the development of error control techniques in both modems and communications software.

The Microcom Network Protocols (MNP) 2 through 4 became the industry's de facto standards for hardware error control. The CCITT caught up with the modem industry in 1988 when it issued the V.42 error control standard. V.42 includes two protocols: The primary one is the Link Access Procedure for Modems (LAPM); the secondary protocol is functionally equivalent to MNP 4.

The desire for greater speed has also led to data compression. During data compression, a program (either communications software or modem firmware) running at one end of the link examines data that's ready for transmission, looking for redundant elements. During transmission, it uses a short data string to replace commonly used characters and redundant data strings.

Microcom's introduction of the MNP 5 protocol for data compression was followed in 1989 by CCITT's release of the V.42bis standard for asynchronous data compression using the Lempel Ziv compression algorithm.

This algorithm offers a significant improvement over the MNP 5 protocol, both in data compression capability and in real-time compensation.

The V.42bis data compression scheme represents the state of the art in single-pass, adaptive compression techniques. It is always better to compress files before transmission using a multipass program like ARC, Lharc, or PKZIP that examines the contents of a file and uses the best compression technique than it is to rely solely on V.42bis compression. V.42bis provides good throughput when no pretransmission compression technique is available, however. Unlike the older MNP 5 compression system still used by many modems (and typically offered as a fallback to the primary compression scheme in V.42bis), V.42bis compression does not slow the transmission of already compressed files.

Both error control and data compression protocols are independent of modulation protocols; that is why you can find MNP, V.42, and V.42bis capabilities in 2,400-bps, 9,600-bps, 14,400-bis, and 28,800-bps modems. Table 11.1 describes the signaling, error control, and data compression standards that apply to modem communications. As you can see, modems and communications programs can conform to a bewildering combination of signaling protocols, error control schemes, data compression schemes, and file transfer protocols. Note also that functions are often redundant—it isn't unusual to use modems that provide error control on the modem-to-modem link in conjunction with software that provides error control over the entire link.

Handling the Data

Both V.42 and MNP error control modems segment data streams into packets. Each outgoing packet includes a 16-bit (optionally, 32-bit for V.42 modems) cyclical redundancy check (CRC), which is a statistical analysis of the packet's contents. The receiving modem performs the same statistical analysis on the incoming packet that the sending modem performed as the packet went out; if it cannot match the CRC, it asks the sending modem to retransmit the frame.

With no error correction, data is sent with a start bit, eight data bits, and a stop bit. This means that it takes 10 bits to send a single byte in asynchronous mode, and a 2,400-bps modem can send only 240 bytes per second. With V.42 or MNP error control employed, you can achieve about 22 percent more throughput, including packet overhead.

Most popular communications software such as Kermit, XModem, YModem, and ZModem offers error control and data compression schemes. These protocols operate only during file transfers, while the MNP 5 and V.42bis firmware in modems work all the time.

Table 11.1

Standards for Modem
Communications

Modem Signaling Protocols	
Bell 103	An almost obsolete standard for signaling at 300 baud
V.21	An international 300-bps signaling standard that is similar to Bell 103
Bell 212	A standard developed by the Bell Operating Companies for operations at 1,200 bps
V.22	An international standard for 1,200 bps operation that is similar to Bell 212
CCITT V.22bis	An international standard for modem signaling at 2,400 bps
CCITT V.32	An international standard for modem signaling at 9,600 bps, with a fallback to V.22bis rates
CCITT V.32bis	An international standard for modem signaling at a maximum rate of 14.4 kilobits per second with a fallback to 12, 9.6, 7.2, or 4.8 kilobits per second
CCITT V.FC	An interim standard for signaling at a rate of 19.2 kilobits per second over dial-up telephone lines
ITU V.34	An international standard for signaling at a maximum rate of 28.8 kilobits per second
Error Control Protocols	
Microcom Network Protocol (MNP) Level 4	A widely adopted scheme for discovering errors in a stream of data and requesting transmission of an appropriate block
Microcom Network Protocol (MNP) Level 10	A system used primarily in Microcom modems for rigorous error control—for example, in cellular telephone modem connections
CCITT V.42	A standard scheme for discovering errors in a stream of data and requesting retransmission of an appropriate block; includes the LAP M and MNP Level protocols
Data Compression Protocols	
Microcom Network Protocol (MNP) Level 5	A widely adopted compression scheme, riding over MNP Level 4 error control, that is often able to give a 3:1 compression advantage; does not work well with precompressed files
CCITT V.42bis	A standard data compression scheme able to give as much as a 4:1 commpression advantage on certain types of files; requires V.42 error control, and is compatible with file precompression techniques

Communications software packages that include their own error control do not provide optimal performance with modems that are already using MNP or V.42 error control connections. To take full advantage of MNP or V.42 error correction, select the software's no-error-correction option when transferring files. YModem-G sends 1,000 bytes per block without software acknowledgment. Using YModem-G, it is common to see throughputs above 270 bytes per second using V.22bis modems with MNP or V.42 error handling.

Data compression provides the potential for even larger savings during file transfers. For both MNP 5 and V.42bis operations, the data throughput speed varies according to the type of data being transmitted, but both ASCII and binary data are compressed. V.42bis offers a potentially better compression algorithm, and is more robust in the way it dynamically adjusts the compression scheme for the data flow.

Most modems on the market today include Microcom's MNP Class 5 data compression protocol. MNP 5 uses two types of data compression algorithms to move certain kinds of files up to twice as fast as they would normally traverse a communications line were they transmitted without any software or hardware compression protocols in place. These two techniques are Huffman encoding and run-length encoding.

Huffman encoding takes advantage of the simple fact that some ASCII characters appear more frequently than others. In a typical data communications session without compression, each character is encoded using a 7- or 8-bit code. Software following the Huffman encoding strategy sends the most frequently used letters in 4-bit groups; less frequently used characters are encoded by as many as 11 bits. Although less frequently used characters can require more bits than uncompressed characters, you still save time with Huffman encoding because the more frequently repeated characters are sent in fewer bits.

When a file is transmitted, the compression software includes information on the length of the encoded character and then the encoded character itself. Because some characters are repeated so often, the data stream containing these common characters is much shorter after compression than it would be using more typical ASCII encoding.

The second type of compression used in MNP 5, run-length encoding, takes advantage of the easy identification of a string of repetitive characters, including nonprinting characters like line feeds, carriage returns, and spaces. When MNP 5 sees at least three of the same characters in a row, it uses run-length encoding. It sends those characters and a count indicating the number of times those characters repeat. Effective handling of repetitive characters provides excellent compression for certain types of files, such as spreadsheets, that use many repeated nonprinting characters for formatting.

Modern modems allow you to disable MNP 5, an important feature when you're downloading compressed files from bulletin boards or transmitting files that have been previously compressed with programs like PKZIP or Lharc. If the MNP 5 protocol on the modem link is active when you're dealing with previously compressed files, it will actually slow the throughput.

MNP 5 software provides data compression and error handling on the entire link, including the segment between each PC's serial port and the attached modem. Nonetheless, other file transfer protocols like XModem and ZModem, which include their own compression and error control, have proven more popular than MNP 5 because they also automate the task of transferring files.

Microcom recently enhanced its data compression technique with the introduction of MNP 7, which encodes characters according to the frequency of character pairs. While MNP 5 provides a 2-to-1 compression ratio for some types of files, MNP 7's compression ratio for similar files is 3 to 1. This means that a modem with a modulation rate of 2,400 bps could provide a throughput of up to 7,200 bps, if it were connected to a high-speed serial port. Still, the Lempel Ziv algorithm used in V.42bis is more efficient than MNP 7 with certain types of files, and Microcom has also implemented V.42bis in its products.

For some applications, the V.42bis protocol is clearly superior to MNP 5. Indeed, on-line services like MCI Mail, CompuServe and GEnie will be expanding their support for V.42bis. If you're thinking about the future, you should consider getting a modem that has both MNP 5 and V.42bis.

Both V.42bis and MNP 5 provide data buffering, which allows your computer port speed to be faster than the signaling rate used between the modems. Modern modems allow you to configure the modem to communicate with the PC at speeds of up to 57,600 bps. To take full advantage of the improved throughput of data compression protocols you have to set the serial port link between the PC and the modem to a speed higher than the connection speed between the modems.

If you're transmitting a file previously compressed with an efficient program like PKZIP or Lharc, V.42bis is significantly faster than MNP 5. MNP 5 protocol on the modem link will actually slow the throughput by constantly searching for ways to compress the already compressed file.

Performance Limitations

The more products push the performance envelope, the more they need a controlled environment. V.34 modems require nearly perfect telephone lines and specially configured serial port connections to reach throughputs near 1 megabit per second when moving a highly compressible file. Typical throughput for text files between same-brand modems hovers at around 30 kilobits per second.

The conditions a modem faces on any dialed telephone call vary widely. Interestingly, some of the worst conditions can occur on calls that are considered local rather than long distance. Local "tail" circuits seldom receive the maintenance given to long distance circuits, so calls within a city or regional area may traverse some of the worst telephone lines. The noise and distortion on a circuit can affect the speed of the connection the modems negotiate and their ability to move data without errors. Error control schemes can catch errors and request retransmission of the bad blocks, but that takes time and reduces effective throughput.

While most people anticipate hostile telephone lines, the limitations built into the PC's serial port often present a surprise bottleneck. You can lose data coming from a fast modem to a PC if you don't have modern hardware, and many communications programs deliberately slow the system's throughput for once sound, but now possibly obsolete, reasons.

Improving Throughput

Because of data compression, the throughput between two modems can be much faster than the signaling rate indicates. Modems signaling at 2,400 bps could be moving files with an effective throughput of 6,000 to 8,000 bps, or even more; however, if you are running your PC's serial port at 2,400 bps, you won't benefit from the increased throughput.

When you configure modems for faster port speed, you must send a setup string to the modem to disable a feature called the BPS Rate Adjust. When this feature is on, it links the port speed to the modem carrier speed. After turning it off, you must also set the Serial Port Flow Control parameter to enable bidirectional control of the RS-232 Clear to Send (CTS) and Request to Send (RTS) lines.

The internal programming in some modems will operate using MNP 5 or V.42bis as a factory default condition, but other modems must be programmed to use these protocols. It's good practice to send a complete setup string to any modem every time it dials. For most modems that follow the Hayes AT commands, the setup string AT\J0\G0\Q3\N2\VI%Cl will disable BPS adjust, disable XON/X-OFF flow control, enable bidirectional RTS/CTS, force a link with MNP error control, show you the status of the MNP connection, and enable MNP 5 data compression. The setup string AT&K3&Q5S46=138WI&R0S48=128 works to initialize Hayes V.42bis modems for the same conditions using a V.42bis connection. Not all V.42bis modems are the same, however. You might have to work with the modem vendor to get the setup string exactly right if it doesn't work out of the box.

Don't forget, you must also set your communications software for the correct port speed and for RTS/CTS flow control. Once you have the serial port, modem, and communications software initialized for optimum performance, your data will be sent and received faster and more reliably.

About the UART

Most serial cards have an 8250 (8-bit) or 16450 (16-bit) UART (Universal Asynchronous Receiver-Transmitter)—both versions operate the same way. When we tested modems in the PC Magazine Labs, we discovered that the UART can be the weak link in the communications chain. The UART problem also occurs with 2,400-bps external modems when the user is operating multitasking programs such as Microsoft Windows.

The UART controls the flow of data through the serial I/O port—it moves data between the serial port and the CPU's parallel data bus. Normally, when a byte arrives at the PC from the modem, the UART signals the CPU with an interrupt. If the CPU is already answering a higher-priority interrupt, the CPU may not immediately respond to the incoming interrupt, which causes the next inbound byte to overwrite the current one. For most asynchronous file-transfer operations, this results in a check-sum error, with the entire data packet being retransmitted.

The 16550AFN UART, a direct replacement for the other chips, solves the overrun problem by creating a first-in, first-out (FIFO) buffer stack. This lets the UART save incoming data until the CPU is ready to process it, but to initiate buffer operations, the 16550AFN needs communications software that can control its FIFO buffer.

At the highest speed of a V.34bis modem, data travels from the modem to the PC at a rate of about 10 characters per millisecond. The buffer in the 16550AFN can hold 16 characters, about 1 millisecond worth of data, provided your communications software turns the buffer on—many of us use programs a year or two old that do not activate the buffer. This 16-character buffer provides enough holding space to allow the UART to survive short periods of inattention from the CPU without losing data. Unfortunately, older UART chips, like the 8250 and 16450, don't have this first-in, first-out buffering.

But sometimes the CPU ignores the UART for more than a few milliseconds. Communications software writers have learned, for example, that some disk drive controllers block interrupts from reaching the CPU for as long as 20 to 40 milliseconds while they access a disk sector. With interrupts blocked, the data can't move from the UART to the CPU, so it is overwritten and lost. Modem error control programs can't prevent these losses because they happen in the PC. For these reasons, communications program designers rely on hardware handshaking—controlling clear-to-send signals on the RS-232 line—to slow the data flow from the modem to the PC. Typically, communications programs tell the modem to stop sending data to the PC whenever they move data to disk or perform other functions that might result in blocked interrupts.

You didn't buy an expensive new V.34 modem to have a communications program slow the data flow, so you must make sure your PC has modern serial port hardware that your communications software can use to get the best possible data flow from a high-speed modem.

External versus Internal Modems

Almost all modem vendors market internal modems that plug into a slot in your PC. Except for their physical configuration, internal and external modems aren't very different. Every organization should have some of each type to meet specific users' needs.

Internal modems offer some significant advantages: Primarily, they come with their own UART and a built-in method of controlling the flow of data between the UART and the modem. The makers of fast modems typically put a 16550AFN UART on the internal modem to reduce overflow problems. Also, since the internal modem combines the serial port and modem in one device, you don't have to hassle with the proper configuration of an RS-232 connecting cable, the modem doesn't occupy desktop space, and you don't have to find a free AC wall plug for it. Because they don't have cabinets and power supplies, internal modems are typically a little less expensive than their external kin. They're cheaper to produce, too, so manufacturers can usually afford to throw in a communications software package. Finally, you can assign most internal modems to COM3 or COM4 to save an existing serial port. On the other hand, the few internal modems that are limited to the alternatives of COM1 or COM2 can be difficult to install if the PC in question already has those ports wired into the motherboard. To use an internal modem at one of these port designations, you'll usually have to run a special program or move jumpers to turn off the internal COM port.

Many people like external modems because the lights installed on the front panel of most models show what is happening. A quick glance at the carrier detect, read data, and terminal ready lights tells you if the circuit is still up and functioning. In addition, it's easy to move external modems between PCs, but changing internal modems is a project.

Again, you can choose between these products based solely on your needs and preferences; however internal modems do provide a way to work around the serial port limitations found in many PCs.

PCMCIA Modems

If you have one of the great new laptop PCs that comes with a PCMCIA slot, you know that PCMCIA modems are fast and easy to carry on the road.

The downside is, they can result in memory conflicts, frozen applications, and frustration. But things are getting better.

PCMCIA slots showed up in volume in laptop computers at the end of 1993. Early on, a lot of products didn't work in a lot of computers. A layer of software called card and socket services (actually as many as three or four programs that logically glue the device into the PC) needed a lot of work. Developers have to tweak buffers, timing loops, and other parameters to get 100-percent interoperability between products. In this respect, though, these programs are no different than LAN card drivers, SCSI drivers, and similar programs.

Your source for the interface software varies. Sometimes the PC comes equipped with these programs; often the software comes with the PCMCIA device. The best advice is always to get the newest version of the card and socket services software from your dealer, the vendor's BBS, or an online forum. The PCMCIA product vendor will typically have better software and support than the computer vendor.

Electrically, PCMCIA modems are similar to internal ISA bus modems. Amazingly, they pack a UART, data pump, line transceiver, and all the other necessary parts inside a credit-card sized package. Almost all the manufacturers seem to have settled on 16550A UART chips, so the PCMCIA modem provides a good alternative to the less capable 8550s that occupy the serial ports in most laptop PCs. Also, the PCMCIA is handy for resetting a hung modem—you can just pull it out and slide it in again.

As you can see in Figure 11.1, the telephone cable connection is the only part of a PCMCIA modem that's visible on the outside, and vendors are already competing over that. Megahertz Corporation pioneered the XJack, a device that retracts out of sight when it's not in use. Other vendors use special external connection cables, that are less fragile, but if you misplace the cable you cannot make a connection.

Memory conflicts are still PCMCIA's biggest problem. The PCMCIA installation programs typically exclude blocks of memory from memory-management programs, so if you're tight on Windows memory, adding PCM-CIA makes things worse. But without these exclusions, the memory manager could load other drivers into the space, and nothing would work. Under DOS 6.0, you can avoid some of these problems by using the [menu] function in CONFIG.SYS to load the PCMCIA drivers and memory configuration selectively when you need them.

PCMCIA devices draw their power from the computer's battery. A modem draws as much as seven watts while in use, but only about one watt in sleep mode. In rough numbers, modem operation can take 10 to 30 percent of your laptop's total power, so using a modem can significantly reduce your battery's life.

Figure 11.1

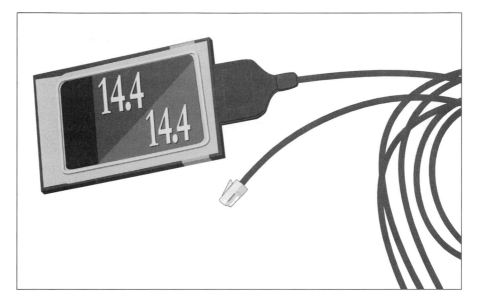

PCMCIA products like this modem are perfect for people who don't want to open their PC to add communications or networking capabilities. However, they can present some memory management challenges because they need special software drivers.

PCMCIA products are maturing, but newly released 32-bit standards may begin the evolution anew. If you're waiting for PCMCIA to come of age, consider portable modems like the Practical Peripherals PM288PKT, Telebit QBlazer, Microcom TravelPorte FAST, or U.S. Robotics WorldPort. They're only slightly bigger, have their own batteries, and are very easy to install.

Preparing Your Modem for Action

Modems for standard telephone lines typically have two RJ-11 telephone jacks, one for a telephone and one for the line that plugs into the wall jack. A few have their RJ-11 jacks wired straight through so you can use either jack for either connection, but in this configuration picking up the phone while the modem is connected can inject noise into the circuit. Other products designate the telephone and line jacks and allow orderly switching between the two devices through a software command or manual switch.

The major setup task for many modems involves determining what commands you must embed in a setup string and send to the modem so it knows what error control and data compression protocols to use, what speed to use on the modem and serial links, and what type of flow control to use on those links. The configurations for a few modems are explicitly included in the setup menus of the most popular communications programs, giving you a point of departure from which to further customize the setup string.

The Hayes Standard AT command set lets you configure any modem for specific operations: You can set the speaker volume, turn it on or off, change the flow control between your PC and modem, or dial telephone numbers. The AT command set also lets you tell the modem whether to use dial tone or pulse, what kind of telephone line (2- or 4-wire) to use, when to answer automatically, and how many rings to allow before answering. For modems with both error control and data compression, the instruction set is extended to control the way the modem negotiates its protocols, as well as specific parameters within the protocols. Most implementations of the Hayes AT command set also allow you to change your modem configuration on the fly and store the change for future use.

There are two good ways to take advantage of the power of V.34 modems: use them with special processors or precompress the files. These products work beautifully over LAN-to-LAN connections between specialized communications boards with high-speed interfaces like bridges and routers. Thus, you can enjoy the low cost of dial-up service while still moving data between LANs at useful speeds. If you want to move data between standalone PCs, make sure you have modern UARTs in the PCs, precompress the data files before transmission using any of the popular programs, and take advantage of the V.34 signaling rate of 28.8 kilobits per second with V.42 error control.

Compared to the vagaries and inconsistencies of modem communications, installing a local area network is simple. Nonetheless, modems are becoming an increasingly important part of and extension to local area networks. Network administrators often encounter modem problems. When you are faced with questions concerning modems, ask the vendors of the communications hardware and software for help. Although some arcane and relatively tiny problems can trip you up, the vendor has probably seen them all.

International Road Warriors

I've focused on North American telephone communications systems, primarily because outside of North America the situation is very confused. If you're an international road warrior, you'll face some unique problems starting with a few that are simply mechanical. For example, there are about 35 types of telephone jacks in use around the world if you include variations like the old Swiss 3-prong and the new Swiss 4-prong. Other challenges are even more arcane. For example, several countries put intermittent pulse tones on the local loop from the central office to trigger metering equipment in the customer's premise. These tones might be optional and might be filtered by a PBX, but they also might interrupt your modem. The best advice I can give you is to phone ahead and ask about modem connections wherever you might be going.

Sharing Telephone Lines

Many people today work in small or home offices with a limited number of telephone lines, but still need the capabilities of voice, data, and fax operation. A product I call a line manager lets you share a phone line among several devices with a minimum amount of hassle.

The line manager looks like a small modem. It connects to the telephone line and to the voice telephone instrument, to a modem, and to a fax machine. In operation, the line manager answers the ringing telephone line, listens for a while, and then decides how to route the call. But if you're thinking "it can't really be that simple," you're correct! It's what happens during the listening period that makes the difference.

The least complex type of line manager shares a voice telephone and a fax machine on a single line. These devices work by listening for the calling (CNG) tone generated by a fax machine when it originates a call. If the line manager hears the CNG tone, it generates a ring to the fax machine. If it doesn't hear the CNG after 3 to 4 seconds, it concludes that the incoming call is a voice call and rings the telephone. Since a person listening as the call goes through might interpret silence as an incomplete call and hang up, the line manager supplies a ringing tone to the caller while it listens for the CNG tone.

You can also use one of these relatively simple devices if you want to share a modem and a fax machine on the same line. Since calling data modems are silent, like calling people, you can attach your modem to the fax line manager port that's designed for a telephone instrument, and it will ring the modem and complete the call after it decides that the incoming call is not a fax. However, make sure modem callers set their software to expect 7 to 10 rings before an answer.

The situation becomes much more more complex if you want to share a line between an answering modem and a voice telephone instrument. Unlike fax machines, calling modems and calling people are both silent, so the fax line manager can't differentiate between them. The usual technique is to have the calling modem dial extra digits—usually a number 4 on the tone pad—just after the line manager answers. The line manager is programmed to look for these tones and to respond by connecting to the answering modem. This technique is tricky because calls to different places and calls placed at different times of day take different periods of time to connect; you have to experiment with the number of commas you put in the dialing string to create a pause, and with the number of times you send the digit 4.

Alternatively, you can program the calling and answering modems to use each other's tones, so that the calling modem originates a set of answer tones. This technique isn't as sensitive to the time needed to complete a call, but the modem commands are more complex. With either technique, you'll have to program the communications software so that the modem makes some noise if you want the line manager to differentiate between voice and modem callers.

A word of caution: All line managers are not compatible with all modems. The modem looks for a ring signal that is a sine wave with a 90-volt amplitude and 20-hertz frequency. Most line managers try to emulate the sine wave by generating a digital signal, but some modems won't respond. If your modem doesn't respond to the line manager's ring, return the line manager for another model; it's not the modem's fault.

■ Communications Software

Dennis Hayes delivered his first modem designed specifically for a personal computer years before IBM shipped the first PC. Yet despite more than a decade spent refining the bonds between modems and communications software, unless you've had a lot of rehearsal or experience you still stand only about a fifty-fifty chance of successfully transferring a file between two PCs on the first try using sophisticated V.34 modems.

There are three types of communications software products: general purpose, network remote access, and front-end access. Network remote access programs fall into two categories: remote node and remote control. Modem remote control packages allow one computer to literally put its keyboard and screen in parallel with the keyboard and screen of another computer for remote control operation. Remote node systems give the calling computer new disk drive letters and, within limits, access to network applications. Front-end access packages are specifically designed to access a single information service such as TAPCIS, ATO, or CISNAV for CompuServe, the Prodigy access software, or the America OnLine access software. I won't discuss front-end access programs here; for more information on them see *PC Magazine Guide to Modem Communications* referenced at the beginning of this chapter.

General Purpose Telecommunications Programs

The biggest category of communications software products consists of the general purpose telecommunications packages. These are "Swiss army knife" programs that do a lot of jobs well. You can use them to access ASCII-based information services, such as CompuServe, MCI Mail, Dialog, and Dow Jones News Service; to access bulletin board systems, ASCII-based private message services like MCI Mail, Unix/VMS-based systems, or mainframe systems (through protocol converters); and, of course, to access other personal computers running DOS.

The general purpose programs offer a host of similar features implemented in a similar way. Pull-down menus, dialing directories, and a variety of file transfer protocols grace virtually all of them. The control screen of CrossTalk Mk.4, shown in Figure 11.2, illustrates many of the options available during data transmission. Generally, you'll find communications programs offered as "shareware"—programs distributed with the hope of a contribution for their use—much more difficult to use than any commercial product. You'll also face a significant challenge when you try to use any of these programs to move files with a high-speed modem that is not on the program's setup list.

Figure 11.2

DCA's CrossTalk MK.4 is a flexible communications program that you can easily customize for each connection you make. This screen shows the degree of detail available for the serial port configuration

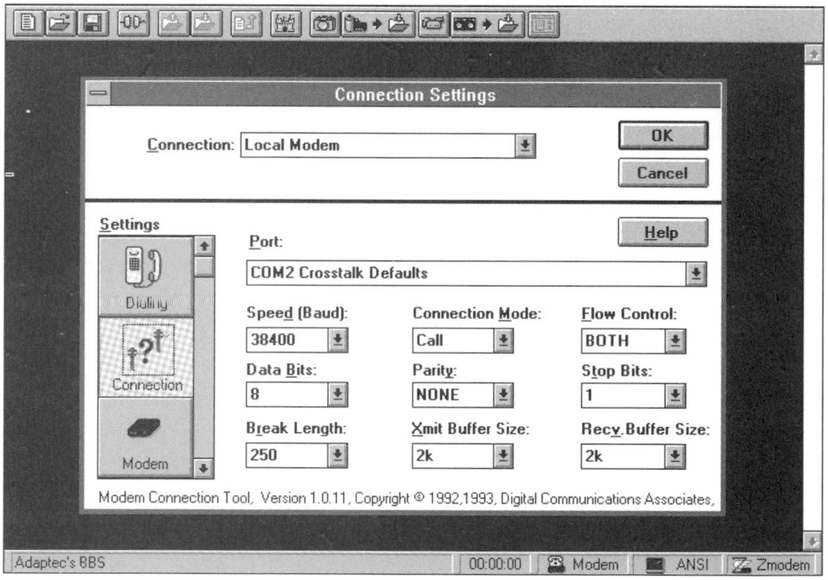

In simplest terms, a telecommunications program turns your PC into a communications terminal that has a screen and a keyboard. The program sends the characters typed on the keyboard out the serial port and displays the characters received from the serial port on the screen. Each of these seemingly simple tasks has unique complicating factors.

Inside the PC, the communications software must activate and manage the functions of the UART as it converts between the parallel data stream used inside the computer and the serial data stream used for connections to the outside world. Typically, the software does this through hardware for the RS-232C signaling and cable connection scheme.

Several generations of chips have been used as UARTs inside PCs, ranging from the 8250 found in the first IBM PCs to the 16550AFN found in top-of-the-line PCs made since about 1990. The operational improvements in the 16550AFN are mainly added registers and buffers that allow the chip to hold data and do work while reducing the load on the PC's CPU; however, the communications software you use must be written to take advantage of the 16550AFN's enhanced capabilities.

Similarly, the data flowing in and out of the serial port requires careful control. PCs typically use either hardware or software methods of flow control with modems. Software flow control relies on sending special characters called XON and XOFF in the data stream that signal the modem or the PC to stop sending data so the receiving device can catch up. Hardware flow control depends on changing voltage levels on certain wires in the RS-232 cabling scheme—typically Request to Send and Clear to Send—which signal the ability to receive data. Hardware flow control is preferred in PC communications systems, because software flow control schemes can be fooled by characters embedded in the streams of data PC users send when they transfer compiled program files or precompressed data files.

Not all modems are ready to use flow control when they come out of the box. Manufacturers ship their modems with a variety of default conditions, so the communications software must send commands to the modem telling it whether to use hardware flow control, software flow control, or both. Unfortunately, the nature of those commands varies not just among manufacturers but even among models of modems from the same manufacturer. When you're using a sophisticated new high-speed modem able to deliver data so fast that flow control is a must, you're often faced with the mystery of how to turn it on. This is a key element in the compatibility issue discussed later in this chapter.

On the incoming side, the communications software also controls the display of received data on the screen. Some computers, particularly mainframe and minicomputer systems like those delivered by Digital Equipment Corporation and IBM, expect special purpose terminals on the other end of the communications link. These machines control the position of the cursor and the display of the characters on the screen through special codes they transmit in the serial data stream. A portion of the communications software called the *terminal emulation package* gives a PC the ability to respond to control codes and to generate special keyboard codes just like a terminal.

The quality of terminal emulators varies widely. While all general purpose communications programs have some terminal emulation capabilities, there are also programs that specialize primarily in terminal emulation functions. General purpose programs typically make PCs respond to a code set specified by the American National Standards Institute (ANSI) and to the commands designed for Digital Equipment Corporation's VT-100 and VT-220 series of terminals.

File Transfers

When PCs link with each other, with information services, or with mini- or mainframe computers, they are often used to send and receive files. There are two ways to move a file from storage into the data communications stream: The first technique is to dump an ASCII file out of the port one character at a time, hoping that some program at the other end will catch it in a buffer which it will then write to disk. The second technique is to set up a file transfer process between the programs on both ends that moves all types of files, including non-ASCII files, in blocks with control over errors introduced in the communications stream and possibly even with data compression. Because these file transfer programs are relatively complex, using statistical analysis techniques to spot errors and compress data, they follow specific protocols, often published and updated by one individual. The common protocols used for error controlled file transfers include XModem, YModem, Kermit, and ZModem. Some information services have also published their own file transfer protocols, such as CompuServe-B.

The universal problem with protocols is that their implementations in programs generally aren't as smooth as their descriptions on paper. When different programmers write code to implement the same protocol, they often come up with programs that don't work together. Additionally, in an effort to improve performance and flexibility, all the protocols have developed options, and programmers often differ on which options should be active in the default setup. The bottom line is, file transfer software can be tricky to use. The different implementations and menu options lead to frustration as often as they do to satisfaction.

Additional Program Features

While controlling the data flow, controlling the screen, and transferring files are the flour, milk, and butter of communications programs, there are many ways to ice the finished cake. All communications packages provide some way to hold frequently called telephone numbers and to associate data like port speed, file transfer protocol, login name, password, and other details with each number.

Every package also provides some way to write scripts to automate the communications sessions. These scripting languages range from simple lists of statements resembling DOS .BAT files to complex programming languages like CASTLE, which is part of DCA's CrossTalk Mk.4. Using a language like CASTLE, you can create complete programs that will automatically place a call, request specific information like stock quotes, analyze the data, and inform you if the information exceeds certain programmed parameters.

Some programs like CrossTalk Mk.4 and CrossTalk XVI, HyperAccess/5, Smartcom, and ProComm Plus even automate the scripting process, recording your keystrokes and the other system's replies during a manual data exchange, and then creating a script to accomplish the same task. Although many people never use the scripting capabilities of their communications packages, some write sophisticated scripts to automate the activities of an entire workgroup or organization.

Compatibility Problems

I surveyed the senior editors of *PC Magazine*, each of whom has used a modem and some kind of communications software practically every day for ten years or more, and asked them about the chances of success for transferring a spreadsheet between two PCs the first time. Their replies, which gave at best a fifty-fifty chance of success, were a microcosm of the anguish less accomplished modem users must feel. As one editor said, "If you have a lot of data to send, the effective throughput of a 1.44-megabyte diskette shipped through a courier service is excellent." Moving data shouldn't be so difficult, but it is. While the companies that produce communications software deserve a lot of the blame, they aren't entirely responsible.

There are three points where a file transfer can break down: in the interface between the PC and the local modem, in the connection between modems, and in the interaction between communications programs. Incompatibilities between modems from different manufacturers are a major problem, particularly with new products. The only cure for this problem is to buy modems of the same make and model, or to give the companies time to work out their incompatibilities. The other two file transfer sticking points are within the control of the communications software, however.

With the exception of Hayes Smartcom, which only works with Hayes modems or their close clones, each communications program contains a listing of the modems it is programmed to set up. Most programs have lists with settings for well over 100 modems; however, a quick search of the product list in the Ziff-Davis Computer Library database turned up over 1,000 modem product names. If your software lists your specific make and model of modem, there's hope that the setup will be correct and detailed enough for all the tasks involved. If your modem isn't on the list, you definitely face a challenge. You can attempt to use a setup for a generic modem following the Hayes AT command setup string, but this might not work for much beyond dialing and automatic answering. Alternatively, you can create a "customized" modem profile for the communications software.

The modems available in today's market have evolved from several distinct ancestors. In the Paleolithic days of the late 1970s and early 1980s there were modems that used % commands, * commands, AT commands, and \ commands. If you are a modem archaeologist and can identify the derivation of your modem from its documentation, you may be able to create your own modem command profile.

If you're fortunate, the software company may have updated information on the modem—often provided by a user like you who has worked through the trial and error process—that the tech support people can read to you or send via fax. Frankly, considering the processing power sitting in the PC on your desktop, this entire process is wasteful and insulting. If the creators of word processing software assumed their users knew as much about printers as the creators of communications programs assume their users know about modems, nothing would ever get printed.

The problem of interfacing LAN adapter cards to networking software is similar to the modem and communications software situation—there are at least three major types of LAN adapters with three major expansion bus interfaces, but in this case the hardware and software companies have worked together to ensure that their products mesh. Unfortunately, there seems to be little such cooperation between the modem vendors and the creators of communications software. In 1990 and 1991, Hayes sponsored seminars on programming the AT command set, but these don't seem to have had much impact. An ANSI modem interface standard has been proposed, but it is broad right where it needs to be narrow—in the area of flow control. The CCITT has a V.25bis standard for modem interfaces, but its commands are limited, and a modem must know the speed and parity of incoming commands before it can read anything. In truth, none of these efforts has had much effect on compatibility—many modems are still a mystery to many communications packages.

For now, the best advice I can offer is to caution that before you buy a new modem—particularly one of the newer V.34 varieties—or a communications program, call the vendor of the communications software and ask them specifically whether that make and model of modem is on their setup menu. If it isn't, look for more compatible products.

■ Network Remote Access

The logic behind the use of remote access products is influenced by time, money, and legislation as much as it is by technology. As any corporate manager who deals with issues of benefits or legality can testify, these forces are often in conflict. But technology and practicality achieve harmony when it comes to remote LAN access products. Giving employees remote access to networks from their homes or hotels improves productivity, reduces costs and makes it easier for U.S. companies to conform to the Clean Air Act, the Family and Medical Leave Act, and to many related state and local regulations.

Studies show that employees produce more and are happier when they can telecommute. In addition, telecommuting allows companies to reduce costs for everything from office space to furniture and utilities, so it also makes good business sense. Apparently Congress thinks telecommuting is a good idea too. The Clean Air Act of 1990 includes provisions that kicked in during late 1993 and surprised senior managers in many companies. The Act decrees that organizations which have over 100 employees and are located in specific metropolitan areas designated by the Environmental Protection Agency must take action to reduce travel to the worksite by 25 percent during peak commute hours.

Similarly, the Family and Medical Leave Act of 1994 provides for up to 12 weeks of unpaid leave each year for specific family and medical reasons. However, because it could benefit both the employer and the employee to get some work done during those weeks of leave, the act also provides for options like telecommuting.

Many products can connect to your network and provide simultaneous access for remote callers. They include Remote LAN Node Turnkey Server from Digital Communciations Associates Inc. (DCA), LAN Distance from IBM Corp., Microcom LANexpress from Microcom Inc., Miniarray Remote Node Server from MultiTech Systens Inc., Dr. Bond-S from NEC America Inc., LanRover/E 2.0 for NetWare from Shiva Corp., Remote Office version 1.2 from Stampede Technologies Inc., and NetBlazer PN4 from Telebit Corp.

Most remote access products are stand-alone, turn-key network devices. Only IBM's LAN Distance, Novell's NetWare Connect, and Stampede's Remote Office require you to add a PC and stir. The phrase *turn-key* is supposed to imply easy, painless installation, but that isn't necessarily so; the so-called turn-key products can have their own sets of problems. The Shiva and Stampede products are both very easy to install, even though the former is a turn-key device and the latter is not. Shiva ships a box that looks like a modem with a LAN port attached. After you snap and plug in the cables, you're practically ready to connect. Stampede ships software and a multiport serial board that you must install in a PC, but they've done such a good job on the installation software that it's very easy to do. At PC Magazine Labs, we generally found that flexibility, in terms of the types of network and PC operating systems a product supports, increases its complexity, making it more difficult to install and manage.

Some installations don't even need separate remote access products. If you choose Microsoft's Windows NT Advanced Server as your network operating system, you'll find a built-in utility called Remote Access Service that works the same as the individual third-party products.

Network remote access products break down into three categories: remote control, remote node, and BBS. Remote control products allow the caller to run programs on a networked PC. Remote mode systems extend the network to programs running on the calling PC. Almost any calling PC will do for remote control, so this technique is appropriate for people who don't have powerful PCs at home or on the road. It also works well for installations where you want to keep all files in a central place, but allow callers to enter orders or take similar actions. Figure 11.3 shows the operation of remote mode and remote control systems.

Figure 11.3

Remote control systems execute programs on the called PC, so the calling PC doesn't need a lot of processing power or memory. Remote node systems execute all programs, including the network communications software, on the calling PC. Remote node operation is best suited to sophisticated computers with plenty of memory and processing power.

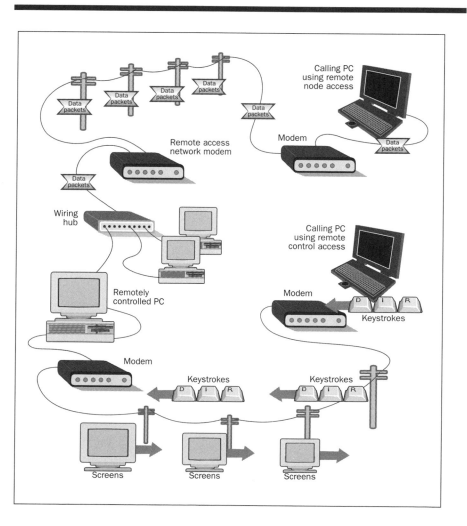

BBS software, programs that answer a call and present a limited menu of options, are part of all major communications packages. They are easy to use and maintain and provide high security. Their best uses are in file transfer and electronic messaging applications.

Modem Remote Control Programs

Whether you want to use the files from your office PC at home or provide technical support to a user in another location, remote computing packages can give you access and control. No matter how many files you manage to fit onto a portable's hard disk, time and again you'll need a file that resides on your office network; having a remote control program installed can be a great relief.

The modem remote control software market is well established, with many competitive products. The latest batch offers some powerful capabilities including enhanced EGA and VGA graphics, multitasking, and the ability to record a session and play it back later. These programs typically include data compression and error control to extract the greatest benefit from the telephone line.

Remote computing uses software, modems, and the phone lines to connect two PCs and make them behave like one machine, even when they are separated by a great distance. The computer whose files and programs are accessed is called the host, and the one that takes control of the host's operations is the remote. While you sit at the remote, it's as if you were also seated at the host; its keyboard and screen become an extension of your own. If another user is actually at the host site, you may feel like a flight instructor giving lessons in a plane equipped with dual controls—you can see everything the student does, while the student can observe your maneuvers and learn by watching.

Remote access to a LAN is one of the most common functions for a remote computing program, but many other imaginative applications are possible. You can work simultaneously with someone on a spreadsheet, database, accounting, or word processing program. If you're a tech support person, you can monitor, control, and troubleshoot software without traveling to the customer's site.

Perhaps the easiest way to exchange data among LANs is through remote control of a networked PC. Applying modem remote control software to a LAN-to-LAN scenario means someone working at a networked PC in city A could use normal dial-up telephone lines to call a modem attached to a networked PC in city B. Once they were connected, the modem remote control software running in both PCs would provide an efficient way for people in city A to make entries in a database, use electronic mail, or copy data files from the city B networks.

A remotely controlled PC allows employees calling from any location, even a non-networked one, to access the full power of the network. The caller can run programs, use printers, access a mainframe computer through a gateway, and otherwise act as a full member of the network. Remote control programs include good security, but they cannot protect against ill-behaved software or human error. Modem remote control programs do not care what network operating system or network adapter cards you use. These packages allow people to span different LAN operating systems easily.

While this type of remote control connection is effective, at some level of activity it becomes uneconomical to dedicate individual networked PCs to receiving dial-in calls. When remote control of a networked PC becomes frequent, it is wise to establish a separate computer system to act as an access server capable of handling many incoming calls simultaneously. If you want callers to be able to run applications off your network, an access server running remote control software is the optimum choice.

The Remote Node Alternative

Until the Windows graphical user interface caught on, the modem remote control method of making a remote connection to a LAN was always much more efficient than another technique called remote node, or remote client. In the remote node method, the calling computer runs all the networking software, including the redirector, with driver programs that send network requests out the serial communications port to a modem connected to a PC on the network. Instead of remotely controlling the networked PC, this method causes the software in the networked PC simply to pass data between its serial port and its network adapter. The calling laptop has a full set of redirected DOS disk drive letters, but the remote client connection must push many layers of messages carrying different network packets and acknowledgments across the relatively slow telephone line.

The remote control connection passes only keystrokes and screen images across the modem connection, so typically it's much faster than the remote client method. Two developments have challenged that superiority, however: First, the multipixel changes that take place in a Windows graphics screen every time you click a mouse take several seconds to traverse even a fast modem link, so the time needed to pass images of dense graphics screens like those used in Windows reduces the efficiency of the remote control approach compared to something like that of the remote node. Second, companies like DCA and Shiva Corp. have come up with ways to reduce the amount of network traffic moving over modems and telephone lines, which significantly reduces the time needed to move data under the remote client arrangement.

Shiva markets a line of products that I call networked modems. Each networked modem has its own network adapter and operates as an autonomous node on the network. A person using a calling PC connected through the networked modem sees a full set of redirected drives and keeps the application's data files on the network file server. Networked modems are new products that will meet the needs of companies dedicated to graphical environments like Windows or OS/2.

The people who create the software for remote client operation through network modems tokenize certain repetitive elements of the NetWare Core Protocol packet within the IPX packet to reduce overhead and improve throughput significantly. This technique gives you the advantage of using your remote computer as part of the LAN while still retaining useful throughput.

Even though the authors of modern remote control programs have learned tricks for improving the slow transmission of graphics screens, remote client and remote control techniques still compete relatively equally in installations where people must run software under Windows or other graphical environments like the OS/2 Presentation Manager.

Remote node products are aimed at client/server applications as diverse as customized ordering and inventory programs, Lotus Notes, and electronic mail programs. They work best when the calling PC has enough memory and processing power to run applications while handling modem communications tasks in the background—typically, that's only on the most modern laptop and desktop PCs. Because these remote node devices push a lot of data across the telephone line, they demand the fastest available modems on both ends.

Do and Do Not!

Modem connections operate with about 1 percent of the signaling speed of network connections, so while the disk drive letters and printer names look the same on a PC connected either through a remote node or through the LAN, they don't work the same. In our tests at PC Magazine Labs, we saw an average throughput for an .EXE file of about 26 kilobits per second. At that rate, it would take about 25 minutes to load Microsoft Word for Windows from the file server, so you obviously don't want to do that.

You must carefully configure the calling PC so that all the large files it needs are on its own hard drive. You only want to push and pull necessary files through the modem. This means login programs, utilities like Novell's MAP.EXE, virus protection programs, and anything else you might normally pull from the file server should be on the calling PC.

Using a remote node product complicates the network administrator's job because the calling PCs may need careful customization to conserve disk space. It also becomes more difficult to update software when network utilities are spread across a large group of traveling machines.

Protocols and LANs

Because remote node access devices extend the network, they're sensitive to the networking protocols used on it. Protocols are agreements about how programs package and exchange data. The two most important protocols in networking are TCP/IP, which is used on the Internet and with Unix computers, and the IPX protocols used by Novell in NetWare. Apple's AppleTalk protocol is also found in many installations. A protocol called NetBEUI, an extension of the older NetBIOS, is important to people using operating systems such as Windows for Workgroups, LANtastic, and POWERlan. Networks running Microsoft's Windows NT and NT Advanced Server are able to use IPX, TCP/IP, or NetBEUI.

DCA's RLN, Stampede's Remote Office, and IBM's LAN Distance function as network bridges. Bridges operate at the Ethernet or Token-Ring level, so they aren't concerned with the differences in the higher-level protocols like IPX or NetBEUI. In theory, bridges should have slower throughput than the other products that act as more selective routers, but in our benchmark tests at the PC Magazine LAN Labs other factors such as software drivers had more influence on throughput.

Products such as Novell's NetWare Connect, MultiTech's MultiCom, and Shiva's LanRover/E for NetWare are essentially single-protocol products. They work well with NetWare's IPX and are relatively simple to se tup.

A few products make it possible to use the networked modems and telephone lines for outgoing calls. NetWare Connect, LanRover/E, and Microcom's LANexpress come with this ability and you can add it to MultiTech's MultiCom. Network dial-out is a feature found in all modern communications software packages. Its main value is in reducing the number of telephone lines you have to run to the desktops in your organization.

Electronic Bulletin Board Systems

Another way to gain remote entry to a LAN is to use bulletin board systems, or BBSs. Although it has different goals and a different lineage than the methods discussed previously, BBS software can be useful not only for connecting users on diverse LANs, but also for promoting wide-area communications in companies whose various offices are not fully or even partially networked.

A menu of messages and functions greets callers when they dial into a BBS. People can easily read and post messages or upload and download files, but they are always under the tight functional control of the BBS software. All the products reviewed in this chapter can store data on a network file server, but a BBS insulates the network from callers; they cannot run programs that might crash the remote system or change important files on the server.

Security and Management

Many managers quake when they think about opening their network to outside access. They fear hackers, viruses, and other threats. All remote access products offer password protection and most have features such as call-back. The LanRover/E and NetWare Connect products integrate with Novell's bindery of names and privileges in NetWare 3.X, so the administrator has only one list to keep straight. In every case, the biggest security threat comes from sloppy password protection rather than technical trickery. IBM's LAN Distance goes the farthest to protect security, allowing for long password phrases and even limiting access according to a physical identification in the calling unit.

As networks grow, network administrators become concerned about managing growing numbers of computer resources and gathering reports for purposes of troubleshooting and budgeting. Products like Microcom's LANexpress and DCA's RLN offer extensive control through the Simple Network Management Protocol (SNMP). Shiva and MultiTech provide their own management programs. Since NetWare Connect runs in a NetWare server, it is managed through NetWare.

All the warnings about software compatibility and the interface to specific makes and models of modems apply to remote control software at the host and remote ends and to network modem software at the remote end. Do not assume any software package will work with any modem, no matter how popular either product is. Always ask software vendors about their product's ability to interface with a specific modem before you make a decision.

Remote Reset

Any remote access device—remote control, remote node, or BBS—can reach a point where it becomes stuck and doesn't respond to commands. These devices need a reboot at the level of the "big red switch" that controls the power to the PC. Similarly, many people don't want their remote access servers to run all the time; they only want the access server up when they want to call in. The folks from Server Technology Corporation have a telephone-activated power control unit called Remote Power On/Off that solves these problems. If you don't want to leave your remote access server on all the time, this affordable product turns it on when the phone rings and off after the call. But if you do leave your access server on all the time, Remote Power On/Off will drop the AC power after a call, wait a few seconds, and then apply power again, which eliminates frustrating problems with "hung" remotely controlled PCs.

Remote Power On/Off detects an incoming call, provides power to devices plugged into its special wall socket adapter, monitors the status of the telephone line, and drops the power at some specified period of time after the telephone connection is broken. Providing you can disable your PC's memory check in ROM BIOS to shorten the boot time, this arrangment will work fine for infrequently called systems.

In many offices, the problem is different. Organizations want to keep PCs acting as access servers running, but applications sometimes freeze. A frozen PC can put an organization's remote access capability out of service until someone physically resets the system, which can be a problem at night and on weekends. The Remote Power On/Off product's reboot feature ensures that the access server will come back up with a fresh reboot after every call. You lose only a few seconds of time between calls and completely avoid the problem of frozen remote access servers.

■ When Computers and Telephones Meet

The links between networks and modems are still primitive, but new relationships are being forged. Your PC itself can't do everything in the modern office, but it should be the place from which you can do everything. You should be able to handle your documents, links to outside information services, e-mail, video conferences, phone calls, voice mail, fax, and all other actions from the keyboard and screen. This doesn't mean that the software for all those functions runs in the PC, only that you can get at what you need from the PC through consistent and integrated interfaces.

The bridges linking the elements of the modern office are under construction. The LAN acts provides the pillars and cables that support it all, but there's much more. Services like ISDN and ATM (Asynchronous Transfer Mode) are laying digital highways to the office. Companies like Microsoft, Novell, and Dialogic are designing the architecture for the bridges, while other companies, which manufacture private branch exchange (PBX) telephone systems, printers, copiers, and fax systems, are turning out the planks.

The LAN cable will join PCs, fax machines, printers, and copiers. Microsoft's At Work architecture has this field to itself and is gaining support. At Work consists of software modules that printer and fax companies load into their products. Microsoft provided the first version of the PC side of At Work in Windows for Workgroups version 3.11, but Windows 4.0 has even more capability. A common interface and communications system make it easy to create, copy, send, and receive documents using a variety of office machines.

On the telephone side, the PBX will remain in its own cabinet, but will have new capabilities. Unfortunately, Microsoft and Novell have different ideas about how a PBX should link to a LAN. Microsoft wants PBXs to be part of At Work, too, but some PBX vendors are skeptical about loading multiple software functions into telephone switches that have a reputation for high reliability at stake. Microsoft also has a series of specifications called the Telephony API (TAPI) that describe how devices and programs on individual PCs interact with the PBX. Their aim is to replace the desktop telephone with the PC.

Novell's NetWare Telephony Services Architecture (NTSA) defines a physical link between a LAN server and the PBX, which maintains an arm's-length relationship that's more comfortable to the PBX vendors. In this scheme, applications running in each PC interact with the PBX just as they do with printers or other networked devices. The telephone stays on the desk, but you can control it from your keyboard. Microsoft's integration is tighter, but Novell's structure makes it less daunting to install the system and to develop applications for the PC and PBX. Figure 11.4 illustrates how LANs and telephone systems meet.

Dialogic Corporation's Signal Computing System Architecture (SCSA) adds smart voice capabilities to both the LAN and the PBX. SCSA is a specification for hardware that talks and listens so you can use software like Vista from ZyBel Microsystems to build interoperable speech recognition and voice synthesis applications. SCSA is compatible with At Work and TAPI, but initially developers will work under Novell's NTSA because it has a bigger market. Many SCSA voice products are designed to slide into a NetWare server.

Videoconferencing is the other major element of desktop information integration. Intel Corp. is leading a group of 12 major vendors in finishing up a PC desktop videoconferencing standard. Real and interoperable products will drift out of these companies throughout the mid 1990s.

Outside of the PC and the LAN, the major technology enabling the integration of desktop information is the introduction (finally) of digital telephone service under an architecture called the Integrated Systems Digital Network (ISDN). ISDN brings data in at 128 kilobits per second and includes many features such as dial-up connections that take only milliseconds to establish. ISDN makes videoconferencing, database replication, and document transfer practical. High software costs for the local telephone companies have slowed ISDN's growth, but according to BellCore, many local telephone companies in the U.S. will have 80 to 90 percent of their lines ready for ISDN in 1995.

The integration of the devices on the typical desktop—particularly the telephone and the PC—is at hand. The more you share resources, the more you reduce costs and increase productivity, so this desktop integration should be heartily welcomed.

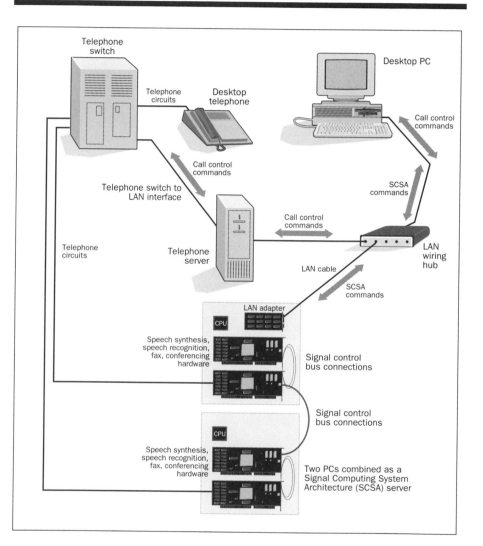

Figure 11.4

Computer Telephony systems integrate LANs with telephone systems, often through a special interface linking the local telephone switch (called a PBX) with a LAN server. Special purpose servers can execute call-handling, fax-on-demand, and other programs for specialized telephony applications.

Less sophisticated computer telephony systems integrate the desktop telephone and PC with or without a LAN.

- *Mainframe and Minicomputer Systems*
- *TCP/IP for Multiplatform Networking*

Linking PCs to Mainframe Systems and Large Networks

TECHNICAL TALE

"It was pretty bad until I got a swivel chair," Gus said. "But now that I can swing back and forth I figure I'm multitasking as good as anyone."

I checked, and he wasn't joking. He had a 3270 mainframe terminal, a 5250 AS/400 terminal, and a PC on his desk, and he swiveled between them, typing information from one system to the other. I'd found him by tracing all the cables going into his office.

Gus had slipped through or hidden from the system, and I wasn't going to reach him by preaching about productivity. He probably liked things just as they stood. But when I looked at his forehead, I saw an approach. "These things generate a lot of heat, don't they?"

"Yeah, the facilities people say they can't do anything about it."

"How about if I could roll all three keyboards and screens into one? You'd have a lot more desk space, and with a new, efficient monitor you'd cut the heat in here by more than two-thirds."

I had him hooked. Once I installed a couple of terminal emulation programs under Windows, I'd show Gus how to cut and paste between the screens. By the time I wrote some software to move the information automatically, Gus would be on the bandwagon. Sometimes network management is equal parts technology and psychology.

The COMPUTER INDUSTRY IS BUZZING WITH THE WORD *DOWNSIZING*. IT REFERS to the process of replacing large, centralized computer installations with networks of PCs. But despite the trend toward downsizing in the development of new applications and systems, organizations have billions of dollars invested in proven programs running on centralized mainframe and minicomputer systems. Replacing these programs is not cost-effective, and there are scientific and engineering applications that will require the power of a mainframe for years to come. Mainframes and minicomputers are going to be around for quite a while, and increasingly, people will want to use PCs to interact with them.

In this chapter I'll describe how to link PCs—and particularly networked PCs—to dissimilar computer systems. I'll provide specifics on the alternative ways you can connect PCs to IBM mainframe computers, along with general information on using a set of protocols called TCP/IP to connect to a variety of computers from different manufacturers.

■ Mainframe and Minicomputer Systems

A mainframe computer system lives up to its label as a "system." Many different pieces of hardware and software must play together in a successful mainframe installation. The system must have at least one central processor, but it isn't unusual for several processors to operate together to share the processing load and to provide backup processing in case one device fails. Such a system might include gigabytes of online data storage and even more storage using tape and other archive systems.

Minicomputer systems are more difficult to define. Only a few years ago you could safely define a minicomputer as a computer with over a megabyte of memory. Today, the PCs many people use on their desktops have more processing power and memory than the minicomputer used by a group of people down the hall. I'm not going to attempt a technical definition of a minicomputer because it will immediately be out of date, but characteristically it is a computer running a multiuser operating system that cannot use DOS, Windows, or OS/2 applications.

People typically interact with modern mainframes and minicomputers through devices called *terminals* that have screens and keyboards. While the terminals include their own processors, memory, and sophisticated video capabilities, they aren't PCs and they don't run application programs. The mainframe applications, which are often written to serve many users simultaneously, run in the mainframe or mini's central processing unit. One terminal can typically have several programs or sessions running on the mainframe at the same time.

Manufacturers offer a variety of connection alternatives for terminals. IBM provides ways for terminals to connect to the central computer system over coaxial cables, through modems, and as part of a local area network.

IBM and the BUNCH

In the 1970s and early 1980s there were many mainframe and minicomputer companies. The "BUNCH"—Burroughs, Univac, NCR, Control Data, and Honeywell——gave IBM a run for its money. Digital Equipment Corp. established itself as the major vendor of minicomputers. Other companies such as Amdahl and Telex cloned pieces and parts of the IBM mainframe systems.

Today, Digital stresses the use of its minicomputers as servers. Unisys, built on the structure of Burroughs and Sperry, continues to have success in certain mainframe market areas, but most PC-to-central-computer products are designed for IBM mainframes.

IBM 3270

Any explanation of how to hook PCs to IBM mainframe computers has to deal with a lot of IBM equipment numbers and describe the IBM network architecture schemes. IBM's major line of terminals, printers, and other communications devices falls into the general category of the "3270 family" of equipment. Each type of device has a specific model number, many of which begin with the digits 327. They're all designed to work in concert to orchestrate access to the mainframe's computing power for users of both PCs and other equipment. Well over 2 million 3270-family terminals were in use in 1990.

IBM's Systems Network Architecture (SNA) is the company's grand scheme for connecting its myriad 3270-family products. It includes a flexible suite of network protocols that can be configured in several ways. Here's how the 3270 family of products fits into various SNA setups.

In a classic 3270 system, each 3278 or 3279 terminal connects to a 3174 or 3274 terminal cluster controller through coaxial cable. The cluster controller acts as a concentrator by gathering messages from the terminals for more efficient transmission to the mainframe.

Groups of cluster controllers attach via a telecommunications line (which can run a few hundred feet locally or even across the country, through leased telephone lines and modems) to another, larger device called a communications controller or a front-end processor (FEP). The common IBM front-end processors are models 3705 and 3725. Other companies, such as ITT Courier, Lee Data, and Memorex Telex, make products that are "plug compatible" and compete with IBM's 3270 devices.

In a relatively recent evolution of the classic plan, IBM gave the 3174 terminal controller, the 3725 FEP, the 3745 communications controller, and other devices the ability to become nodes on a Token-Ring network. This architecture requires relatively expensive adapters and more memory on the 3270 hardware. Because the IBM Token-Ring Interface Coupler mainframe hardware has the acronym TIC, this architecture is usually called a "tick" or "tick connection."

PUs and LUs

In IBM's SNA connection scheme, each terminal or printer connected to the controller is called a *physical unit*, or PU. Different kinds of PUs have different capabilities. The front-end processor expects to send certain kinds of data to and get specific kinds of responses from each type of PU.

Each PU holds one or more *logical units*, or LUs; these address and interact with the host in an SNA network. It is actually the LU—typically a program—that does the work that's transmitted over the communications link. IBM's Virtual Telecommunications Access Method (VTAM) software, which runs in the mainframe, works with the Network Control Program (NCP) in the front-end processor to recognize, configure, and communicate with the LUs.

During operation, the 3278/9 terminals send messages called scan codes to the cluster controller each time a key is pressed. The cluster controller echoes the keystrokes back to the terminal so that they are confirmed and displayed on the screen. Data from the mainframe host steps through the front-end processor, to the cluster controller, and then into a display buffer in the terminal.

Data coming to the terminal for screen presentation is handled in blocks called fields; these can vary in length from a few characters to a whole screen. The size and characteristics of a field depend on what the terminal finds in the display buffer. Characteristics like blinking, reverse video, seven-color displays, and underlining are defined by modified characters containing extended-attribute bytes. These bytes give different meanings to incoming characters to let them represent functions not ordinarily handled in the 8-bit data alphabet the 3270 terminals use.

Easy Transfers

Simple file transfers between a PC and a mainframe are often performed using an IBM editing utility called IND$FILE on the mainframe. This method of moving data is effective, but slow. Companies like Attachmate, DCA, and Wall Data sell software for both the PC and the host that speeds file transfers between them.

Making mainframe data easily available to PC applications is another task for paired PC/host software. Companies as diverse as Lotus Development

Corp. and Martin Marietta market software for the PC that extracts data from mainframe systems for PC applications.

One Screen for All and All Screens for One

Today, people have PCs on their desktops. Personal computers offer a flexibility and responsiveness the mainframe systems can't touch, but many people with PCs also need access to mainframe systems. People from system programmers to administrative assistants make good use of multiple mainframe sessions. Some people continually monitor mail systems (such as IBM's popular PROFS) in one session while using a scheduling program in a second session and a major mainframe application in a third one. People developing applications often have multiple sessions active to receive error messages and to simulate several users.

People don't want screens and keyboards for both terminals and PCs on their desktops, though, and there are many ways application programs running in a PC can use information distilled by a mainframe application, so the logical thing to do is to make the PC act like a terminal. Some of the most successful and long-lived PC add-on products, such as DCA's IRMA terminal emulator, give PCs the ability to serve as terminals for IBM mainframes.

Before a PC and an IBM mainframe can communicate and exchange data with each other, some major obstacles must be circumvented. For example, the PC's keyboard doesn't have as many keys as a 3270 terminal does, and the terminal has several special graphics characters that aren't in the PC's screen repertoire. The PC also lacks an appropriate communications interface, and it uses the ASCII data alphabet instead of IBM's standard mainframe alphabet, the Extended Binary Coded Decimal Interchange Code (EBCDIC).

Currently, there are three basic ways to overcome these difficulties: by adding a plug-in card combined with software and/or hardware that makes the PC act like a 3270 terminal when it is attached to a cluster controller; by connecting a protocol converter between the PC and the mainframe that translates the mainframe's data into a form usable by the PC; or by using a network to link the PC and the mainframe.

Connecting the PC to a 3174 or 3274 terminal cluster controller through coaxial cable is a popular technique because it is simple and requires no action at the mainframe end. The technique of using a separate computer called a protocol converter to interface the PC and the mainframe has lost its appeal because it is expensive, and today's powerful PCs can handle the terminal-emulation tasks very well. Given the subject of this book, you can guess that I'll focus on using a LAN to link PCs and mainframes.

Regardless of the connection scheme, these terminal-emulation products let you touch a key to toggle between local DOS programs and mainframe processes. You don't even have to consider finding desk space for both a PC and a mainframe terminal.

Terminal-Emulation Functions and Features

The terminal-emulation portions of the various products on the market differ mainly in the variety of IBM terminals they ape. Some products act like simple character-mode terminals, while others let the PC, driven by mainframe programs, display excellent color graphics screens. All of them give you the option to remap the PC's keyboard so that various keystroke combinations send the messages expected from the special function keys on IBM terminals.

A PC acting as a terminal operates in one of several modes. A CUT (Control Unit Terminal) can have a single session with the mainframe. In the DFT (Distributed Function Terminal) mode, the 3270 terminal can have up to five concurrent sessions with the mainframe. IBM has another, related mode it calls MLT (Multiple Logical Terminal), that allows multiple sessions with CUT-mode terminals through IBM's 3174 terminal cluster controller.

An application program interface, or API, looks for inputs from other programs. When an API is available, people who write applications like accounting, inventory, and communications programs can use simple commands to move data through the network to the mainframe and to interact with mainframe applications. The API converts the relatively simple commands that have been written in C or some other high-level programming language into the complex actions needed to move, verify, and store data.

IBM has defined several APIs for use with mainframe applications. Some of them require software running on both the PC and the mainframe, but others work locally in the PC. For instance, IBM's 3270-PC API and the High-Level-Language Application Program Interface (HLLAPI) run only on the PC; Advanced Program-to-Program Communications (APPC) requires software on both the PC and the mainframe, but it allows for a high degree of integration between PC and mainframe applications.

These products also have the ability to record and replay *macros*, sets of recorded keystrokes that are stored and always ready to replay. Macros make it easy to use applications that normally require many keystrokes to start. The programs can memorize the keystrokes you use and store them as a macro that you can easily initiate. Attachmate Corp.'s facility for creating macros is particularly handy because you can easily create a macro that will pause, wait for keyboard input, and then continue. This is useful for entering a date, a password, or some other piece of information.

3270 under Windows

The topic might sound dry, but products providing 3270 terminal emulation under Windows are exciting to see because they display the full activities of several mainframe programs simultaneously in small windows you can easily read.

Under Microsoft Windows, 3270 terminal emulators can shrink the window displaying a 3270 session almost to postage-stamp size and still provide a usable and readable display. You can monitor the activity in as many mainframe sessions as you're likely to have and still use other local applications.

Such 3270 emulators thrive in the Windows environment. They let you make icons to launch mainframe applications, provide interesting icons to show mainframe activity, and use three functions of Windows—DDE, DLL, and the clipboard—to link mainframe and Windows applications.

The dynamic data exchange (DDE) capability of Windows allows different applications to share data. The techniques used are called *hotspot* and *hotlink*. Under the hotspot technique, you can control mainframe applications with your mouse. The terminal-emulation program understands cursor movements and mouse inputs over screen elements generated by the host. In other words, you can double-click your mouse on a screen element generated by the host application or mainframe communications software, and the Windows terminal-emulation software will tell the host to take a corresponding action.

Under the hotlinks scheme, a specially written application can accept messages in predefined areas of a display generated by the host computer. For example, Microsoft Excel can hotlink to the host display session and react to the information displayed on the screen.

The 3270 emulation programs running under Windows can also benefit from Dynamic Link Libraries (DLLs). DLLs are a group of functional program elements, such as device drivers, shared by all Windows applications. The sharing action provides for efficient use of memory.

Another way applications can share data is through the Microsoft Windows clipboard. All of the products in this market include an edit feature that allows the user to copy portions of the host display to the clipboard in Windows and then paste the same data to another application's Windows session. This differs from DDE in that the clipboard requires user intervention in moving the data between applications.

The graphical interface also helps reduce problems associated with remapping the PC keyboard to emulate the much larger 3270 keyboard. On-screen keyboard maps make it easy to realign the keyboard and to use the mouse instead of keystrokes to select special "keys."

The Coaxial Terminal Connection

The coaxial adapter card architecture, pioneered by DCA and now offered by a dozen companies, supplies each PC with a direct coaxial attachment (common to IBM 3270 terminals) for the mainframe's terminal cluster controller. The PC runs software that makes it act like an IBM terminal, and the mainframe regards it as such. Data is transmitted via standard IBM 3270 cables. The terminal-emulation software in the PC not only lets you transfer files between the PC and the mainframe, it typically lets you toggle between mainframe sessions and DOS programs.

Because this type of architecture calls for a dedicated port for each PC on the mainframe's terminal cluster controller—whether or not it is active—connecting a large number of PCs via this method becomes expensive. The performance (measured in terms of throughput and response time) is good, and the installation easy, but the costs for mainframe hardware are high. Additionally, the 3270 coaxial adapter is, like a LAN adapter, another device that you must integrate into each PC—it takes an expansion slot, an interrupt, and some portion of RAM.

LAN Connections

If you use a LAN to connect to a mainframe, you avoid the expense of putting a 3270 coaxial adapter in every PC, the problems of installing such adapters, and the cost of buying additional terminal cluster controllers for the PCs. There are two distinctly different ways of using a LAN to connect to a mainframe: a direct connection and a gateway. The gateway connection scheme includes several options.

Many gateways use a relatively slow SNA synchronous data link control (SDLC) connection operating at 19.2 kilobits per second (kbps). Connection options such as coaxial attachment or attachment over a Token-Ring network between the gateway and the mainframe create a link that operates at speeds up to 16 megabits per second (mbps).

During our testing of gateway products at PC Magazine Labs, we found that the throughput over the shared 19.2-kbps SDLC line adequately supports a dozen or more PCs acting as terminals. While the overhead created by gateway activity on a typical network is negligible, if the PCs do more than terminal emulation—for example, exchanging files or engaging in program-to-program communications—the throughput over the shared link quickly becomes a limiting factor. You can install more gateways on the network to divide the load, but that means a greater cash outlay for PCs and possibly mainframe hardware. It also means adding to the network manager's workload.

The LAN gateway alternative significantly reduces the cost of mainframe hardware needed for multi-PC-to-mainframe installations. One PC, usually dedicated to the task, acts as the gateway—a specific type of communications server. This is the only machine that connects directly to the mainframe. The mainframe regards this gateway as a terminal cluster controller and talks to it over one of a variety of communications links.

A LAN gateway product consists of a special card that fits into the gateway station's interface bus, software that runs in the gateway station and links the card to the LAN, and terminal-emulation software that runs on each PC on the LAN. The emulation software and gateway software communicate through the network's communications services software.

If you use NetWare as your network operating system, Novell's IPX/SPX will route the mainframe data between each client PC and the gateway PC. Other networks will use a transport-layer protocol like NetBIOS or TCP/IP to carry the data. These communications services work from node to node and are totally separate from the file-server software. You can set up and use a LAN gateway on a network that doesn't even have a file server. Just be sure the gateway product you choose supports the communications services of your network.

In a LAN gateway configuration, the networked client PCs run terminal-emulation software and share the single mainframe connection through the gateway. If you use the network for other tasks, like file- and printer-sharing, the per-PC cost of attaching to a mainframe can be very low. The primary cost factors are the prices of the gateway computer, the gateway/terminal-emulation software, and the connection scheme you choose.

Other Gateway Connections

Today, a typical gateway uses a relatively slow SDLC link to connect to the mainframe hardware suite, but there are two other gateway-to-mainframe connection schemes you should consider: Token-Ring (IEEE 802.2) and IBM 3299 multiplex. Figure 12.1 will help you understand the network-to-mainframe connection alternatives.

The Token-Ring gateway—which DCA and others call an 802.2 gateway, with reference to the IEEE standard—links the gateway PC and mainframe over a Token-Ring network. The mainframe element is TIC-equipped, and the PC gateway houses one or more network adapter cards, which connect the gateway to the network stations over Ethernet, ARCnet, Token-Ring, or any other wiring scheme. Another LAN adapter card in the gateway PC makes the Token-Ring connection to the TIC. You might establish a "PC Token-Ring to mainframe Token-Ring" gateway to reduce the number of physical units polled by the mainframe.

Figure 12.1

PCs acting as 3270 terminals can connect to the mainframe through an SDLC gateway, a Token-Ring gateway, and a direct Token-Ring connection. A large mainframe installation might include all these attachment schemes.

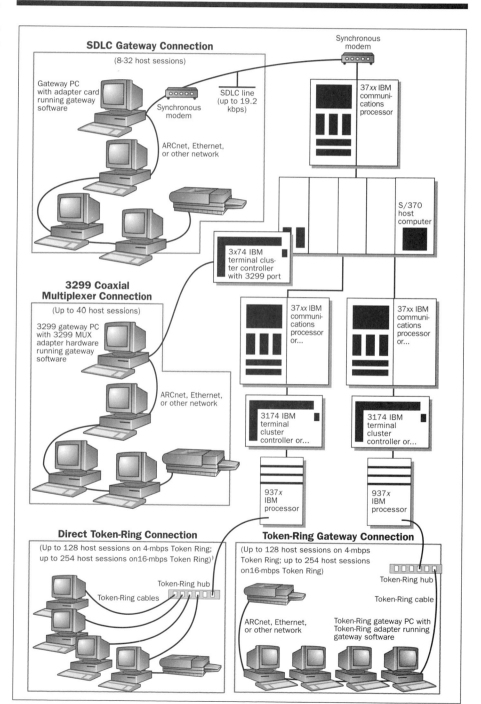

Attachmate, Banyan, DCA, IBM, and Novell either market separate 802.2 gateway products or include 802.2 gateway capabilities in their direct Token-Ring attachment packages. These products are priced in different ways, but they average between $250 to $350 per attached station.

You have to add the cost of the PC acting as a gateway, but typically even an unloved 4.77-MHz PC can do the job. The cost of the TIC-equipped mainframe components varies widely depending on what equipment you want to use, how you get support, and how you buy the equipment. If you don't have TIC-equipped mainframe components, there is still a gateway alternative that offers a high-throughput link to the mainframe.

Several companies market gateways that emulate IBM 3299 multiplexers. The real IBM 3299 multiplexer is designed to make it easier to connect a group of terminals to a mainframe over several thousand feet of cable. The multiplexer combines the data from eight coaxial cables onto one cable to reduce the cost of wiring.

Each of IBM's 3174 terminal cluster controllers has one of its four primary channels configured for an IBM 3299 connection. You can economically upgrade controllers with a microcode change to give 3299 service.

When a gateway PC on a network emulates a 3299 with appropriate software and a special coaxial adapter card, it uses a high-speed connection to the IBM 3174. The gateway can distribute up to forty simultaneous mainframe sessions to its attached PCs running terminal-emulation software. Our testing has shown that the 3299 gateway architecture provides throughput at least as good as the Token-Ring connection, with the potential for significantly lower cost.

There are many options you can look for in gateway systems, including pooled sessions, sessions divided by groups of users, security controls, and trace/dump utilities. Several companies offer good management packages, with varying abilities to audit and retire unused mainframe sessions and control the use of resources.

Installing any LAN gateway requires collaboration between the LAN system administrator and folks with special skills on the mainframe end—the system programmers. People on both sides of the link must set numerous electrical and software parameters to ensure effective terminal operation and file transfer through the gateway. While the software does contain menus to make life easier, the initial installation and configuration of both systems takes the full attention of someone who has complemented a good practical knowledge of MS-DOS with a three- to five-day, vendor-run course on the LAN software.

TIC Trick

The method of PC-to-mainframe connection IBM's sales force most frequently recommends is direct Token-Ring connection. The TIC endows IBM mainframe equipment—including the 3174 terminal cluster controller, several front-end processors, the AS/400 processor, and the 9370 mainframe—with the ability to connect to an IBM Token-Ring network directly. Since PCs can also connect directly to a Token-Ring network, PCs and mainframes can interact as peers on the same network as long as each machine runs the appropriate software. This eliminates the need for gateways, dedicated coaxial-cable connections, and slow-speed communications channels.

The TIC generates fast response times. Our tests show that you can initiate a file transfer from the mainframe to your PC and receive a 50K file through the network in one second. The throughput rates we measured for Token-Ring connection were, in some cases, 80 times as fast as when the same hardware was connected through an SNA SDLC LAN gateway. Graphics screens sent by the mainframe seem to snap into place as soon as you hit the Enter key.

You're right if you suspect there's a catch to this too-good-to-be-true situation. In fact, there are several.

First, you must use Token-Ring network cards and cables. While Token-Ring installations are robust and able to survive cable problems that disrupt other types of networks, the installation is expensive. Not only does the cable itself cost about 40 percent more per foot than thin Ethernet cable, but you also need many times the amount of cable for the same number of nodes. And for every eight nodes you install on a Token-Ring network, you need a Token-Ring wiring hub. Such hubs stack together in a relay rack; you need a room just for the rack and the centralized wiring ducts.

In addition, TIC equipment is not available for older versions of IBM's terminal cluster controllers or front-end processors. If you want to use the TIC architecture, you might have to upgrade to new mainframe communications equipment.

Using the direct Token-Ring connection requires close coordination between the people managing PCs and the people living with the mainframes. The system programmers tending the mainframe must explicitly define each SNA physical unit (that is, each connected PC) in the mainframe software. This means you have to coordinate the addition and deletion of PCs with the mainframe system programmers and wait until they make the changes to their software before the PCs can be serviced.

Finally, if you use a network gateway to connect PCs and mainframes, only one physical unit is defined; that unit distributes many logical units or sessions to the connected PCs. You can add networked PCs in back of a gateway at any time, and they can immediately use 3270 SNA sessions. If you have been in this business for more than a few years, you know that configuration freedom was one of the driving factors behind the popularity of PCs. While the TIC option may appear simple, it can make management more complex.

PC-to-mainframe products for Token-Ring connections are solely software-based. Since Token-Ring adapter cards supply the electrical connections to the mainframe, the PC-to-TIC products consist of 3270 terminal-emulation programs, various utilities, application programming interfaces, and driver software that carries data to and from the Token-Ring adapter cards. The typical retail price for these packages is between $200 and $300 per station.

Linking to IBM's AS/400 Family

IBM's AS/400 family of minicomputers offers flexibility and a large time-tested library of software for many businesses. In its standard configuration, the AS/400 connects to separate IBM 5250-series terminals over a specialized dual coaxial cable called "twin-ax." People sitting at these terminals run programs in the shared processor and memory of the AS/400. Eventually, almost all organizations using AS/400s want to link PCs to the minicomputer. If you have only a few PCs, you can install a special adapter in each PC for the AS/400 twin-ax cables, load 5250 terminal emulation, and switch between running local applications and running software on the AS/400. AS/400 port connections are expensive, though; since many PCs in offices are networked, it makes sense to use the network connection to get to the AS/400.

There are several good ways to link a LAN running Novell's NetWare, for example, to an AS/400, and there are also a lot of things to consider. Your options include a direct network attachment over either Token-Ring or Ethernet, direct attachment of each PC to the AS/400, or attachment through either of two types of gateways. Then you can choose to use IBM's software with any of the attachment schemes or you can buy third-party software. In all, it's a situation with a lot of options.

First, you can do things the "IBM way." IBM would like you to buy a Token-Ring adapter for your AS/400 and then run 5250 terminal-emulation software on each PC that works over Token-Ring.

If you want to take the Token-Ring attachment route, your present Ethernet LAN doesn't present a problem; you can establish a router in a NetWare server to combine the Ethernet links to the PCs with a Token-Ring link to the

AS/400. The primary advantage of the AS/400 Token-Ring connection scheme is that it doesn't require the addition of expensive twin-ax ports on the AS/400.

You can, of course, equip each networked PC with a twin-ax adapter, load 5250 terminal-emulation software, and make a direct connection to the AS/400 from each PC. Since you can attach up to seven terminals or PCs acting as terminals to each AS/400 twin-ax port, you can daisy-chain the wiring to keep costs down. However, choosing this alternative means that you'll have two cables—a LAN cable and an AS/400 twin-ax cable—going to each PC, and that you'll need to have enough AS/400 twin-ax ports to service all the PCs that could ever be on at the same time.

A LAN gateway holds down costs and lets you share the twin-ax port connections. You set up a single PC on the LAN as a gateway to the AS/400. This gateway machine can be an older, recycled PC with an 80286 processor; you don't have to buy a new computer for this role. A single twin-ax adapter in the gateway PC is the only connection to one port on the AS/400, so the gateway can access seven AS/400 connections that it distributes to networked PCs on a first-come, first-served basis. You can put as many as three twin-ax adapters in the gateway, so it can give access to twenty-one PCs simultaneously across the LAN.

Many companies make AS/400 gateway products. The leading vendors of twin-ax gateways and twin-ax adapters for individual PCs include Andrew Corp., AST Research, Emerald Systems, IDEAssociates, and Micro-Integration Corp.

Frankly, the choice between these attachment schemes is a matter of economics. How many free twin-ax ports have you already bought and paid for on the AS/400? If you have a lot of ports standing idle, the direct attachment or gateway approaches become more appealing. Do you have a spare PC you can use as a gateway? If so, that reduces costs. Is it more economical to add a Token-Ring adapter to the AS/400 than it is to buy more twin-ax ports and an individual twin-ax board for each PC? Is it more economical to add a Token-Ring adapter to the AS/400 and establish a Token-Ring link to a router than it is to establish a gateway between the Ethernet LAN and twin-ax ports? You only have to do some simple addition to come up with the numbers for each attachment alternative.

IBM's PC Support software consists of a package for the AS/400 and a package for the PC. The avowed purpose of the system is to provide IBM's Advanced Program to Program Communications (APPC) services between programs running on the PC and programs running on the AS/400. Few organizations have real APPC applications, however, so the most common function of PC Support is to move files between PCs and the AS/400. Typically, AS/400 system managers only run the AS/400 side of PC Support when they need to do a specific job.

IBM has made a smart move by marketing Wall Data's Rumba as a Windows front end to PC Support. The Rumba front end lets you use the multitasking capabilities of Windows, cut and paste between Windows applications, and use a context-sensitive help system. There are alternatives to PC Support, but since most AS/400 sites already have it, you'll probably learn to live with it.

More than IBM

So far I've described in detail how you can connect networks of PCs to IBM mainframe systems, particularly PCs running under IBM's Systems Network Architecture and connected to AS/400 minicomputers. But while IBM's hardware is widely popular, network designers often need to integrate computers from many manufacturers into a practical information management and transfer system. To do that, they need more than IBM's proprietary SNA.

■ TCP/IP for Multiplatform Networking

One of the most difficult problems system integrators and managers face is connecting different types of computers in a network. As the number of PCs in an organization grows, so does the need to link those PCs to any of several minicomputer and mainframe systems.

In an ideal world, every computer would exchange information freely with every other computer, regardless of the name on the front panel or the processor and operating system inside. In the real world, even computers from the same manufacturer are often unable to exchange data.

There is, however, one Rosetta stone of the computer world that can link a wide variety of mainframe, minicomputer, and PC systems. That common denominator is called TCP/IP, and anyone who deals with PCs every day will appreciate its power. Just imagine a $250 to $500 software package that provides easy file transfers and simple electronic-mail services between PCs and many kinds of dissimilar computer systems.

TCP/IP stands for Transmission Control Protocol/Internet Protocol. Protocols are procedures for communications, described on paper and agreed to by the people who design products. The TCP/IP standards are brought to life in software sold by many companies.

The DoD Drives Common Protocols

The TCP/IP protocols were developed by the U.S. Department of Defense when DoD scientists were faced with the problem of linking thousands of dissimilar computers. The Defense Advanced Research Projects Agency (DARPA) is a small organization occupying leased office space in the Virginia suburbs a couple of miles from the Pentagon, but its impact on technology in general and on data communications in particular has been huge.

In the mid-1970s, DARPA saw the need to interlink dissimilar computers across the nation to support research efforts. Back then, computers usually used point-to-point leased lines and vendor-specific protocols to communicate. DARPA contracted with several organizations to develop a standard set of nonproprietary protocols that would provide easy communications between computers connected in a multinode network. This open protocol predates the current work of the International Standards Organization by a decade.

The TCP/IP protocols evolved from work done at MIT with the participation of several companies, and from healthy rounds of industry comments. In 1980, DARPA installed the first TCP/IP modules on computers in its networks. It mandated that all computers attached to the growing nationwide ARPANET network had to use TCP/IP by January 1983. But DARPA's planners didn't expect TCP/IP to flourish just because they said it should.

DARPA and other organizations, such as the Defense Communications Agency, contracted with several companies to deliver TCP/IP modules for the computers and operating systems commonly used by the government. They paid companies like Honeywell, IBM, and Sperry (now Unisys) to develop TCP/IP software for specific computer-and-operating-system combinations used in the government. This seed money was well spent because it motivated these and many other companies to use their own funds to get onto the TCP/IP bandwagon.

DARPA also contracted with Bolt Beranek and Newman to develop software for Unix machines. This contract allowed universities to acquire TCP/IP inexpensively and to work with the protocols in many environments. Perhaps most importantly, the Defense Communications Agency began a program of testing and certifying software for compliance with the DoD's TCP/IP standard.

The problem with many products that claim to follow a standard (like the EIA-standard RS-232C ports on some printers, for example) is that they are incomplete. The designer of the product leaves out "unneeded" features to save money or adds a little twist to keep the product unique. The Defense Communications Agency checked and certified TCP/IP products to make sure they met the standard and really were interoperable. This testing program ended in 1987, but the result of the effort was hundreds of products for many dozens of computers and operating systems that are certified to meet a specific standard.

Many corporations and almost all federal government organizations and universities in the U.S. have taken advantage of the availability and standardization of TCP/IP software. The managers of the TCP/IP program also recognize the International Standards Organization's efforts to develop an extensive set of non-vendor-specific protocols, and they openly support that program. Plans have been made for TCP/IP to evolve into something called Transport Class 4 or TP4 under the ISO's program, but few people who manage active networks will jump quickly from a tested and proven network protocol to one that is still evolving. TCP/IP has a long and bright future, but best of all, it works well today.

TCP/IP Online

In a typical TCP/IP network, a cabling and signaling scheme like Ethernet provides the basic links between dissimilar machines. Ethernet adapters are available for practically every type of computer data bus. The cable delivers data wrapped in an Ethernet packet to each machine. Computers with different operating systems and architectures that strip away the Ethernet packet do not know what to do with data they receive from foreign machines unless they find further instructions. TCP/IP provides those instructions; the packets receive standardized handling when they arrive, regardless of the operating environment on the receiving side.

The TCP/IP module used by each machine must be customized for the computer and its operating system but standardized for the network. TCP/IP modules are available for hundreds of mainframe and minicomputer systems and for many PC networks.

National and international networks of dissimilar computers are assembled in basically the same way as Ethernet networks, except that long-distance transmission schemes (such as X.25 packet switching) carry the data instead of Ethernet carrying it. X.25 gateways on a LAN can provide TCP/IP-equipped PCs with both local and long-distance connection capabilities.

Hooking Up

PCs using TCP/IP to communicate with non-PCs usually talk over a local area network. Intelligent Ethernet adapter cards play an important role in the success of TCP/IP on the PC.

But TCP/IP isn't limited to Ethernet. IBM has an active program to provide TCP/IP connections over its Token-Ring adapters. The success of Token-Ring, despite its high cost and cabling hassles, makes the marriage of TCP/IP and Token-Ring increasingly important. The ability to run TCP/IP over Token-Ring and provide seamless connections to IBM hardware is an important IBM marketing lure.

There are two ways networked PCs can use TCP/IP. The first involves loading a TCP/IP software module into every machine on the network. The second configuration uses one machine as a gateway to the TCP/IP network or high-powered computer.

If your network has a great deal of interaction between different types of machines, it makes sense to give every PC its own TCP/IP module. The penalties you pay for putting the software on every machine are greater RAM use and increased network overhead.

As the power of the average computer on an office desktop increases, it becomes increasingly practical to use more than one network communications protocol stack in the PC. It is often useful to load a TCP/IP protocol stack in the PC along with some other network protocol stack like the IPX used with Novell's NetWare.

Setting up a TCP/IP gateway is the best solution for a homogeneous network of PCs that sometimes need access to a specific TCP/IP network or machine. The PCs on this kind of network do most of their work together using whatever PC-to-PC communications protocol the network provides. PC applications needing TCP/IP services send data through the gateway. The gateway translates between the PCs' network-protocol environment and the TCP/IP environment. The TCP/IP software typically runs on a machine dedicated to the gateway task.

The throughput of the TCP/IP gateway is more limited by the speed of the connection to the TCP/IP network than by its own translation activities. The connection between the gateway and the TCP/IP system can be through Ethernet coaxial cable, public data networks like Tymnet or Telenet, private networks like the DoD's ARPANET, or by other means. If a TCP/IP gateway connects two Ethernet networks, it is called an *Internet router*. Since these networks are so common in TCP/IP installations, the phrase *TCP/IP router* is frequently encountered.

TCP/IP Network Particulars

The heart of the IP portion of TCP/IP is a concept called the *Internet address*. This is a 32-bit number assigned to every node on the network. There are various types of addresses designed for different-sized networks, but you can write every address in base 10 using this form: 128.22.5.13. These numbers identify the major network and subnetworks a node is on. The address identifies a particular node and provides a path that gateways can use to route information from one machine to another.

Although data-delivery systems like Ethernet or X.25 bring their packets to any machine electrically attached to the cable, the IP modules must know each others' Internet addresses to communicate. A machine acting as a gateway between different TCP/IP networks will have a different Internet address on each network. Internal look-up tables and software based on another standard called the Address Resolution Protocol are used to route the data between networks through a gateway.

Another piece of software works with the IP-layer programs to move information to the right application on the receiving system. This software follows a standard called the User Data Protocol (UDP). It is helpful to think of the UDP software as creating a data address in the TCP/IP message that details exactly what application the data block is supposed to contact when it reaches the address described by the IP software. The UDP software provides the final routing for the data within the receiving system.

The TCP or Transmission Control Protocol portion of TCP/IP comes into operation once the packet is delivered to the correct Internet address and application port. Software packages that follow the TCP standard run on each machine, establish a connection to each other, and manage the communications exchanges. A data-delivery system like Ethernet makes no promises about successfully delivering a packet. Neither IP nor UDP knows anything about recovering packets that aren't successfully delivered, but TCP structures and buffers the data flow, looks for responses, and takes action to replace missing data blocks. This concept of data management is called "reliable stream" service.

Conceptually, software that supports the TCP protocol stands alone. It can work with data received through a serial port, over a packet-switched network, or from a network system like Ethernet. In concept, it doesn't need or even know about IP or UDP, but in practice TCP is an integral part of the TCP/IP equation and is most frequently used with IP and UDP.

Above TCP/IP

TCP/IP delivers data in a standard format and makes that data available for use in higher-level programs. The DoD standardized the protocol specifications for several other programs that take data from TCP/IP and do useful things with it. These protocols include the File Transfer Protocol (FTP), the Simple Mail Transfer Protocol (SMTP), and a terminal-emulation and communications program called TELNET. The specifications for these protocols are carefully described in DoD standards publications MIL-STD-1780, -1781, and -1782. In addition, efforts are underway to standardize the NetBIOS interface that was originally developed by IBM and Sytek. Figure 12.2 shows the relationship between the protocols in the TCP/IP suite.

Programs supporting the FTP protocol give people the ability to log onto dissimilar machines across a network, use a standard command to list available directories and files, and exchange files with the remote machine. FTP can perform some simple data-translation tasks, like converting data between the standard ASCII alphabet and IBM's EBCDIC. FTP is controlled either through responses to command-line prompts or by commands passed from an application program.

Figure 12.2

This diagram is patterned after the typical ISO seven-layer protocol stack used to identify network structure. It shows the upward path through software and hardware that makes TCP/IP a viable means of data transfer among dissimilar machines linked in a network.

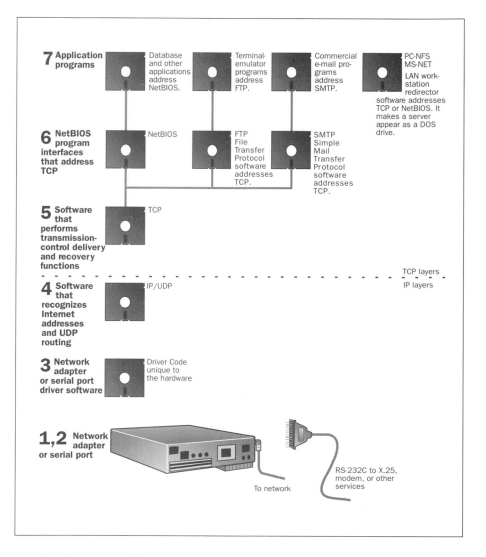

The Simple Mail Transfer Protocol lives up to its name. Programs supporting this protocol do little more than follow a strictly defined script used to enter and retrieve e-mail messages. Several companies market SMTP programs for different kinds of computers. The real advantage of this protocol is that the commands that save and retrieve e-mail messages are the same regardless of what machine acts as the host.

The TELNET protocol describes the operation of a communications program that knows how to call for services from the TCP and IP software. The main purpose of software that implements the TELNET protocol is usually to convert the computer it runs on into a minicomputer terminal. Most of the companies include at least a DEC VT-100 terminal emulator in their TEL-NET packages. Some companies let you run special versions of popular terminal-emulation programs like Walker Richer and Quinn's Reflection on top of their TELNET software. This combination provides sophisticated emulation of Hewlett-Packard and other terminals.

Almost all of the products that support these higher-level protocols are designed to communicate with a large host computer. You can't get on a network and communicate between two PCs acting as peers using FTP, SMTP, or TELNET; however, some companies (such as ftp Software) include host programs that let a single PC become a host and conduct multiple simultaneous sessions with other PCs running FTP, SMTP, or TELNET software.

File-Server Software

There are no federal standards for higher-level file-server software like NetWare or Microsoft's Windows NT, but several of the companies marketing TCP/IP software have drivers that can be compiled into the NetWare operating system.

Sun Microsystems markets file-server software called NFS for computers running the Unix operating system. The NFS software package allows machines wearing many different nameplates to interact as file servers and clients through TCP/IP.

Our experiences at PC Magazine Labs show that PCs fit into TCP/IP networks very gracefully. Many companies will sell you TCP/IP software for the PC and for specific PC network environments. TCP/IP software provides a fast and efficient way to exchange data with computers of different architectures running different operating systems.

- *Fat Cables*

- *Extending and Segmenting the Network*

- *The Linking Media*

- *ISDN*

- *X.25: Versatile, Efficient, International, and Necessary*

- *ATM*

- *Linking LANs: A New Frontier*

Linking LANs

TECHNICAL TALE
Stephen, my 11-year old, likes what he calls "classical science fiction." When I told him we were linking our networks, he asked when the system would become "self-aware." At the time, I'd smiled tolerently. Now, I wondered.

My screen kept flashing, "You do not have rights on this network." I was feeling oppressed. "Rights?" I typed.

The screen blanked and then I read, "The network has determined that you don't have the right to see the information stored here."

I hastily logged off and looked around. Finally, I called the network manager over and said, "Can this thing think?"

"It knows how to drive me crazy!" she replied.

After I showed her my example of sentient awareness, she said, "You're in the help screens! That message probably came from the router's help system. People still make the decisions here." A few keystrokes and I had regained my rights on the network.

I was reassured until a week later when I was working late at my desk. After I tried to open a new file, the screen said, "It's after your normal work time, and you no longer have rights on this network." Maybe the message came from server or router security, but I distinctly heard a hollow laugh from somewhere as I was dumped off the network.

In THE FIRST CHAPTER I INTRODUCED THE IDEA THAT INFORMATION IS THE RAW material, inventory, and processed product of many modern organizations. Computer networks are the production line, the warehouse, and even the retail point of sale for the information products generated by many businesses. These networks act as local, regional, and even international distribution systems for modern commerce. They form a commercial infrastructure for businesses, countries, and multinational economies.

If local area networks are like the in-house production lines of manufacturing plants, then computer networks using leased telephone lines, metropolitan-area networks (MANs), and wide-area networks (WANs) are the equivalent of the trucking, rail, barge, and air freight systems needed to support smokestack industries. Like those transportation systems, MANs, WANs, and private networks have different capacities, economies, and even regulatory problems.

Some manufacturing companies own their own trucks and boxcars, while others contract for all transportation services. Similarly, some organizations own their MAN and WAN facilities, while others lease these specialized services from commercial suppliers. The suppliers include long-haul carriers like AT&T and MCI, specialized companies such as Tymnet and Telenet, and others such as the local telephone exchange and cable television companies.

When managers of smokestack industries leave the control of transportation systems totally to specialists, they risk inefficiency and unpleasant surprises. Because computer communications systems are so important to the operation of many modern companies, these systems too call for the attention of high-level management. Unfortunately, well-designed networks aren't highly visible, and generally networks are cloaked in technical jargon, but they are both critically important and expensive to run. Managers of organizations that rely on computer networks need a generalized understanding of these networks to supervise information-system professionals effectively.

This chapter is aimed at the general manager who wants a tutorial and reference for wide-area networks, and at the computer-support professional who needs to link LANs across a campus, across town, or across an ocean. In it, I'll describe the devices used to extend local area networks and the systems used to link LANs over long distances. Along the way, I'll revisit some concepts from earlier chapters such as connections between dissimilar electronic-mail systems, network management, and TCP/IP. I'll also introduce products called bridges, routers, and brouters—products that are easier to use than to explain!

■ Fat Cables

Local area networks have a wide bandwidth; they can pass millions of bits of data per second. The concept is easy to understand if you picture a LAN as a fat cable that can move a lot of data quickly. Because the signals needed to represent the 0s and 1s on a fast LAN are closely spaced, the equipment cannot tolerate signal degradation or noise in the data stream.

Unfortunately, copper cables accumulate electrical noise as they travel over longer distances, and the pulses of electricity or light representing the data bits lose their sharpness and strength as they travel through copper or fiber-optic cables. Induced noise and signal degradation are the two primary factors that limit the fat LAN cable's coverage to several kilometers under the best conditions.

Typically, longer communications links must move data more slowly because of induced noise and degraded signals. Multiplexers, repeaters, and other special equipment allow the transmission of data at high speed over long distances, but this kind of equipment is expensive, so the combination of signaling speed and distance work together to increase costs. You can buy and install your own cable to run data at 10 megabits per second for less than $1 per foot at distances of several thousand feet. But you'll have to pay about $15,000 per year to lease a 1.5-megabit-per-second link from New York to San Francisco, and the equipment to interface your computers to the leased line may cost you several thousand dollars more up front.

Still, many organizations need to move a lot of data over distances greater than a few thousand feet, so managers need to learn the techniques of extending and linking LANs. The techniques you use to link LAN segments depend on the distance and speed you need, the network communications protocols you use, and your business philosophy regarding leasing versus owning facilities.

■ Extending and Segmenting the Network

The first category of products I'll describe—repeaters, bridges, and routers—enables you to extend and segment your network's fat, or high-speed, cable. You can easily understand why you might want to extend the LAN cable; you might need to span 40 stories in an office building or two miles of a college campus. Devices called *repeaters* enable you to extend your network cable to several thousand feet by retiming and regenerating packets or frames so they can continue over such distances.

The reasons for segmenting a LAN may be less clear. Workers in all organizations interact in groups based on common interests. Most communications follow specific paths and take place within these workgroups; however, people also need ways to communicate between workgroups. The simplest scheme is to put all the people in all the workgroups on the same cable and let them communicate and interact as business requires. But this arrangement quickly consumes the cable's resources. It doesn't make sense to clog the LAN cable serving the accounting department with all the traffic generated in the engineering department simply because engineers sometimes need to share budget programs with accountants. Organizations with busy networks need a device that can link workgroup LANs while exercising discretion over which traffic passes between the various workgroups.

This kind of discretionary device is known as a *bridge*. Unlike a repeater, which passes all data between cable segments, a bridge links cable systems while passing only certain specified traffic between them. A *router* is a more complex linking device that has a greater ability to examine and direct the traffic it carries Figure 13.1 shows the basic concept behind each of these three LAN-linking devices.

Each of these devices functions at a different level of the ISO's OSI model. The repeater looks only at packets or frames generated by adapters operating at the physical level. Bridges use the specific station addresses generated by firmware in the data-link layer. Routers use information provided by software following specific network-layer protocols. As Table 13.1 shows, a fourth type of device (the LAN gateway discussed in Chapter 14) operates at higher levels of the OSI model to translate data formats and open sessions between application programs.

Table 13.1

Linking Devices in the
Network Layers

Layer	Functions	Linking Device
7 Application	Applications move files, emulate terminals, and generate other traffic.	Gateway
6 Presentation	Programs format data and convert characters.	Gateway
5 Session	Programs negotiate and establish connections between modes.	Gateway
4 Transport	Programs ensure end-to-end delivery.	None
3 Network	Programs route packets across multiple inter-LAN links.	Router
2 Data Link	Firmware transfers packests or frames.	Bridge
1 Physical	Firmware sequences packets or frames for transmission.	Repeater

Figure 13.1

In simple terms, a repeater moves all traffic in both directions between LAN segments. A bridge moves specified traffic between segments. A router makes decisions about the path traffic will take between segments.

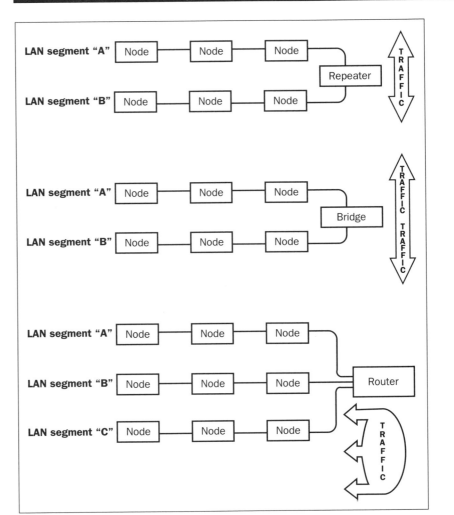

While the names, concepts, and uses of bridges and routers are relatively simple, selecting one of these products involves enough options to keep a committee busy for a long time. I'm going to give you the classic descriptions of these devices and a number of explanations and examples. But companies keep bringing out products that go beyond the classic descriptions. The concepts are clear, but their practical application can make the classic definitions fuzzy in real installations.

Repeaters

The differences among the products you can use to extend your local area network cable are sometimes subtle, but they are all based on the concept of the multiple layers of communications protocols. Typically people refer to the ISO's OSI model, but Digital Equipment Corp. and IBM have communications models and network equipment that don't exactly fit the ISO model.

A repeater, like the one shown in Figure 13.2, is typically a humble little box, about the size of a small PC, that connects between two segments of network cable, retimes and regenerates the digital signals on the cable, and sends them on their way again. These functions are typical of those described in the physical layer of the ISO model, so it's common to say that a repeater is a physical-layer device.

Figure 13.2

The PICnic LANrepeater links separate LAN segments to allow extension of the Ethernet LAN cable beyond the single 500-foot span described in the IEEE 802.3 specifications.

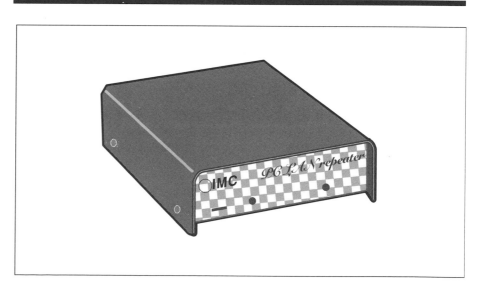

The actions of a repeater allow you to increase the geographical coverage of your LAN. For example, the Ethernet standard specifies that a signal may travel over a maximum cable length of 500 meters for a single segment, but with repeaters interconnecting five segments, a signal on an Ethernet network could reach a maximum distance of 2,500 meters of cable. The slightly different IEEE 802.3 standard allows for up to four repeaters connecting five cable segments, to a maximum of 3,000 meters (1.8 miles), with a total cumulative delay of 950 nanoseconds introduced by the transmission media.

Certain repeaters, such as the Cabletron LR-2000 shown in Figure 13.3, can interconnect cable segments using different physical media such as thin Ethernet coaxial cables and fiber-optic cables. Similarly, repeaters for Token-Ring networks can translate between electrical signals on shielded or unshielded twisted-pair wiring and light pulses on fiber-optic cabling. In modern installations you'll often find repeater modules housed in the central wiring hubs of 10BaseT and fiber-optic cable systems. But repeaters don't provide a feature called *traffic isolation*. They dutifully send every bit of data appearing on either cable segment through to the other side, even if the data consists of malformed packets from a malfunctioning Ethernet adapter or packets not destined for use off the local LAN segment.

Figure 13.3

The Cabletron LR-2000 is one of a family of repeaters that can move packets between different media such as unshielded twisted-pair wire, coaxial cable, or fiber-optic cable.

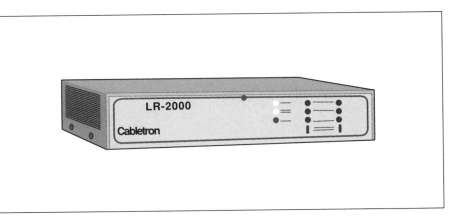

Modern repeaters have features such as light-emitting diodes to display network operation, and they are available in a variety of physical configurations including stand-alone or rack-mount. Costs range from just under $1,000 for simple Ethernet equipment to well over $2,000 for Token-Ring devices.

Bridges

While repeaters always link elements of a local area network, bridges can link local cable segments, but can also link the fat cable of a LAN to networks of thinner media such as leased telephone lines. The two main purposes of a bridge are to extend the network and to segment traffic. Like repeaters, bridges can send packets and frames between various types of media. But unlike repeaters, bridges forward traffic from one cable system only if it is addressed to devices on the other cable system; in this way, they limit the nonessential traffic on both systems. A modern bridge reads the destination address of the network packet and determines whether the address is on the same segment of network cable as the originating station. If the destination station is on the other side of the bridge, the bridge sequences the packet into the traffic on that cable segment.

The functions of bridges are those associated with the media-access control (MAC) sublayer of the data-link layer (layer 2) in the ISO model. For example, bridges can read the station address of an Ethernet packet or of a Token-Ring frame to determine the destination of the message, but they cannot look deeper inside the packet or frame to read NetBIOS or TCP/IP addresses. Thus, they're often called MAC-layer bridges.

As Figure 13.4 illustrates, bridges are categorized as *local* or *remote*. Local bridges link fat cable segments on a local network. Remote bridges link fat local cables to thin long-distance cables to connect physically separated networks. The important point is that you need only one local bridge to link two physically close cable segments, but you need two remote bridges to link two cable segments over a long interconnecting span of media.

Figure 13.4

A local bridge directly connects two LAN segments. Remote bridges operate in pairs, connecting the LAN cable segments using an intermediary interLAN link such as a leased telephone line.

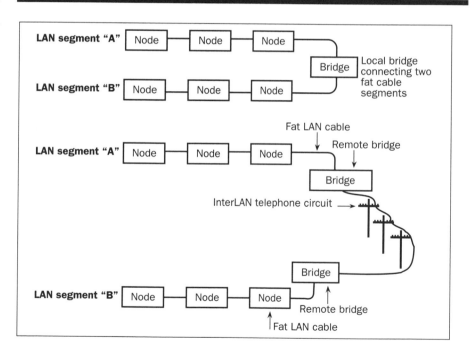

How Bridges Learn

As with many aspects of internetworking, it's reasonably simple to generalize: Bridges only relay messages from one cable destined for a station on the other cable. But if you ask, "How does it know?", you uncover a pretty complex subject.

The simplest bridges use a routing table, created by the network manager and contained in software, to decide whether to pass or hold data messages.

But people move their computers and change their offices and jobs frequently. Making someone update the routing table in the network bridges every time a computer is moved down the hall creates too much administrative overhead, so bridges typically have software with a learning algorithm.

Bridges, like the CentreCOM products from Allied Telesis shown in Figure 13.5, learn about the stations on the network by sending out a broadcast message that creates a reply from all stations. The bridge listens to all traffic on the attached cable segments and checks the source addresses of all packets and the locations of the sending stations. The routing software builds a table of the stations and cable segments and then decides when to forward messages and when to drop them.

Figure 13.5

The Allied Telesis family of CentreCOM bridges includes various network-management options.

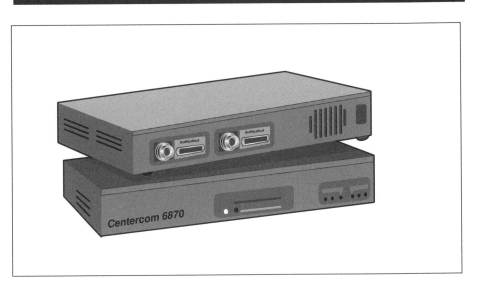

This function is relatively simple when a bridge links only two segments of a network, but it becomes much more complex as networks grow. For example, consider the case of a company with networks on the first, third, and fifth floors of a building. These networks could be connected in one of two ways: in a *cascade* or through a *backbone*. If the segments are cascaded, the first-floor LAN is bridged to the third-floor LAN, and the third-floor LAN is bridged to the fifth-floor LAN. The cascaded bridge topology loads the intermediate LAN segment with traffic destined for the third LAN segment, but it requires only two bridges.

The backbone bridge topology links bridges dedicated to the various LAN segments through a separate backbone cable. The backbone cable is often a fiber-optic link, which allows for relatively great distances. Figure 13.6 illustrates the cascade and bridge topologies. A less common *star* topology, not shown in the diagram, uses a single multiport bridge to link multiple cables and is typically used with lighter traffic loads.

Figure 13.6

The cascade bridge topology requires fewer routers and less connecting equipment than the backbone bridge topology. But the cascade topology must move all data from LAN segment A through segment B to get to segment C. The backbone topology reduces the overall traffic load because it can discriminate between types of traffic going to various segments.

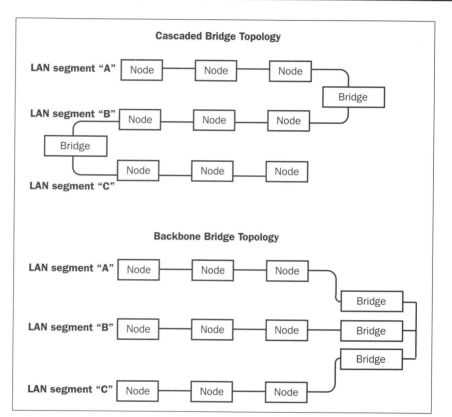

It's possible, either through error, through a desire for redundancy, or through independent connections to some common point like a mainframe computer, for the first- and fifth-floor LAN segments to become connected by a redundant path. In theory, packets could then be recirculated by the bridges and an overload condition called a *broadcast storm* could result. Engineers have developed several intelligent algorithms to detect multiple paths and shut them down.

Logical Algorithms for Bridges

Software operating in each bridge determines the most efficient path between network segments and adopts it as the primary route. If the primary route fails, the bridges use the next-best alternative path. This redundancy is particularly valuable when network segments are connected by long-distance circuits that are subject to interruption.

The software in all the bridges on the LAN must follow one of several logical algorithms to decide which path to use. The IEEE 802.1 Network Management Committee has adopted a standard for a technique called the Spanning Tree Algorithm that was originally developed by Digital Equipment Corp. and Vitalink Communications Corp. Products supporting this algorithm are used primarily by local bridges; the technique isn't economical for use over leased telephone circuits connecting remote bridges. The logic in the Spanning Tree Algorithm lets you link two LAN spans with two bridges for reliability, while avoiding the problems of multiple packets being broadcast by both bridges.

Remote bridges, like the Cabletron units shown in Figure 13.7, use different techniques called source routing and protocol-transparent routing. *Source routing* is a technique used mostly on Token-Ring networks and backed primarily by IBM. In the source-routing system, the source node sends test frames over the network until they arrive at the destination station. Each network bridge along the way adds its own address. The destination station sends the test frames it receives back to the source station. Finally, the source station uses that information to determine the fastest path and sends the entire message over that path.

Figure 13.7

Cabletron Systems'
family of remote bridges
can use various types of
interLAN media to
establish links between
LAN segments on
different floors of a
building, in different
parts of the country, and
on different continents.

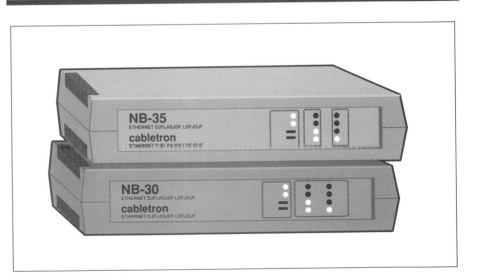

The source-routing technique ensures that messages take the fastest path and balances traffic on long-distance links, but it generates network traffic and requires a lot of processing at the nodes.

The *protocol-transparent routing* technique puts the workload on the bridges. Each bridge maintains a map of the entire network and forwards each packet to the correct network segment. If the bridge hasn't yet learned the location of the destination station, it forwards the packet to all the LAN segments until the destination replies. This is known as *forward-if-not-local* logic. Routers use the opposite, *forward-only-if-known-remote* logic.

The IEEE 802.1 Network Management Committee and the 802.5 Token-Ring Committee have developed ways to use both source routing and protocol-transparent routing on the same network.

No Translation Services

Like repeaters, bridges can only link similar networks, but bridges and repeaters concentrate on different similarities. A bridge doesn't deal with the physical-layer hardware and drivers handled by repeaters. You can use a repeater to link one Ethernet network to another Ethernet network, despite the type of cabling they use, because the Ethernet packets and the media-access control protocols are the same. But bridges can link LAN segments using completely different LAN adapters and media-access protocols as long as the networks use the same communications protocol; for instance, NetBIOS to NetBIOS, IPX to IPX, or DECnet to DECnet.

Bridge Requirements

Bridges often run inside PCs. Companies like Eicon Technology Corp. sell hardware and software kits that link LAN segments through several kinds of thick and thin LAN connections. The price of these kits depends on what kinds of media you're linking. The software and hardware needed to create an Ethernet-to-Ethernet bridge cost less than $1,000.

Unlike other kinds of network communications servers I've described in this book, bridges have a lot of work to do and need all the computing power a fast PC can supply. If you set up a bridge in a PC, make sure it has at least an 80386 processor running at 16 MHz, and don't plan on using the computer for any other tasks.

Many companies, including Retix and 3Com Corp., offer bridges that have their own processors and don't need a PC. These devices, often about the size of a small pizza box, vary widely in price. Depending on the type of connections they make, these bridges can cost anywhere from just over $1,000 to about $10,000.

Bridges can be important elements in network-management systems. Because bridges read the destination and source of every packet, they can collect statistics and report on and control traffic conditions exceeding specific criteria. Many bridges can generate reports in the format of the CMIP or SNMP network-management systems described in Chapter 9.

Routers

Just as bridges improve on the functionality of repeaters, so routers improve on bridges. Routers read the more complex network addressing information in the packet or token and may add more information to get the packet through the network. For example, a router might wrap an Ethernet packet in an "envelope" of data containing routing and transmission information for transmission through an X.25 packet-switched network. When the envelope of data comes out the other end of the X.25 network, the receiving router strips off the X.25 data, readdresses the Ethernet packet back, and sequences it on the attached LAN segment.

Routers make very smart interconnections between the elements of complex networks. Routers can choose among redundant paths between LAN segments, and can link LAN segments using completely different data-packaging and media-access schemes. Primarily because of their complexity, however, routers move data more slowly than bridges.

Routers work at the network layer (layer 3) of the ISO model. Unlike bridges, routers don't know the exact location of each node. Instead, a router knows only about subnetwork addresses. It reads the information contained in each packet or frame, uses complex network addressing procedures to determine the appropriate destination, and then repackages and retransmits the data. The router doesn't care what kinds of hardware the LAN segments use, but they must run software conforming to the same network-layer protocol. Some of the products sold by vendors include routers for DECnet, IP, IPX, OSI, and XNS. Telebit Corp.'s NetBlazer, shown in Figure 13.8, combines an IP router with other functions.

Some companies, including Cisco Systems and Wellfleet Communications, sell multiprotocol routers that allow you to combine protocols like IP and DECnet in the same network. The Wollongong Group sells an effective router that combines the popular NetWare IPX protocol and the IP portion of the TCP/IP protocol. However, there are no standards for these implementations, and you'd better be ready to buy all your multiprotocol routers from one company.

Routers aren't transparent like bridges. They take a lot of setup and management. Typically, you won't consider dealing with the complexities of routers until you have LAN segments of 20 or more nodes, or segments using complex protocol suites like TCP/IP.

The addressing scheme used by routers allows administrators to break the network into subnetworks. This architecture can accommodate many different topologies including a highly reliable ring of leased circuits, like the one shown in Figure 13.9. Routers receive only specifically addressed packets or frames from originating stations or from other routers. They don't read every packet or frame on every attached LAN segment as a bridge

Figure 13.8

Telebit's NetBlazer is an integrated communications server designed to act as an IP router; it can use both leased and dial-up telephone-line connections for simultaneous interLAN communications. This product can be configured with up to three Ethernet connections, 26 modem connections, and one 56-kilobit-per-second leased line.

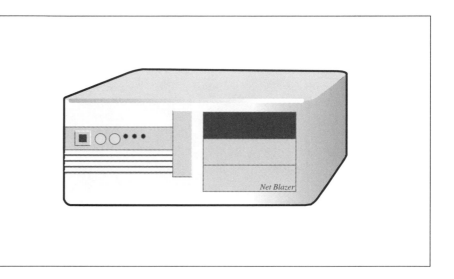

does. Because they don't pass or even handle every packet or frame, routers act as a safety barrier between network segments. Bad data packets or broadcast storms simply don't make it through the router.

When it relays a packet between LAN segments, a router decides what path the data packet will follow by determining the number of hops between internetwork segments. Usually the router software chooses the route that requires the fewest hops. A router that always picks the shortest route typically uses a routing table a programmer has created for a specific network. This kind of device, known as a *static router*, works fine in many networking systems.

Some administrators want to give the router more options. A category of devices called *dynamic routers* can examine factors such as the cost of sending traffic over specific links and the amount of traffic on specific links and decide to send packets or frames over an alternate route. Of course, the more thinking a router does before it forwards a packet or frame, the longer it takes to get the data to its destination. The throughput you get from a local router depends on the complexity of its routing tables and the CPU power available to run its software. The throughput of remote routers is typically limited by the speed of the media linking them together.

Data Compression and Routers

As I explain later in this chapter, you have to pay thousands of dollars a month to lease a circuit to link LAN segments. The cost is driven by the speed of the data you want to send across the link. Therefore, it makes sense

Figure 13.9

Routers in a large
interLAN network can use
the interconnecting
circuits as alternative
routes for traffic. If the
circuit between LAN
segment A and segment
B breaks down, the
routers can send traffic
around the long way to
retain connectivity.

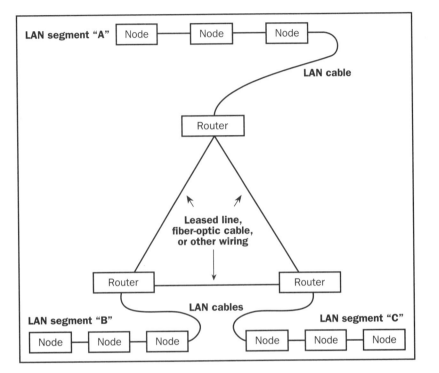

to invest in equipment at both ends of the link that can use the expensive circuit most efficiently.

Because routers strip off the LAN MAC-layer address information before they send a packet from one LAN to another, they reduce the total number of bits going across the interLAN communications link. The remote router at the receiving end restores the correct MAC-layer address back onto the packet before moving the data into its local LAN segment. Because of this action, routers send information across the interLAN circuit more effi ciently than bridges.

As an example, the Ethernet MAC-layer address is 18 bytes, or 3 percent of the maximum-sized packet carried under NetWare's IPX. Since most packets on a LAN of DOS-based PCs are very small, the address can constitute over 50 percent of many packets. Simply removing the MAC-layer address can reduce the percentage of transmitted data significantly. Additionally, companies such as Newport Systems Solutions include software using compression algorithms that can compress certain kinds of data to improve throughput by as much as a factor of four.

Gateways

If you have to link very different kinds of networks, such as a network of IBM mainframe computers and a network of PCs, you might elect to use a device called a *gateway*. Gateways function at the high end of the OSI model; they totally repackage and sometimes even convert the data going between the two networks. Routers add addressing information to the packets or frames they move and don't change the content of the message. Gateway programs often do change the format of the message to make it conform to the application program at the receiving end.

I described PC-to-mainframe gateways in Chapter 12, but the most common LAN-to-LAN gateways are those used by the electronic-mail systems described in Chapter 10. These gateway programs move electronic-mail messages from the format and coding of one program, sometimes through an intermediate common format, into the format of the receiving program.

The X.400 messaging standard is becoming an increasingly important part of LAN-to-LAN connectivity. X.400 is an international standard aimed at providing a global system for exchanging electronic mail. The standard describes a rather complex model of programs called *message transfer agents* (MTAs); these work together to move a message from someone using one kind of e-mail program, called a *user agent* (UA), to someone using a different type of user agent. The UAs and the MTAs all communicate according to one of three protocols. X.400 is one of the best examples of the complexity that evolves from the design of a committee, but many people have made X.400 work for high-level interLAN connectivity.

Novell, in partnership with Retix and Touch Communications, produces a NetWare MHS-to-X.400 electronic-mail gateway. The gateway moves electronic-mail messages from any MHS-compatible electronic-mail program into an X.400 service. Companies such as MCI and U.S. Sprint provide X.400 environments as subscription services.

A unique company called Soft-Switch, Inc. makes its sole business the movement of electronic-mail messages using X.400 and other proprietary protocols. The company supplies hardware and software products to construct electronic-mail backbone systems and corporate e-mail networks. It markets one package called Softswitch, a high-performance electronic-mail software package that can be integrated into an existing IBM mainframe computer system to support a huge network of interactive PC-and-mainframe e-mail programs.

The primary advantage of using a gateway (like an e-mail gateway) to link LANs at a very high level is that the interLAN communications circuit doesn't have to carry a lot of data. The MHS system works well with dial-up telephone lines and 2,400-bit-per-second modems. Because the computers acting as gateways do so much processing, the interconnecting circuits do not have to carry nearly as much data.

WAITS

In a *PC Magazine* article published in the middle of 1990, I christened a new category of products *Wide Area Information Transfer Systems*, or WAITS. WAITS programs use PCs to move files economically and efficiently between LANs. They can be viewed as a type of gateway, primarily because they are applications and completely insensitive to any underlying protocols.

Automated, unattended operation is key to the WAITS concept. Typically, PCs running WAITS software contact each other and move information at scheduled times, although most allow the option of simply moving files when they are ready. They usually connect over dial-up telephone lines because they don't need high data rates, but they can use any interconnecting circuits.

The XcelleNet Wide Area Network Management System, marketed by XcelleNet, is certainly the most sophisticated WAITS product. XcelleNet uses an OS/2-based multitasking master station to interrogate and control remote nodes running under any of several other operating systems. For really big operations, several XcelleNet master stations in the same location can coordinate their operations across the LAN.

WAITS products can solve the interLAN communications problems of many people who only need to move files between networks and don't need more sophisticated computing capabilities involving multiple layers of protocols. These products are inexpensive to install and invisible to the people who benefit from receiving the latest updated data with very little fuss or recurring expense.

■ The Linking Media

So far, we've described the logic and devices used to move frames and packets between LAN segments. If the LAN segments are physically close together, bridges and routers are useful to extend the fat cable, to control LAN traffic, and to perform administrative management functions. But many organizations need to link LAN segments over distances greater than a few thousand feet. In these cases, the fat cable ends and some kind of interconnecting communications circuit must carry the data using one of several types of signaling schemes. I'm going to start out describing the transmission circuits you can use to link LANs, and then introduce the signaling schemes associated with each type of media.

Remember that it is difficult and expensive to send data quickly over long distances. In all of the decisions you make regarding linked LANs, you'll have to balance throughput against distance and cost. Because the cost of the internetwork segment is typically the driving factor in the equation, it's often advisable to make a significant investment in network hardware that makes the best use of the long-distance media.

The internetwork media available to link LAN segments includes telephone lines, satellite networks, microwave radio, fiber-optic networks, and perhaps cable television coaxial systems.

Telephone-Line Systems

Stated a little simplistically, there are two types of telephone lines: those going to the public dial network (dial-up lines) and those leased for long-term dedicated use. When you dial a long-distance telephone number, the computers in the telephone switches route your call and set up a temporary dedicated connection. Leased lines provide a full-time dedicated connection that does not pass through the system of switches.

As usual, real products blur the simple definitions by offering, for example, circuits in the dial-up network that virtually appear to be dedicated lines. These virtual private networks (VPNs), offered by AT&T, U.S. Sprint, and other long-distance companies, allow the telephone carriers to make optimal use of the switched telephone system while providing users with service equivalent to full-time leased lines.

You can use dial-up telephone lines to link LANs. The MHS electronic-mail system is an e-mail gateway that can use dial-up lines to transfer messages. Using the latest high-speed modems meeting the V.34 signaling standard and V.42bis data-compression standard, you can move electronic-mail messages at a respectable throughput of 50 kilobits per second or better over a standard dial-up telephone line.

Competition in the long-distance telephone industry within the United States has driven down the price of dialed long-distance service, so making dialed calls to link LANs on a temporary basis is a practical alternative for many organizations. In the U.S., it is often practical and economical to dial up a link between two routers or bridges for several hours a day to update databases or application programs on LANs. But in many other countries, calling long distance is still expensive, and in some cases the circuits can't pass high-speed data effectively.

Leasing Lines

Selling leased telephone lines has been an important business for the long-distance telephone industry since the 1930s, but in the United States the process became more complex after Bell Telephone System's divestiture and the

Federal Communications Commission's Computer II decision, which defined the roles of the various companies in the industry.

In the U.S., a person who wants to lease a single full-period telephone line across state boundaries might have to coordinate the efforts of three different companies to get the long-distance circuit, the "tail" circuit from the long-distance vendor's equipment to the customer's premises, and the necessary terminating equipment. Even with this need for coordination, it is often possible to install a leased line within a few days, or a few weeks at the most, after the companies get their service orders.

People in countries outside the U.S. can often get the complete long-distance service package from one vendor—typically a government monopoly—but in many cases they have to wait months for the service to appear.

Leased lines for digital data transmission are available in various grades of service. The grade of service relates to how fast you want to move data over the line. Leased data lines are specially configured or "conditioned" for data transmission in several speed ranges.

In the U.S., companies selling long-distance services are often called *interexchange carriers* because their circuits carry service between the major telephone exchanges. The companies that sell the service between buildings and homes and the exchanges are called the *local carriers*. In countries outside North America, there is often no differentiation between these carriers. AT&T is a regulated interexchange carrier whose rates or "tariffs" are subject to the supervision of the Federal Communications Commission. Other long-distance carriers, like Lightnet, MCI, and U.S. Sprint, do not have to file a schedule of public tariffs, but their rates are almost always competitive with AT&T's published tariff rates.

T1 Service

You can lease point-to-point circuits certified for data rates ranging from 2,500 bits per second to over 45 megabits per second. The basic unit of measure for data service, used both by engineers to specify service and by salespeople to price service, is the *T1* channel. A T1 channel can carry 1.544 megabits of data per second, and conforms to certain technical characteristics for signaling and termination of the circuits.

You can establish your own circuits following the T1 channel specifications to move data across a campus or within a large building, but network designers and managers typically think of T1 as a service traversing hundreds or thousands of miles over leased long-distance facilities. AT&T and other carriers will charge you about $5,000 per month for a dedicated T1 circuit spanning 1,000 miles. A T1 line only 500 miles long still costs about $3,000 a month, but T1 service over 2,000 miles costs about $8,000, or somewhat less than twice the price of the 1,000-mile service. Generally, the formula is cost = base monthly rate + (monthly charge per mile × the number of miles).

If your organization needs even faster service, it isn't cheap. A T3 link, which provides 45-megabit-per-second service, costs over $50,000 per month on a 1,000-mile path.

In addition to the leased-line charge, you may also pay several hundred dollars a month for the connection from the interexchange carrier to your facilities and for the termination equipment.

You can use the entire capacity of a T1 circuit to link two LAN segments, but the terminating equipment typically gives you the option of breaking the circuit into several parts. For planning purposes, a channel for one voice conversation takes 64 kilobits per second. So if you lease a T1 circuit between different branches of your organization, you could, for example, use 768 kilobits of the 1.544-megabit capacity to carry 12 voice connections between the PBX telephone systems at each end and still have another 768 kilobits per second available to link the LAN segments through a router or bridge at each end.

As a footnote: Because AT&T encodes certain supervisory information in the data stream, that company has typically provided 56-kilobit-per-second service to its customers—although it is evolving to 64-kilobit service. You should also know that equipment is available from several companies to compress a voice conversation into a 32- or even 16-kilobit-per-second channel, making the space on the T1 link even more economical for voice as well as data transmission. Even 8-kilobit-per-second voice channels are available, but the voice quality is clearly inferior to that of the faster 16- or 32-kilobit services, and few organizations find this voice compression option desirable.

As the demands of your organization change, even on an hourly basis, you can adjust the amount of T1 capacity you allocate to voice and data traffic. There are some problems with shifting between voice and data because the two services have different error and delay tolerances, but many organizations find it efficient to balance their use of T1 channels between voice and data.

Fractional T1

A packaging scheme called *fractional T1* makes it economical to lease circuits for data-communications service slower than the full 1.544-megabit-per-second T1 channel. The basic rate of service for fractional T1 is a channel speed of 64 kilobits per second. Interexchange carriers commonly sell fractional T1 service at rates of 384, 512, and 768 kilobits per second. A 1,000-mile 512-kilobit-per-second service costs about $2,000 per month, plus the fees for terminating circuits and equipment.

Reliability

Redundancy provides reliability. Experienced network administrators know that long-distance links are the major cause of internetwork outages. Routers, bridges, and other network devices seldom fail, but the leased long-distance circuits linking them often do. You typically don't have to pay the fee for the circuit during the malfunction, but this is little consolation for people who can't move the data that is the lifeblood of their business.

If you buy a couple of full or fractional T1 circuits from different interexchange carriers, your network routers can automatically use whatever links are available in the event of a failure. Some routers even use the dial-up telephone lines to back up the leased lines. The data-transmission rate over the remaining or alternative route might be slower than the primary route, but slow internetwork connectivity is far better than no connectivity.

Connecting to High-Speed Channels

When you connect a remote bridge or router to a high-speed T1 or fractional T1 communications channel, an adapter board in the bridge or router changes the network traffic into a stream of data meeting one of several standards for connection and signaling. The output might follow the EIA RS-232, RS-449, or CCITT V.35 standards. Somehow, you need to connect that output to a device called a *multiplexer* that interfaces with the high-speed communications line.

The job of a multiplexer is to subdivide the available single fast communications channel into multiple channels of voice and slower data communications. Companies such as Network Equipment Technologies, Newbridge Networks, StrataCom, Timeplex, and Verilink Corp. provide multiplexer equipment. The Micom Marathon 5K shown in Figure 13.10 combines the capabilities of a multiplexer with other LAN connectivity products in one box.

You'll hear people talk about a *channel service unit* (CSU), the side of the equipment connected to the communications channel, and a *data service unit* (DSU), the side of the equipment connected to the bridge or router. As Figure 13.11 shows, the DSU converts all the incoming data into the proper format for transmission over the T1 or fractional T1 circuit, while the CSU terminates the high-speed circuit and keeps the signals in phase and properly timed. Some bridge products contain a DSU, so all you need is an inexpensive CSU.

The cost of typical DSU/CSU equipment starts at about $2,500 and climbs to many times that amount for sophisticated multiplexers with numerous network-management and reporting functions.

Figure 13.10

The Marathon 5K from Micom Communications Corp. is an example of a product that defies typical definitions. It is a high-quality statistical multiplexer that can mix voice, data, and fax signals on a single fractional T1 circuit. You can insert optional bridge or router modules into the same chassis to make it a router/ multiplexer combination.

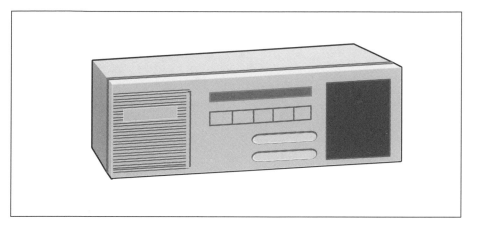

Figure 13.11

This diagram shows a complex and a simple termination for a T1 or fractional T1 circuit. The top diagram shows a system mixing voice and LAN data on the same T1 link through the services of a multiplexer. The bottom diagram shows a router with a built-in DSU connecting directly to the CSU used to terminate the T1 or fractional T1 circuit.

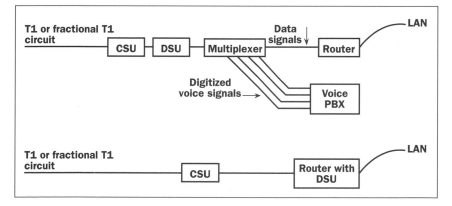

Here are a few facts to remember about T1 circuits:

- T1 is a way of packaging service in increments of 1.544 megabits per second.

- T1 service is provided by many kinds of companies, but primarily by the long-distance or "interexchange" carriers.

- Fractional T1 delivers service in 64-kilobit-per-second increments.

Satellite Communications

The interexchange carriers like AT&T, MCI, and U.S. Sprint use ground-based copper and fiber-optic circuits for nearly all of their connections. But instead of leasing long-distance circuits from the telephone carriers, many organizations, including companies like K-Mart Corp. and Wal-Mart Stores, use their own private satellite radio systems to carry data between their widely separated enterprises. Chrysler Corp. is said to have the largest private satellite network in the world, linking over 6,000 locations.

Companies such as Alascom, AT&T, Comsat World Systems, Contel ASC, and GTE Spacenet Corp. offer a wide variety of satellite services for private industry and governments, ranging from on-call emergency backup services to point-to-point data services, at rates from 19.2 kilobits per second to multiple T1 rates.

Communications satellites are typically in a geosynchronous orbit around the Earth's equator, so from the ground they appear to be stationary in the sky. Each satellite has a number of transponders that relay communications signals. A transponder takes in a weak signal broadcast from an Earth station, cleans it up, amplifies it, and rebroadcasts the signal back to Earth. Because of the satellite's 23,300-mile (35,810-kilometer) vantage point, the rebroadcast signal can cover most of Europe, North America, or South America—depending on the antennas used on both the satellite and ground sides of the link.

This large area of coverage is one of several potential advantages that leased satellite communications circuits have over terrestrial leased circuits. Satellite communications companies don't charge for their circuits according to distance as the terrestrial companies do. The people in the industry say that satellite circuits use "distance-insensitive" pricing, while prices for terrestrial circuits are "distance-sensitive." The satellite companies charge for access to the transponder and possibly add charges based on the amount of bandwidth, a measure of the data transmission rate you use. You should note that leased terrestrial links are typically usage-insensitive; you pay the same monthly charge for the terrestrial lines regardless of how much or how little data you move through them.

The general rule of thumb is that satellite links can't compete on a cost basis with leased terrestrial links under distances of 500 miles. At distances over 500 miles, the satellite links become increasingly competitive with leased lines.

Another advantage of satellite service for many organizations is ease of installation. You don't have to worry about the coordination between the interexchange carrier and the local carrier or the time needed to install service. For satellite communications, a very small *aperture terminal* (VSAT) with an antenna size of 1.2 to 2.8 meters can be installed on a rooftop or in a parking lot within a few hours. Obviously, such systems are also relatively portable and allow you to avoid telephone-line installation charges for temporary operating locations.

Moreover, satellite services offer reliability that terrestrial services can't match. The signal paths to and from the satellite are unaffected by all but the heaviest precipitation, and as long as your Earth station is operational, natural disasters can't take out your circuits. Even the terrestrial carriers use satellite circuits to back up their copper-wire and fiber-optic links.

So if you need to link a LAN in your organization's Chicago headquarters to LANs in branch offices in London and Houston, you could equip each location with a small Earth-station antenna and radio system on the roof or in the parking lot, bring a wire from the Earth station into the building, connect it to the network's remote bridge or router, and let the packets or frames fly through space.

Reality is a little more complex than the concept. There are two significant drawbacks to using a satellite to link LANs: relatively slow throughput and a factor called *satellite delay*.

Typically the low-cost VSATs can transmit only at 19.2 kilobits per second, so they are a slow link between LANs. This speed is fast enough for many kinds of applications, but there are some jobs that need faster inter-LAN links. If you want faster service from a satellite, even up to multiple T1 speeds, you'll need a larger and more expensive antenna. The exact size of the antenna depends on the distance from the satellite's position on the equator and other factors, such as the surrounding radio-frequency environment, but T1 service typically requires a 3- to 4-meter antenna, and the installation might require special permits and planning.

Because of the distance from Earth to the satellite and back again, it takes 0.27 seconds for the signal to make the round trip, even at the speed of light. This satellite delay can be significant to people using certain kinds of applications over interLAN circuits. Satellite circuits are fine for automated updates performed by electronic-mail systems, file transfers done by database or accounting programs, and other program-to-program tasks. But if someone in the loop is entering keystrokes into a program and trying to receive immediate replies, the slow speed of typical satellite circuits and the delay imposed by the extraterrestrial signal paths probably limit the acceptability of this transmission alternative.

Because of the need to conserve the power and resources of the satellite transponder, satellite links typically operate in a star topology like the one shown in Figure 13.12. In this configuration, the transponder receives a number of incoming signals, combines them, and beams them back toward the Earth in one economical data stream. One Earth station serves as a hub, exchanging data with a number of smaller stations situated almost anywhere within the signal footprint of the satellite.

Figure 13.12

In this example, the New York LAN segment serves as a hub, using fractional T1 radio circuits of 256 and 768 kilobits per second to move data between the satellite and the four ground stations.

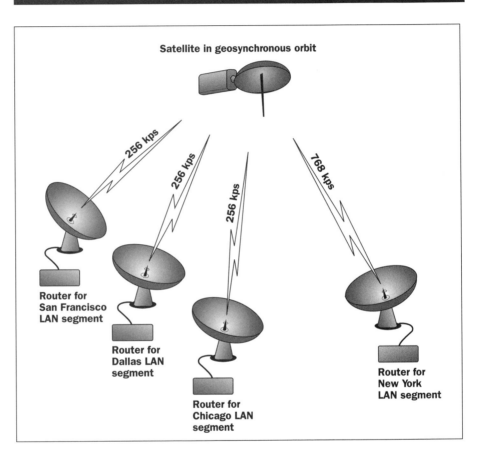

The hub station has a larger antenna than the others, so it can receive the signal from the satellite with less noise and handle a fat data stream with an acceptable level of errors. Many cities have satellite "parks," like New York's Teleport, where several companies share a few large antennae. When several organizations share a single large Earth station, they also share the burdens of installation cost and maintenance problems.

Satellite circuits aren't a perfect interLAN solution for every organization, but they offer unique features and geographic flexibility that no other service can match.

MANs and FDDI

So far, in this chapter I've described how you can lease high-speed services in 64-kilobit increments from terrestrial carriers and satellite carriers. But other companies will sell you circuits to interconnect your facilities within metropolitan areas. For planning purposes, you can think of a metropolitan area as a circle with a 100-kilometer (62-mile) circumference.

As I've explained before, there is the technically ideal way to link LANs and there are the practical alternatives. The IEEE 802.6 committee is developing a standard—the technically ideal solution—for *metropolitan-area networks* or MANs. But organizations as diverse as railroads and cable television companies will also sell you local circuits to link your LANs.

The IEEE 802.6 committee is working on a standard called the Distributed Queue Dual Bus (DQDB). The DQDB topology includes two parallel runs of cable—typically fiber-optic cable—linking each node (typically a router for a LAN segment) on the system. This dual-cable system provides high reliability and high signaling rates, typically in the vicinity of 100 megabits per second. Each ring of cable is independent and moves small 48-byte packets around the ring from node to node; this packet size is specified in other draft standards, such as a high-speed ISDN which is still evolving.

The DQDB system allocates system capacity to each node in 125-microsecond segments. The IEEE 802.6 MAN is designed to be a metropolitan utility serving a large number of organizations across a large area. In the U.S., IEEE 802.6 MANs will probably be installed and run by the local telephone companies. The standards for DQDB are still evolving, and the installation of equipment will take years.

Right now you are more likely to see a service called Fiber Distributed Data Interface (FDDI) providing a backbone of communications services across town. In the grand scheme, FDDI networks will act as traffic-gathering points to feed the larger DQDB network. FDDI systems have a sustained throughput of about 80 megabits per second and are limited to smaller areas than DQDB. FDDI operates over distances limited to about 100 kilometers of cable in each ring, and the nodes can't be farther than 2.5 kilometers apart. FDDI systems can be economically installed using existing equipment by organizations that need them, or by companies that want to sell a service to anyone in the extended neighborhood.

The FDDI architecture uses two rings of fiber—the primary ring and secondary ring—to carry data, as shown in Figure 13.13. The rings are in a physical hub topology similar to the one described in the IEEE 802.5 Token-Ring architecture. All nodes attach to the primary ring, but since the secondary ring is designed primarily to provide a backup connection in case of primary-ring failure, some nodes—called *Class B stations*—might not attach to the secondary ring for reasons of economy.

Some organizations, such as Advanced Micro Devices (AMD), promote using FDDI to deliver data to desktops instead of limiting it to internetwork links. There are movements underway to use shielded and even unshielded twisted-pair media for FDDI.

Figure 13.13

The FDDI hub topology uses a primary ring for data and a secondary ring as a backup. In this simplified diagram, one node is not on the secondary ring and cannot benefit from its redundancy. On the other hand, a node with a single connection has a low cost for installation and equipment.

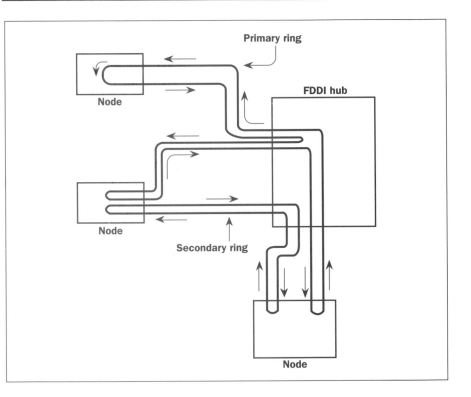

FDDI is an excellent technology for metropolitan network coverage. The ability of fiber-optic cable to ignore electrical interference and to be relatively inert makes it possible to pull cable in all sorts of unlikely places. Railroads are laying FDDI cables along their rights-of-way, while innovative companies are pulling glass fiber through the steam pipes under major office buildings and, in Chicago, in the abandoned tunnels under the city, once used to cart coal to building basements.

Other Carriers

If your organization needs to connect LANs in a metropolitan area, you might look for communications circuits from unlikely carriers. A few cable television companies have installed two-way coaxial cables and can carry data at high speed. Railroads often have excess microwave radio or fiber-optic channels installed along their routes. I've even seen television stations with excess capacity on their private microwave systems. These organizations and others might be able to sell you a service that can link your LANs.

Specialized companies in many metropolitan areas offer circuits for MAN connectivity. For example, Metropolitan Fiber Systems sells fiber-optic MAN circuits in Baltimore, Boston, Chicago, Houston, Los Angeles, Minneapolis, New York, San Francisco, and other cities. Diginet Communications sells circuits in Chicago and Milwaukee, and Bay Area Teleport sells circuits—primarily carried over microwave radio—throughout central California. The Teleport Communications Group offers fiber-optic service throughout the New York City commercial area.

Finally, you can be your own carrier within a metropolitan area, particularly if you have at least one office with a top-down view of the skyline. Several companies, including M/A-Com, Microwave Networks, and Motorola Microwave sell microwave radios operating at 23 GHz that you can literally set on a desktop and point out the window toward the distant LAN. These products can only span line-of-sight distances, for a maximum of 3 to 5 miles, but they can provide throughput of 1.544 megabits per second, and since you can typically buy the equipment for around $10,000 per set, there are no monthly leased-line charges.

■ ISDN

We've looked at interLAN circuits you can lease over terrestrial lines, satellite links, and MAN systems like FDDI. The next interLAN connectivity alternative, the Integrated Services Digital Network (ISDN), uses copper wires to move data down the hall, across town, or across the country. ISDN is more than just circuits; the ISDN specification also covers what kinds of signaling travel over those circuits.

ISDN is one of the best-funded and broadest-reaching programs to come out of the high-technology industry in the late twentieth century. The goal of the program is to link every home and organizational desktop with high-speed digital data services carried over copper telephone wires. This movement has the potential to influence how people in Western Europe, Japan, and North America work, study, communicate, and conduct commerce.

The banners waving on the front lines of ISDN carry the colors of some of the largest international corporations, including AT&T, Hitachi, Northern Telecom, Siemens, government-controlled telephone monopolies, and every U.S. Regional Bell Company.

Today, ISDN is most important to you if your organization is around Atlanta, Boston, Chicago, Houston, Huntsville, Orlando, St. Louis, Sunnyvale, Tampa, Washington, and many cities served by U.S. West. Service is available in many other areas, but these are ISDN "hot spots."

Of the Regional Bell Operating Companies, U.S. West, Ameritech, Bell South, and Southwestern Bell have taken leadership positions in ISDN. You can order ISDN service from U.S. West in Olympia, Washington, and Great Falls, Montana, but you will have a hard time getting ISDN service from NYNEX in New York City outside of a few neighborhoods. However, all of the Bell Operating Companies have made a commitment to ISDN, and the number of service areas is growing every month.

ISDN Technology

This international Integrated Services Digital Network program sets standards for the complete digitization of the telephone systems in Western Europe, Japan, and North America. The plan calls for converting the present analog signaling circuits and systems to digital circuits and systems circulating 0s and 1s instead of analog voice frequencies.

This isn't as radical as it sounds. Modern phone systems are already mostly digital. When you hit the keys on a Touch-tone phone, you program a sophisticated computer in the telephone company's central office and tell it to connect your phone to the desired destination. Your local telephone company's central office computer communicates digitally with computers from other companies, both nationally and internationally, to move your voice.

Digital computer-based telephone switches are the rule in most communities in North America. Many organizations have PBXs that convert analog voice signals to digital 0s and 1s right in the telephone. Many of us use all-digital phone systems already.

Since you've come so far in this book, you should be quick to ask, "If digital switches are so common, why do I have to use a modem to change my PC's digital signals to analog tones for the telephone lines?" The answer is that modern telephone systems are only modern up to the dial central office. From the dial central office to homes and businesses, they drop back to technology that Alexander Graham Bell would recognize. This local wiring, the "local loop," was designed for analog telephones and signals. Special line cards in the dial central office's telephone switch translate between the digital signals in the switch and the analog signals in the phone line. You must convert your PC's new-technology digital signals into old-technology audio tones with a modem so they can be converted back to digital signals, in a different form, at the switch.

Advertisements from long-distance telephone carriers aside, most of the noise you hear on a telephone call comes from the analog local loops on each end. Make these local loops digital and the noise disappears. Of course digital square waves get clipped and distorted, but you can fix digital signal problems by regenerating the signals at intermediate stops. Analog noise is additive throughout the system.

Using digital local loops means you need digital phones at each end. Does that mean you have to throw out your existing phones to use ISDN?

Yes, probably. You could use an adapter to integrate an old-style analog phone into ISDN service, but you would miss the convenience of several ISDN services, which I'll describe a little later. Even on a digital local loop, your PC still needs a modem-like adapter to use ISDN. The unique signaling scheme and voltage levels of ISDN create the need for a digital-to-digital ISDN adapter in each PC.

By the way, when your phone is digital it needs a source of local power. If you don't have a back-up power source for the phone, when the lights go out, so does the phone service.

When you make the local loops digital, you eliminate the bandwidth problems that force us to use sophisticated and high-priced computer-controlled modems to move data at anything over 300 bits per second. Using data compression and sophisticated signaling techniques, modern modems advertise throughputs of up to 48 kilobits per second over dial-up lines, but not with every file and certainly not with everybody's modem. If you make the local loop digital, you can easily send over 140 kilobits per second over the telephone lines.

Sometimes it's easy to make the local loops digital, and sometimes it's very hard. If the premise (home or office) is within 6 to 10 miles of the dial central office, as it would be in most cities and towns, copper cables link the premise and the central office. Copper cables can carry high-speed data, but presently devices called *loading coils* designed to minimize distortion of the analog signals make it impossible to send digital signals over the copper cables. Converting the cabling for digital signaling can be as easy as clipping off the loading coils.

For premises farther from the dial central office, engineers use other techniques, including radio repeaters, to carry the voice signals. These repeaters don't have digital capabilities and are expensive to replace.

For these and other reasons, ISDN will grow first in the cities and in new communities installing telephone systems for the first time. Since the initial market for ISDN services comes from organizations in the cities, the availability of service and the demand for service will grow hand in hand.

Who Is Calling?

What does ISDN bring the average telephone user besides higher-quality voice calls? The answer the telephone industry loves to demonstrate is the ability to know who is calling before you answer the phone.

Because an ISDN telephone call is digital, the phones and switches can pass a lot of information about the call. A key ISDN buzzword is ICLID or *incoming call ID*. The ICLID message goes from the calling phone's ISDN switch to the called phone. ISDN telephone sets typically have an LCD panel showing the number of the calling phone. With a small amount of internal memory augmentation and your own programming, the phone can display the calling person's name, ring differently for calls from certain people, and route incoming calls to other numbers or services based on who is calling.

The next step in the application of this technology is to route the originating number of an incoming call to a local computer, which then displays the credit record, buying history, or other caller-related information before you answer the call. This technique can save valuable minutes in order-taking or other heavy call-handling situations.

Let Computers Talk

The ICLID is an oversold aspect of ISDN. There are other ways to get incoming call information from modern telephone switches without using the ISDN technology. The bright future of ISDN, which few telephone people see, is in serving as the pipe that links millions of PCs, minis, and mainframes across neighborhoods, cities, and oceans on demand. The applications that will use these communications links include executive information systems, electronic mail, database access, printer sharing, and the rest of the growing list of networked workgroup productivity applications on modern LANs. People using PCs and other computers need to communicate easily and at high speed beyond the typical 1,000-foot boundaries of local area networks.

The designers of ISDN developed a standard dividing the available bandwidth into three data channels. Two of the channels move data at 64 kilobits per second, although many long distance ISDN calls will actually be carried at 56 kilobits per channel because that is the data rate of the interexchange carriers. The third channel operates at 16 kilobits per second and provides a path for telephones to send requests to the ISDN switch while moving data from applications at full speed on the data channels.

In ISDN parlance, the 64-kilobit-per-second data channels are called "B-channels" and the slower, 16-kilobit-per-second signaling channel is a "D-channel." The typical type of desktop ISDN service is called 2B+D or "basic rate" service. These services are illustrated in Figure 13.14.

A computer looks at the ISDN line as a wide-open pipe for the transfer of data at nearly 150 kilobits per second. People who are used to reading about 10-megabit-per-second Ethernet and 16-megabit-per-second Token-Ring might assume that ISDN is slow in comparison, but LAN schemes like Ethernet and Token-Ring use sophisticated media-access protocols to control the access of each node to the cable. LAN nodes must wait, retry, repeat, and perform many overhead tasks to share the cable. These actions cut the LAN throughput of even the fastest computer to hundreds of kilobits per second instead of megabits.

Figure 13.14

ISDN carries voice and data over standard telephone lines digitally. Several different rates of service, each combining 19.2- and 64-kilobit-per-second signaling, can link subscriber locations and the central telephone equipment. PCs with ISDN terminal adapters and special telephones with RS-232 connections can combine voice and data on the same desktop.

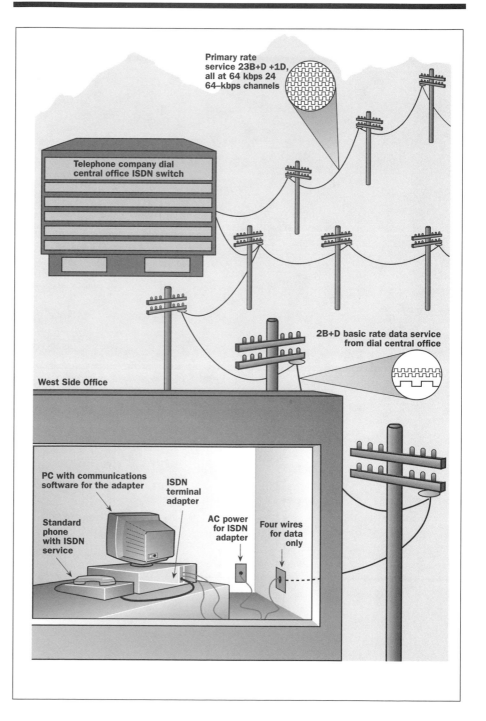

Figure 13.14

(Continued)

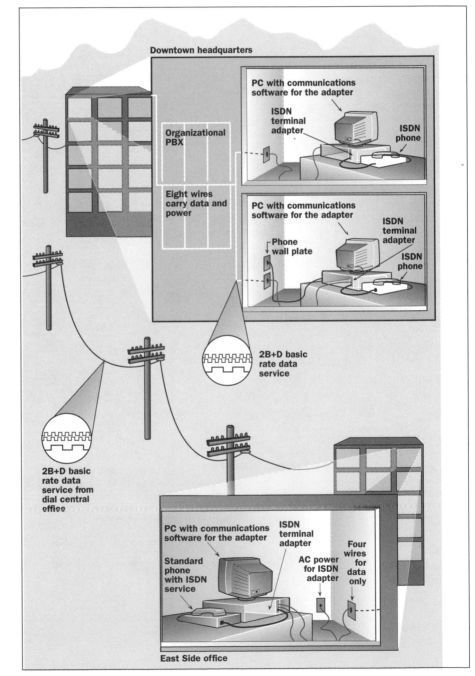

Suddenly the ISDN pipe doesn't look so thin. You can move a lot of data quickly over a high-quality ISDN circuit because other nodes don't share or contend for its service.

The Bright Lights

There are companies that realize the potential of ISDN as a communications platform for computer-based applications. Companies like AT&T and NCR have PC adapters for ISDN available for shipping to system integrators and technically sophisticated customers. The packages range from little more than a bare board begging for third-party application software to tightly integrated and sophisticated products with software that can provide video conferencing or LAN-to-LAN connections across ISDN links.

In their early versions, these ISDN adapters are not economical for linking individual PCs. Prices of over $1,500 per machine seem to be the norm. In addition, if you get ISDN service from a Regional Bell Company instead of from your own PBX, you must pay tariffed service charges. Various regulatory jurisdictions use different rate packages based on connection time, packet counts, and completed call charges.

The pricing of ISDN adapters is more typical of products like SNA and X.25 gateways than PC-to-PC products or LAN interface cards. It seems likely that based on price alone, many people will initially use ISDN connections to link traditional LANs rather than replace them.

Right now, the ISDN adapters from different manufacturers cannot communicate with each other. The adapters and application programs use the empty ISDN data channel in unique and proprietary ways. In particular, these products vary in the way they compress data and in the way they interact with the network operating systems.

ISDN Coming to You

If you manage a group of PCs in one of the increasing number of ISDN geographic areas, you need to know how this alternative can serve you to link PCs, mainframes, and existing LANs across the miles, and eventually across thousands of miles, with fast digital service. Today ISDN is economical mainly for linking LANs, but in the near future it may displace today's traditional local area network in many installations.

■ X.25: Versatile, Efficient, International, and Necessary

You should be aware of a protocol called X.25, which defines how communications devices like bridges and routers package and route data over a connecting circuit. You can use X.25 data packaging and routing over any of the terrestrial, satellite, or ISDN communications circuits I've described. You can use the data-packaging and data-handling aspects of X.25 over any type of point-to-point circuits, but the protocol is better-known for its packet-switching capabilities.

Packet switching is one of three major switching classes. The others are *circuit switching* and *message* or *store-and-forward switching.* You use circuit switching every time you make a telephone call. The lines the call traverses are dedicated to you and the person you called, and they remain fixed until you hang up. These lines are unavailable to anyone else, even when neither party is talking. In store-and-forward switching, the complete message, like a Western Union telegram, is sent from switch to switch. When the message reaches the destination switch, it is printed out and delivered.

Packet switching breaks messages into small bundles or packets (for instance, 128 characters). These packets are sent out as they are built in a *packet assembler/disassembler* or PAD. A PAD may be nothing more than a special kind of adapter board with its own processing capability and software. A PAD can reside in a PC, and Hayes even builds a PAD into its VSeries of Smartmodems. The packets coming from a PAD are interleaved on a circuit with packets from other sources to make maximum use of the available bandwidth.

To make matters confusing, several different packet-switching protocols are used both in LANs and in wide-area networks. These include protocols as diverse as IBM's Systems Network Architecture (SNA), Token-Ring, and FDDI. The most widely used, internationally agreed-on protocol for packet switching is X.25. The X.25 standard was first adopted as an international standard in 1976 and has been revised and updated every four years since then.

The protocol for X.25 details a specific exchange of packets required to pass information. These packets have structured contents and precede the passing of information. A *call request packet* is sent to the requested host, which can grant permission for the exchange by issuing a *call accepted packet.* The call is set up and information exchanged in the form of packets that contain addressing information. Of course, these packets also contain the actual data that the sender wishes to transmit. The call is ended when a *call clear packet* is sent and a *clear confirmation packet* is received in acknowledgement. Each of the packets in this exchange has a specified structure, and each field is defined. Special *reset* and *restart packets* add to the robustness of X.25. These, along with other prescribed packets such as the *diagnostic packet*, make X.25 extremely versatile and easy to use.

X.25: Good and Stubborn

Several companies, such as AT&T, Telenet, and Tymnet, manage networks of minicomputers spread across the nation and across the world that connect together with high-speed data-communications lines. These companies sell their networks' data-handling and transmission capabilities to subscribers under several pricing schemes. Outside the U.S., national telephone companies in many countries offer X.25 services, sometimes at lower rates than leased lines or dial-up lines.

Because these networks use software conforming to the X.25 protocols to ensure the accuracy of the data they carry, and because they can offer other associated services, they are called *value-added networks* or VANs.

Because X.25 packet-switched VANs route each packet to any destination on the fly, they create the ability to link thousands of locations simultaneously. You see this best in on-line services like CompuServe, where people calling in from locations around the world simultaneously communicate with the central database computers.

When you use X.25 VANs to link LANs, you gain error-free simultaneous connections to multiple locations. This capability should make X.25 VANs perfect for LAN-to-LAN connections. Unfortunately, traditional and short-sighted policies in the management of these networks lead to two problems: limited throughput and what I call a "centralized connection" mentality.

Artists often depict an X.25 network as a "cloud" with connections in and out. They use the cloud to obscure the complexity of the minicomputers inside the VAN and their interconnections. There are two types of connections going into the "cloud." The first is a high-speed leased line that can carry 19.2, 56, or 64 kilobits per second, or even 1.544 megabits per second, from the computer to the cloud, using full X.25 protocols. This is an expensive connection, usually reserved for the busy host computer. The other type of connection is a dial-up telephone line that does not provide full X.25 data handling between the computer and the network.

Unfortunately, X.25 vendors haven't installed modern V.32bis modems on many dial access ports so that people can call in at 9,600 bits per second or better. They have few ports that can handle even a maximum speed of 2,400 bits per second. It isn't practical to make interLAN connections at only 2,400 bits per second.

The limitation on connection speed is made worse by the double error-checking used when Novell IPX packets travel over X.25. Both IPX and X.25 have built-in error correction. Novell designed IPX with the "Did you get what I sent?" concept in mind. Therefore, a lot of X.25 packets consist of IPX confirmations to packets that X.25 already confirmed, at least at the X.25 network level, so you need all the throughput you can get to carry the overhead. While the X.25 confirmation is redundant to the higher IPX confirmation, the additional X.25 packet information is needed for the VAN routing.

The other problem with using X.25 VANs to link LANs comes from the traditional use of VANs to make one-to-many connections. In the past, multiple clients used VANs to get to one host. The fee structure and programming of the networks reflect and perpetuate this scheme, but this isn't the best structure for LAN-to-LAN connections.

Despite the limitations on speed and on connection options, X.25 networks are appropriate for many LAN-to-LAN applications. Pressure from users should force the managers of these systems to implement more features for the LAN-to-LAN market.

Public versus Private X.25 Networks

X.25 packet-switching networks provide effective solutions for many applications. For example, X.25 works well where multiple protocols must be handled, low delay is required, or users need to connect to multiple hosts for short periods of time.

A familiar example of an X.25 network application is the processing of credit-card charges you see in stores daily. The electronic transaction from the card reader is frequently carried over an X.25 network. This permits short messages (which include your account number, store identification, and the amount to be charged) to be sent to the proper bank and receipt of the transaction to be acknowledged by the bank. The X.25 network allows this to occur without the use of costly, dedicated connections from each store to each bank that issues credit cards.

Packet-switching services can be obtained by building private networks or through the use of public data networks. As the name implies, a private network is one where network resources are usually dedicated to a small number of applications or a restricted set of users, as in a corporate network. The network resources include the access circuits, the network interfaces between the user and the packet switches, the packet-switching nodes (PSNs) and the trunk circuits that connect them, and the control systems for the network.

Private network access is typically handled through dedicated circuits. With public data networks, network resources are owned by a third party (such as Tymnet or Telenet) and leased on a usage basis to many users, serving many applications. Access to public networks is typically through dial-up circuits.

The decision to use a private or public network is primarily based on economics and, to some extent, on desired network performance. From a performance perspective, public networks are sufficient for many uses, but specific applications may require a specialized customized network. In these cases, a private network provides the flexibility to incorporate the necessary performance capabilities.

In public networks, costs to a user are determined by the amount of time the user is connected and by the number of packets the user sends and receives. Although various cost algorithms are employed, generally the more you use, the more you pay. In private networks, user costs are driven by the initial capital investment and network operations costs.

Usage must also be viewed in terms of traffic volume and transaction size. For example, comparing interactive transactions and large transmissions (such as file transfers) over a range of traffic volumes yields "regions" where either private or public packet networks are more cost-effective.

Frame Relay

The X.25 protocol is a conservative design that numbers, acknowledges, and supervises every packet and even asks network switches to retransmit packets that don't make the trip across the network. This conservative approach protects data, but requires a lot of expensive computing and communicating resources within the network to do all the extra work involved. A less careful, but less burdensome, protocol called *frame relay* has moved into the WAN market so forcefully that, in the U.S., almost all new WAN connections use frame relay instead of X.25.

The frame-relay protocol design takes advantage of the fact that modern transmission systems are quiet and reliable by reducing the protective overhead to allow more throughput at lower cost without unacceptable data loss.

The frame-relay concept transfers some of the responsibilties of the switches in the X.25 network to the terminal equipment on each end. If there is a problem with a packet—for example, if bits are lost or if a node is so congested that it receives more packets than it can process—the frame-relay network discards the data and expects the terminal equipment to take corrective action. Typically, this involves retransmitting the data that failed to make it across the network. Because LAN protocols like Novell's SPX/IPX have their own error control that is redundant with the error control in X.25, they fit nicely into the frame-relay architecture.

But on the down side, the end-to-end recovery scheme can be costly because it increases traffic on the network. If frame-relay packets are discarded because of congestion, retransmitting the data can merely aggravate the problem. So even though the terminal equipment can recover discarded blocks, it's still important to minimize frame discards.

Since LAN traffic tends to flow in bursts, the probability of occasional congestion is high (unless the user overconfigures both the lines and the switches and pays more than necessary for network costs), so it's important for a frame-relay network to have excellent congestion management features. The frame-relay standards include several nonmandatory suggestions about how the network can signal congestion and how the LAN portal devices should react. Because these suggestions aren't mandatory, companies can field devices that conform to the frame-relay protocols but don't have congestion control capabilities.

Two important frame-relay congestion control systems involve using the *discard eligibility* (DE) bit in the frame-relay format and establishing an estimated rate of traffic called the *committed information rate* (CIR).

Setting the DE bit to a binary 1 marks the frame as eligible for early elimination in the event of congestion. The DE bit could be set by a LAN portal device on lower-priority traffic or traffic that can withstand a few seconds of delay, like electronic mail. Marking potential sacrificial frames with the DE bit provides a good way to let higher-priority traffic pass.

The committed information rate represents an estimate of the normal amount of traffic coming from a node in a busy period. In a commercial network, the higher the CIR the higher the monthly cost. In private networks, the CIR is still an important budgeting and management tool. The network measures the traffic coming from each node. If the load is less than the CIR, it passes the frames untouched if possible; however, if the load exceeds the CIR, the network sets the DE bit on the excess frames. If the network experiences congestion, frames that exceed their own CIR are eliminated before those that don't have the DE bit set. Because congestion control is so important, we strongly suggest you select products that provide DE and CIR capabilities along with other forms of node-to-node communications.

■ ATM

The newest, and therefore to lovers of status technology, the hottest, technology for linking LANs is called *Asynchronous Transfer Mode* (ATM). ATM is a packet-switching technology like X.25 and frame relay, but with a few twists.

The advantages of ATM include the ability to create a seamless and fast network reaching from the desktop out across limitless wide areas. In its full splendor, ATM would do away with routers, allocated bandwidth, and contention for the communictions media. Believers in ATM include the world's largest telecommunications and computing corporations, but who really needs ATM and what makes it necessary?

The answer is, only organizations that need to deliver synchronized video and sound can really see the grandeur of ATM. This category includes movie and entertainment players such as Time-Warner and Viacom International, who want to deliver 500 channels of on-demand video and sound to your home.

Organizations that only need to move a lot of computer data will pay a penalty for ATM's overhead. For moving data that doesn't demand millisecond synchronization, there are better and more efficient technologies, like the widely available and proven frame relay. My advice is, wait and then wait some more before applauding ATM.

In some ways ATM benefits from the related frame-relay technology, but in other ways it's a throwback. Good connections and smarter software at the higher levels allow frame-relay packets to move data reliably and more efficiently than X.25. Every vendor of wide-area packet-switching services from CompuServe to Wiltel, Sprint, AT&T, and MCI can provide frame-relay subscriber service at DS-1 (1.544 Mbps) and European standard E1 (2.048 Mbps) speeds. Service at DS-3 (44.736 Mbps) rates is available, but is not as widely used.

The advantage of frame relay is that it makes the best use of the available bandwidth by packaging the data in variable-length packets for transmission across the network. It is commonly accepted that variable-length packets suit the bursty nature of computer data transmissions.

On all types of communications links, from the slowest 300-baud modem connection to multimegabit local networks, the engineering goal is always to bundle the data into big packets that have little overhead (data bits that provide routing, error-checking, timing, and other information) for the most efficient throughput and lowest communications-channel cost. Low overhead with big packets is the concept behind X-Modem 1K, Z-Modem, Microsoft's NetBEUI/SMB, and Novell's Burst Mode IPX protocols.

Packet-switched architectures that use large packets have two problems: First the packet switches must buffer packets of different sizes. This juggling act requires sophisticated software that consumes processing power and memory, so the cost of the switch goes up. Second, as big packets make their way through the switch they hold up other packets. In technospeak, these switches have a high *latency*, that is, there can be irregular gaps of several milliseconds between the arrival of packets in a stream. If you are running a time-sensitive application like videoconferencing, unsynchronized packets can make lips move without sound and images jerk on the screen.

Two switched-circuit services are related to, predecessors of, and today sometimes carriers of ATM: Switched Multimegabit Data Service (SMDS) and Broadband ISDN (BISDN). SMDS is a LAN-bridging service, weakly marketed by local telephone companies, that provides transmission at DS-1 or DS-3 rates. Beautifully designed to use copper or fiber-optic cabling, it was integrated into the IEEE 802.6 specification for metropolitan area networks.

Never heard of SMDS? The telephone companies were supposed to market it to meet your data needs, but they failed to work out the long-distance side of the connections. A few cutting-edge companies use SMDS in metropolitan networks, but there are competing technologies, such as the privately owned fiber-optic loops available in Chicago and other cities, that offer higher speed and excellent economy in metropolitan settings.

Broadband ISDN is that shy and never-blooming perennial, the Integrated Services Digital Network, piped over fiber-optic cable at 155 Mbps. ATM was first described within the BISDN architecture and BISDN serves as a carrier for ATM packets.

Some of the hot data communications ideas that preceded ATM, like frame relay, are designed to squeeze the best value out of the communications channel. Technologies like SMDS and BISDN, which have been very slow to take hold in the market, enhance the channel by adding intelligence to the fabric of the network. So far, that approach hasn't hit it big because people favor adding intelligence to the ends of the network, at prices they can control. It remains to be seen whether ATM will fare any better.

ATM Facts and Fallacies

If you listen to the cheerleading for ATM, you'll hear that ATM gives you a high-speed, scalable architecture that works from desktop to WAN without all the sticky protocol changes and transmission techniques commonly used today. You'll also hear that the small packets ATM uses provide low latency, so sound and picture arrive together. All of these benefits are real.

Another theoretical advantage of switched technologies like X.25, frame relay, and ATM is that they facilitate multipoint networks. Technologists call these *meshed* networks, meaning that traffic flows through all levels. But in the real world, despite the reengineering of corporations, traffic flow is typically still centralized or hierarchical. The advantage of meshed-network communications is lost on most organizations moving computer data today.

If you listen well to the ATM boosters, you'll notice that ATM is always mentioned in the same breath as high speed and broad bandwidth. There's an unspoken assumption that ATM somehow creates high speed, which isn't true. ATM is associated with high-speed signaling primarily because the protocol is simple and flexible enough to work over a broad range of speeds. Nothing is free, though; even with ATM high speed costs more, and ATM imposes significant overhead costs of its own.

The unrelenting fact of physics is that costs escalate dramatically as you increase signaling speed, distance, or both. ATM doesn't change that equation; however, it does allow companies with the largest networks to pay less for their switches, to use their wide-bandwidth fiber-optic links, and to manage their entire networks—from desktop to distant desktop—as one end-to-end entity. All of which means that these carriers can increase margins, or lower prices, while selling more services.

ATM's cell-switching technology appeals to today's telephone companies because ATM can handle both data and voice on the same network, something X.25 and frame relay cannot do. In fact, the design of the ATM cell was driven by requirements imposed by voice telephone transmission.

ATM gives these carriers an intelligent network to resell. Sprint Corp. was the first to make ATM services commercially available, and other carriers such as AT&T, MCI, and Wiltel weren't far behind.

ATM Overhead

If you're going to pay many tens of thousands of dollars a month for a fast digital service, you'll want to squeeze every bit of data through that channel you can, so let's look at the efficiency of different transmission techniques.

The X.25 and frame-relay packet switched architectures follow a protocol called the Link Access Procedure Balanced (LAPB) that is built on the well-known High Level Data Link Control (HDLC). Generally, the user data—the useful cargo in the frame—can occupy as many as 4,096 bytes, but the default is 128 bytes. If you add about four bytes for address- and control-field overhead in frame relay, the resulting packet has as little as .08 percent and an average of just 3 percent overhead.

The ATM packet totals 53 bytes of which 5 bytes, or a little more than 9 percent, are overhead. In some cases, timing added by the ATM adaptive layer can raise the overhead to 13 percent. So the smaller ATM packets use at least 6 percent more of the communications channel than frame-relay packets to move the same data. To put this into perspective, 6 percent of a DS-3 channel is 2.68 Mbps, or about forty 64-Kbps channels in ATM overhead.

Admittedly, this analysis is simplistic—there are other factors involved—but it's generally accurate and conservative. To the end user or network manager, the major advantage of ATM is its low latency—its small packets can move through a congested switch with minimal delay—but that single advantage can cost you a lot of wasted bandwidth and a lot of money.

ATM Fever

If there is one difference between ATM and competing technologies like frame relay, it's the number of companies that have delivered early ATM products. These companies aren't motivated by a pure desire to move your computer data. They know that ATM will be a critical part of the heralded convergence of television and data, so they're betting on their ability to carry entertainment and information to future homes and offices—but they'll settle for computer data until the future rolls around.

Fore Systems in Pittsburgh, PA and Newbridge Systems in Herndon, VA are ATM pioneers. Both of these companies have development and marketing arrangements with better-known vendors in the PC industry. Fore is teamed with 3Com and Cabletron, and Newbridge is working with ODS and Xyplex

IBM has also taken a strong pro-ATM position. The company is shipping products that use ATM at 25 Mbps over unshielded twisted-pair wire. Frankly, I think this is a smart move because it brings ATM to the desktop while minimizing cabling worries.

The prices of ATM hardware are going down due to competition among chip manufacturers, a factor that never emerged to improve the price of hardware for technologies like ISDN. IBM has announced that it will develop its own chips and license them to other manufacturers. AT&T, National Semiconductor and Texas Instruments are in the same business. PMC-Sierra has built a chip set under the guidance of a consortium of about 20 telecommunications switching-equipment vendors including Fore Systems, Synoptics, and Newbridge.

On the long-distance network side, AT&T and Wiltel followed Sprint's lead and began offering DS-3 ATM services in early 1994. Even CompuServe, which has a substantial X.25 and frame-relay service business, has announced plans to buy ATM switches.

Ask Yourself about ATM

Is ATM for you? Here are some simple questions to ask yourself:

- *Do I need to deliver voice or synchronized voice and video in real time?* If not, first investigate Ethernet switching or 100 Mbps Ethernet systems.

- *Do I need to send data more than two or three miles, but still keep it within the U.S.?* If you need to move data only a few miles, look at microwave or fiber-optic cable options. If you need to go outside the U.S., look at leased lines or frame-relay public data network options because ATM will be accepted more slowly outside the U.S.

- *Do I need to deliver data to many locations or is my need point-to-point?* If your enterprise-network is a pyramid with few interconnections, circuit-switched services like Switched 56, Switched T-1, or SMDS will probably be more cost effective than pure ATM.

- *Do I have a budget of tens of thousands of dollars for a testbed?* If not, look at Ethernet switches.

- *Am I willing to commit myself to one vendor for several years?* Compatibility is an issue. If you like to mix and match vendors, stick with more mature technologies.

If you answered yes to each of these questions, you may be ready to climb on the leading edge of ATM. But despite the clamor it's generated, at present only a few corporations reap great benefits from ATM technology.

■ Linking LANs: A New Frontier

The number of organizations that need to expand their information-processing systems by linking LANs across tens or thousands of miles is growing. Some companies, particularly the aggressive manufacturers of routers and bridges, are responding to this lucrative market for data-transport services. Other companies, particularly the local telephone exchange carriers, are looking the wrong way and missing some tremendous opportunities for new business.

In the mid-1990s, new technologies are providing circuits for interLAN connections. These include

- Higher-powered satellites that can provide higher data rates with smaller Earth-station antennae

- Digital cellular radio systems

- More powerful private-branch-exchange telephone systems with direct links to LANs

No book can tell you everything you need to know about linking LANs. You'll need help both from the companies making the routers and bridges and from the companies that sell long-distance circuits. But the information in this chapter should give you a basis for sound choices and decisions about the architecture you will use to connect LAN segments.

- *Convergence around a Point?*
- *The Internet*
- *Of the Future*

The Internet and the
Information Superhighway

TECHNICAL TALE

"Road kill, on-ramp, tool booth, stop sign, U-turn, narrow bridge... What other highway words can I use?"

"What are you writing?" Steve asked.

"Oh, it's an article on the information highway and I want to be clever," Scott replied.

Well, if you really want to be clever, stop trying to stretch a point and just tell the people what it's all about," Steve advised.

"Okay, what is it all about?"

"It's about social change as much as technical advances—fast connections, fast processors, interoperable protocols, new ways of doing business, and new life styles all coming together at once. Futurists like Alvin Toffler understand it better than politicians. All this 'highway' stuff is political hype, just a code word for another round of pork-barrel politics."

"Ahhh," Scott replied, "I've got you—you're the school crossing guard on the info highway." He ducked the book that sailed across the room, but Steve's point had already hit home.

O KAY, I USED THE "INFO HIGHWAY" PHRASE TO GET YOUR ATTENTION, BUT THE slick analogy of a highway quickly falls apart, so that's the last time you'll hear it from me. It's more useful to think of the coming changes in how we interact as the convergence of powerful processing, improved bandwidth, massive storage, and a social need to communicate. The concept of convergence is important because it both allows and forces change to happen. In this chapter we'll examine the mix of technologies supporting the current convergence, as well as its impacts and some of its products. We'll look at the Internet, video conferencing, and other network-based products that can boost your connectivity productivity. To get things rolling, we'll present some ideas designed to put you in a convergent frame of mind. Thanks probably to the profit motive, there is no shortage of thoughts about the impact of technology on the way we work. Some of the following ideas relate to technology and others are more concerned with the process of doing business. As you'll see, these observations don't all point in the same direction; the best I can do is lay them out and add my comments on how they might impact the way you work for a living.

- *You either ride the tiger or the tiger eats you!* Anyone running a business today can relate to this piece of Eastern wisdom. The pace of change is increasing, and many old ways of doing business will now get you into trouble. The current roaring tiger ready to snack on would-be leaders of commerce is information technology. The processes of storing, creating, retrieving, distributing, and using information are a significant and often major part of most new jobs.

- *Moore's Law has changed business and commerce forever.* Gordon Moore observed that the number of gates (transistors) on new integrated circuits doubles every 18 months. This literally means that organizations can affordably double their processing power and data storage capacity that frequently. In many cases, new processing capability changes the business so that entire lines of products or ways of doing business last only a year and a half. Today, processing power and a long communications reach allow us to quickly modify the way we create, market, distribute, and pay for products, and the cycle shows no sign of slowing.

  It's important to understand that doubling your processing power means more than simply paging your documents faster on the screen. Doubling your processing power also means that you double the speed of your modems and halve the amount of bandwidth needed to send full-motion video. Processing power and transmission capability go hand-in-hand.

- *You can get what you want when you want it! Mass production gives way to mass customization.* Before the industrial age, most goods were custom made. Within the limits of material and time, people who had enough wealth could hire skilled workers to make things just for them. When industrialization and mass production came along, workers could create more goods at a much more reasonable price. Large numbers of people could afford to buy the things they wanted—as long as they wanted a Model T Ford that was black like everyone else's. Today, information technology is making it practical to customize goods on a massive scale. Modern milling machines are controlled by microprocessors with programs that can change on-the-fly. While printing tens of thousands of copies of a magazine, computer-driven printing presses create special editions tailored to the needs of specific individuals. As the links between the buyers, manufacturers, and designers of products get faster, buyers will gain the ability to order products that will be fabricated on-demand, customized from within a wide set of options, and shipped overnight. We already buy desktop computers that way. In the coming age, clothes, appliances, and many other items will be ordered, custom manufactured, and delivered on-demand.

- *The "ilities" have met the "ologies" and nothing will ever be the same.* Some of the standard "ilities" of business include manageability, profitability, and sustainability. Since these factors have met information technology, the sociology of flexible organizations and business relationships have inevitably changed. Technology hasn't forced the changes, but it made them possible. These changes aren't necessarily positive or negative. For example, the concept of manageability will continue to evolve from dictatorship toward leadership, which is probably a desirable evolution, but one that could have some negative impacts on individual productivity. Because leadership organizations value intelligent employees with strong skills, many businesses now compete as fiercely for talented employees as they do for new customers. The meaning of the word "profitability" won't change in the future, but modern companies will need information technology to maintain profit margins. The paths to profitably are new and will continue to evolve swiftly. Sustainability—the ability to hold on to business in the future—is becoming very difficult to achieve as modern corporations profit from fast reactions and speed. Customers are growing increasingly fickle because it's so easy for them to develop new sources of supply.

- *Information technology helps to flatten organizations.* Branch offices and middle managers exist to glean, cache, sort, and squeeze information. As wide and local area networks make information more generally available throughout an organization, the gleaners and squeezers become redundant. Modern organizations are horizontal structures linked by information technology. They need fewer people, but those people must have greater information skills.

- *Virtual corporations rely on business connections.* Modern enterprises survive by speedily reacting to opportunities. Maintaining internal corporate speed requires a network of external links to suppliers, distributors, customers, lawyers, and accountants. This group forms an ever changing and highly responsive "virtual corporation" that can grow into and withdraw from business areas in rapid response to market pressures.

- *Inventory is an obsolete concept.* Any inventory, whether it is a stock of parts or a warehouse full of finished products, represents money that isn't working. Today, many manufacturers practice "just-in-time" delivery to keep their inventories low. In the coming years, inventories will shrink even more as manufacturing systems report their production activity directly to suppliers who will then be responsible for replenishment.

- *The cost of moving information will be so low that getting the audience's attention will be the major problem.* Businesses won't have any problem reaching customers, but they will have a problem being recognized over the competition. As electronic links to homes and businesses expand, marketing will change in ways that are impossible to predict. In this highly competitive environment, a new business model that pays addressees to look at advertising messages might become commonplace.

- *Information is not a consumable.* For the first time in the history of commerce, we have a raw material that doesn't diminish with use. Specific combinations of information might have more value at one time than another, but no matter how much they're used they are never depleted. The ability to spot and fill new niches for information and products already marks successful companies, and this trend will continue.

- *Presentation is as important as content.* Because of the unique nature of information, this observation means even more than Marshall Mcluhan's famous statement, "The media is the message." As some new technologies increase the volume of delivery, others must provide ways to extract useful information from the vast fund of available data. The odds are good that virtual reality will become a useful way to present business information. Immersed in a world of symbols and images, people will understand the patterns of finance, supply, and demand intuitively and more profoundly than they could by simply looking at charts or reading columns of numbers.

- *An increasingly large percentage of workers won't go to work.* Earthquakes, floods, and storms in the 1990s have proven that many people don't have to "go to" work in order to do their jobs. Improved information access links make it effective and economical for people to work from home or from neighborhood work centers equipped with appropriate technology. Working at home or locally can help to alleviate some social and economic problems while actually improving the productivity and profit margins of commercial organizations.

- *Corporate classrooms close.* While hiring and training good workers will continue to be a major corporate problem, making people sit in a classroom won't be part of the solution. Information technology will provide "just-on-time" training through a variety of mediums. As people work their way through their jobs, tutorial programs will be available to answer questions and provide guidance. Broad information links create broad avenues for training.

- *A modern bank is only as good as its information network…but is it any more than its network?* Today, information about money is often as good as money itself. When individuals have totally secure and validated means of communications, the act of pooling money to loan can assume a whole new form. Future banks may be institutions without a building. While these virtual banks will offer some guarantees and unique services and provide anonymity, they will become more visible as brokers between those with money and those who want to use it.

■ Convergence around a Point?

So where will we see the effects or benefits of this convergence of new technologies and sociologies with business practices? Some companies are betting that people will want interactive sports, movies on request, work at home, and endless access to caches of information. Will one of these be the "killer application" that makes convergence a commercial success instead of a technical curiosity? Or will the killer application be something less elegant like people self-publishing their own life stories to send to other people?

Your view of convergence depends on your starting point. If your company makes network file servers like those made by Hewlett-Packard, convergence means using hardware based on the PA-RISC processor with Fast and Wide SCSI-2 drives capable of delivering 40 Mbps from multigigabyte disk farms to create a video server. Pacific Telesis is using this HP hardware to supply video-on-demand shopping and entertainment services in California.

Companies with a television orientation see everything in terms of TV. Scientific Atlanta, Inc., Kaleida Labs, and Motorola, Inc. have joined forces to produce the Malibu Graphics Controller for TV-top systems, which may be your buffer to convergence. Scientific Atlanta and Silicon Graphics, Inc. are already working with cable TV giant Time Warner, Inc. to deliver video-on-demand to 4,000 customers in Orlando, Florida. The TV-top boxes are high-powered, typically with an embedded PowerPC processor but a relatively inflexible front-end for television sets. Basically, they're products for the technophobic that provide only a limited set of functions in a flashy format.

In my view, only the PC has the power, familiarity, and broad focus needed to bring in the total picture. The PC already acts as a smart terminal for information services, a place to transmit and receive faxes, a portal to electronic mail, and a creation station for personal and commercial documents. The TV focused smart-box companies, who are starting from scratch, will ultimately capture only a narrow slice of the convergence interface market.

Of course, the average PC still has a way to go before it becomes the perfect gateway to convergence, but our industry moves fast. The convergence PC requires full 64-bit capabilities controlled by a multitasking operating system, a fast I/O bus for communications devices, fast video, and lots of storage. But the price of machines with these capabilities is already within reach of most technically inclined people.

Microsoft, IBM, Intel, and Novell are developing new industry standards and products for the convergent PC. The Intel Pentium, harried by the IBM/Apple PowerPC, is being demonstrated at 150 MHz. The Peripheral Component Interface (PCI), a new PC architecture, is a good move toward a configuration that allows independent actions by the processor, memory, and communications peripherals.

Intel is making important improvements in PC-based videoconferencing including its Indeo video compression technology. Novell's NetWare Video brings client/server technology to multimedia. It allows client PCs to access any CD-ROM title that conforms to the Microsoft Video for Windows standards on a NetWare video server.

The PC needs connections that can lead it into the convergence zone. Soon PCs will have to interact with many information pipes including both improved cable television services and improved telephone services. Wireless connections and even power lines are also in the running for information transmission. There won't be a single pipe that brings all the traffic into the home or office. We'll do our tasks with the tools at hand, but the PC will bring them all together.

Companies like Intel (working with General Instruments) and Zenith are delivering devices designed to link PCs into improved cable television services. These so-called cable modems—a technically incorrect but catchy name—are being used to provide two-way cable connections to the Prodigy and America Online services.

Telephone companies are upgrading their capacity and services by installing ISDN, laying ever more fiber optic cabling, and using techniques such as AT&T's Very High Bit Rate Digital Subscriber Line (VHDSL) to offer 3 Mbps subscriber service over all types of copper cables. Telephone growth plans often must clear regulatory hurdles, but regulators too are feeling the pressure for new technology.

Asynchronous Transfer Mode (ATM) is a communications technique that delivers sound and images in synchronization. Although ATM was developed as a part of ISDN, ATM can run over cable coaxial links, telephone unshielded twisted-pair wire, and LAN cables, so the PC doesn't care where it gets its voice and video data.

The technology convergence—or digital highway if you care to use that phrase—isn't mysterious. It's simply a product of human ingenuity and the PC's continued growth.

■ The Internet

Throughout this book, I focus primarily on techniques for moving information within an organization. This internal movement is extremely important because it allows flexibility and quick responsiveness, but the leverage that means success in business often comes from outside the organization. In the second half of the 1990s, external links to information bases will be extremely important. Among the oldest, and certainly the most successful, links to outside resources is the Internet. You can't write about modern converging connectivity architectures without discussing it, but talking about the Internet is like trying to paint a moving train—it changes as you look at it.

I'm not positioning the entire Internet as a model for external networking. Indeed, its present structure doesn't include many things a commercial service needs, such as a good billing scheme. However, the events and techniques that have shaped the Internet will certainly spin off into unforeseen products and technologies. The pace of change on the Internet is accelerating and it started out pretty fast!

In the late 1970s, the terminal on my desk was attached to a computer that could exchange messages over something called the Defense Advanced Research Projects Agency Network or ARPA Net. At that time, this network linked over 600 universities, companies, and government agencies for the purpose of information sharing. Frankly, a lot of the network traffic—particularly after dark—was either game playing or personal messages from college students, but even that proved useful, because it helped stress and test the network in many ways and also trained a generation of technophiles to love getting online. In the 1980s the Department of Defense turned to more secure networks and sponsorship for the Internet moved to the National Science Foundation. As commercial uses of the Internet have grown, various commercial organizations are literally laying a new network over the older, government-sponsored one.

The basic components of the Internet are the same devices described in Chapter 13: communications lines and routers. An Internet server installation can be as simple as the one shown in Figure 14.1—a Unix-based computer with some terminals and a router connected to a leased line. In the U.S., clusters of major Internet service points are in the Washington D.C., Boston, and Silicon Valley areas, but there are major subnetworks around the world.

Figure 14.1

An Internet node might be nothing more than a computer running Unix attached to a router over an Ethernet cable. If you add more computers to the cable, the same computer can provide Internet access for an entire organization. The other side of the router connects to a leased line that travels to a back–bone router typically located in Washington D.C. or California.

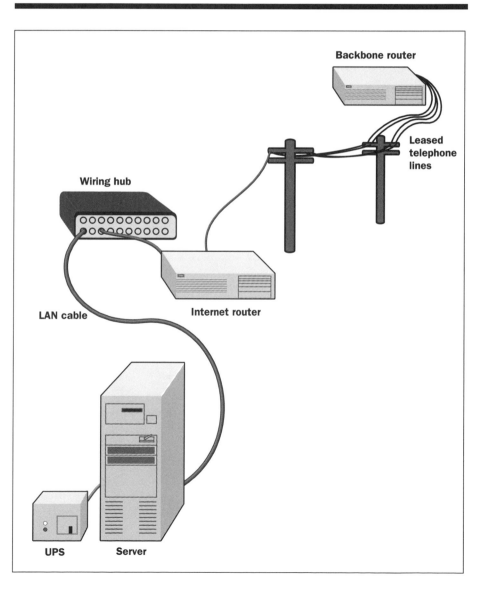

An Internet server has two roles: It offers services—typically in the form of information databases and program libraries—to users connecting across the backbone, and it offers backbone access to locally connected users. These servers can range from PCs with less power than the one on your desktop to mainframe systems with huge disk storage subsystems.

Internet servers can hold databases that perform many different functions. The three most popular general functions are electronic mail, newsgroups, and special server programs. Electronic mail systems on the Internet conform to the Simple Mail Transfer Protocol (SMTP). Each user has a mailbox name that is associated with a specific server. For example, I might be fderfler@frank.com. This fairly simple address identifying my account on my own access server is a rarity on the Internet. More typical addresses include several levels of network and server names. By the way, the @ sign is pronounced "at" when you say your Internet e-mail address.

Newsgroups are special interest groups whose files reside on servers across the network. They are similar to special interest forums on CompuServe and many bulletin board services, but many of them deal with very technical or very far out subjects. There are newsgroups for practically every interest in the world, and many people spend most of their online time simply browsing newsgroups in search of the interesting, arcane, or peculiar. Figure 14.2 shows a newsgroup reader.

Figure 14.2

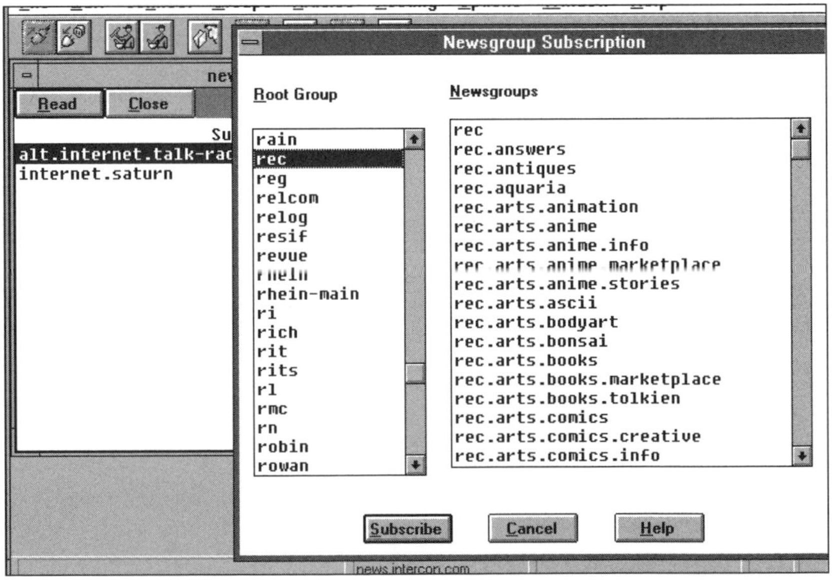

Newsgroup reader software provides a way to browse through the newsgroups made available by your Internet access provider. Your access provider typically copies hundreds of megabytes of text daily so it is available with a fast response.

Special server programs use software that looks for matching special-purpose client programs. Together, the client/server programs perform tasks, typically conducting searches for files and information. I'll discuss these programs in a little more depth later in this chapter.

Getting Access

Since buying a router and leasing telephone connections into an Internet backbone router are expensive—the leased line can easily run $1,000 per month—people have found ways to share Internet access. Instead of attaching terminals to a computer connected to a router, you can have the computer service a number of modems to provide dial-in access service, or you can use a separate communications server like the one in Figure 14.3 to handle multiple incoming callers simultaneously, which is the way many Internet access providers operate.

The sophistication of the software you use to make the modem connection into the Internet computer determines the quality of service you receive, and the quality of your service determines what nifty things you can do with Internet access. You'll want an Internet connection that uses the Serial Line Internet Protocol (SLIP) or the Point to Point Protocol (PPP) so you can use interesting Internet tools like MOSAIC and Gopher. The SLIP and PPP connections arrange the data in packets and do error-checking so you can send binary data over the telephone line; however. you need special software in your computer to make these connections.

A number of commercial companies now operate their own subnetworks of the Internet. They essentially have large computers with many types of access ports (including LANs for locally connected computers) that feed into the common Internet backbone. An umbrella organization called the Commercial Internet Exchange Association (CIX) sets some policies for these operations. Among the first subnetworks are AlterNet from UUNET Technologies, CERFnet from General Atomics, and PSInet from Performance Systems International. MCI, IBM, and Sprint have also been active on the commercial side of Internet operations. Companies like CompuServe and America Online offer Internet connection in addition to their own extensive information bases. There are also dozens of companies around the world providing regional Internet access. Some charge per minute of connection while others charge a flat fee for service.

Internet Tools

Once you have Internet access, you'll want to know what tools are available to you. The TCP/IP suite includes its own set of tools, now more than a decade old, that allow you to perform some basic tasks. The file transfer protocol (ftp)

Figure 14.3

A large-scale access provider typically establishes a communi– cations server to handle incoming callers. The communications server establishes a link to the callers using either the SLIP or PPP protocols to allow the transfer of binary packetized data.

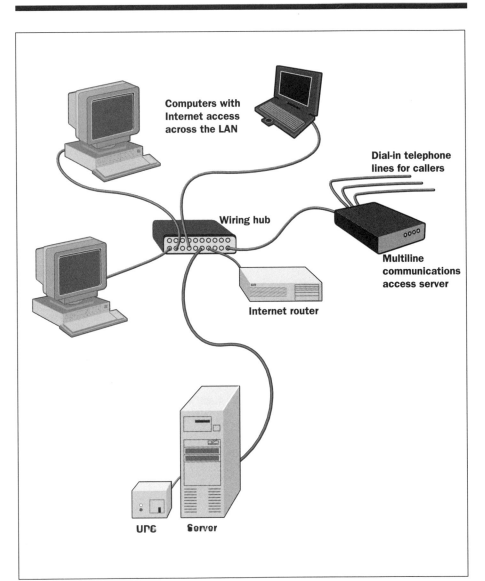

provides a way for you to go out and find files and bring them back to your sys- tem. Figure 14.4 shows an ftp session. TELNET is a program that lets you con- nect to a host computer across the Internet; this isn't much different from a terminal connection to a minicomputer. A little more sophisticated is the news- reader, a generic program that allows you to read specific newsgroups. TEL- NET and ftp are basic tools of the trade based on teletypewriter technology, but the interesting technologies on the Internet—the technologies that will have the greatest impact on the rest of the convergent technologies—make it easier to find and display data.

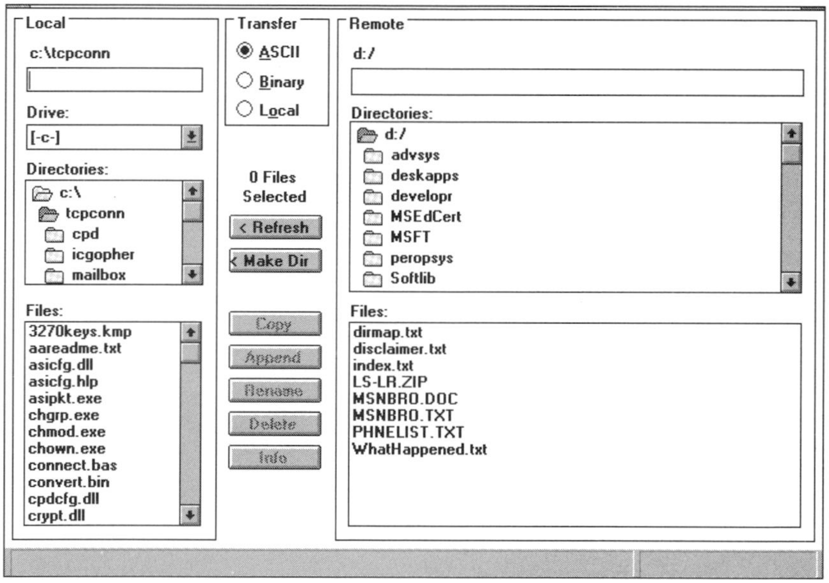

Figure 14.4

The ftp utility isn't much to look at, but its basic commands allow you to draw down files from servers throughout the Internet. Almost all TCP/IP software packages include the ftp utility, and it is also included in many desktop operating systems such as Windows NT.

The Wide Area Information Service (WAIS) is a text-searching engine that can zip through libraries, specially indexed files contained in multiple databases. You can direct WAIS to look for specific words or text strings in many different libraries. Some libraries have specific rules about how many searches you can make or how many documents you can download, but generally WAIS is a researcher's dream.

Early on, it became apparent that the sheer number of information sources in the Internet made it difficult to search intelligently. So some enterprising folks began to setup special purpose servers that collect information on "what's out there" and present it in a searchable way. A service called Archie was one of the first. You can attach to an Archie server using TELNET, ask it to search its database for a specific match, and it will try to find the files you want. Then you have to connect to the computer holding the files and use ftp to pull them down.

The next step in the evolution of finding and retrieving information is Internet Gopher, shown in Figure 14.5. Like Archie servers, Gopher servers know the locations of hundreds of thousands of files; they can supply file names and even file descriptions. Unlike Archie, the Gopher provides user software for PC, Mac, or Unix computers that presents a nice set of menus to help you frame your search, and Gopher servers help you to retrieve files without a lot of maneuvering around the network. Gopher servers can contact less capable Internet servers and bring files to you through the Gopher user software. In effect, they are powerful agents that can execute all the arcane ftp, TELNET, and other commands for you.

Figure 14.5

This Gopher software connects to special servers that help you find and copy the data and program files you want. Gopher servers can execute the lower-level ftp and TELNET commands to capture data, so you don't have to know anything about their syntax or use.

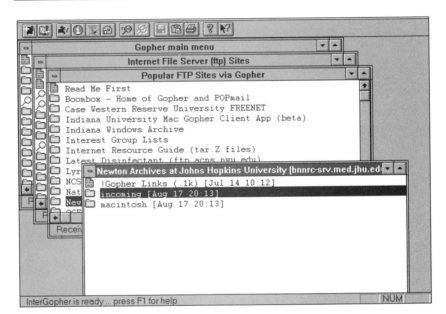

The latest development in the evolution of Internet services is the World Wide Web (WWW). The Web uses a concept called *hypertext* to good advantage. The idea for hypertext has been around for quite a while, but it was terribly hard to make it work in **print**. If this were an electronic hypertext document, you would be able to click (or touch or blink at or otherwise indicate) the bold word **print**, and you would branch into a discussion of printing. Hypertext links between subjects can become very complex; while they're the very devil for writers or designers to create, they are extremely useful to readers. A few hypertext books have been published, with tabbed pages leading to linked subject matter, but creating—and using—this kind of document has to be a labor of love. Creating hypertext documents on a computer also requires a lot of detailed work, but at least it's practical.

Specially designed screens on WWW servers interface with client programs to present topics in a hypertext format. You need a computer with a graphical interface like a Macintosh or a PC running under Windows to take full advantage of its features, but when you see the Web in action, you'll see the future.

Figure 14.6 shows MOSAIC, the most popular WWW client program. MOSAIC started life as a shareware program—it was given away across the Internet. Recently, several companies have licensed MOSAIC with the intent of turning it into a commercial product, so you may encounter several versions of MOSAIC with different sets of features.

Figure 14.6

The MOSAIC program hides its power behind the "home page" screens of specific MOSAIC servers. These screens contain icons, pictures, and specially highlighted text that can lead users to related subject matter.

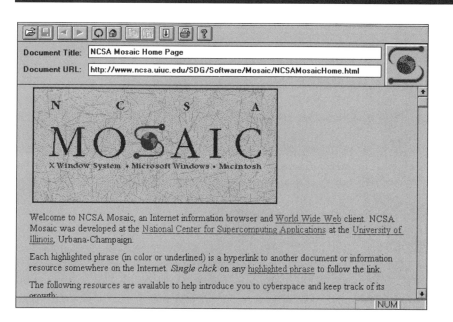

Under MOSAIC, the hypertext concept has evolved into a sophisticated interactive system that uses icons, pictures, and other devices to indicate linked subjects. You can use MOSAIC to navigate through a world of related subjects as the WWW server draws upon its vast stores of information to meet your needs. Because the screens of MOSAIC servers are very specialized, they typically serve a specific special-interest subject area. MOSAIC is a great front-end for commercial enterprises that want to showcase their products in the most effective way. A MOSAIC catalog is pretty spectacular, both in concept and in execution.

■ Of the Future

The Internet is more of an incubator than a model. It is a hothouse of ideas blooming in a favorable environment. As technologies converge, concepts developed within the Internet will find practical uses in many areas.

Linking the Parts of Your Desktop

Whether you work in a traditional office building or at home, your PC should be the place where you do everything. You should be able to handle documents, links to outside information services, e-mail, video conferences, phone calls, voice mail, faxes, and all the other components of a modern office from your keyboard and screen. Remember, this doesn't mean that the software for all these functions runs in your PC, only that you can get what you need from the PC through consistent and integrated interfaces.

In Chapter 11, I talked about the bridges being built to link the elements of the modern office. Increasingly, the LAN cable will connect PCs, fax machines, printers, and copiers. While the PBX will remain in its own cabinet, the integration of PCs and telephones is at hand, as are interpretable speech recognition and voice synthesis applications.

The introduction of digital telephone service under ISDN is finally making videoconferencing, database replication, and document transfer practical. With Intel currently leading a group of 12 major vendors in establishing a PC desktop videoconferencing standard, we should soon see a number of real and interoperable videoconferencing products.

Video in Your Office

In the mid-1980s I took part in a program that built videoconferencing rooms at military bases around the world. Each room had large display screens, special desks, controlled lighting, a microphone system, a tangle of cables and controls, and its own satellite terminal that used proprietary signaling schemes. Modern videoconferencing facilities don't require as much space, equipment, or furniture—your desktop and a PC will do the job. And instead of $50,000 per seat, the cost is less than $5,000 per desktop, assuming you already have a PC or Macintosh.

The confluence of powerful PCs, modern video compression protocols, new standards, and digital switched communications services has begun to make desktop videoconferencing affordable and effective. Figure 14.7 shows the components of a typical dekstop video system. You probably won't be comfortable making a commitment to purchase videoconferencing equipment until the latter half of the 1990s, but it isn't too early to start budgeting and establishing some trial installations.

Figure 14.7

Several components, including a camera and communications adapter, make up a basic desktop videoconferencing system. Adding a scanner and other graphics devices improves the systems's flexibility.

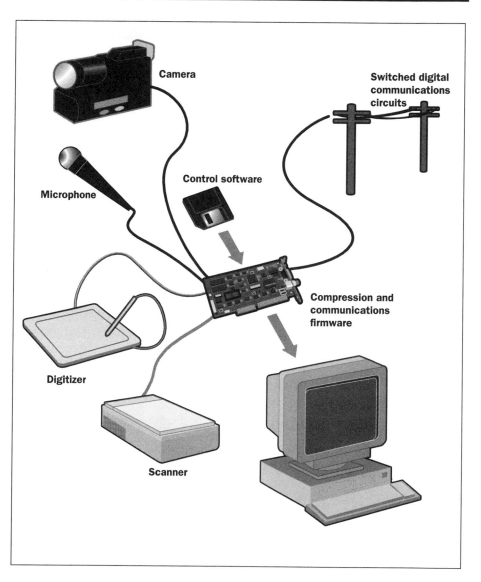

Camera

Switched digital communications circuits

Microphone

Control software

Digitizer

Compression and communications firmware

Scanner

Down to the Desktop

There is a real difference in the kind of videoconferencing you participate in when you sit in a big video room and what you accomplish when you have a desktop video connection. Videoconferencing between rooms is really a meeting of two meetings. There are as many social protocols as communications protocols in operation. When you make a desktop video connection, you are literally linking your major productivity desktop tools, the PCs and their software, and merging their power. The PC-to-PC links assume equal importance with the person-to-person links. Indeed, the programs controlling these links provide a way to trade-off person-to-person video definition for PC-to-PC performance if you have limited interconnecting bandwidth.

In an effective video conference, both sides can fine-tune the numbers in the same spreadsheet, make changes to the same diagram, and edit the same text while also exchanging signs in spoken and body language. With videoconferencing, you can communicate through your mouse, keyboard, scanner, and digitizer pad as well as through your voice and facial expressions. If you add a clear LCD panel to your PC, you can also project the output using an overhead projector to gain some group meeting capability.

PC-based videoconferencing systems have one short term limitation: The present systems can't provide low cost multipoint connections. Today, you can have $5,000 per desktop point-to-point video connections or $25,000 per location multipoint connections using proprietary communications hardware. PictureTel Corp., VideoTelecom Corp. and Compression Labs Inc. dominate the multipoint videoconferencing market. Lower-cost multipoint hardware conforming to international standards should be available soon, and will bring more buyers into the market.

If you're considering videoconferencing over your organization's computer network, there are three reasons to think again. First, the need for video communications typically extends beyond the fast local area network cabling system. If you're on the local network, you can probably walk to a face-to-face meeting and access the programs and data you want through the LAN when you get there. It's hard to justify the cost of videoconferencing within a building or campus.

Second, video transmissions quickly saturate the capacity of a local or wide area network. Video traffic presents a high and sustained level of data, as opposed to computer programs that create bursts of traffic, but maintain a low average traffic load. Under the sustained load of video transmissions, the average network utilization shoots up and overall network performance crumbles. In particular, it doesn't make economic sense to saturate expensive internetwork routers and leased interLAN telephone lines with sustained video traffic.

The high average throughput of video traffic is a prime motivation behind the development of 100-megabit signaling technologies for LANs, asynchronous transfer mode networks, and a technology called *isochronous Ethernet* that is being developed separately by IBM and National Semiconductor. Networks with faster signaling have more bandwidth to share, so they can tolerate the high sustained throughput of video transmission. Isochronous Ethernet supports the transmission of voice, data, and video by adding 6 mbps of throughput to the 10 mbps of today's Ethernet.

The third reason to reconsider the wisdom of videoconferencing over a LAN or WAN is that videoconferencing often extends beyond the organization. We live in an era of virtual organizations and collaboration among corporations. Commercial television proves the value of video selling every day. You'll want to conference with clients, suppliers, distributors, and consultants as much as with people in your own organization, and only dialed-up telephone connections provide this flexibility.

To use PC desktop videoconferencing, you'll need either Switched 56 services or ISDN basic rate services. Fortunately, Switched 56 is widely available and easy to order throughout the U.S. as part of a service called Digital Centrex, and ISDN's availability is improving. Digital connection services are also commonly part of campus-wide and company-wide private branch exchange (PBX) telephone services. That's why companies like Northern Telecom and AT&T are pushing videoconferencing products.

The Picture on Standards

The International Telecommunication Union has been busy in the area of video transmission standards, but remember, compliance with standards doesn't necessarily mean compatibility between products. Five ITU standards, known collectively as Px64, but often referred to by the title of the primary standard H.261, define videoconferencing. H.261, adopted in December 1990, describes the compression and decompression algorithms used for video.

Other standards within Px64 include the framing protocol and video/audio multiplexing protocol H.221, the call set-up and tear-down protocol H.242, and the control and indication signaling protocol H.230.

Px64 defines two screen formats known as the Common Intermediate Format (CIF) and the Quarter Common Intermediate Format (QCIF). CIF uses 288 lines with 352 pixels per line and QCIF uses 144 lines with 176 pixels per line. A QCIF picture will fill about one-quarter of a standard VGA screen—yet another reason to invest in a large monitor.

In 1991, the Motion Picture Experts Group (MPEG), working with the Joint Photographics Expert Group (JPEG) of the International Standards Organization, sponsored the development of an additional ITU standard that rolls high-resolution still-frame and VCR-like capabilities such as control of fastforward and reverse into the Px64 standard. Although it is still evolving, the total package is known as ITU H.320 and you should shop for H.320-compliant products. The revised H.320 specification also includes multipoint capability.

On Camera

You can divide PC videoconferencing technology into two areas: in front of the PC and inside the PC. Each side of the system has its own technology and buzzwords.

In front of the PC, you use standard data input tools such as a mouse and keyboard during a conference, but you'll also want a scanner to capture documents and a digitizer pad for drawing. Of course you'll need a camera and microphone on each end of the circuit too. While many types of cameras (camcorders included) will do, the best cameras for this purpose have a high sensitivity to light—2 lux or better—so you don't need special lighting, and a good depth of field so you stay in focus. It's often useful to have a macro focus lens on the camera so you can use it to display small three-dimensional items that you can't run through the scanner. The ability to focus to within an inch of the lens is useful. You'll also want a camera that has standard RCA jacks for video, so you can use it for other purposes.

Inside the PC, the videoconferencing system includes three major functional pieces of hardware and the integrating software. The functional hardware elements are a coder/decoder or CODEC that digitizes the video and audio signals; a compression engine that compresses and decompresses the video and audio during transmission; and a communications card that integrates the video and audio data stream with data from the PC and formats it into a serial connection—typically this would be an ISDN port or a V.35 serial port used to connect to a Switched 56 interface.

The integrating software does everything from maintaining a telephone book of commonly called numbers to controlling shared screen displays and file transfers. The software is also valuable in helping you trade movement for detail in the televised images. Despite improved compression techniques, it still takes time to move a video image across a communications line. Commercial television systems transmit 30 frames per second (fps) over wide bandwidth cable and radio systems. At 30 fps, the human eye sees smooth movement. Desktop videoconferencing systems don't have that bandwidth, so the videoconferencing software typically allows you to exchange image quality for image smoothness. If you want high-quality pictures, perhaps because you have the camera aimed at a stationary object, you can choose a rate of 6 to 10 frames per second for the best resolution. But if you are viewing people, the slower rates produce too much blur. PC desktop systems typically can reach a rate of 15 fps. At that speed you can see facial expressions and all but the fastest hand movements clearly.

The Macintosh market has been years ahead of the PC market in handling video. On the Mac, QuickTime is a standard for video hardware integration and for the development of tools for video programming: creating video messages, clips, and features. However, Microsoft compressed the PC's time line with the introduction of Video for Windows. The API for this Microsoft software describes, among other things, the special system calls used for video and the Audio Video Interleaved (AVI) file format. Apple responded with QuickTime for Windows, which can bring video programs created on the Mac into a PC running Windows. While videoconferencing and video programming are two different activities, their hardware requirements overlap so you can often use your videoconferencing gear to create and store other types of video programs and to broadcast prerecorded programs.

Companies selling videoconferencing products package the elements in different ways. Northern Telecom's VISIT bundles everything together and provides an integrated system that takes a single expansion slot. IBM's videoconferencing system revolves around its Person-to-Person/2 software package, but the company sells each part of the system separately, and overall it takes two expansion slots. AT&T's Personal Video System bundles technology from AT&T and NCR into one package that also takes two slots.

Video Convergence

Desktop videoconferencing is yet another technology that can change the way your organization works. Like electronic mail, videoconferencing won't totally replace travel or face-to-face meetings, but it does provide another dimension of communication. Convergence pulls together sound, video, and fast services, as well as new technologies and sociologies for information sharing. You don't have much choice about getting involved in convergence—unless you choose to live a techno-hermit's life, it will find you—but you can determine how much your company will leverage convergence to your benefit. Leaning out over the edge of technology may show you a whole new way to run your organization.

■ Appendix

Product and Vendor Directory

Electronic Mail and Associated Products

cc:Mail
Lotus Development Corp.
800 W. El Camino Real
Mountain View, CA 94044
800-448-2500, 415-961-8800
fax: 415-961-0840

• Electronic mail system for PC LANs. Supports WAN connectivity with any combination of server-to-server, LAN-to-LAN, and remote PC-to-LAN messaging, as well as connection to other e-mail systems. Includes notification of new mail messages by bell tone and either flashing desktop icon or pop-up dialog box. Also provides distributed mail server software, a single common post office, encrypted compressed messages and user directory files, paper mail terminology and tools, automatic conversion among popular graphic displays, and remote PC access.

tPost LAN (V.5.1)
Coker Electronics
1430 Lexington Ave.
San Mateo, CA 94402
415-573-5515

• Electronic mail package for LANs and multiuser systems with built-in gateway to remote LANs and stand-alone field PCs. Includes function-key driven routines, private and public distribution lists, attachments, remote command execution, an e-mail-to-fax option, and a forms option.

Cross+Point (V.5.24)
Cross International Corp.
854 Walnut St., Suite B
Boulder, CO 80302
303-440-7313
fax: 303-442-2616

• Electronic mail system with groupware, computer conferencing, or thought processing. Includes bulletin board, online messaging, and windowing. Provides encryption and pop-up notification as well as a fax/e-mail interface to many PC-fax boards. Handles internetworking for LAN-to-LAN communications.

DaVinci eMAIL for DOS and Windows (V.2.5)
DaVinci Systems Corp.
PO Box 17449
Raleigh, NC 27619
800-328-4624, 919-881-4320
fax: 919-787-3550

• Memory-resident electronic mail program. Provides pull-down menus, mouse support, and security. Any number of files can be attached to any message. Receivers are notified of incoming messages by pop-up dialog box and by tone.

All-In-1 Desktop for MS-DOS (V.1.1)
Digital Equipment Corp.
146 Main St.
Maynard, MA 01754-2571
508-493-5111
fax: 508-493-8780

• Allows MS-DOS-based PC users to access All-In-1 applications on VAX. Includes individual and group calendaring, group conferencing, electronic mail, a facility for launching applications from within All-In-1, an auto-dial function, a phone book, a facility for logging phone numbers called and length of calls, and decision-support tools.

Edge Office
Edge Systems, Inc.
1245 Corporate Blvd., Fourth Floor
Aurora, IL 60504-6420
708-898-0021
fax: 708-898-5406

• Consists of integrated modules including Event Notification, File Cabinet, Telephone Book, Telephone Message Notepad, Electronic Mail, Time Manager, Reverse Polish Notation Calculator, ASE Editor, and Document Routing.

Futurus MAIL Plus (V.2.11)
Futurus Corp.
211 Perimeter Circle Pkwy., Suite 910
Atlanta, GA 30346
800-327-8296
fax: 404-392-9313

• Peer-to-peer e-mail system including phone messaging and real-time chat modules. Available in both Windows and DOS platforms. Provides instant notification of all module functions. User-configurable options allow for individual needs and tastes. Offers access to faxes, including zoom in/zoom out, flipping, and printing. Offers seamless plug-and-play communication with all mainframe e-mail packages.

The Major BBS (V.5.11)
Galacticomm, Inc.
4101 Southwest 47th Ave., Suite 101
Ft. Lauderdale, FL 33314
305-583-5990
fax: 305-583-7846

• Multiuser bulletin board system. Provides file upload and download, teleconferencing, classified ads, system information, electronic mail, user information display/edit, shopping, and entertainment/games. Supports up to 256 simultaneous users. E-mail offers file attachments, carbon copies, return receipts, message forwarding/quoting, and distribution lists.

PROFS Extended Mail
IBM
Old Orchard Rd.
Armonk, NY 10504
800-426-3333, 914-765-1900

• A proven electronic mail system able to run on a variety of host hardware from mainframes to PCs.

Officepower
ICL Business Systems
9801 Muirlands Blvd.
Irvine, CA 92718
714-458-7282
fax: 714-458-6257

• Multifunctional office management system. Offers word processing, electronic filing, electronic mail, appointment calendars, telephone and address dictionaries, phone message log and routing, full-function math, accounting, and electronic spreadsheets. Optional PC, Mac, or Unix integration with GUI.

PostMark E-Mail
Network Associates
80 East 100 North
Provo, UT 84606
801-373-7888

• Combines MHS-compatible e-mail system with ASCII-standard word processor. Performs standard e-mail functions and group discussions.

Notes
Lotus Development Corp.
55 Cambridge Pkwy.
Cambridge, MA 02142
800-343-5414, 617-577-8500
fax: 617-225-1299

• High-powered groupware with strong e-mail. Its high price and heavy maintenance costs may deter you, but its unique detailed features are alluring.

Microsoft Mail
Microsoft Corp.
One Microsoft Way
Redmond, WA 98052
800-227-4679

• Integrated system that sends messages, spreadsheets, faxes, and any type of file. Sends and receives messages through remote electronic mail systems (REMS) account to IBM PROFS, DEC VAX-mail, All-In-1, Wang Office, 3Com 3+ Mail, and CompuServe. A usable form of this product is included in the latest versions of Microsoft's Windows operating system.

Wildcat! (V.4.0)
Mustang Software, Inc.
PO Box 2264
Bakersfield, CA 93303
800-999-9619, 805-395-0223
fax: 805-395-0713

• BBS system. Offers electronic mail, file transfer, questionnaires, and bulletins. Provides customizable display files and security for 50 levels of users. Messaging capabilities include ability to reply, forward to third parties, send carbon copies, request return receipt, and print. Net/multiline available. Versions supporting 1 to 250 lines are available with or without Pro! series utilities.

Notework
ON Technology Group
1 Cambridge Center, Kendall Square
Cambridge, MA 02142-9773
800-697-9273, 617-374-1400
fax: 617-374-1433

• Pop-up e-mail program. Includes pop-up telephoning, messaging, and file transfer. Allows user to print, export, and confirm receipt of messages, customize editing commands, attach files to notes, notify others of incoming calls, and send urgent messages.

X.400 Gateway
Xsoft (Division of Xerox Corp.)
3400 Hillview Ave.
Palo Alto, CA 94303
800-428-2995, 415-424-0111
fax: 415-813-7162

• Provides communications connectivity between TCP and OSI electronic mail networks. Exchange of mail messages between X.400-based electronic mail services and Unix mail applications is transparent. Conforms to government's GOSIP standard and complies with Defense Communications Agency's OSI migration strategy.

QuickTalk
SilverSoft, Inc.
1301 Geranium St., NW
Washington, D.C. 20012
202-291-8212

• Calls up electronic mail system and enters text directly into word processor or spreadsheet. Uploads or downloads file while in background. Converts up to 40 strings of characters while reading file or text.

OfficeNet
Source Data Systems, Inc.
950 Ridgemount Dr., NE
Cedar Rapids, IA 52402-7222
800-553-7305, 319-393-3343
fax: 319-393-5173

• Includes word processing, electronic mail, scheduling and calendars, spreadsheet, file management, phone list, notepad, and calculator functions.

CompletE-MAIL/MHS
Transend Corp.
884 Portola Rd.
Portola Valley, CA 94025
415-851-3402
fax: 415-851-1031

• LAN-based e-mail system. Supports mail handling service standard. Creates, exchanges, and manages messages, DOS files, and electronic files. Intuitive, icon-based windowing user interface. Incorporates word processor or imports data from user's word processor.

LAN Office
Wang Laboratories, Inc.
One Industrial Way, Mail Stop 014-A1B
Lowell, MA 01851
800-225-0654, 508-459-5000

• Includes electronic mail, time management, directory services, note services, user profile customization, and menu modification. Compatible with Banyan VINES, Novell Advanced NetWare, 3Com 3+ Share, and IBM PC LAN Program.

WordPerfect GroupWise
WordPerfect Corp.
1555 N. Technology Way
Orem, UT 84057
800-321-4566, 801-225-5000
fax: 801-222-4477

• Office automation package for LANs. Includes shell menu for integration of programs, clipboard, electronic mail, notebook with auto-dial feature, scheduler, file manager, calculator, calendar, macro editor, and program editor. Includes Novell's wide-area message handling service (MHS). Includes WPScheduler, WPNotebook, and WPFile Manager.

LAN Fax Gateways and Related Products

FaxPress
Castelle
3255-3 Scott Blvd.
Santa Clara, CA 95051
800-289-7555, 408-496-0474
fax: 408-496-0502

• Price: $3,295–$4,595

- Number installed to date: 1,000
- Date announced: 1994
- Shareable devices: Facsimile
- Network compatibility: Ethernet, IBM Token-Ring

GammaFax CP-4/AEB/LSI

GammaLink
1314 Chesapeake Terrace
Sunnyvale, CA 94089
800-FAX-4PCS, 408-744-1400
fax: 408-744-1900

- Price: $2,995
- Date announced: 1993
- Group compatibility: CCITT Group 3
- Document transmit rate: 14.4 Kbps
- Standard features: Broadcasting, background operation, auto cover page, scheduling

NetFax FaxServer

OAZ Communications, Inc.
44920 Osgood Rd.
Fremont, CA 94539-6101
800-NET-FAX3, 510-226-0171
fax: 510-226-7079

- Price: $1,995
- Release Date: 1992
- System compatibility: PC-MS/DOS, OS/2
- Network compatibility: Novell
- Networked-based computer fax solution for sending, receiving, viewing and managing fax messages. Includes fax board, fax server software and fax client software for DOS and Windows users.

PureFax Plus Fax Server

Pure Data, Inc.
1740 S. I-35
Carrollton, TX 75006
800-662-8210, 214-242-2040
fax: 214-242-9487

- Price: $995
- Date announced: 1993
- Network compatibility: Ethernet, Token-Ring
- Shareable devices: Facsimile

ISDN Adapters and Equipment

Pipeline 50 Workgroup Access Server

Ascend Communications, Inc.
1275 Harbor Bay Pkwy.
Alameda, CA 94502
800-ASCEND-4, 510-769-6001
fax: 510-814-2300

- Price: $1,495–$1,695
- Date announced: 1994
- Description: Ethernet to BRI ISDN router
- Local or remote: Remote
- Configuration: Stand-alone
- Number of LAN interfaces: 1
- Network compatibility: Ethernet
- IEEE standard: IEEE-802.3 10Base2, 10BaseT
- LAN speed: 10 Mbps
- Protocols supported: IP, IPX, PPP
- Number of WAN interfaces: 1
- Serial interfaces supported: T1, ISDN, 56 Kbps services

Everyware STD/BRI Bridge CB-400
Combinet, Inc.
333 W. El Camino Real
Sunnyvale, CA 94087
800-967-6651, 408-522-9020
fax: 408-522-4600

- Price: $2,190
- Date announced: 1991
- Description: ISDN BRI to Ethernet bridge
- Local or remote: Remote
- Number of LAN interfaces: 1
- Network compatibility: Ethernet
- Media type: Thin coax; UTP
- LAN speed: 10 Mbps
- Number of WAN interfaces: 1
- Serial interfaces supported: RS-232
- Packet filtering rate: 14,400 pps

PC IMAC
DigiBoard
6400 Flying Cloud Dr.
Eden Prairie, MN 55344-3322
800-344-4273, 612-943-9020
Direct Sales: 800-437-7241

- Price: $795–$895
- Date announced: 1993
- Description: ISDN Terminal adapters
- Compatibility: ISA, EISA, MCA
- Line access standard: Basic Rate Interface (2B+D)
- Physical interfaces supported: RJ-45
- Central office switch supported: AT&T 5ESS, Northern Telecom DMS-100
- Command set: Hayes AT
- Additional Features: Circuit switched data

IMAC
DigiBoard
6400 Flying Cloud Dr.
Eden Prairie, MN 55344-3322
800-344-4273, 612-943-9020
Direct Sales: 800-437-7241

- Price: $1,695
- Date announced: 1991
- Network compatibility: Ethernet
- Configuration: Stand-alone
- Serial interfaces supported: RS-232
- Number of LAN interfaces: 1
- LAN speed: 10 Mbps
- IEEE standard: IEEE-802.3 10Base2, 10Base5, 10BaseT
- Number of WAN interfaces: 1
- Packet filtering rate: 14,400 pps
- Packet forwarding rate: 250 pps
- Additional features: Inverse multiplexing, ISDN protocol analysis, IP host

LD-LAN E-101
Extension Technology Corp.
30 Hollis St.
Framingham, MA 01701-8616
800-856-2672, 508-872-7748

- Price: $1,195
- Description: ISDN Terminal Adapters
- Date Announced: 1992
- Compatibility: ISA
- Line access standard: Basic Rate Interface (2B+D)
- Physical interfaces supported: RS-232C
- Rate adaptation standard: V.120
- Central office switch supported: AT&T 5ESS, Northern Telecom DMS-100

LD-LAN E-201

Extension Technology Corp.
30 Hollis St.
Framingham, MA 01701-8616
800-856-2672, 508-872-7748

- Price: $1,495
- Description: ISDN Terminal Adapters
- Date Announced: 1992
- Compatibility: EISA
- Line access standard: Basic Rate Interface (2B+D)
- Physical interfaces supported: RS-232C
- Rate adaption standard: V.120
- Central office switch supported: AT&T 5ESS, Northern Telecom DMS-100

LANline 5240I

Gandalf Systems Corp.
9 North Olney Ave., Cherry Hill
Industrial Center-9
Cherry Hill, NY 08003-1688
800-Gandalf, 609-424-9400
fax: 609-751-4376

- Price: $2,695
- Date announced: 1994
- Description: Bridge to Ethernet
- Local or remote: Remote
- Configuration: Stand-alone
- Number of LAN interfaces: 1
- Network compatibility: Ethernet
- LAN speed: 10 Mbps
- Number of WAN interfaces: 1
- Serial interfaces supported: RS-232, V.35
- Additional functions: Integral ISDN terminal adapter

ISDN PC Adapter

Hayes Microcomputer Products, Inc.
5835 Peachtree Corners, E
Norcross, GA 30092-3405
800-96-HAYES, 404-840-9200
fax: 404-441-1213

- Price: $1,199
- Date announced: 1990
- Compatibility: ISA
- Line access standard: Basic Rate Interface (2B+D)
- Reference point: S/T Interface
- Physical interfaces supported: RJ-11
- Rate adaption standard: V.120
- Central office switch supported: AT&T 5ESS, Northern Telecom DMS-100, National ISDN-1
- Command set: Hayes AT
- Additional features: Circuit switched data, packet switched data, built-in diagnostics

RemoteExpress ISDN LAN Adapter

Intel Corp.
5200 NE Elam Young Pkwy.
Hillsboro, OR 97124-6497
800-538-3373, 503-629-7354
fax: 503-629-7580

- Price: $499
- Date Announced: 1994
- Compatibility: ISA
- Line access standard: Basic Rate Interface (2B+D)
- Physical interfaces supported: RS-232C

Network Operating Systems

LANtastic (V.6.0)
Artisoft, Inc.
2202 N. Forbes Blvd.
Tucson, AZ 85745
800-846-9762, 602-670-7100
fax: 602-670-7101

• Peer-to-peer LAN that connects up to 500 users. Provides printer, disk, CD-ROM, and file sharing, as well as e-mail and local and network disk backup. Supports NetBIOS–compatible adapters, chat and voice mail with sounding board adapters on each PC. Includes resource caching and a despooling feature.

CorStream
Artisoft, Inc.
2202 N. Forbes Blvd.
Tucson, AZ 85745
800-846-9762, 602-670-7100
fax: 602-670-7101

• Server for the LANtastic operating system that combines LANtastic NLM and Novell NetWare OS. Provides fault tolerance, file system/media management, mission-critical reliability, and applications capability. Built on 32-bit multitasking, multithread OS, and can seek data across multiple disk drives. Allows user to install as much memory as needed for optimal throughput.

VINES (V.5.54)
Banyan Systems, Inc.
120 Flanders Rd.
Westboro, MA 01581-1033
800-222-6926, 508-898-1000
fax: 508-898-1755

• Integrated, distributed network OS for local or global internetworking and management of PCs, minicomputers and mainframes. Creates enterprise-wide, multivendor networks. Offers transparent WAN and LAN bridging. Provides fine-grained security, expanded printer support, and high-capacity disk support.

OS/2 LAN Server (V.3.01)
IBM
Old Orchard Rd.
Armonk, NY 10504
800-426-3333, 914-765-1900

• Supports OS/2 Requestor portion of IBM's OS/2 Extended Edition (V.1.2). Includes most of Microsoft LAN Manager's capabilities. Supports 16- and 32-bit OSs. Provides double-byte character set, Windows support, and OEM enabling, as well as disk mirroring/duplexing and local server security. CD-ROM version available.

InvisibleLAN (V.3.44)
Invisible Software, Inc.
1142 Chess Dr.
Foster City, CA 94404
800-982-2962, 415-570-5967
fax: 415-570-6017

• Peer-to-peer network OS. Designed for use over industry-standard coaxial cable and twisted-pair wiring. Operates with both DOS and Windows. Includes expanded memory managers, menu-driven or command-line installation and initialization, online help, disk-caching utilities, file sharing, printer spooling, e-mail, security and automatic reconnection.

Windows NT
Microsoft Corp.
One Microsoft Way
Redmond, WA 98052-6399
800-426-9400, 206-882-8080
fax: 206-883-8101

• Client/server 32-bit preemptive multitasking OS. Runs 32-bit, MS-DOS, Windows, POSIX and character-based OS/2 1.X applications. Accesses up to 2GB of virtual memory per application and terabytes of storage. Includes event viewer for monitoring the system, security and applications event logs, and an event logger for displaying details. Provides point-and-click access to file manager, printer manager, control panel, user manager, disk administrator, event viewer, performance monitor, backup, and command prompt.

NetWare (V.4.2)
Novell, Inc.
122 East 1700 South
Provo, UT 84606-6194
800-453-1267, 801-379-7000
fax: 801-429-5155

• LAN OS. Various levels for enterprise-wide and workgroup computing. Provides user transparent connectivity, internetworking capabilities, multiple remote connections, LAN-to-host communications, data protection, resource accounting, security, and programming tools. Available on CD-ROM.

PowerLAN
Performance Technology
800 Lincoln Ctr, 7800 I-10, W, Suite 800
San Antonio, TX 78230
800-443-LANS, 210-979-2000
fax: 210-979-2002

• Peer-to-peer network OS that supports up to 255 users. Features printer sharing and network disk sharing, low memory requirements, administrative tools, and printing capabilities.

Network Management Suites

Monitrix—The Network Manager (V.3.0)
Cheyenne Software, Inc.
3 Expressway Plaza
Rosyln, NY 11577
800-243-9462, 516-484-5110
fax: 516-484-3446

• Network management VAP or NLM. Tracks file server, network printers, and individual network nodes. Provides alarm capabilities to indicate when disk-drive capacity drops below a certain threshold, when printer goes off-line, or when a problem with a network node is detected. Performs diagnostic tests by checking transmission paths between two network nodes. Offers topology map.

Lanscope (V.2.1d3)
Connect Computer Co., Inc.
9855 West 78th St., Suite 270
Eden Prairie, MN 55344
612-944-0181
fax: 612-944-9298

• LAN management system. Provides menuing security, usage tracking, software-usage control, network resource management, printer spooling, user productivity, and network management. Modules include menuing system, Audit Trail, Hot Key Workstation Utilities, and Turnstyle Software Metering.

Frye Utilities for Networks—NetWare Management (V.2.0)
Frye Computer Systems, Inc.
19 Temple Pl.
Boston, MA 02111-9779
800-234-3793, 617-451-5400
fax: 617-451-6711

• Allows user to retrieve and edit information needed to troubleshoot, diagnose, and manage network. Edits and updates Syscon, Pconsole, Fconsole, Printcon, Printdef, Volinfo and Filer information. Offers detailed explanations of all errors and terms and recommendations for solutions. Provides a single screen to show all the server's user activity in real-time graphic, numeric, and text formats.

Brightwork Utilities for Netware (V.1.0)
McAfee Associates, Inc.
2710 Walsh Ave., Suite 200
Santa Clara, CA 95051-0963
800-866-6585, 408-988-3832
fax: 408-970-9727

• Suite of applications for small and medium-sized LANs. Tracks network software and hardware. Allows user to support and troubleshoot Windows or DOS workstations on a LAN. Monitors system performance, security, capacity, and configuration. Provides LAN users with access to printers attached to any PC on the network.

LANalyzer Network Analyzer
Novell, Inc.
2180 Fortune Dr.
San Jose, CA 95131
800-243-8526, 408-434-2300
fax: 408-435-1706

• Provides protocol analysis to mid-sized networks. Captures network packet data on NetWare 3.X LANs and performs limited amount of decoding. Troubleshoots IBM mainframes and AS/400 computers, networked applications running on IBM equipment, and related front-end devices.

SaberLAN Workstation (V.5.0)
Saber Software Corp.
5944 Luther Lane, Suite 1007
Dallas, TX 75225
800-338-8754, 214-361-8086
fax: 214-361-1882

• Integrated set of Network utilities. Provides tools for designing customized menus, tracking software licenses, managing disk space, and catching potential trouble spots. Offers graphical and object-oriented front end to Windows. Includes printer management utilities for DOS and Windows.

Norton Administrator for Networks (V.1.0)
Symantec Corp.
10201 Torre Ave.
Cupertino, CA 95014-2132
800-441-7234, 408-253-9600
fax: 408-446-9750

- Allows network managers to control software and hardware inventory, distribute software, and manage licensing system security and antivirus protection from a central console. Automatically builds a database of information each time a user logs onto a machine, capturing information on system resources and configuration.

Printer Sharing Devices (Data Switches)

PrintDirector Silver Series
Digital Products, Inc.
411 Waverly Oaks
Waltham, MA 02154
800-243-2333, 617-647-1234
fax: 617-647-4474

- Price: $595–$1,695
- Number installed to date: 3,000
- Date announced: 1990
- Allows multiple PCs to share multiple printers. Provides 1 to 4MB print buffer. Available in 6-, 10-, and 16-port configurations.

Data Switches
Rose Electronics
10850 Wilcrest, Suite 900
Houston, TX 77099
800-333-9343, 713-933-7673
fax: 713-933-0044

- An extensive family of printer-sharing devices.

Data Switches
Western Telematic, Inc.
5 Sterling
Irvine, CA 92718-2517
800-854-7226, 714-586-9950
fax: 714-583-9514

- An extensive family of printer-sharing devices.

TCP/IP and Related Products

LANtastic for TCP/IP (V.2.1)
Artisoft, Inc.
2202 N. Forbes Blvd.
Tucson AZ 85745
800-846-9726, 602-670-7100
fax: 602-670-7101

- Provides terminal emulators that enable users to access applications, share printers, and transfer and manipulate files residing on remote hosts as if users were directly connected.

BW-Connect NFS for Windows NT
Beame & Whiteside Software, Inc.
706 Hillsborough St.
Raleigh, NC 27603-1655
800-INFO-NFS, 919-831-8989
fax: 919-831-8990

• 32-bit multithread kernel implementation of NFS client. Allows Windows NT users to access file and print resources on other systems using NFS protocol. Includes client/server TCP/IP applications such as FTP and Telnet.

SNMPc (V.3.3)
Castle Rock Computing, Inc.
20863 Stevens Creek Blvd., Suite 530
Cupertino, CA 95014
800-331-7667, 408-366-6540
fax: 408-252-2379

• Incorporates Simple Network Management Protocol (SNMP) to help user oversee TCP/IP networks by monitoring network performance and status and by reporting on network faults. Provides a hierarchical map of the network that graphically displays each node and network segment. Part of the map is always displayed in the main window, which can be scaled and moved at any time. Includes real-time graphical or tabular display of counters that trigger alarms when preset limits of network elements are exceeded. Works in Microsoft Windows environment.

Super TCP for Windows
Frontier Technologies Corp.
10201 N. Port Washington Road
Mequon, WI 53092
414-241-4555
fax: 414-241-7084

• TCP/IP connectivity package for Windows. Features Windows DLL, Windows sockets API, NFS client/server, FTP/TFTP client/server, multisession VT320 tn3270, e-Mail, WinSock 1.1 compliancy, News Reader, NetPrint, Talk, fax client/server, SNMP/MIB and SLIP.

TCP/Connect II for Windows
InterCon Systems Corp.
950 Herndon Pkwy., Suite 420
Herndon VA 22070
800-638-2968, 703-709-5500
fax: 703-709-5555

• Allows Windows users to communicate with varied computer systems using TCP/IP protocols. Provides terminal emulation, file transfer, e-mail, electronic news, print services and SNMP agent. Implemented as a DLL. Provides VT220 and tn3270 terminal emulation.

cc:Mail Link to SMTP
Lotus Development Corp. (cc:Mail Division)
800 W. El Camino Real
Mountain View, CA 94040
800-448-2500, 415-961-8800
fax: 415-961-0840

• Provides communication link between cc:Mail users of Simple Mail Transfer Protocol-based mail systems. Enables users to prepare and send messages as if they were sending to someone on the same e-mail system. Works as a TCP/IP node connected to an

Ethernet network. Includes all TCP/IP and FTP software required on PC side. Users can communicate with users of Unix Mail, Internet, Bitnet, IBM PROFS, DEC VMSmail, DEC VAX All-In-1, DG AOS/VS Mail, and HP DeskMate. Transfers binary and text files and fax items as mail attachments.

PC/TCP Network Software
FTP Software, Inc.
2 High St.
North Andover, MA 01845-2620
800-282-4FTP, 508-685-4000
fax: 508-794-4488

• Communicates with computers supporting the TCP/IP family of protocols. Contains utilities for file transfer, terminal emulation, mail, NFS file sharing, remote backup, printing, and network testing.

TCP/IP for OS/2 EE (V.1.1)
IBM
Old Orchard Rd.
Armonk, NY 10504
800-426-3333, 914-765-1900

• Allows an OS/2 EE V.1.2 system attached to an IBM Token-Ring, IEEE 802.3 LAN, or Ethernet V.2 LAN to interoperate with other systems in TCP/IP networks. Incorporates Transmission Control Protocol (TCP), Internet Protocol (IP), Internet Control Messaging Protocol (ICMP), TELNET client/server, Simple Mail Transfer Protocol (SMTP) client/server, Trivial File Transfer Protocol (TFTP) client/server, and remote execution client/server. IBM number 73F6071, 73F6072, 73F6073, 73F6074, 73F6075.

LAN Workplace
Novell, Inc.
122 East 1700 South
Provo, UT 84606-6194
800-453-1267, 801-429-7000
fax: 801-429-5155

• Provides users with concurrent access to LANs and TCP/IP hosts. Gives access to Unix systems and other network resources using the TCP/IP protocol suite.

OpenConnect/FTP
OpenConnect Systems Corp.
2711 LBJ Freeway, Suite 800
Dallas, TX 75234-6400
214-484-5200
fax: 214-484-6400

• Allows bidirectional file transfer between IBM systems and TCP/IP hosts in Interactive and Batch mode. FTP Server allows file transfer to and from TCP/IP hosts and supports log-on security validation as well as binary and ASCII file transfers.

SmarTerm
Persoft, Inc.
465 Science Dr.
Madison, WI 53744-4953
800-EMU-LATE, 608-273-6000
fax: 608-273-8227

• Emulates DEC VT320, 220, 100, 52, and TTY. Includes ASCII, binary file transfer, and Kermit, Xmodem, and PDIP error-free file transfer as well as background operations, softkeys, pop-up windows, and 132-column support. Also includes LAT protocol and TELNET with support for multiple sessions and named services for popular PC implementations of TCP/IP, including

Wollongong's WIN/TCP and Excelan's LAN Workplace for DOS.

TCP
3Com Corp.
PO Box 58145, 5400 Bayfront Plaza
Santa Clara, CA 95052-8145
800-638-3266, 408-764-5000
fax: 408-764-5001

• Allows PCs to communicate and share resources within diversified TCP/IP environments. Allows users to link to TCP resources while still maintaining connections to NetWare and other workgroup servers.

Chameleon
UniPress Software, Inc.
2025 Lincoln Hwy. Suite 209
Edison, NJ 08817
800-222-0550, 908-287-2100
fax: 908-287-4929

• TCP/IP package for MS Windows. Includes terminal emulation, file transfer, advanced networking, chameleon NFS, electronic mail, and NetRoute IP router.

TCP Connection
Walker Richer and Quinn, Inc.
1500 Dexter Ave., N
Seattle, WA 98109-3051
800-872-2550, 206-217-7500
fax: 206-217-0293

• Add-on for WRQ's Reflection package. Designed for PC-to-host connections using TCP/IP networking software. Includes TCP/IP stack and LAT and Telnet Connections.

3270 Terminal Emulation Products

Extra! Connectivity Software: Entry Level
Attachmate Corp.
3617 131st Ave., SE
Bellevue, WA 98006-1332
800-426-6283, 206-644-4010
fax: 206-747-9924

• Provides 3270 terminal single-session functions with low memory usage. Includes file transfer, screen print, and program interfaces. Connects to mainframe via coaxial cable, LAN, modem, or Token-Ring interface coupler.

IRMA
Digital Communications Associates, Inc. (DCA)
1000 Alderman Dr.
Alpharetta, GA 30202-4199
800-348-3221, 404-442-4000
fax: 404-442-4366

• Communications software that supports a variety of connections to SNA hosts and peer computers. Provides 10, 3270 sessions, IBM IND$FILE file transfer support, 3287 print emulator, and DCA productivity features.

Access for Windows 3270/5250 (V.3.21)
Eicon Technology Corp.
2196 32nd Ave.
Montreal, QB, CD H8T 3H7
800-803-4266, 514-631-2592
fax: 514-631-3092

• Terminal display and printer emulation product for Windows desktops. Includes file transfer and support for multiple gateways and direct connections to host. Supports host-based graphics along with multiple document interface and IBM EHLLAPI interface.

PC 3270 Emulation (V.3.0)
IBM
Old Orchard Rd.
Armonk, NY 10504
800-426-3333, 914-765-1900

• Allows PCs to emulate IBM 3270 display terminals, transfer files with host, automate processes via emulator APIs and function as a LAN gateway. Supports IPX/SPX and TCP/IP.

MicroGate 3270/SNA
MicroGate Corp.
9501 Capital of Texas Hwy., Suite 105
Austin, TX 78759
800-444-1982, 512-345-7791
fax: 512-343-9046

• Provides remote 3270 terminal emulation for PCs. Remote PCs can access SNA hosts to conduct on-line 3270 sessions. Includes a script language for automating date entry and background IND$FILE file transfer and High-Level Application Program Interface. Supports SyncLink communications cards and modems.

TN3270 for LAN WorkPlace
Novell, Inc.
122 East 1700 South
Provo, UT 84606
800-453-1267, 801-429-7000
fax: 801-429-5155

• Add-on to the LAN WorkPlace product. Provides DOS and Windows users with virtual terminal service to an IBM environment. Allows users to log into an IBM mainframe as a 3270 terminal and run Telnet sessions. Includes IBM 3270 terminal emulator and API.

Rexxterm (V.2.3)
Quercus Systems
PO Box 2157
Saratoga, CA 95070-0157
408-867-7399

• Provides VT100 and 3270 terminal emulation and supports Xmodem, Ymodem, Zmodem, Kermit, and CompuServe-B file transfer protocols. Uses the REXX scripting language. Includes ASCII file upload capability, a built-in editor, a data capture buffer, host mode, keyboard reconfiguration, and unlimited dialing directory files.

Rumba (V.3.0)
Wall Data, Inc.
17769 Northeast 78th Pl.
Redmond, WA 98052
800-487-8622, 206-883-4777
fax: 206-861-3175

• A Windows communications program. Lets a PC act as a distributed function terminal and supports extended data streams. Runs multiple 3270 mainframe sessions while maintaining applications in other windows, and gives data-sharing capability to applications running in Windows. Facilitates file transfers and macro customization. Features Hotlinks, which updates data downloaded from host into a Windows application, and Hotspots, which allows users of local Windows programs to execute mainframe functions or previously created macros by clicking on corresponding menu items. Uses 39K of RAM for the first session and 25K for each additional session. EGA or higher video adapter required.

Zero Slot LAN Products

Coactive Connector
Coactive Computing Corp.
1301 Shoreway Rd., Suite 221
Belmont, CA 94002
800-488-1717, 415-802-1080

- Price: $150
- Date announced: 1993
- External module designed to enable printer and file sharing between PCs and/or Apple Macintoshes. Includes DOS and Windows software. Attaches to the PC's parallel port and supports up to 32 computers. Allows the network to operate at distances of up to 1,000 feet.

Timbuktu for Windows (V.1.1)
Farallon Computing, Inc.
2470 Mariner Square Loop
Alameda, CA 94501-1010
800-425-4141, 510-814-5100
fax: 510-814-5020

- Provides network-based, cross-platform information exchange and resource sharing for Windows systems and Macintoshes. Allows users to share information on Ethernet and LocalTalk networks. Includes Farallon's PhoneNet PC version 3.0, which provides underlying connection for AppleTalk.

LapLink V
Traveling Software, Inc.
18702 N. Creek Pkwy.
Bothell, WA 98011
800-343-8080, 206-483-8088
fax: 206-487-1284

- File transfer that can be used remotely via modems or network. Features pull-down menus and includes Traveling's Universal Communications Object, which allows two PCs to communicate regardless of the hardware connecting them. Corporate version available.

LAN Analysis Products

Traffic Monitoring Software
LT Stat (V.3.0)
Blue Lance, Inc.
1700 West Loop South, Suite 1100
Houston, TX 77027
800-TKO-BLUE, 713-680-1187
fax: 713-622-1370

- LAN utility that manages disk utilization, security, and system configuration. Generates reports including server, user and group configuration, trustee assignment, accounting reports, effective rights, menu file, NetWare message and error, log-in scripts, directory, volume and user utilization, duplicate file, and last updated file.

FRESH Utilities (V.2.3)

Fresh Technology Group
1478 N. Tech Blvd., Suite 101
Gilbert, AZ 85234
800-545-8324, 602-497-4200
fax: 602-497-4242

• Assortment of 11 utility programs designed to allow network administrators or users to monitor activity and maximize productivity on a network. Includes online help. Enables network administrators to generate reports on the activity of server, groups, users, and queues. Command-line utilities include FTLight, FTLogout, FTDirsiz, and others.

LANWatch Network Analyzer (V.3.1)

FTP Software, Inc.
2 High St.
North Andover, MA 01845-2620
800-282-4FTP, 508-685-4000
fax: 508-794-4488

• Network analyzer for LANs. Useful for developing and debugging protocols and for installing, troubleshooting, and monitoring networks. Includes an analyzer that increases the amount of data, speed, and ways to manipulate data.

BindView Network Control System (NCS) (V.3.5)

The LAN Support Group, Inc.
2425 Fountainview Dr., Suite 390
Houston, TX 77057
800-749-8439, 713-789-0881

• Management and reporting utility for Novell NetWare LANs. Prints custom-tailored, professional audit and management reports detailing file server configurations. Documents system configuration and user configuration data as a safeguard against lost or damaged bindery. Allows customization.

TXD (TC8310) (V.1.01)

Thomas-Conrad Corp.
1908R Kramer Lane
Austin, TX 78758
800-332-8683, 512-836-1935
fax: 512-836-2840

• Analyzes network performance and diagnoses problems on Novell NetWare LANs. Determines internetwork configuration, interrogates all nodes, analyzes critical data from one or all nodes, and reports unusual activity levels with interpretations of what the levels represent. Executes point-to-point communication testing.

NetProbe

3Com Corp.
3165 Kifer Rd.
Santa Clara, CA 95052-8145
800-638-3266, 408-562-6400
fax: 408-970-1112

• Network analyzer designed for pinpointing problems in Ethernet and Token-Ring networks. Locates non-responding workstations, internet route malfunctions, network failures, and overloaded network servers. Requires 3Com's EtherLink, EtherLink Plus, or TokenLink adapter board.

Network Traffic Analyzers

LANProbe II
Hewlett-Packard Co.
3000 Hanover St.
Palo Alto, CA 94304-1181
800-752-0900, 415-857-1501
fax: 800-333-1917

- Price: $2,995–$3,995
- Date announced: 1994
- Function: Protocol analyzer
- Protocols supported: Ethernet, Token-Ring
- Power provision: Through interface

Pentascanner
MicroTest, Inc.
4747 North 22nd St.
Phoenix, AZ 85016-4708
800-526-9675, 602-952-6400
fax: 602-952-6401

- Price: $4,195
- Date announced: 1993
- Function: Protocol analyzer
- Packaging: Portable/handheld
- Protocols supported: 10BaseT, 10Base2, 4 Mbps Token-Ring, 16 Mbps Token-Ring, ARCnet, Fast Ethernet, AppleTalk, ATM
- Interfaces supported: T1, F1, ISDN
- Visual monitors provided: Backlit LCDs
- Printer interface provided: No
- Disk storage provided: No

Expert Sniffer Portable Analyzer
Network General Corp.
4200 Bohannon Dr.
Menlo Park, CA 94025
800-695-8251, 415-473-2000
fax: 415-321-0855

- Date announced: 1994
- Function: Protocol analyzer
- Packaging: Desktop/stand-alone
- Protocols supported: Token-Ring, Ethernet, FDDI
- Interfaces supported: RS-232C
- Visual monitors provided: Compaq DeskPro 486/66, 486/66M display
- Power provision: AC and battery
- Printer interface provided: Yes
- Disk storage provided: Yes

LAN Remote Control Software

Remotely Possible/LAN for Windows (V.4.0)
Avalan Technology
116 Hopping Brooke Park
Holliston, MA 01746
800-441-2281, 508-429-6482
fax: 508-429-3179

- Native Windows LAN remote control software that allows master PC on any network to remotely control slave PC via mouse. Features multiple levels of password protection and user ID.

NETremote+ (V.5.2)
McAfee Associates, Inc.
2710 Walsh Ave., Suite 200
Santa Clara, CA 95051-0963
800-866-6585, 408-988-3832
fax: 408-970-9727

• Remote access and user support software for LAN. Allows network manager to provide instant support for users anywhere on a LAN or WAN by viewing the remote user's screen and controlling the remote user's keyboard. Includes built-in diagnostics and an async module that lets user dial into or out of the network.

Remote2 (V.3.0)
DCA
1000 Alderman Dr.
Alpharetta, GA 30202
800-348-3221, 404-442-4000
fax: 404-442-4366

• Allows remote operation of PC and software from any location via terminal or PC. Supports CrossTalk and Xmodem file transfers. Includes a guard utility that allows the host user to restrict access of guests to drives, directories, and individual files.

ReachOut/Network (V.4.0)
Ocean Isle Software, Inc.
1201 19th Pl., 2nd Floor
Vero Beach, FL 32960-0631
800-677-6232, 407-770-4777
fax: 407-770-4779

• Remote control application that allows an administrator to monitor and control a client and to pinpoint and fix problems on a user's PC without leaving the desk. Features include remote mouse support, a chat window, pull-down point and shoot menus, and context-sensitive help.

Norton pcAnywhere/LAN (V.4.5)
Symantec Corp.
10201 Torre Ave.
Cupertino, CA 95014-2132
800-441-7234, 408-253-9600
fax: 408-446-9750

• PC-to-PC remote communications software for network-based PC users. Permits one workstation to control another on a LAN and to control communications with off-site PCs, laptops, and terminals.

Close-Up/LAN—The Network Remote
Norton-Lambert Corp.
PO Box 4085
Santa Barbara, CA 93140
805-964-6767
fax: 805-683-5679

• Allows a user to share screens and keyboards with one, many, or all users on a network. Enables users on a LAN to share printers, modems, faxes, and computers. Can be used for teaching, training, and conferencing.

CO/Session LAN II (V.6.2)
Triton Technologies, Inc.
200 Middlesex Turnpike
Iselin, NJ 08830
800-322-9440, 201-855-9440
fax: 201-855-9608

• Remote control software that allows remote users to run local applications and exchange files on home office LANs.

LAN Remote Comm Servers

LAN Distance
IBM
Old Orchard Rd.
Armonk, NY 10504
800-426-3333, 914-765-1900

• Allows a portable computer or remote PC to access a LAN as if it were on a network. Consists of the LAN Distance Remote and the LAN Distance Connection Server.

LANexpress Remote LAN Access System (V.1.0)
Microcom, Inc.
500 River Ridge Dr.
Norwood, MA 2062-5028
800-822-8224, 617-551-1000
fax: 617-551-1021

• Hardware/software package that lets mobile users dial into their host LANs via cellular or land lines and launch remote nodes and remote control applications from the Windows interface on one call. Includes LANexpress Remote, LANexpress Server, eight built-in DeskPorte Fast or TravelPort modems, expressWatch, SNMP-based management software, and Microcom's Carbon Copy for Windows.

LANRover
Shiva Corp.
63 Third Ave., Northwest Park
Burlington, MA 01803
800-458-3550, 617-270-8300
fax: 617-270-8599

• Provides remote access to NetWare, TCP/IP, or NetBEUI protocols. Available with four or eight external modems.

NetModem/E
Shiva Corp.
63 Third Ave., Northwest Park
Burlington, MA 01803
800-458-3550, 617-270-8300
fax: 617-270-8599

• Remote access to NetWare protocols via V.42 bis/V.32 bis modems.

Network Access Servers

Communique
CommVision
510 Logue Ave.
Mountain View, CA 94043
800-832-6526, 415-254-5720
fax: 415-254-9320

• Price: $11,495–$16,495
• Network compatibility: Ethernet
• LAN speed: 10 Mbps
• Shareable devices: Integrated NetWare based remote node, remote control dial-in/out, gateway, fax, e-mail, and bulletin board services

ERS/FT
Cubix Corp.
2800 Lockheed Way
Carson City, NV 89706 0719
800-829-0554, 702-883-7611
fax: 702-882-2407

• Price: $23,000
• Multiple CPUs in a single cabinet

ChatterBox/Plus
J&L Information Systems, Inc.
9600 Topanga Canyon Blvd.
Chatsworth, CA 91311
818-709-1778
fax: 818-882-1424

- Price: $2,695–$5,095
- Shareable devices: Printer, modem,
  hard disk
- Network compatibility: Ethernet,
  Token-Ring
- LAN speed: 4, 10, 16 Mbps

■ ˉGlossary

access method   A protocol that determines which device in a local area network has access to the transmission media at any instant. CSMA/CD is an example of an access method. IBM uses the same term for specific kinds of communications software that include protocols for exchanging data, constructing files, and other functions.

access protocol   The traffic rules that LAN workstations abide by to avoid data collisions when sending signals over shared network media; also referred to as the *media-access control (MAC) protocol*. Common examples are carrier sense multiple access (CSMA) and token passing.

ACK   A positive acknowledgment control character. This character is exchanged between system components when data has been received without error. The control character is also used as an affirmative response for setting up a communications exchange. ACK is also used as the name of a message containing an acknowledgment.

acoustic coupler   The portion of a modem that physically holds a telephone handset in two rubber cups. The cups house a small microphone and speaker that "talk" and "listen" to the telephone handset.

ADCCP (Advanced Data Communications Control Procedures)   A bit-oriented ANSI-standard communications protocol. It is a link-layer protocol.

A/D converter   A device that converts analog signals to digital.

address   A unique memory location. Network interface cards and CPUs often use shared addresses in RAM to move data from each card to the PC's processor. The term can also refer to the unique identifier for a particular node in a network.

Address Resolution Protocol (ARP)   A protocol within the Transmission Control Protocol/Internet Protocol (TCP/IP) suite that "maps" IP addresses to Ethernet addresses. TCP/IP requires ARP for use with Ethernet.

Advanced Communications Function (ACF)   An IBM program package to allow sharing computer resources through communications links. It supports SNA.

Advanced Communications Service   A large data communications network developed by AT&T.

AFP (AppleTalk File Protocol)   Apple's network protocol, used to provide access between file servers and clients in an AppleShare network. AFP is also used by Novell's products for the Macintosh.

alphanumeric   Characters made up of letters and numbers; usually contrasted with graphics characters made up of dots in terminal emulation.

analog   Commonly refers to transmission methods developed to transmit voice signals. These methods were designed only for the bandwidth of the human voice (up to about 3 kHz); this limits their capability to pass high-speed digital signals.

ANSI (American National Standards Institute)   An organization that develops and publishes standards for codes, alphabets, and signaling schemes.

API (application program interface)   A set of standard software interrupts, calls, and data formats that application programs use to initiate contact with network services, mainframe communications programs, or other program-to-program communications. For example, applications use APIs to call services that transport data across a network.

APPC (Advanced Program-to-Program Communications)   An IBM protocol analogous to the OSI model's session layer; it sets up the necessary conditions that enable application programs to send data to each other through the network.

APPC/PC   An IBM product that implements APPC on a PC.

AppleTalk   An Apple networking system that can transfer data at a rate of 230 kilobytes per second over shielded twisted-pair wire. Superseded by the term *LocalTalk*.

application layer   The highest (seventh) level of the OSI model. It describes the way that application programs interact with the network operating system.

applications processor   A special-purpose computer that enables a telephone system to furnish special services such as voice mail, messaging services, and electronic mail.

ARCnet (Attached Resources Computing)   A networking architecture (marketed by Datapoint Corp. and other vendors) using a token-passing bus architecture, usually on coaxial cable.

ARPANET (Advanced Research Projects Agency Network)   A network originally sponsored by the Defense Advanced Research Projects Agency (DARPA) to link universities and government research centers. The TCP/IP protocols were pioneered on ARPANET.

ARQ   A control code that calls for the retransmission of a block of data.

ASCII (American Standard Code for Information Interchange)   The data alphabet used in the IBM PC to determine the composition of the 7-bit string of 0s and 1s that represents each character (alphabetic, numeric, or special).

ASR (automatic send/receive)   A term left over from teleprinters that punched messages on paper tape. Now, it is sometimes used to indicate any terminal that has a storage capability.

asynchronous   A method of transmission in which the time intervals between characters do not have to be equal. Start and stop bits are added to coordinate the transfer of characters.

attenuation   The decrease in power of a signal transmitted over a wire, measured in decibels. As attenuation increases, the signal decreases.

automatic number identification (ANI)   A feature that passes a caller's ten-digit telephone number over the network to the customer's premises so that the caller can be identified.

background program (background mode)   A program that performs its functions while the user is working with a different program. Communications programs often operate in background mode. They can receive messages while the user works with other programs. The messages are stored for later display.

balun (BALanced UNbalanced)   An impedance-matching device that connects a balanced line (such as a twisted-pair line) and an unbalanced line (such as a coaxial cable).

bandwidth   The range of frequencies a circuit will pass. Analog circuits typically have a bandwidth limited to that of the human voice (about 300 Hz to 3 kHz). The square waves of a digital signal require a higher bandwidth. The higher the transmission rate, the greater the bandwidth requirement. Fiber-optic and coaxial cables have excellent bandwidths. Also, in common usage, *bandwidth* refers to the upper limit of the rate that information can be transferred over a network.

base address   The first address in a series of addresses in memory, often used to describe the beginning of a network interface card's I/O space.

baseband   A network that transmits signals as a direct-current pulse rather than as variations in a radio-frequency signal.

basic-rate interface (BRI)   The ISDN standard governing how a customer's desktop terminals and telephones can connect to the ISDN switch. It specifies two B-channels that allow 64-kilobit-per-second simultaneous voice and data service, and one D-channel that carries call information and customer data at 16 kbps.

baud   A measure of transmission speed; the reciprocal of the time duration of the shortest signal element in a transmission. In RS-232C ASCII, the signaling element is 1 bit.

BBS (bulletin board system)   An electronic message system.

BCD (binary-coded decimal)   A coding scheme using a 6-bit (six-level) code.

B-channel   A "bearer" channel that carries voice or data at 64 kilobits per second in either direction and is circuit-switched.

benchmark test   A program used to measure system speed or throughput.

Bindery   A database maintained by Novell's NetWare operating system that holds information on users, servers, and other elements of the network.

Bisynchronous Communications   Also abbreviated as BSC, this protocol is one of the two commonly used methods of encoding data for transmission between devices in IBM mainframe computer systems. Data characters are gathered in a package called a *frame,* which is marked by 2 synchronization bits (bisync). The more modern protocol is SDLC.

bit   The smallest unit of information. In digital signaling, this commonly refers to a 0 or a 1.

block   A number of characters transmitted as a group.

BNC connector   A small coaxial connector with a half-twist locking shell.

boot ROM   A read-only memory chip allowing a workstation to communicate with the file server and to read a DOS boot program from the server. Stations can thus operate on the network without having a disk drive.

bps   Bits per second.

bridge   An interconnection device, sometimes working within a PC and sometimes within a special-purpose computer, that can connect LANs using similar or dissimilar data links such as Ethernet, Token-Ring, and X.25. Bridges link LANs at the data-link layer of the OSI model. Modern bridges read and filter data packets and frames, and they pass traffic only if the address is on the same segment of the network cable as the originating station.

broadband   Refers to a network that carries information riding on carrier waves rather than directly as pulses, providing greater capacity at the cost of higher complexity.

broadcast   To send a message to all stations or an entire class of stations connected to the network.

brouter   A device that combines the functions of a bridge and a router. Brouters can route one or more protocols, such as TCP/IP and XNS, and bridge all other traffic. Contrast with *bridge, router,* and *gateway.*

buffer   A temporary storage space. Data may be stored in a buffer as it is received, before or after transmission. A buffer may be used to compensate for the differences between the speed of transmission and the speed of processing.

buffered repeater   A device that amplifies and regenerates signals so they can travel farther along a cable. This type of repeater also controls the flow of messages to prevent collisions.

bus topology   A "broadcast" arrangement in which all network stations receive the same message through the cable at the same time.

byte   A group of 8 bits.

C   A programming language used predominantly by professional programmers to write applications software.

cache   An amount of RAM set aside to hold data that is expected to be accessed again. The second access, which finds the data in RAM, is very fast.

call packet   A block of data carrying addressing and other information that is needed to establish an X.25 switched virtual circuit (SVC).

carrier signal   A tone or radio signal modulated by data, usually for long-distance transmission.

CCITT X.25 Recommendation   An international standard defining packet-switched communication protocols for a public or private network. The recommendation is prepared by the Comite Consultatif International Telegraphique et Telephonique (CCITT). Along with other CCITT recommendations, the X.25 Recommendation defines the physical-, data-link-, and network-layer protocols necessary to interface with X.25 networks. The CCITT X.25 Recommendation is supported by most X.25 equipment vendors, but a new CCITT X.25 Recommendation is published every four years.

CCS 7   A network signaling standard for ISDN that incorporates information from databases in order to offer advanced network services.

central office (CO)   The telephone-switching location nearest to the customer's premises. It serves the businesses and residences connected to its loop lines.

channel   A path between sender and receiver that carries one stream of information (a two-way path is a *circuit*).

character   One letter, number, or special code.

CICS (Customer Information Control System)   This IBM software runs on a mainframe and makes a variety of services available for application programs. It furnishes easy ways for programs to enter mainframe files and find data within them.

circuit switching   A method of communicating in which a dedicated communications path is established between two devices, the bandwidth is guaranteed, and the delay is essentially limited to propagation time. The telephone system uses circuit switching.

clear packet   A block of data containing a command that performs the equivalent of hanging up the telephone.

client/server computing   A computing system in which processing can be distributed among "clients" on the network that request information and one or more network "servers" that store data, let clients share data and programs, help in printing operations, and so on. The system can accommodate standalone applications (word processing), applications requiring data from the server (spreadsheets), applications that use server capabilities to exchange information among users (electronic mail), and applications providing true client/server teamwork (databases, especially those based on Structured Query Language, or SQL). Before client/server computing, a server would download an entire database to a client machine for processing. SQL database applications divide the work between machines, letting the database stay on the server.

cluster controller   A computer that sits between a group of terminals and the mainframe, gathering messages and multiplexing over a single link to the mainframe.

CMIP (Common Management Information Protocol)   An OSI-based structure for formatting messages and for transmitting information between data-collection programs and reporting devices. This was developed by the International Standards Organization and designated as ISO 9596.

CMOT (CMIP Over TCP/IP)   An Internet standard defining the use of CMIP for managing TCP/IP networks.

coax or coaxial cable   A type of network media. Coaxial cable contains a copper inner conductor surrounded by plastic insulation and then a woven copper or foil shield.

codec (coder/decoder)   A device that transforms analog voice signals into a digital bit stream (coder) and digital signals into analog voice (decoder) using pulse-code modulation.

collision   An attempt by two units to send a message at one time on a single channel. In some networks, the detection of a collision causes all senders to stop transmissions, while in others the collision is noticed when the receiving station fails to acknowledge the data.

common carrier   A transmission company (such as a telephone company) that serves the general public.

communications controller   A programmable computer dedicated to data communications and serving as the "front end" in the IBM SNA network.

concentrator   See *wiring hub*.

contention   The condition when two or more stations attempt to use the same channel at the same time.

control character   A character used for special signaling; often not printed or displayed, but causing special functions such as the movement of paper in a printer, the blanking of a display screen, or "handshaking" between communicating devices to control the flow of data.

COW interface (character-oriented Windows interface)   An SAA-compatible user interface for OS/2 applications.

cps   Characters per second.

CPU (central processing unit)   The functional "brain" of a computer; the element that does the actual adding and subtracting of 0s and 1s that is essential to computing.

CRC (cyclic redundancy check) A numeric value derived from the bits in a message. The transmitting station uses one of several formulas to produce a number that is attached to the message. The receiving station applies the same formula and should derive the same number. If the numbers are not the same, an error condition is declared.

crosstalk The spillover of a signal from one channel to another. In data communications it is very disruptive. Usually, careful adjustment of the circuits will eliminate crosstalk.

CRT (cathode ray tube) A video screen.

CSMA (carrier sense multiple access) A media-sharing scheme in which stations listen in to what's happening on the network media; if the cable is not in use, a station is permitted to transmit its message. CSMA is often combined with a means of performing collision detection, hence *CSMA/CD*.

current loop An electrical interface that is sensitive to current changes rather than voltage swings; used with older teleprinter equipment.

cursor The symbol indicating the place on the video screen where the next character will appear.

customer premises equipment (CPE) A general term for the telephones, computers, private branch exchanges, and other hardware located on the end user's side of the network boundary, established by the Computer Inquiry II action of the Federal Communications Commission.

D/A converter A device that changes digital pulses into analog signals.

Data Access Protocol A specialized protocol used by Digital Equipment Corp.

datagram A packet of computer-generated information that includes a complete destination address provided by the user, not the network, along with whatever data the packet carries.

data-link control A communications layer in SNA that manages the physical data circuits.

data-link layer The second layer of the OSI model. Protocols functioning in this layer manage the flow of data leaving a network device and work with the receiving station to ensure that the data arrives safely.

data packet   In X.25, a block of data that transports full-duplex information via an X.25 switched virtual circuit (SVC) or permanent virtual circuit (PVC). X.25 data packets may contain up to 1,024 bytes of user data, but the most common size is 128 bytes (the X.25 default).

data set   **1.** A file, a "set" of data. **2.** The name the telephone company often uses for a modem.

DB-25   The designation of a standard plug-and-jack set used in RS-232C wiring: 25-pin connectors, with 13 pins in one row and 12 in the other row.

DCE (data communications equipment)   Refers to any X.25 network component that implements the CCITT X.25 standard.

D-channel   The "data" channel of an ISDN interface, used to carry control signals and customer call data in a packet-switched mode. In the basic-rate interface (BRI), the D-channel operates at 16 kilobits per second; in the primary-rate interface (PRI), the D-channel is used at 64 kbps.

DDCMP (Digital Data Communications Message Protocol)   A byte-oriented, link-layer protocol from Digital Equipment Corp., used to transmit messages over a communications line.

DDD (direct distance dialing)   Use of the common long-distance telephone system.

DECnet   A communications protocol and line of networking products from Digital Equipment Corp., compatible with Ethernet and a wide range of systems.

delay   Commonly, a pause in activity. Delay can also be a kind of distortion on a communications circuit. Specifically, it is the property of an electrical circuit that slows down and distorts high-frequency signals. Devices called *equalizers* slow down the lower frequencies and "equalize" the signal.

demodulation   The process of retrieving data from a modulated carrier wave; the reverse of *modulation*.

dial-up line   A communications circuit established by dialing a destination over a commercial telephone system.

digital   In common use, on/off signaling; signals consist of 0s and 1s instead of a great multitude of analog-modulated frequencies.

disk duplexing   A fault-tolerant technique that writes simultaneously to two hard disks using different controllers.

disk mirroring   A fault-tolerant technique that writes data simultaneously to two hard disks using the same controller.

DISOSS (Distributed Office Supported System)   An integrated package of electronic-mail and document-preparation programs from IBM, designed for IBM mainframe computer systems.

distortion   Any change to the transmitted signal. Distortion can be caused by crosstalk, delay, attenuation, or other factors.

Distributed Systems Architecture (DSA)   A Honeywell architecture that conforms to the Open Systems Interconnection model proposed by the ISO. It supports X.25 for packet switching and X.21 for packet-switched and circuit-switched network protocols.

DQDB (Distributed Queue Dual Bus)   A proposed IEEE 802.6 standard for metropolitan-area networks (MANs).

driver   A software program that interfaces between portions of the LAN software and the hardware on the network interface card.

DTE (data terminal equipment)   Refers to any end-user device that can access an X.25 network using the CCITT X.25 standard, LAP/LAB, and X.25 PAP.

duplex   1. In communications circuits, the ability to transmit and receive at the same time; also referred to as *full duplex*. Half-duplex circuits can receive only or transmit only. 2. In terminals, a choice between displaying locally generated characters and echoed characters.

EBCDIC (Extended Binary Coded Decimal Interchange Code)   The data alphabet used in all IBM computers except the PC; it determines the composition of the 8-bit string of 0s and 1s representing each character (alphabetic, numeric, or special).

echoplex   A method of transmission in which characters are echoed from the distant end and the echoes are presented on the terminal; this provides a constant check of the communications circuit to the user.

echo suppressor   A device used to eliminate the echo effect of long-distance voice transmission circuits. This suppressor must be disabled for full-duplex data transmission; the modem answer tones turn the suppressor off automatically.

ECMA (European Computer Manufacturers' Association)   A trade association that provides input to international standards-forming organizations.

EDI (electronic data interchange)   The communication of orders, invoices, and similar transactions electronically between organizations.

EIA (Electronic Industries Association)   An organization of U.S. manufacturers of electronic parts and equipment. The organization develops industry standards for the interface between data-processing and communications equipment.

802.X   The Institute of Electrical and Electronics Engineers (IEEE) committee that developed a set of standards describing the cabling, electrical topology, physical topology, and access scheme of network products; in other words, the 802.X standards define the physical and data-link layers of LAN architectures. IEEE 802.3 is the work of an 802 subcommittee that describes the cabling and signaling for a system nearly identical to classic Ethernet. IEEE 802.5 comes from another subcommittee and similarly describes IBM's Token-Ring architecture.

EISA (Extended Industry Standard Architecture)   A PC bus system that serves as an alternative to IBM's Micro Channel Architecture (MCA). The EISA architecture, backed by an industry consortium headed by Compaq, is compatible with the IBM AT bus; MCA is not.

elevator seeking   A method of optimizing the movement of the heads on the hard disk in a file server.

EMA (Enterprise Management Architecture)   Digital Equipment Corp.'s company-specific architecture, conforming to ISO's CMIP.

emulation   Simulation of a system, function, or program.

equalization   Balancing of a circuit so that it passes all frequencies with equal efficiency.

Ethernet   A network cable and access protocol scheme originally developed by Xerox, now marketed mainly by Digital Equipment Corp. and 3Com.

EtherTalk   **1.** The Apple Ethernet adapter for the Macintosh II computer. **2.** The software driver used by the Macintosh to communicate with Ethernet adapters.

facsimile (fax)   The transmission of page images by a system that is concerned with patterns of light and dark rather than with specific characters. Older systems use analog signals; newer devices use digital signals and may interact with computers and other digital devices.

fault   A physical or logical break in a communications link.

fault management   One of the five basic categories of network management defined by the International Standards Organization (ISO). Fault management is used for the detection, isolation, and correction of faults on the network.

fault tolerance   A method of ensuring continued operation through redundancy and diversity.

FCC   Federal Communications Commission.

FDDI (Fiber Distributed Data Interface)   A specification for fiber-optic networks operating at 100 megabits per second. FDDI uses wiring hubs, and the hubs are prime candidates to serve as network monitoring and control devices.

FEP (front-end processor)   A computer that sits between groups of cluster controllers and the mainframe, concentrating signals before they are transmitted to the mainframe.

fiber optics   A data-transmission method that uses light pulses sent over glass cables.

field   A particular position within a message frame. Positions are labeled as the control field, flag field, and so on. Bits in each message have a meaning for stations on the network.

file lock   See *locking.*

file server   A type of server that holds files in private and shared directories for LAN users. See *server.*

flow control   A convention used to regulate communications between two nodes. Hardware and software techniques are available.

foreign exchange   A telephone line that represents a local number in a calling area quite removed from the telephone's actual termination. If your office is in the suburbs but many of your customers are in the city, you might have a foreign-exchange line with a city telephone office.

four-wire circuit   A transmission arrangement where two half-duplex circuits (two wires each) are combined to make one full-duplex circuit.

frame   A data packet on a Token-Ring network. Also denotes a data packet on other networks such as X.25 or SNA.

frequency-agile modem   A modem used on some broadband systems that can shift frequencies to communicate with stations in different dedicated bands.

frequency converter   In broadband cable systems, the device that translates between the transmitting and receiving frequencies.

frequency-division multiplexing   A technique for combining many signals on one circuit by separating them in frequency.

frequency-shift keying   A transmission method using two different frequencies that are shifted to represent the digital 0s and 1s; used in some common modems.

FTAM (File Transfer Access and Management)   An OSI protocol that provides access to files stored on dissimilar systems.

FTP (File Transfer Protocol)   A protocol that describes how one computer can host other computers to allow transferring files in either direction. Users can see directories of either computer on the host and perform limited file-management functions. Software for the FTP client function is usually a part of TCP/IP packages for the PC; some vendors also provide FTP host software for the PC. See *TFTP*.

full duplex   The ability for communications to flow both ways over a communications link at the same time.

functional-management layer   A communications layer in SNA that formats presentations.

gateway   A device that serves as a shared point of entry from a local area network into a larger information resource such as a large packet-switched information network or a mainframe computer.

GOSIP (Government OSI Profile)   The U.S. government's version of the OSI protocols. GOSIP compliance is typically a requirement in government networking purchases.

ground   An electrically neutral contact point.

half duplex   **1.** Alternating transmissions; each station can either transmit or receive, not both simultaneously. **2.** In terminals, describes the condition when a terminal displays its own transmissions instead of a remote-end echo. **3.** The configuration option in some modems allowing local character echo.

handshaking   Exchange of control codes or specific characters to control data flow.

HDLC (High-level Data Link Control)   A comprehensive standard developed by the International Standards Organization (ISO). It is a bit-oriented link-layer protocol.

high-speed modem   A modem operating at speeds from 2,400 to 9,600 bits per second.

HLLAPI (High-Level-Language Application Program Interface)   A scripting language (that is, a set of verbs) that allows programmers to build transparent interfaces between 3270 terminals and applications on IBM mainframes.

HotFix   A Novell program that dynamically marks defective blocks on the hard disk so they will not be used.

Hz (hertz)   Cycles per second.

ICMP (Internet Control Message Protocol)   The TCP/IP process that provides the set of functions used for network-layer management and control.

IEEE 802   A large family of standards for the physical and electrical connections in local area networks, developed by the IEEE (Institute of Electrical and Electronics Engineers).

IEEE 802.1D   An IEEE media-access-control-level standard for interLAN bridges linking IEEE 802.3, 802.4, and 802.5 networks.

IEEE 802.2   An IEEE standard for data-link-layer software and firmware for use with IEEE 802.3, 802.4, and 802.5 networks.

IEEE 802.3 1Base5   An IEEE specification matching the older AT&T StarLAN product. It designates a 1-megabit-per-second signaling rate, a baseband signaling technique, and a maximum cable-segment distance of 500 meters.

IEEE 802.3 10Base2   This IEEE specification matches the thin Ethernet cabling. It designates a 10-megabit-per-second signaling rate, a baseband signaling technique, and a maximum cable-segment distance of 185 (nearly 200) meters.

IEEE 802.3 10BaseT   An IEEE standard describing 10-megabit-per-second twisted-pair Ethernet wiring using baseband signaling. This system requires a wiring hub.

IEEE 802.3 10Broad36   This IEEE specification describes a long-distance type of Ethernet cabling with a 10-megabit-per-second signaling rate, a broadband signaling technique, and a maximum cable-segment distance of 3,600 meters.

IEEE 802.4   This IEEE specification describes a LAN using 10-megabit-per-second signaling, token-passing media-access control, and a physical bus topology. It is typically used as part of networks following the Manufacturing Automation Protocol (MAP) developed by General Motors. This is sometimes confused with ARCnet, but it is not the same.

IEEE 802.5   This IEEE specification describes a LAN using 4- or 16-megabit-per-second signaling, token-passing media-access control, and a physical ring topology. It is used by IBM's Token-Ring systems.

IEEE 802.6   This IEEE standard for metropolitan-area networks (MANs) describes what is called a Distributed Queue Dual Bus (DQDB). The DQDB topology includes two parallel runs of cable—typically fiber-optic cable—linking each node (typically a router for a LAN segment) using signaling rates in the range of 100 megabits per second.

impedance   An electrical property of a cable, combining capacitance, inductance, and resistance, and measured in ohms.

IND$FILE   A mainframe editing utility, commonly used to make PC-to-mainframe file transfers; a logical unit in an SNA network that addresses and interacts with the host.

interface   An interconnection point, usually between pieces of equipment.

Internet   A collection of networks and gateways including ARPAnet, MILnet, and NSFnet (National Science Foundation net). Internet uses TCP/IP protocols.

interrupt   A signal that suspends a program temporarily, transferring control to the operating system when input or output is required. Interrupts may have priority levels, and higher-priority interrupts take precedence in processing.

I/O   Input/output.

I/O bound   A condition where the operation of the I/O port is the limiting factor in program execution.

IP (Internet Protocol)   A standard describing software that keeps track of the Internet address for different nodes, routes outgoing messages, and recognizes incoming messages.

IPX (Internet Packet Exchange)   NetWare's native LAN communications protocol, used to move data between server and/or workstation programs running on different network nodes. IPX packets are encapsulated and carried by the packets used in Ethernet and the similar frames used in Token-Ring networks.

IRQ (interrupt request)   A computer instruction that causes an interruption of a program for an I/O task.

ISDN (Integrated Services Digital Network)   As officially defined by the CCITT, "a limited set of standard interfaces to a digital communications network." The result is a network that offers end users voice, data, and certain image services on end-to-end digital circuits.

ISO (International Standards Organization)   A Paris-based organization that developed the Open Systems Interconnection (OSI) model.

jam signal   A signal generated by a card to ensure that other cards know that a packet collision has taken place.

jumper   A plastic-and-metal shorting bar that slides over two or more electrical contacts to set certain conditions for operation.

k   Used in this book to represent a kilobyte (1,024 bytes).

kernel   The heart of an operating system, containing the basic scheduling and interrupt handling, but not the higher-level services, such as the file system.

LAN Manager   The multiuser network operating system codeveloped by Microsoft and 3Com. LAN Manager offers a wide range of network-management and control capabilities.

LAN Manager/X (LM/X)   LAN Manager for the Unix environment.

LAN Server   IDM's proprietary OS/2-based network operating system. LAN Server is compatible with LAN Manager, codeveloped by Microsoft and 3Com.

LAP-B   Link access procedure (balanced), the most common data-link control protocol used to interface X.25 DTEs with X.25 DCEs. X.25 also specifies a *LAP*, or link access procedure (not balanced). Both LAP and LAP-B are full-duplex, point-to-point bit-synchronous protocols. The unit of data transmission is called a *frame;* frames may contain one or more X.25 packets.

leased line   A communications circuit reserved for the permanent use of a customer; also called *private line.*

light-wave communications   Usually, communications using fiber-optic cables and light generated by lasers or light-emitting diodes (LEDs). The phrase can also refer to systems using modulated light beams passing through the air between buildings or other adjacent locations.

link layer   The second layer in the OSI architecture. This layer performs the function of taking data from the higher layers, creating packets, and sending them accurately out through the physical layer.

local   Refers to programs, files, peripherals, and computational power accessed directly in the user's own machine rather than through the network.

local area network (LAN)   A computer communications system limited to no more than a few miles and using high-speed connections (2 to 100 megabits per second).

local area transport (LAT)   A DECnet protocol used for terminal-to-host communications.

local loop   The connection between a customer's premises and the telephone company's central office.

LocalTalk   The 230.4-kilobit-per-second media-access method developed by Apple Computer for use with its MacIntosh computer.

locking   A method of protecting shared data. When an application program opens a file, *file locking* either prevents simultaneous access by a second program or limits such access to "read only." DOS Versions 3.0 and higher allow an application to lock a range of bytes in a file for various purposes. Since DBMS programs interpret this range of bytes as a record, this is called *record locking*.

low-speed modem   A modem operating at speeds up to 600 bits per second.

LU 6.2 (Logical Unit 6.2)   In IBM's SNA scheme, a software product that implements the session-layer conversation specified in the Advanced Program-to-Program Communications (APPC) protocol.

MAC (media-access control)   See *access protocol*.

mainframe   A large centralized computer.

MAN (metropolitan-area network)   A public high-speed network (100 megabits per second or more) capable of voice and data transmission over a range of 25 to 50 miles (40 to 80 kilometers).

MAP (Manufacturing Automation Protocol) A token-passing bus LAN originally designed by General Motors and now adopted as a subset of the IEEE 802.3 standards.

mark A signaling condition equal to a binary 1.

MAU See *medium attachment unit* and *Multistation Access Unit.*

MCA (Micro Channel Architecture) The basis for IBM Micro Channel bus, used in high-end models of IBM's PS/2 series of personal computers.

media Plural of *medium*; the cabling or wiring used to carry network signals. Typical examples are coax, fiber-optic, and twisted-pair wire.

media-sharing LAN A network in which all nodes share the cable using a media-access control (MAC) scheme. Contrast with *circuit switching* or *packet switching.*

medium attachment unit (MAU) A transceiver that attaches to the AUI port on an Ethernet adapter and provides electrical and mechanical attachments to fiber-optic, twisted-pair, or other media.

medium-speed modem A modem operating between 600 and 2,400 bits per second.

message switching A routing technique using a message store-and-forward system. No dedicated path is established. Rather, each message contains a destination address and is passed from source to destination through intermediate nodes. At each node, the entire message is received, stored briefly, and then passed on to the next node.

MHS (Message Handling Service) A program developed by Action Technologies and marketed by that firm and Novell to exchange files with other programs and send files out through gateways to other computers and networks. It is used particularly to link dissimilar electronic-mail systems.

MIB (management information base) A directory listing the logical names of all information resources residing in a network and pertinent to the network's management.

midsplit A type of broadband cable system in which the available frequencies are split into two groups, one for transmission and one for reception. This requires a frequency converter.

modem (modulator/demodulator)   A device that translates between electrical signals and some other means of signaling. Typically a modem translates between direct-current signals from a computer or terminal and analog signals sent over telephone lines. Other modems handle radio frequencies and light waves.

modem eliminator   A wiring device designed to replace two modems; it connects equipment over a distance of up to several hundred feet. In asynchronous systems, this is a simple cable.

modulation   A process of varying signals to represent intelligent information. The frequency, amplitude, or phase of a signal may be modulated to represent an analog or digital signal.

multiple name spaces   The association of several names or other pieces of information with the same file. This allows renaming files and designating them for dissimilar computer systems such as the PC and the Mac.

multipoint line   A single communications link for two or more devices shared by one computer and more than one terminal. Use of this line requires a polling mechanism. It is also called a *multidrop line*.

Multistation Access Unit (MAU)   IBM's name for a Token-Ring wiring concentrator.

NAK   A control code indicating that a character or block of data was not properly received. The name stands for *negative acknowledgement*. See *ACK*.

Named Pipes   A technique used for communications between applications operating on the same computer or across the network. It includes a relatively easy-to-use API, providing application programmers with a simple way to create interprogram communications using routines similar to disk-file opening, reading, and writing.

N connector   The large-diameter connector used with thick Ethernet cable.

NCP   **1.** (NetWare Core Protocol) The data format of the requests NetWare uses to access files. **2.** (Network Control Program) Special IBM software that runs in a front-end processor and works with VTAM on the host computer to link the application programs and terminal controllers.

NDIS (Network Driver Interface Specification)   A device driver specification codeveloped by Microsoft and 3Com. Besides providing hardware and protocol independence for network drivers, NDIS supports both DOS and OS/2, and it offers protocol multiplexing so that multiple protocol stacks can coexist in the same host.

NetBIOS (Network Basic Input/Output System)   A layer of software originally developed by IBM and Sytek to link a network operating system with specific hardware. It can also open communications between workstations on a network at the transport layer. Today, many vendors either provide a version of NetBIOS to interface with their hardware or emulate its transport-layer communications services in their network products.

NetVIEW   IBM's company-specific network-management and control architecture. This architecture relies heavily on mainframe data-collection programs and also incorporates PC-level products running under OS/2.

NetWare   A popular series of network operating systems and related products made by Novell.

network   A continuing connection between two or more computers that facilitates sharing files and resources.

network-addressable unit (NAU)   In SNA, a device that can be the source and destination of messages.

network layer   The third level of the OSI model, containing the logic and rules that determine the path to be taken by data flowing through a network; not important in small LANs.

NFS (Network File System)   One of many distributed-file-system protocols that allow a computer on a network to use the files and peripherals of another networked computer as if they were local. This protocol was developed by Sun Microsystems and adopted by other vendors.

NLMs (NetWare Loadable Modules)   Applications and drivers that run in a server under Novell's NetWare 386 and can be loaded or unloaded on the fly. In other networks, such applications could require dedicated PCs.

NMP (Network Management Protocol)   An AT&T-developed set of protocols designed to exchange information with and control the devices that govern various components of a network, including modems and T1 multiplexers.

NNTP (Network News Transport Protocol)   An extension of the TCP/IP protocol that provides a network news transport service.

node   A connection or switching point on the network.

ODI (Open Data-link Interface)   A standard interface for transport protocols, allowing them to share a single network card without any conflicts.

OfficeVision   IBM's set of applications designed to bring a uniform user interface to the company's various lines of computing products. OfficeVision works in conjunction with IBM's Systems Application Architecture.

online   Connected to a network or a host computer system.

ONMS (Open Network Management System)   Digital Communications Associates' architecture for products conforming to ISO's CMIP.

Open Systems Interconnection (OSI) reference model   A model for networks developed by the International Standards Organization, dividing the network functions into seven connected layers. Each layer builds on the services provided by those under it.

OpenView   Hewlett-Packard's suite of a network-management application, a server platform, and support services. OpenView is based on HP-UX, which complies with AT&T's Unix system.

OPT (Open Protocol Technology)   Novell's strategy for complete protocol independence. NetWare supports multivendor hardware with this approach.

OSF (Open Software Foundation)   A consortium of industry leaders working to standardize the Unix operating system.

OSI   See *Open Systems Interconnection.*

OS/2 (Operating System/2)   An operating system developed by IBM and Microsoft for use with Intel's microprocessors. Unlike its predecessor, DOS, OS/2 is a multitasking operating system.

OS/2 Extended Edition   IBM's proprietary version of OS/2; it includes built-in communications and database-management facilities.

OverVIEW   Proteon's architecture for products conforming to SNMP.

packet   A block of data sent over the network transmitting the identities of the sending and receiving stations, error-control information, and a message.

packet filter   A feature of a bridge that compares each packet received with specifications set by the network administrator. If the packet matches the specifications, the bridge can either forward or reject it. Packet filters let the administrator limit protocol-specific traffic to one network segment, isolate electronic-mail domains, and perform many other traffic-control functions.

packet switching   A transmission technique that maximizes the use of digital transmission facilities by transmitting packets of digital data from many customers simultaneously on a single communications channel.

PAD (packet assembler/disassembler)   An X.25 PAD. A hardware-and-software device, sometimes inside a PC, that provides users access to an X.25 network. CCITT Recommendations X.3, X.28, and X.29 define the PAD parameters, terminal-to-PAD interface, and PAD-to-X.25 host interface.

PAP (packet-level procedure)   A protocol for the transfer of packets between an X.25 DTE and an X.25 DCE. X.25 PAP is a full-duplex protocol that supports data sequencing, flow control, accountability, and error detection and recovery.

parallel transmission   Simultaneous transmission of bits down parallel wires; for example, *byte parallel transmission* requires eight wires. See *serial port*.

parity   In ASCII, a check of the total number of 1 bits (as opposed to 0's) in a character's binary representation. A final eighth bit is set so that the count, when transmitted, is always even or always odd. This even or odd state can easily be checked at the receiving end; an incorrect parity bit can help reveal errors in the transmission.

passive head end   A device that connects the two broadband cables of a dual-cable system. It does not provide frequency translation.

PBX (private branch exchange)   A telephone system serving a specific location. Many PBX systems can carry computer data without the use of modems.

PDS (Premise Distribution System)   AT&T's proprietary buildingwide telecommunications cabling system.

peer-to-peer resource sharing   An architecture that lets any station contribute resources to the network while still running local application programs.

physical layer   The lowest layer of the OSI model. It consists of network wiring and cable and the interface hardware that sends and receives signals over the network.

PING (Packet Internet Groper)   An exercise program associated with TCP/IP and used to test the Internet communications channel between stations.

pipe   A communications process within the operating system that acts as an interface between a computer's devices (keyboard, disk drives, memory, and so on) and an applications program. A pipe simplifies the development of application programs by "buffering" a program from the intricacies of the hardware or the software that controls the hardware; the application developer writes code to a single pipe, not to several individual devices. A pipe is also used for program-to-program communications.

polling   A method of controlling the transmission sequence of communicating devices on a shared circuit by sending an inquiry to each device asking whether it wishes to transmit.

presentation layer   The sixth layer of the OSI model, which formats data for screen presentation and translates incompatible file formats.

Presentation Manager   The portion of the operating system OS/2 providing users with a graphical-based rather than character-based interface. The screens are similar to those of Microsoft Windows.

primary-rate interface (PRI)   In ISDN, the specification for the interface at each end of the high-volume trunks linking PBX and central-office facilities or connecting network switches to each other. The primary rate consists of 23 B or "bearer" channels (operating at 64 kilobits per second) and a D or "data" channel (also functioning at 64 kbps). The combined signal-carrying capacity is 1.544 megabits per second—equivalent to that of a type T1 channel.

print server   A computer on the network that makes one or more attached printers available to other users. The server usually requires a hard disk to spool the print jobs while they wait in a queue for the printer.

print spooler   The software that holds print jobs sent to a shared printer over a network when the printer is busy. Each file is saved in temporary storage and then printed when the shared printer is available.

PROFS (Professional Office System)   Interactive productivity software developed by IBM that runs under the VM/CMS mainframe system. PROFS is frequently used for electronic mail.

propagation delay   The delay between the time a signal enters a channel and the time it is received. This is normally insignificant in local area networks, but it becomes a major factor in satellite communications.

protocol   A specification that describes the rules and procedures that products should follow to perform activities on a network, such as transmitting data. If they use the same protocols, products from different vendors can communicate on the same network.

PSDN   Packet-switched data network.

PU (physical unit)   In an SNA network, usually a terminal or printer connected to the controller.

public data network   A commercially owned or national-monopoly packet-switched network, publicly available as a service to data-processing users.

pulse-code modulation (PCM)   A common method for digitizing voice signals. The bandwidth required for a single digitized voice channel is 64 kilobits per second.

PVC   See *VC (virtual circuit)*.

query language   A programming language designed to make it easier to specify what information a user wants to retrieve from a database.

queue   A list formed by items in a system waiting for service. An example is a *print queue* of documents to be printed in a network print server.

RAM (random access memory)   Also known as *read-write memory*; the memory used to execute application programs.

record locking   A feature that excludes other users from accessing (or sometimes just writing to) a record in a file while the first user is accessing that record.

redirector   A software module loaded into every network workstation; it captures application programs' requests for file- and equipment-sharing services and routes them through the network for action.

repeater   A device that amplifies and regenerates signals so they can travel on additional cable segments.

restart packet   A block of data that notifies X.25 DTEs that an irrecoverable error exists within the X.25 network. Restart packets clear all existing SVCs and resynchronize all existing PVCs between an X.25 DTE and X.25 DCE.

reverse channel   An answer-back channel provided during half-duplex operation. It allows the receiving modem to send low-speed acknowledgments to the transmitting modem without breaking the half-duplex mode. This is also used to arrange the turnaround between modems so that one ceases transmitting and the other can begin.

RF (radio frequency)   A generic term referring to the technology used in cable television and broadband networks. It uses electromagnetic waveforms, usually in the megahertz (MHz) range, for transmission.

RFS (Remote File Service) One of the many distributed-file-system network protocols that allow one computer to use the files and peripherals of another as if they were local. Developed by AT&T and adopted by other vendors as a part of Unix V.

ring A network connection method that routes messages through each station on the network in turn. Most ring networks use a token-passing protocol, which allows any station to put a message on the network when it receives a special bit pattern.

RJE (Remote Job Entry) A method of submitting work to an IBM mainframe in a batch format. Though superseded by the 3270 system, it is still widely used in some installations.

RJ-11/RJ-45 Designations for commonly used modular telephone connectors. RJ-11 is the 8-pin connector used in most voice connections. RJ-45 is the 8-pin connector used for data transmission over twisted-pair telephone wire.

RO (receive-only) Refers to a one-way device such as a printer, plotter, or graphics display.

ROM (read-only memory) Memory containing preloaded programs that cannot be rewritten or changed by the CPU.

router An interconnection device that is similar to a bridge but serves packets or frames containing certain protocols. Routers link LANs at the network layer of the OSI model. Modern routers handle multiple protocol stacks simultaneously and move packets or frames onto the right links for their destinations. For example, an X.25 router will wrap an Ethernet packet back into an Ethernet system.

RPC (Remote Procedure Call) A set of software tools developed by a consortium of manufacturers and designed to assist developers in creating distributed applications. These tools automatically generate the code for both sides of the program (client and server) and let the programmer concentrate on other portions of the application.

RS-232C An electrical standard for the interconnection of equipment established by the Electrical Industries Association; the same as the CCITT code V.24. RS-232C is used for serial ports.

RS-449 An EIA standard that applies to binary, serial synchronous, or asynchronous communications systems.

RU (request unit or response unit) A message that makes a request or responds to one during a session.

SAA (Systems Application Architecture) A set of specifications written by IBM describing how users, application programs, and communications programs interface. SAA represents an attempt to standardize the look and feel of applications and the methods they use to communicate.

SDLC (synchronous data link control) The data-link layer of SNA, SDLC is a more efficient method than the older bisync protocol when it comes to packaging data for transmission between computers. Packets of data are sent over the line without the overhead created by synchronization and other padding bits.

serial port An I/O port that transmits data 1 bit at a time; contrasted with a *parallel transmission*, which transmits multiple bits (usually 8) simultaneously. RS-232C is a common serial signaling protocol.

server **1.** A computer with a large power supply and cabinet capacity. **2.** Any computer on a network that makes file, print, or communications services available to other network stations.

session The name for the connection between a mainframe terminal (or a PC emulating a mainframe terminal) and the mainframe itself when they are communicating. The number of sessions that can be run simultaneously through a LAN gateway is limited by the gateway software and the hardware configuration.

session layer The fifth layer of the OSI model, which sets up the conditions whereby individual nodes on the network can communicate or send data to each other. The functions of this layer are used for many purposes, including determining which side may transmit during half-duplex communications.

SFT (system fault tolerance) The capability to recover from or avoid a system crash. Novell uses a Transaction Tracking System (TTS), disk mirroring, and disk duplexing as its system recovery methods.

SMB (Server Message Block) A distributed-file-system network protocol that allows one computer to use the files and peripherals of another as if they were local. Developed by Microsoft and adopted by IBM and many other vendors.

SMTP (Simple Mail Transfer Protocol) A protocol that describes an electronic-mail system with both host and user sections. Many companies sell host software (usually for Unix) that will exchange SMTP mail with proprietary mail systems, such as IBM's PROFS. The user software is often included as a utility in TCP/IP packages for the PC.

SNA (Systems Network Architecture) IBM's scheme for connecting its computerized products so that they can communicate and share data.

SNADS (SNA Distribution Services) An IBM protocol that allows the distribution of electronic mail and attached documents through an SNA network.

SNMP (Simple Network Management Protocol) A structure for formatting messages and for transmitting information between reporting devices and data-collection programs; developed jointly by the Department of Defense, industry, and the academic community as part of the TCP/IP protocol suite.

space The signal condition that equals a binary 0.

SPX (Sequenced Packet Exchange) An enhanced set of commands implemented on top of IPX to create a true transport-layer interface. SPX provides more functions than IPX, including guaranteed packet delivery.

SQL (Structured Query Language) A formal data sublanguage for specifying common database operations such as retrieving, adding, changing, or deleting records. SQL is pronounced "sequel."

STA (Spanning Tree Algorithm) A technique based on an IEEE 802.1 standard that detects and eliminates logical loops in a bridged network. When multiple paths exist, STA lets a bridge use only the most efficient one. If that path fails, STA automatically reconfigures the network so that another path becomes active, sustaining network operations.

StarLAN A networking system developed by AT&T that uses CSMA protocols on twisted-pair telephone wire; a subset of 802.3.

start bit A data bit used in asynchronous transmission to signal the beginning of a character and indicate that the channel is in use. It is a space signal lasting only for the duration of 1 bit.

star topology A network connection method that hooks up all links to a central node.

stop bit A data bit used in asynchronous transmission to signal the end of a character and indicate that the channel is idle. It is a mark signal lasting at least for the duration of 1 bit.

store and forward See *message switching.*

Streams An architecture introduced with Unix System V, Release 3.2, that provides for flexible and layered communication paths between processes (programs) and device drivers. Many companies market applications and devices that can integrate through Streams protocols.

strobe   An electrical pulse used to call for the transfer of information.

SVC   See *VC (virtual circuit)*.

sync character   A character (two or more in bisync) sent from a transmitting station for synchronizing the clocks in transmitting and receiving stations.

synchronous   Refers to a transmission system in which characters are synchronized by the transmission of initial sync characters and a common clock signal. No stop or start bits are used.

T1   A 1.544-megabit-per-second communications circuit provided by long-distance communications carriers for voice or data transmission. T1 lines are typically divided into 24 64-kilobit channels.

tap   A connector that couples to a cable without blocking the passage of signals down the cable.

TCAM (Telecommunications Access Method)   An IBM system for controlling communications.

T-connector   A coaxial connector, shaped like a T, that connects two thin Ethernet cables while supplying an additional connector for a network interface card.

TCP (Transmission Control Protocol)   A specification for software that bundles and unbundles sent and received data into packets, manages the transmission of packets on a network, and checks for errors.

TCP/IP (Transmission Control Protocol/Internet Protocol)   A set of communications protocols that has evolved since the late 1970s, when it was first developed by the Department of Defense (DOD). Because programs supporting these protocols are available on so many different computer systems, they have become an excellent way to connect different types of computers over networks.

Telex   An international messaging service, marketed in the United States by Western Union.

TELNET   A terminal-emulation protocol. Software supporting TELNET usually comes as a utility in a TCP/IP package, and all TELNET programs provide DEC VT-100 terminal emulation. Many companies either provide or allow other add-in emulators.

10Base2   IEEE's specifications for running Ethernet over thin coaxial cable.

10Base5   IEEE's specifications for running Ethernet over thick coaxial cable.

10BaseT   IEEE's specifications for running Ethernet over unshielded twisted-pair wiring.

terminal adapter (TA)   An ISDN phone or a PC card that emulates one. Devices on the end of a basic-rate interface line are known as *terminals*.

terminator   A resistor used at each end of an Ethernet cable to ensure that signals do not reflect back and cause errors. It is usually attached to an electrical ground at one end.

TFTP (Trivial File Transfer Protocol)   A simplified version of FTP that transfers files but does not provide password protection or user-directory capability. It is associated with the TCP/IP family of protocols.

thick Ethernet   A cabling system using relatively stiff, large-diameter cable to connect transceivers. The transceivers connect to the nodes through flexible multiwire cable.

thin Ethernet   A cabling system using a thin and flexible coaxial cable to connect each node to the next node in line.

3174, 3270, and so on   Appear at the end of the alphabet in this glossary.

3+Open   A family of 3Com networking products built around the LAN Manager file/print server. 3+Open includes connectivity, messaging, and network management services.

TIC (Token-Ring Interface Coupler)   An IBM device that allows a controller or processor to attach directly to a Token-Ring network. This is an optional part of several IBM terminal cluster controllers and front-end processors.

time-division multiplexing (TDM)   A method of placing a number of signals on one communications circuit by allocating the available time among competing stations. Allocations may be on a microsecond basis.

time domain reflectometry (TDR)   A method of sending a radio pulse down a wire or cable to detect a shorted or open condition. High-priced devices can pinpoint a fault within inches; lower-priced devices often provide widely varying results when they try to pinpoint the distance to a fault.

T interface   A standard basic-rate interface using four copper wires.

token passing   An access protocol in which a special message (token) circulates among the network nodes, giving them permission to transmit.

Token-Ring   The wire and the access protocol scheme whereby stations relay packets in a logical ring configuration. This architecture, pioneered by IBM, is described in the IEEE 802.5 standards.

TOP (Technical and Office Protocol)   An implementation of OSI standards in office and engineering environments. TOP, developed by Boeing and other firms, employs Ethernet specifications.

topology   The map or plan of the network. The physical topology describes how the wires or cables are laid out, and the logical or electrical topology describes how the messages flow.

TP-4 (Transport Protocol 4)   An OSI layer-4 protocol developed by the National Bureau of Standards.

transceiver   A communicating device capable of transmitting and receiving.

transmission control   The layer in SNA that controls sessions and manages communications.

transport layer   The fourth layer of the OSI model. Software in this layer checks the integrity of and formats the data carried by the physical layer (1), managed by the data layer (2), and perhaps routed by the network layer (3).

tree   Refers to a network arrangement in which the stations are attached to a common branch or data bus.

TTS (Transaction Tracking System)   A log of all file activity in NetWare

twisted-pair Ethernet   See *IEEE 802.3 10BaseT*.

twisted-pair wiring   Cable comprised of two wires twisted together at six turns per inch to provide electrical self-shielding. Some telephone wire—but by no means all—is twisted-pair.

Type 3 cable   An unshielded twisted-pair wire that meets IBM specifications for use in 4-megabit-per-second Token-Ring networks.

UDP (User Datagram Protocol)   A TCP/IP protocol describing how messages reach application programs within a destination computer. This protocol is normally bundled with IP-layer software.

U interface   A standard basic-rate interface using two copper wires.

Unix   A multitasking, multiuser operating system for minicomputers that was developed by AT&T and has enjoyed popularity among engineering and technical professionals. Unix is finding new uses as the basis of file-server operating systems for networks of PCs.

UNMA (Unified Network Management Architecture)   AT&T's company-specific architecture conforming to the ISO's CMIP.

UUCP (Unix-to-Unix Copy Program)   A standard Unix utility used for information exchange between two Unix nodes.

VAN (value-added network)   A privately owned packet-switched network whose services are sold to the public. See *PSDN*.

VC (virtual circuit)   An X.25 VC is a PAP logical connection between an X.25 DTE and an X.25 DCE. X.25 supports both *switched VCs* (SVCs) and *permanent VCs* (PVCs). SVCs are analogous to dial-up lines; that is, they allow a particular X.25 DTE to establish a connection with different X.25 DTEs on a per-call basis. By contrast, PVCs are analogous to leased lines because they always connect two X.25 DTEs.

VINES (Virtual Networking Software)   A Unix-based network operating system from Banyan Systems.

virtual circuit   A temporary connection path, set up between two points by software and packet switching, that appears to the user to be available as a dedicated circuit. This "phantom" circuit can be maintained indefinitely or can be ended at will.

voice channel   A transmission path usually limited to passing the bandwidth of the human voice.

VTAM (Virtual Telecommunications Access Method)   An IBM standard for software that runs on the host mainframe computer and works with the Network Control Program to establish communications between the host and the cluster controllers. Among other things, VTAM sets the pacing and LU characteristics.

WAN (wide-area network)   A type of network that connects computers over areas potentially as wide as the entire world.

wideband   Refers to a channel or transmission medium capable of passing more frequencies than a standard 3-kHz voice channel.

wideband modem   A modem that operates at over 9,600 bits per second.

wiring hub   A cabinet, usually mounted in a wiring closet, that holds connection modules for various kinds of cabling. The hub contains electronic circuits that retime and repeat the signals on the cable. The hub may also contain a microprocessor board that monitors and reports on network activity.

X.25   A CCITT standard that describes how data is handled in and how computers can access a packet-switched network.

X.400   The CCITT designation for an international electronic-mail distribution system.

X.500   The CCITT designation for a directory standard to coordinate the dispersed file directories of different systems.

XNS (Xerox Network Services)   A multilayer protocol system developed by Xerox and adopted, at least in part, by Novell and other vendors. XNS is one of the many distributed-file-system protocols that allow network stations to use other computers' files and peripherals as if they were local.

X/Open   A consortium of computer-industry vendors, chartered to specify an open system platform based on the Unix operating system.

X Window   A network-based windowing system that provides a programmatic interface for graphic window displays. X Window permits graphics produced on one networked workstation to be displayed on another.

3174   A new version of the 3274 terminal cluster controller.

3270   The generic name for the family of interoperable IBM system components —terminals, printers, and terminal cluster controllers—that can be used to communicate with a mainframe by means of the SNA or bisync protocols. All of these components have four-digit names, some of which begin with the digits 327.

3274/3276   The most commonly used cluster controller. This device links as many as 32 3270-type terminals and printers to a mainframe front-end processor.

3278   The most commonly used terminal in the 3270 family. It features a monochrome display and offers a limited graphics set.

3279   A color terminal that is part of the 3270 family.

3287   The current series of printers in the 3270 equipment family.

3705 A common front-end processor, typically used to link several 3274s to a mainframe.

3725 A common front-end processor, intended for linking groups of cluster controllers to a mainframe.

3745 A new communications controller that combines the functions of a cluster controller and a front-end processor. The 3745 can interface simultaneously with as many as 8 Token-Ring networks, 512 terminals or printers, and 16 1.544-megabit-per-second communications lines.

■ Index

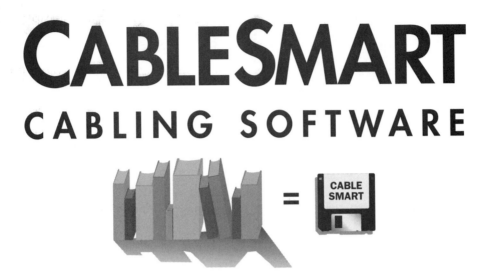

Networking Protocols and St[...]

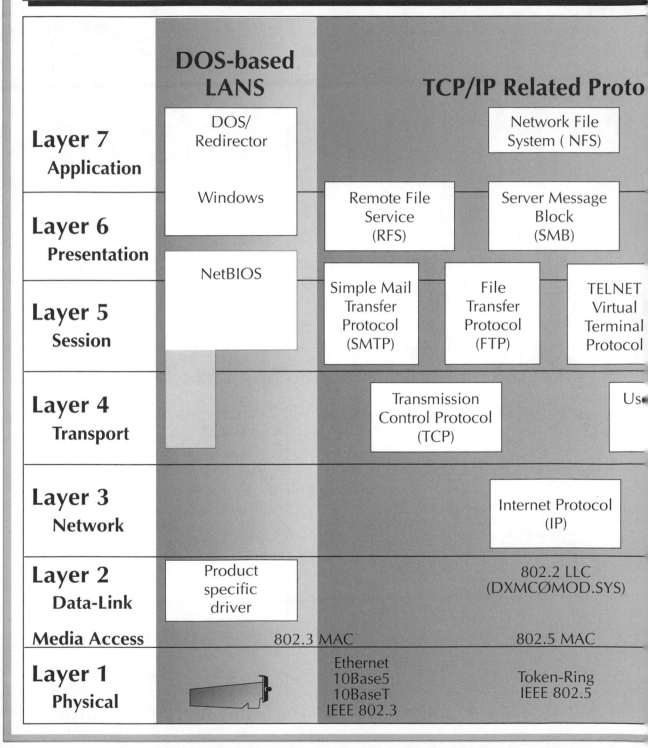

	DOS-based LANS	TCP/IP Related Proto[...]			
Layer 7 Application	DOS/ Redirector Windows				Network File System (NFS)
Layer 6 Presentation		Remote File Service (RFS)		Server Message Block (SMB)	
Layer 5 Session	NetBIOS	Simple Mail Transfer Protocol (SMTP)	File Transfer Protocol (FTP)		TELNET Virtual Terminal Protocol
Layer 4 Transport			Transmission Control Protocol (TCP)		Us[...]
Layer 3 Network				Internet Protocol (IP)	
Layer 2 Data-Link	Product specific driver		802.2 LLC (DXMCØMOD.SYS)		
Media Access	802.3 MAC		802.5 MAC		
Layer 1 Physical		Ethernet 10Base5 10BaseT IEEE 802.3		Token-Ring IEEE 802.5	

with THE Connectivity Decision Tree

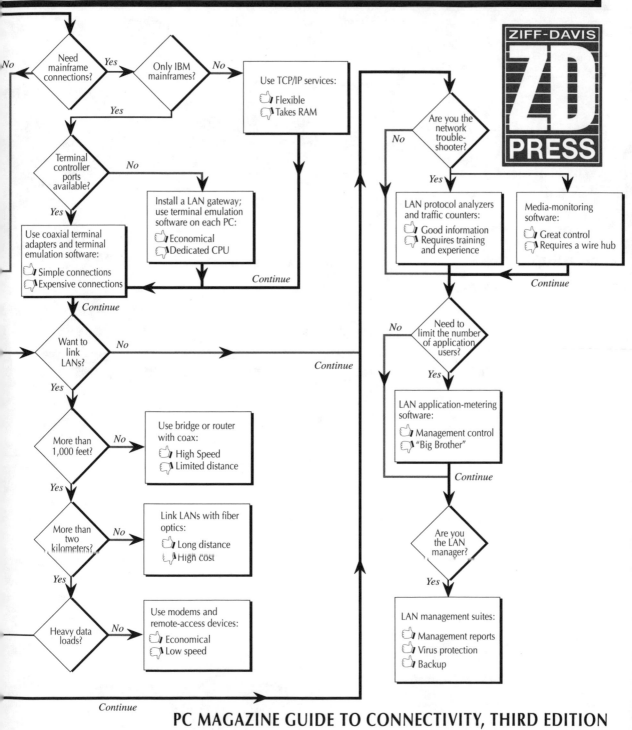

ZIFF-DAVIS
ZD
PRESS

Need mainframe connections? — **No** →

Yes → Only IBM mainframes? — **No** → Use TCP/IP services:
👍 Flexible
👎 Takes RAM

Yes ↓

Terminal controller ports available? — **No** → Install a LAN gateway; use terminal emulation software on each PC:
👍 Economical
👎 Dedicated CPU

Yes ↓

Use coaxial terminal adapters and terminal emulation software:
👍 Simple connections
👎 Expensive connections

Continue

Want to link LANs? — **No** → *Continue*

Yes ↓

More than 1,000 feet? — **No** → Use bridge or router with coax:
👍 High Speed
👎 Limited distance

Yes ↓

More than two kilometers? — **No** → Link LANs with fiber optics:
👍 Long distance
👎 High cost

Yes ↓

Heavy data loads? — **No** → Use modems and remote-access devices:
👍 Economical
👎 Low speed

Continue

Are you the network trouble-shooter? — **No**

Yes ↓

LAN protocol analyzers and traffic counters:
👍 Good information
👎 Requires training and experience

Media-monitoring software:
👍 Great control
👎 Requires a wire hub

Continue

Need to limit the number of application users? — **No**

Yes ↓

LAN application-metering software:
👍 Management control
👎 "Big Brother"

Continue

Are you the LAN manager?

Yes ↓

LAN management suites:
👍 Management reports
👍 Virus protection
👍 Backup

Continue

Make Your Best Connection

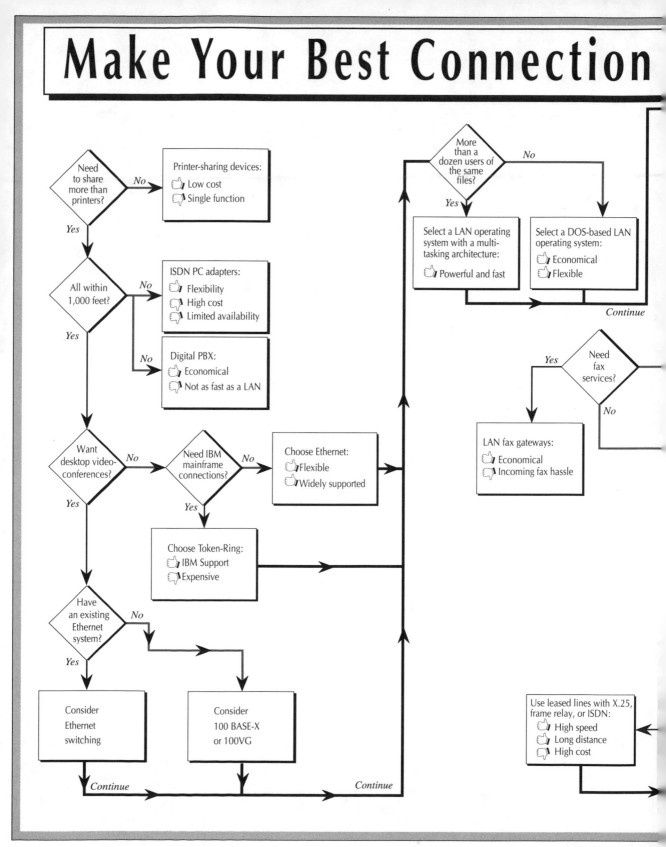

andards

This chart illustrates the relationships of common network protocols and standards. The left-hand column divides the protocols according to the seven layers of the OSI model for reference, but most families of protocols don't fit cleanly into that model. The devices at the physical layer can be used by any of the stacks of protocols. The chart depicts typical families of protocols, but in practice you'll find more complex combinations.

cols	Novell NetWare	Banyan VINES		Microsoft Windows NT
	NetWare shell	Redirector		Redirector
Network File System (NFS)	Network Core Protocols (NCP)	VINES Remote Procedure Calls	Server Message Block (SMB)	Server Message Block (SMB)
Simple Network Management Protocol (SNMP)	NetBIOS Emulator	NetBIOS Service		Internet Packet Exchange (IPX) or Transmissions Control Protocol (TCP)
r Datagram Protocol (UDP)	Sequenced Packet Exchange (SPX)	VINES Interprocess Communications Protocol (VIPC)		
X.25 Packet-Level Protocol	Internet Packet Exchange (IPX)	VINES Internet Protocol (VIP)		
Link Access Protocol Balanced (LAPB)	Open Data-link Interface (ODI)	Product specific driver	Network Driver Interface Specification (NDIS)	Network Driver Interface Specification (NDIS)
RS-232 RS-449 V.35				